W9-BCI-265

The Copperheads in the Middle West

THE COPPERHEADS

THE MIDDLE WEST

By

Frank L. Klement

THE UNIVERSITY
OF CHICAGO PRESS

Library of Congress Catalog Number: 59-11622

THE UNIVERSITY OF CHICAGO PRESS, CHICAGO 37
Cambridge University Press, London, N.W. 1, England
The University of Toronto Press, Toronto 5, Canada

© *1960 by The University of Chicago. Published 1960*
Composed and printed by THE UNIVERSITY OF CHICAGO
PRESS, *Chicago, Illinois, U.S.A.*

To Laurel
and
Paul, Richard, and Kenneth

Preface

T HE APOTHEOSIS of Lincoln and the intensification of nationalism have affected the writing of Civil War history. In the postwar
decades there was a tendency to justify and glorify that which had
happened. Lincoln became both a historical figure and a legend.
Grant, Sherman, and other military men had their buttons shined
and their reputations enhanced. Radical Republicans, like "Thad"
Stevens, had their names written in gold ink. The Copperheads,
Democratic critics of the Lincoln administration, were depicted
as irrational men who flirted with treason and who expressed pro-
Southern sympathies. The war was described as glorious, noble,
and inevitable. Nationalist history, à la James Ford Rhodes, enjoyed its golden era.

Our own generation has rewritten much of the history of the
Civil War. Lincoln has been realistically reassessed. Some of the
starch has been taken out of the Radical Republicans. The military leadership has been criticized and re-evaluated. Those who
had once argued that the war was "inevitable" or "irrepressible"
have been challenged by those who described the war as "needless." Only the Copperhead story remains quite the same—those
critics of the Lincoln administration are still viewed as men whose
hearts were black, whose blood was yellow, and whose minds
were blank. It has remained a favorite practice to collect Copperhead quotations and to hang them on the line of treason. Furthermore, newspaper charges made by Republican editors in Civil

War days have been accepted at face value by historians. Even the Golden Circle legends remain respectable.

I have attempted to re-examine the Copperhead movement in the upper Midwest. It defies a definitive analysis, for it is compounded out of complex and intangible ingredients. Its sectional, economic, social, religious, and political roots are deeply planted and its aspects difficult to refine. As historians, we trespass upon the periphery of fact when we assign motives to an individual or attempt to explain group action. Yet, if history is a cause-effect process, interpretation cannot be bypassed and an attempt to explain the "why" of midwestern Copperheadism must be attempted.

Two simple statements form the foundation for this discourse: (*a*) midwestern Copperheads, like supporters of the Lincoln administration, were human beings—motivated by the same wants and emotions that have been possessed by people throughout the ages, and (*b*) the midwestern Copperheads were conservatives who opposed the changes which the war was bringing to America —as individuals they swam against the current.

Beginning in the graduate seminars of Professor William B. Hesseltine, I have pursued the fascinating subject of midwestern Copperheadism for a long time—sometimes wandering down by-paths or getting lost on sideroads. A grant-in-aid-of-research, made by the National Social Science Research Council, enabled me to spend a summer in the Library of Congress and the National Archives. A fellowship granted by the Fund for the Advancement of Education (established by the Ford Foundation) made it possible for me to do research in Washington, D.C., and in some twenty midwestern libraries. A grant by the Committee on Research of Marquette University underwrote help in preparing the manuscript for publication.

The courtesies and assistance offered by members of library staffs—often far beyond the line of duty—cannot be repaid by words of thanks or kind words. To fail to mention by name those who were most helpful may be an injustice, but there were so many and they were uniformly co-operative.

I am indebted to such scholars as Charles H. Coleman, Harvey L. Carter, Ray Billington, Rev. Edward J. Drummond, S.J., Forrest L. Seal, William B. Hesseltine and the late Harry Pratt for inspiration and encouragement given or materials loaned. A number of graduate assistants checked footnote and bibliographical items. Another graduate assistant, Ekkehard Eickhoff of Brunswick, Germany, helped to examine the files of the Milwaukee *See-Bote*. Portions of the first draft of the manuscript were typed by Miss Cleoria Serritella (now Mrs. Karl Springer) and Laurel M. Klement. The latter also gave invaluable assistance in the preparation of the Index.

While appreciating the help of various agencies, institutions, and individuals, I alone assume responsibility for any errors of fact or interpretation which may appear in this specialized study.

Contents

List of Illustrations

I

Emergence of Opposition to the
Lincoln Administration

THE CIVIL WAR was far more than a contest between armies clad in blue and gray. Those crucial years helped to give a new meaning to the term "democracy," and the doctrine of equality crossed new frontiers of American thought. The war years also witnessed the transformation of a federal union into an American nation, for the dogma of states' rights was buried at Appomattox. On the economic scene, industry made gains over agriculture— the high tariff policy and the philosophy of industrialism became integral parts of postwar America.

All Northerners did not favor the changes which the war was bringing to America. Most of the midwestern Democrats put themselves on record as critics of change. In a sense, those Democrats were conservatives; they thought that the wheel of revolution turned too fast and too far. Their wartime slogan, "The Constitution as it is, the Union as it was," proved that they looked toward the past and feared the changes which the war foisted upon the country.

Those Democratic critics of change and of the Lincoln administration came to be called "Copperheads." They seized upon every argument and every angle to make their protest effective. They sought to gain control of the political machinery and to turn the populace against the party in power. In a sense, there was a war within the war.

It is true that partisanship seemed to disappear in the opening days of the Civil War. When news of the surrender of Fort Sumter swept over the Midwest in April of 1861, a wave of patriotism and hysteria engulfed the countryside. Flags flew on every hand "till the whole Northern heavens seemed a perfect aurora borealis of stars and stripes."[1] Count Adam Gurowski, writing from his observation post in the nation's capital, recorded his impressions in a diary: "I am not deceived in my faith in the North; the excitement, the wrath is terrible. Party lines burn, dissolved by the excitement. Now the people is fusion, as bronze."[2] Prominent Democrats like Stephen A. Douglas of Illinois and Horatio Seymour of New York actively preached patriotism and encouraged men to volunteer for army duty. It did seem as if patriotism had triumphed over partisanship. "The Democrats generally as well as the Republicans," wrote a member of Lincoln's cabinet, "are offering themselves to the country."[3]

Time tempered the emotions—aided considerably by such forces as political reality, economic grievances, and western sectionalism. Those who opposed change were alarmed by the howls of the abolitionists, by President Lincoln's extraordinary measures, and by the turn of events. When Republicans took steps to write their Chicago platform of 1860 into law, they gave the partisan Democrats a chance to complain. When President Lincoln found it necessary to take action for which there was no precedent, sometimes venturing on questionable constitutional ground, western conservatives became alarmed. Partyism, consequently, returned to the midwestern scene. President Lincoln's rabid supporters contended that all who refused to give unqualified support to the administration gave aid to the enemy; they tried to pin the tail of treason on the Democratic donkey. Midwestern conservatives and Democratic partisans, on the other hand, distinguished between the administration and the government; they publicly affirmed their opposition to the former and their loyalty to the latter. Thus, while Confederate and Federal forces clashed upon the battlefields, political rivals engaged in verbal combat on the home front.

Partisan opposition to the Lincoln administration and to the direction of events existed in all sections of the country. In the Midwest, however, it had a distinct sectional flavor, and there it made headlines more often. Clement L. Vallandigham, the Ohioan who later became the best-known Copperhead, helped to put midwestern Copperheadism in the spotlight. Furthermore, the most intense struggles between the critics and the supporters of Lincoln took place in Ohio, Indiana, and Illinois. In those states the Copperhead movement began to take shape in 1861 and 1862. Economic factors gave strength to the movement.

The economic depression of 1861–62 in the upper Mississippi Valley was a Hydra-headed monster. The river trade collapsed. Farm prices plunged as food surpluses glutted the market. A bank panic wiped out much of the paper money. Business houses by the hundreds closed their doors, and unemployment brought hardship to the homes of many workingmen. Bankruptcies were numerous in spite of the fact that the panic of 1857 had weeded out the weaker houses and the appearance of war clouds upon the horizon late in 1860 had introduced caution everywhere.[4]

The Mississippi River blockade, imposed by the War Department, helped to depress farm prices. Midwestern farm surpluses intended for the Southern market remained in granaries or in warehouses and elevators. Wheat, flour, packed pork, and distilled spirits begged for buyers. In some sections, corn prices dipped to less than ten cents a bushel. Some farmers, rather than dispose of their surplus corn at ruinous prices, burned it as fuel. Potatoes could be had by the hundred bushels for the asking. Butter was a drug on the market, and in 1861 hog prices were halved.[5]

Many midwestern farmers deplored the turn of events which closed the Southern market and brought on the agricultural depression of 1861–62. It was easy for them—especially those of the Democratic faith—to blame the Lincoln administration for the economic crisis. The editor of an Illinois newspaper typified the Democratic critics. He blamed the Republicans for the loss of the Southern market and for the distraught state of affairs. He entitled an editorial "Western Farmers, What Are Your Interests[?]" and boldly asked, "Will the fighting farmers of the Upper Mississippi ever find out that it is the Lincoln blood-and-murder party who has killed their 'goose with the golden eggs'?"[6]

The Mississippi River blockade did more than depress farm prices. It raised havoc with the many commercial firms and manufacturing companies whose business depended upon the down-river trade. Such cities as Cincinnati, Louisville, Cairo, and St. Louis entered upon a period of hard times. Cincinnati was especially hard hit; its trade "was paralyzed," "many of the stores and shops were closed," and there was "much poverty" among the working classes. Louisville suffered even more as sixty-eight out of seventy jobbing houses closed their doors; its population decreased by ten thousand in the first year of the war.[7] A loyal Kentuckian testified: "All kinds of business here is prostrated. We can sell no kind of stock for money, having no market for anything. The country is in great commotion and confusion."[8]

The business depression in the states of the upper Mississippi Valley was aggravated by the bank panic which visited that region in 1861. The paper money of most midwestern states was largely based on Southern bonds which the bankers had deposited with state auditors. Wisconsin and Illinois banks, for example, relied heavily upon "Missouri Sixes," "North Carolina Sixes," and the state bonds of Louisiana, Virginia, and Tennessee to validate their paper currency. The coming of secession and civil war caused the Southern bonds to depreciate in value. Many banks fell into bankruptcy. By mid-July of 1861, thirty-eight Wisconsin banks had declared bankruptcy, and a score more were in precarious straits. The crisis was even more acute in Illinois. Of 112 banks functioning in Illinois before the war, only seventeen survived the panic of 1861.

These bank failures placed a heavy burden on the struggling economy of the upper Midwest. There was a shortage of currency to finance the fall harvests. Furthermore, much of the direct loss was borne by farmers who held stock in the defunct banks or who had had the depreciating or worthless notes passed into their hands by wary and wiser middlemen. Workingmen, too, were victims of questionable practices. Sometimes they were paid in notes which unscrupulous bankers passed on to the public. Bank riots and public protests proved that discontent existed, and people blamed the Lincoln administration for the hard times and the depressed prices.

The business plague caused some to translate their economic grievances into political bitterness. A contemporary, who visited Cincinnati late in 1861, found that Lincoln's name was anathema in some business circles. He wrote to his political mentor:

Matters look blue enough here; business men have long faces and short money receipts. One Jim Brown & Co. say they have lost $40,000 since the election by depreciation in stock. There are three of them and they each voted for Lincoln, "God & Liberty," and say now they "wish Lincoln and all political parties were in hell." . . .[9]

Democrats, of course, tried to capitalize upon the hard times and blamed the Republicans for all of the nation's ills. The editor of the Dubuque *Herald,* who later became one of the most outspoken critics of the Lincoln administration, bluntly blamed the state of affairs upon Lincoln's election. "Grain has gone down till it won't pay hauling charges," he wrote. "So much for electing a man—the exponent of Personal Liberty Bills, Nigger Suffrage and Equality, Beecherism, Stoweism, Niggerism and a dozen isms and Tom fooleries upon which the entire North under the lead of Abolitionized Massachusetts has gone mad."[10] Some Democrats assumed a serves-you-right attitude. They thought that some suffering would teach the fickle public a political lesson. "The times are hard now . . . but they will be a good deal harder before next December," wrote a Democratic editor, "and a world of good will be done to thousands of people by having their noses held upon the grindstone for some time to come."[11] At their political conventions and party rallies Democratic speakers often compared previous "Democratic prosperity" with "Republican misery." Thomas A. Hendricks, prominent Indiana Democrat, exemplified those who tried to bid for votes by blaming the "farm crisis" and the "troublous times" on his political opponents. At the Indiana

State Democratic Convention of 1862 he blamed Republican policy for the agricultural depression and the general hard times. Democratic policy, he asserted, would bring back prosperity.[12]

The hard times and the state of affairs gave Democratic politicians in the upper Mississippi Valley a chance to stir the coals of sectionalism anew. Western sectionalism, of course, existed long before the Civil War began. The West had begun to develop its own culture and was fully aware of its own interests. Westerners sometimes were as section-conscious as the Southern planters or the New England Yankees. Clement L. Vallandigham was an avowed western sectionalist. He once bragged brazenly, "I am as good a Western fire-eater as the hottest salamander in this House." He closed a famous pro-western speech with a sectional pledge: ". . . I am not a Northern man, nor yet a Southern man; but I am a *Western Man* by birth, by habit, by education; and although still a United States man with United States principles, yet within and subordinate to the Constitution, am wholly devoted to Western interests. . . . I became and am a *Western sectionalist,* and so shall continue to the day of my death."[13]

Western sectionalism became an important ingredient of that concoction called midwestern Copperheadism. Many Copperheads prided themselves on their loyalty to their section and publicly proclaimed that the Lincoln administration had sold its soul to New York capitalists and New England manufacturers. They claimed that some of the administration measures made the Midwest the slave and servant of the Northeast and that the "revived Whiggery" espoused by the Lincoln administration was as abominable to the agricultural West as it was to the plantation South.[14] In addition to berating the "economic exploitation" of the Midwest, western sectionalists claimed that a gulf existed between Yankeedom and midwestern culture. The high literacy of New Englanders and their determination to refashion the westerner in the Yankee image made them unpopular with most westerners. Vallandigham, self-proclaimed sectionalist, contended that he was "inexorably hostile to Puritan domination in religion or morals or literature or politics."[15]

Democrats who posed as western sectionalists had many opportunities to appeal to anti–New England prejudice in the early years of the war. The Morrill Tariff Act of February 20, 1861, drew the fire of nearly every Democratic editor and politician. The editor of the Cincinnati *Enquirer* stated the case of the western sectionalists succinctly:

The spirit in which the measure is gotten up is to oppress the agricultural interests of the West. . . . It well deserves the name "The Bill of Abominations" and it will never be submitted to by the West. . . . It is a New England measure, and is an evidence of the way the West will be treated in a Confederacy of which she [New England] is the dictator. . . . She is determined that the whole country shall be subservient to the interests of her manufactures; and, having driven the South out of the Union, she wants additional burdens put upon the West to make up for the loss of the Southern market. Her policy is extremely selfish and injurious to the interests of the North-West, who, we are confident, will resist it to the last extremity. Such oppressive taxation for the benefit of the few is almost sufficient to drive any people to rebellion.[16]

The same sectional argument was repeated in hundreds of editorials and upon many political platforms. Samuel Medary, founder of the Columbus *Crisis,* repeatedly stated that the tariff policy "enriched the manufacturer" at the expense of western farmers and western workingmen.[17] The editor of the German-language Milwaukee *See-Bote* steadily condemned all tariff acts as sectional measures which exploited the West. He headlined a long editorial "The Irrepressible Conflict between East and West" and interpreted midwestern Copperheadism as the westerners' reaction to New England's program of "revived Whiggery."[18] When the editor of the Hastings *Democrat* labeled the Morrill Tariff "a monster of iniquity and injustice," harmful "especially to the West,"[19] he merely restated the views of hundreds of midwestern editors. The outspoken editor of the Canton, Ohio, *Stark County Democrat* showed less restraint than most of his colleagues. His hatred of New England showed in all of his anti-tariff arguments, and he concluded an anti-tariff tirade saying that "the crazy descendants of Plymouth Rock" had hearts "as bloodless as the Rock."[20]

Vallandigham, of course, had opposed the Morrill Act in Congress and seldom missed an opportunity to denounce it as an anti-western measure. He even gave notice that he intended to introduce a repeal resolution during the next session of Congress.[21] Frederic W. Horn, a respected and well-known Democratic leader in Wisconsin, resigned his captaincy in the state militia rather than fight in a war which he believed would subjugate the Middle West to "Pennsylvania's Iron mongers and New England manufacturers."[22] Horn's views seemed to correspond with those of a prominent Indianapolis merchant and free trader who criticized the proposed tariff bill and threatened, "If that tax is levied, it will make me disloyal."[23] James A. Craven, who represented a southern Indiana district in Congress and thought the tariff program unfair to his constituents, said that it might be necessary for the Midwest to "cut loose from the New England states." He thought his section would have to choose between the free-trade policy of the Southern Confederacy and the high-tariff policy of the industrialized Northeast.[24]

Instead of heeding the voices of protest coming out of the West, eastern protectionists demanded an even higher tariff wall. An amendment to the Morrill Tariff, passed in August of 1861, levied duties upon coffee, tea, sugar, spices, and other household items. The tariff act of July 14, 1862, reduced the free list and increased the rates on many items already on the protected list. Both acts increased the cost of living for western farmers and laborers at a time when the Midwest was suffering from an economic recession. These acts gave western critics of the administration another opportunity to expound their sectional argument and to appeal to the anti–New England prejudice so widespread in portions of the upper Mississippi Valley. One sarcastic editor of a western weekly newspaper suggested that the best way the mistaken Republicans could support a mistaken president was by "drinking lots of coffee at thirty and thirty-five cents a pound."[25]

Western Democrats like Lambdin P. Milligan and Daniel W. Voorhees never ceased to condemn the "cupidity" of New England protectionists. Milligan, arrested for "disloyalty" late in the war, always proclaimed his devotion to free trade and to the West while he denounced New England capitalists and manufacturers— the "lords of the looms."[26] Voorhees, sometimes, called the leading Copperhead of Indiana, branded midwestern congressmen who supported protection as "apostates to their section" and "unfaithful servants" who espoused "a tariff policy of protection" which enriched the "manufacturing monopolists" by "subjecting the great agricultural West to onerous and unequal burdens."[27]

The same westerners who spoke out against the tariff as a sectional and discriminatory measure also condemned the proposed excise taxes on distilled spirits and malt liquors. They believed that New England underwrote both the excise measures debated in Congress in 1862 and the temperance crusade. Westerners generally opposed both. Some western sectionalists contended that the distilling industry was an important part of their section's economy. Western farmers produced the wheat, corn, and barley used in making beer and whiskey. Peoria's eleven distilleries of 1860, for example, sometimes used 11,650 bushels of grain daily. Vallandigham, though a teetotaler, never missed an opportunity to condemn New England and to defend his section, and he labeled the excise proposal as discriminatory and unfair. Another midwesterner, a Chicagoan who asked his congressman to oppose the excise proposal debated in Congress in early 1862, wrote that the excise bill was proof positive that New England expected the West to pay for the war and do most of the actual fighting as well.[28] It was common practice for midwestern Copperheads to blame New England for the war, the tariff, and the excise taxes written into the revenue act of July 1, 1862.[29] They resented New England's efforts to put puritan morality into law and to tax the agrarian economy of the West.

Midwestern Democrats who sought votes in the field of sectional prejudice condemned eastern capitalists as well as New England manufacturers. Eastern capital owned most of the midwestern railroads, especially the east-west trunk lines which were expected to carry western farm surpluses to market. The closing of the Mississippi River put the western farmers at the mercy of the railroads. The railroads made the most of the opportunity. Freight rates were more than doubled in 1861 and further increases were added in 1862. It seemed unfair to farmers of southern Illinois that the cost of shipping a barrel of produce to New York City should increase from $1.20 in July of 1861 to $3.00 by January 15, 1862.

Complaints against excessive freight rates and eastern capital echoed from all parts of the upper Mississippi Valley. Iowans complained that it cost "more than *five times* as much to transport a bushel of wheat from Iowa to New York as the farmer received for it."[30] Samuel Medary, editor of the *Crisis*, complained against the "brutally skinning despotism of Eastern railroads," predicting that administration policy and the "capitalists' greed" would make "Western people paupers and slaves forever."[31] One letter-writer who complained against the "extortions" of the "railroad companys" warned that "empty cribs make biting horses." Disgusted, he added: "If our country retrogrades as much in the next two years as it has done in the last two years, Russia would be a desirable place to emigrate to compared to the United States."[32]

The strangle hold which the east-west rail lines and the Great Lakes shipowners had on midwestern farmers nurtured Copperheadism. It also sowed the seeds of Grangerism, which bloomed full flower in the postwar years.[33] The Copperhead-controlled Illinois state constitutional convention of 1862 revealed the sectional interests existing in the Midwest. Members took turns denouncing the "rapacity of the railroads," claiming that the python-like conspiracy of the railroads and elevators squeezed them to death. They contended that railroad rates were discriminatory, favoring some shippers and some communities. They condemned the promotional practices of railroad companies and the "forced loans" foisted on local governmental units and individual farmers. They protested against the lobbying tactics employed by railroad promotors, and some denounced the "free pass system" (free passes to legislators and state officials) as a form of bribery. They censured pooling and stock-watering for tending to produce higher freight rates. Some delegates asked for state regulation of the rail-roads and establishment of state railroad commissions.

The constitution the delegates drafted was loaded with anti-railroad provisions; it even contained a Granger-like statement that all private property was "subservient to the public welfare."[34] The newly drafted constitution failed its ratification test, partly because the railroad and banking interests threw their weight against the document.[35] Agrarian discontent, anti-railroad sentiment and western sectionalism blended together. One western letter-writer stated the situation briefly:

Our State is very much more of a political ferment than people at the East seem to be aware of. The extraordinary toll levied on all products by the Rail roads and the Erie Canal management is producing bad fruit, creating a feeling which however senseless it may be is nevertheless a very passionate one and may result in much evil. An union with a Southern Confederacy is openly talked of by even moderate men. Practically we cannot reach the seaboard either by the Mississippi or via the East—and it is ruin to our farmers.[36]

Even some Republicans recognized that midwestern Copper-headism had some economic roots. One who reviewed the primary needs of his section discounted the charges of "disloyalty" which propagandists circulated in the press. "It is not a question of loyalty," he wrote, "but . . . one of bread and butter."[37] In mid-year of 1862 General John A. McClernand toured the Midwest to find out why that section was flooded with dissatisfaction and discontent. McClernand, as the President's special envoy, ascribed the anti-Administration sentiment to high freight rates and low farm prices. He immediately urged military operations to reopen the Mississippi and regain New Orleans as an outlet for midwestern farm surpluses.[38] Certainly the political revolt of 1862 and the spread of midwestern opposition to the Lincoln administration owed much to the economic conditions of 1862, to the rebirth of western sectionalism, and to the westerners' belief that eastern industry and capital were writing their wishes into law.

Democratic politicians who sought votes in an area suffering from economic discontent soon learned that other measures also possessed vote-getting qualities. Negrophobia and midwestern opposition to the slavery policies of the Lincoln administration also produced votes. Midwestern Democrats even saw the image of New England in the abolition crusade, and they tried to stigmatize both in the same breath. The prominence of William Lloyd Garrison and Wendell Phillips in the abolition movement enabled Midwestern conservatives to label it a New England heresy and to denounce Garrison and Phillips as its high priests.

Conservative Democrats of the upper Mississippi Valley learned to hate abolition long before the Civil War. They blamed the New England Emigrant Aid Society for stirring up strife in Kansas, they condemned abolitionists for destroying the comity of sections, and they berated John Brown for lighting the fires of violence at Harpers Ferry. They denounced the efforts of New England to canonize Brown, and they were incensed when their children came home from school singing "John Brown's Body." They feared for their country when fanaticism became respectable. Vallandigham protested the "sanctification" of Brown: "Thirty years ago, John Brown, hung like a felon, would have been buried like a dog."[39] To some conservatives it appeared that the abolitionists had brought the Republican party into being in order to transform their ideals into law.

A few prominent midwestern Democrats even defended slavery as an institution. Jesse Bright of Indiana and George Wallace Jones of Iowa had at one time owned slaves. John Reynolds of Illinois and Rev. C. F. W. Walther (genius of the Missouri Synod of the Lutheran Church) had written treatises in defense of slavery.[40] The majority of Democrats, however, were not sympathetic to the institution of slavery. With one voice they condemned both the abolitionists of the North and the extremists of the South. "The irrepressible conflict is about to be realized," stated the venerable William Allen of Ohio, "not as the natural result of the institution of slavery . . . but the result of the perversion of public sentiment by mad partisans. . . ."[41] Vallandigham and Stephen A. Douglas condemned "Southern Fire-eaters" and "Northern fanatics" with equal vehemence.

During the first year of the war western conservatives found little to criticize in President Lincoln's stand on the controversial abolition measures. They indorsed his revocation of General John C. Frémont's proclamation which threatened to confiscate the property of all rebels within his jurisdiction and to free their slaves.[42] Conservative Democrats applauded again when Simon Cameron, who had suggested the use of Negro troops, resigned his cabinet portfolio.[43] They protested, however, when Congress, in the early months of 1862, considered the advisability of abolishing slavery in the District of Columbia, of repealing the Fugitive Slave Act, and of practicing abolition via federal confiscation acts.[44]

Denouncing abolitionists and abolition became a favorite Democratic technique. Democratic strategists recognized that early in 1862 most midwesterners were opposed to abolition. Negrophobia, they saw, was an extensive and powerful prejudice, and they cultivated it zealously.

The anti-abolition argument had a strong appeal to three elements of the Midwest's population. The Irish-Americans in the cities feared that abolition would release a flood of cheap labor that would envelop the North and compete for the crumbs on their tables. When employers used free Negroes as strikebreakers or utilized "contraband labor" to beat down wages, Irish-Americans became violent and vociferous. It was the Irish-Americans who brought about the anti-Negro riots in such cities as Detroit, Chicago, Cincinnati, and New York. The Irish detested the abolitionists, voted the straight Democratic ticket, and became the backbone of the Copperhead movement in the cities.[45]

German-Americans, especially those who labored for a living, also joined the Copperhead ranks. Centered in such cities as Milwaukee, St. Louis, Chicago, and Cincinnati, they had the same fear of "cheap labor" as the Irish. While the "forty-eighters" agitated for abolition and waved Republican party banners, the rank-and-file German immigrant, who joined the Irish workmen on construction jobs or in the factories, listened to Democratic politicians denouncing abolition. "The jealousy of the low Germans

and Irish against the free negro," wrote a touring foreign correspondent, "was sufficient to set them against the war which would
have brought four million of their black rivals into competition
for that hard and dirty work which American freedom bestowed
on them."[46] The Milwaukee *See-Bote* warned Germans against the
dangers of abolition. The editor, plagued by Negrophobia, entitled an editorial "Abolition, the Worst Enemy of the Free White
Laborer" and warned his readers that employers (most Milwaukee
employers were Republicans) desired abolition in order to create
a pool of "cheap labor." He even issued a call to action: "Workmen! Be Careful! Organize yourself against this element which
threatens your impoverishment and annihilation."[47] The *Crisis,*
the Chicago *Times,* the Cincinnati *Enquirer,* and the Detroit *Free
Press,* as the leading Copperhead papers of the Midwest, repeated
the same theme and endeavored to keep the Irish-Americans and
the German-Americans from voting the Republican ticket.[48]

Southern immigrants who had crossed the Ohio River to pre-
empt the poorer soils of southern Ohio, Indiana, and Illinois
formed the third element of the Midwest's population easily
affected by Negrophobia. They brought their anti-Negro prejudice
with them and supported state bills which would restrict the influx of Negro migrants or deny them citizenship rights. In Ohio
the Copperhead country was characterized by smaller homesteads,
poorer soils, and more widespread illiteracy. The same trade-
marks were stamped on much of the Copperhead country of
southern Indiana, Illinois, and Iowa. Anti-abolition speeches appealed to the prejudices which were part of the cultural patterns
of these poorer people.[49]

When Lincoln espoused compensated emancipation, he lost the
confidence of conservatives who several months earlier had pronounced him "sound on the nigger question."[50] They argued that
emancipation was unconstitutional and impractical; they feared
it would damage the Union movement in the border states; and
they claimed it violated the President's inaugural pledge and the
original objectives of the war.[51]

As the abolition crusade gathered momentum, conservative midwesterners became more apprehensive and more bitter. Some lost their equanimity and turned to public abuse of all abolitionists and Republicans. The editor of the La Crosse *Democrat* cursed abolitionists for "fiddling while Rome burned."[52] An Ohio editor, John W. Kees, referred to abolitionists as "damned disunionists," and he wanted them hung "till the flesh would rot off their bones and the winds of Heaven whistle yanky doodle through their loathsum skelitonz."[53] Disconsolately the Ohio editor added, "It is a pity that there is not a more tormenting hell than that kept by Beelzebub for such abolition fiends."[54] Democratic critics of abolitionism and the Lincoln administration made much of the argument that the war was being fought to save the Union and not to free the slaves. They condemned abolition as a heresy which threatened "to pervert" the objective of the war. They produced a torrent of anti-abolition editorials, speeches, resolutions, and pamphlets. Some helped to circulate Professor Christy's book, *Pulpit Politics*.[55] Others turned to verse and ridicule as a way to slay the "abolition ogre"; one minced no words when he laid the lash to "Black Republicanism":

> Come all treacherous Abolitionists, and join in
>   hostile band,
> You're going to invade the Southern men and drive
>   them from their land;
> Disunion is your motto, and Satan is your guide,
> So jump into the wagon and all take a ride.[56]

Some publicly warned Lincoln that if he accepted abolition as official governmental policy, he would jeopardize unity in the war effort. One wrote that the President's flirting with Miss Abolition had "weakened" his loyalty to the administration and the government "to an extent" he "dare hardly confess."[57]

Democratic hostility toward abolition failed to silence the Radical Republicans or check the movement. President Lincoln, caught in the vise (Democrats would have preferred the word "vice") of abolition pressure, finally yielded in September of 1862 when he issued his preliminary proclamation of emancipation. While Radical Republicans rejoiced, Democrats and conservatives expressed their disgust and indignation. The editor of the Chatfield *Democrat* labeled Lincoln's proclamation of September 22, "a piece of fanatical folly";[58] Joseph J. Bingham, editor of the Indianapolis *State Sentinel,* called it "a blunder . . . fraught with evil";[59] the outspoken editor of the Milwaukee *See-Bote* denounced the document as "a ridiculous and unsavory piece of writing";[60] the outraged editor of the Louisville *Journal* labeled the measure "a gigantic usurpation."[61]

These spokesmen of midwestern conservatism advanced a variety of arguments against Lincoln's preliminary proclamation of emancipation. They charged that the President had violated both his previous pledges and his oath to uphold the Constitution. They predicted that unionism would suffer in the border states and that the proclamation would divide the North and unify the South. Some argued that Lincoln was taking a step toward a "Robespierrian tyranny." Some predicted that a "black flood" would sweep away the jobs of white laborers.[62]

In some sections of the Midwest the protest was one of action as well as words. Minor violence flared in many cities. In Plainfield, Illinois, white workers walked off the job and declared they "would not work with niggers."[63] In the same state Ogle County farmers organized a vigilante group to arrest every "contraband" (free Negro) brought into their area.[64] In Indiana a mob surrounded the house of a farmer who had hired a "contraband" and kidnapped the trembling Negro, ordering him out of the community.[65]

The preliminary proclamation of emancipation provided midwestern Democrats with a fiery election issue and stirred them to political activity. Critics of Lincolnian policy predicted that the public would repudiate abolitionism and Lincoln's proclamation of September 22 at the polls. Midwestern conservatism and Negrophobia undoubtedly played a role in bringing forth the political revolt of 1862. After the October elections jolted the Lincoln administration in Indiana and Ohio in 1862, the editor of the Indianapolis *State Sentinel* wrote the headline "Abolition Slaughtered."[66] When the November elections continued the anti-administration trend, anti-abolition headlines became even more popular. The Democratic editor of the Springfield *Illinois State Register* formulated the headline: "The Home of Lincoln Condemns the Proclamation."[67] "The Lord sent us *sunshine* in the late election," wrote the aged patriarch (John Reynolds) of Illinois politics; "we must drive back the abolitionists into the same hole they came out of."[68] Reynolds interpreted the election results as a repudiation of Lincoln's emancipation policy. Even some Republicans confessed that the independent voters had refused to swallow the administration's abolition medicine.[69]

Although anti-abolitionism and economic unrest contributed much to the development of anti-administration sentiment in 1862, there were other issues which emboldened the Democrats and turned citizens into Copperheads. Public reaction to arbitrary arrests and to the centralizing tendencies of the federal government also enabled Democratic politicians to grind political grist in their mills.

Democrats who looked for opportunities to criticize the Lincoln administration found them soon after the first Republican president moved into the White House. In the eighty days between Lincoln's call for troops and the convening of Congress on July 4, 1861, he took some unprecedented and extraordinary actions. He proclaimed a blockade of Southern ports, authorized the increase of the regular army, ordered the expenditures of governmental moneys without congressional approval or appropriation, and suspended the writ of habeas corpus. Democrats like Samuel Medary of the Columbus *Crisis* and Dennis Mahony of the Dubuque *Herald* wrote learned treatises in protest. "The step between this [Lincoln's directive increasing the size of the regular army] and *coup d'etat* of a despot," wrote Mahony, "is short and easily taken."[70] Mahony and Medary liked to remind their readers that civil wars in Europe had ended in dictatorships. Therefore, they reasoned, Americans must guard their liberties vigilantly and allow no venturing on unconstitutional ground. "We are embarking on a course," warned a Democratic prophet, "that will certainly produce some Cromwell or Napoleon who will crush beneath his iron heel the democratic legacy we have so long enjoyed."[71]

When Lincoln or his agents arbitrarily arrested many residents in Kentucky and Maryland to keep those states in the Union, the same Democratic critics again raised their voices in protest. When Chief Justice Roger B. Taney wrote his decision in the much-publicized case *Ex parte Merryman,* he gave the critics solid ground for their arguments against arbitrary arrests.

These early Democratic protests, however, failed to stir the public, which was interested in revenge for the Fort Sumter affair and hypnotized by a swell of patriotism. As the tide of patriotism, however, receded before the economic depression of 1861–62 and the dangers of abolition, the voices of the Democratic critics of administration measures again became audible. Fault-finding editors became more numerous, resolutions denouncing arbitrary arrests increased in number, and those who condemned the centralizing tendencies of the government became more popular. Samuel Medary wanted the President impeached because he ordered or sanctioned the arbitrary arrests.[72] Vallandigham introduced a bill in Congress to "imprison" the President if he allowed any more arrests to be made in the border states or the loyal states.[73] Democrats in Congress gave full support to a resolution which called on President Lincoln and the State Department to produce the record of, and the explanation for, arbitrary arrests already made; but a party vote buried the resolution in committee.[74] When their protests were stifled in the halls of Congress, Democratic congressmen turned to a public "Address" which harshly criticized the arbitrary arrests and the trend toward "Despotism." The Hon. William A. Richardson, well-known congressman from Illinois, helped to draft the "Address" and such prominent Democrats as Vallandigham, James C. Robinson, Daniel Voorhees, William J. Allen, and George H. Pendleton put their signatures upon the controversial document.[75]

If midwestern Democrats expected documents (addresses, editorials, or resolves), the court decision in *Ex parte Merryman,* or excursions in platform oratory to stay the arrests and to create a new respect for the writ of habeas corpus, they were badly mistaken. In August and September of 1862 a new wave of arrests swept over the Midwest. The net of an overly zealous federal marshal in southern Illinois produced nearly forty political prisoners. Several of the victims (like William J. Allen, Amos Green, and Andrew Duff) were known throughout the state for their devotion to the Democratic party and their critical attitude toward the Lincoln administration.[76] Then there were many smaller political fish. Five county political leaders had expressed their views too freely at the Williamson County barbecue sponsored by the Democrats. In northern Illinois another federal marshal arrested Madison Y. Johnson and David Sheean, two prominent Galena lawyers who had taken steps to check military authority in an area where the civil courts were functioning.[77]

Most of those arrested in neighboring Iowa were newspaper editors who had earned the wrath of H. M. Hoxie, the federal marshal who doubled as a member of the Republican State Central Committee. The Iowa victims included the ubiquitous Dennis A. Mahony, editor of the Dubuque *Herald* and director of Democratic opinions among the city's Irish residents. Lesser known politicos were arrested in Indiana, including Dr. Theodore Horton (a Democrat who had previously served in the state legislature) and Jason B. Brown. The latter was arrested while he was making a political speech at Seymour. Edson B. Olds, a respected Lancaster, Ohio, resident who believed that the war had turned into an abolition crusade, was the best known of the Ohioans who were seized and escorted to prison in 1862.[78] In border states like Kentucky and Missouri the arrests were conducted wholesale. Military authorities in these states, anxious to control elections and cow their critics, took many citizens into custody. Since these generals and their subordinates interpreted any criticism of the Lincoln administration as disloyalty, the traditional rights of citizens were constantly ignored and violated.

If the arrests were intended to intimidate Democrats and silence Lincoln's critics, they failed to achieve their objective. Democrats gained a chance to pose as the champions of individual liberties, and others made deliberate bids to don the cloak of martyrdom. It seemed that it became an honor to feel the hand of the law. After Daniel Sheward, the Iowan who edited the Fairfield *Constitution and Union,* was arrested and shipped to an eastern prison, his wife complimented him upon the "honors" that were bestowed upon him: "Oh, I tell you that your arrest is the greatest honor that they could confer upon you. I feel proud of the day that you was arrested and your friends think the same."[79] After Archibald McGregor, bluff Ohioan and editor of the *Stark County Democrat,* felt the hand of the law and sat inactive in a prison cell, his revengeful wife's editorials proved much more vicious and vituperative than her husband's. She proclaimed that the administration was drunk with power, addicted to tyranny, characterized by imbecility, and "reveling in the ruin of the country."[80]

The defiant Democrats of the upper Midwest retaliated by nominating some of those held in prisons for public office. William J. Allen of Illinois and Mahony of Iowa, for example, were nominated *in absentia* for congressional seats, and Amos Green (Illinois) and Dr. Edson Olds were proposed by their party for membership in their respective state legislatures.

The many arbitrary arrests and the suppression of individual rights gave members of the opposition party an opportunity to depict themselves as the defenders of civil liberties and as Jeffersonian Democrats. They read the Declaration of Independence and the Bill of Rights at public rallies. They drafted resolutions and addresses which deplored the trend toward "tyranny" and centralization. They scanned the words and writings of Jefferson to substantiate their criticisms of the Lincoln administration. They redeveloped the states' rights argument as they exposed the Republican record, enumerating instances where the Constitution had been violated and individual rights stifled. The "Address" to the Democracy of Wisconsin, prepared before the fall elections of 1862, and its Michigan counterpart relied heavily upon Jefferson for arguments and phraseology. Both were learned disquisitions on government, states' rights, and constitutionalism. Both argued reasonably and rationally against the practice of arbitrary arrest.

They condemned the policy of expediency pursued by the President and the doctrine of necessity used to justify unconstitutional measures.[81]

Throughout the war these Democratic critics, as conservatives who opposed change, remained strict constructionists. They set themselves up as defenders of states' rights and individual rights. Throughout the war, Thomas Jefferson remained their guide and Jeffersonian Democracy their ideal. They recognized that the government was being transformed from a federal union into a truly national state. Furthermore, they did not trust the man in the White House; they did not know what he had in his heart. They did not know that Lincoln basically objected to the arbitrary arrests and that the blame for the excesses rested on his marshals and generals or on jittery Republican governors.

Democrats made the question of arbitrary arrests one of the major issues in the elections of late 1862. Illinois Democratic spokesmen, especially, asked the electorate to repudiate "the reign of terror," the policy of intimidation and arrest.[82]

Naturally, the victorious Democrats interpreted the October and November election returns as a popular repudiation of Lincolnian policy. Some, like Charles Mason, believed that the Democratic landslide had saved the United States from becoming "a dictatorship."[83] Wilbur F. Storey, the editor-owner of the Chicago *Times* and a Democrat who had given the Lincoln administration qualified support early in the war, interpreted the election results as a repudiation of "Radicalism" (abolition) and "unconstitutional government" (arbitrary arrests).[84] The editor of the Democratic party's official organ in Indiana wrote in a like vein. He saw it as "an emphatic repudiation" of "Abolitionism generally" and "a condemnation of arbitrary arrests, of the suspension of the writ of habeas corpus, and [suspension] of the right of trial by a jury where the civil law and the courts had not been obstructed."[85] Mrs. Archibald McGregor, whose husband was still confined behind bars without charge, expressed her pleasure at the Democratic upsurge; she, too, interpreted it as the public's repudiation of arbitrary arrests.[86] Political prisoners like Dennis A. Mahony, Madison Y. Johnson, Dr. Edson B. Olds, and Archibald McGregor said "Amen!"

Those critics of the Lincoln administration who condemned arbitrary arrests most loudly did more than gloat over the election results. They added to the embarrassment suffered by Lincoln's party in a variety of ways. They gave heroes' welcomes to political prisoners freed soon after the votes were counted. An estimated 10,000 cheering partisans welcomed home Dr. Edson B. Olds. He had been elected *in absentia* (while a prisoner of state) to the Ohio state legislature and now strutted and swaggered enjoying his moments of glory.[87] At Canton, Ohio, when Archibald McGregor, editor of the *Stark County Democrat*, returned from prison, he was met by an "enormous crowd" at the railway depot. His friends escorted him in honor through the streets of the city and ended the occasion with a rally garnished with partisan speeches.[88] The homecoming accorded to Dennis A. Mahony in Dubuque was also a gala celebration. Democratic politicians in Dubuque County made capital out of the affair, much to the consternation of Lincoln's staunch supporters. The Republican editor of the Dubuque *Times* called the celebration a "most preposterous, treasonable, and disgraceful exhibition."[89] The wild reception given to David Sheean and Madison Y. Johnson, when they returned home after incarceration in Fort Lafayette, threw a blanket of gloom over Galena Republicans. Adding insult to injury, Sheean's friends induced him to be their candidate for mayor, and he was elected by a two to one majority.

Those Democrats who were most critical of the administration's arbitrary arrests carried their policy of embarrassing the President into Congress. On the first day of the new session, heartened by the election returns, the Hon. William A. Richardson of Illinois introduced a resolution calling for a congressional "inquiry" into political arrests and the treatment accorded political prisoners.[90] Democrats who supported the resolution spoke of "bastiles" and of *"lettres de cachet."* Vallandigham introduced a similar resolution and supported it with an able and restrained address. Garrett Davis, an able congressman from Kentucky, spent the entire afternoon of one day condemning President Lincoln for suspending the writ of habeas corpus and reviling what he called "the trend toward absolutism."[91] Although the Republicans readily prevented the passage of the various resolutions of inquiry, Lincoln's congressional critics had a chance to berate the administration. They loudly proclaimed that the election returns repudiated the practice of arbitrarily arresting Democrats and holding them without charge.

The widespread political arrests made before the election of 1862 backfired and embarrassed the administration. The public reaction expressed through the ballot palsied the hands of federal officials who had earlier been so bold and insulting. After the election it was again honorable to be a member of the opposition party. The editor of one midwestern newspaper portrayed the situation in his usual immoderate way:

For once in two years one can walk the streets without insult. The war of proscription is over. Political and social tyranny are about dead. Intolerant Knaves are silent; it is well they are. . . . King Bomba don't reign here now, and never will again. The people have closed the flood gates of tyranny, and mean to keep them closed.[92]

Although the popular reaction to arbitrary arrests, the general resentment against the acceptance of abolition as official policy, the economic depression of 1861–62, and midwestern sectionalism all contributed to Copperheadism in the upper Mississippi Valley, the basic ingredient was political partisanship. Democrats were inclined to view administration policy and Lincoln's every act through colored spectacles. Their concern for their party's welfare, their mistrust of Republicans, and their political prejudices colored their thinking. In some instances, the chief opposition to administration measures was rooted in rank partisanship. Democrats naturally tried to turn public sentiment to political advantage. Republicans, of course, were often guilty of the same sin.

The role of the minority or opposition party in a time of war defies any detailed delineation. Should the minority party dissolve? Should the majority party cease to practice partisanship? Should the two-party system be retained? No Marquis of Queensberry rules for political prize fights or for wartime elections had been drafted before the Civil War began. Democrats thought it their duty to win elections, to maintain the two-party system, and to criticize the Lincoln administration. They thought that a dictatorship would come to pass if they did not. The Democrats, as the "outs," were anxious to become the "ins"; they sought political office and political power.

The Republicans, on the other hand, were in no mood to surrender the offices and power they had won earlier at the polls. They wished to write their Chicago platform into federal law. They wished to enjoy political rewards which the election of 1860 placed at their disposal. They were reluctant to share patronage with the "outs" or to divide the spoils of office. They wanted the Democrats to support the Lincoln administration, but they did not want to give the opposition party a hand in shaping policy.

From the beginning of the war, the Democrats claimed that talk of unity was contradicted by Republican partisanship. Democrats who held federal appointments before President Lincoln took office lost their jobs as fast as the Republican political machine could furnish replacements. Democrats by the score claimed that the Republicans waged a constant war upon their party. One Democratic editor wrote:

Not a day passes but Administration organs are whining in our ears that there is no party now, the North is a unit, no more removal from office now except for cause, and all that kind o' stuff. And all this time passes, but the machinery of removals and appointments is run up to its utmost limit of execution. Would to God that this war on the rebels was carried on with half the activity and success that characterized this bloodless civil war on Democrats.[93]

The theme that the Lincoln administration practiced rank partisanship became a popular Democratic chant. The many political arrests made before the election of 1862 seemed to give some substance to that complaint. The Ohio state legislature, in Republican hands, redistricted the state disgracefully and brazenly—a partisan maneuver which led to Vallandigham's defeat in the congressional elections of 1862.[94] In several midwestern states, Republican legislatures devised voting-in-the-field schemes so soldier votes could be manipulated and counted in the Republican columns. Lincoln's Republican supporters pretended that the government and the administration were one, and they demanded unqualified support for the latter. Governor Oliver P. Morton of Indiana had no scruples when it came to turning events to the advantage of his party, and his narrow partisanship helped to precipitate a constitutional crisis in the Hoosier State. Governors Richard Yates of Illinois and Samuel Kirkwood of Iowa took advice from their party's state chairmen and drove Democrats to take retaliatory measures.

Democrats were as guilty of mudsill machinations and rank partisanship as their Republican brethren. They tried to cultivate votes in the field of war weariness and out of the defeats suffered by Federal armies on various battlefields. They tried to turn economic discontent into Democratic votes and blamed the party in power for all of the economic ills of the Midwest. They appealed to the sectional pride in midwestern hearts and tried to depict the Yankee as intolerant, grasping, and bigoted. They claimed that the Lincoln administration was creating a Frankenstein that would make the Midwest a slave to New England. Democrats appealed to racial bigotry and the evil spirit of Negrophobia to build up a distrust of the Lincoln administration. It was a favorite Democratic practice to label the opposition "Black Republicans." They tried to depict Lincoln as a tyrant in order to scare independent voters into Democratic party ranks. They pretended that Republicans had brought on the war, that compromise was easily possible, and that the South could not be conquered. They raised the cry over "oppressive taxation," "general ruin," and empty pocketbooks; they tried to make voters think of personal rather than national problems. They catered to the prejudice against the draft which existed in some communities.

Democratic efforts to capitalize on fear of the draft were best illustrated in Wisconsin. The draft of 1862 occurred only in those states which failed to provide enough volunteer regiments, and it was conducted under state, not federal, auspices. The Wisconsin counties which had failed to provide enough volunteers were peopled mainly by immigrants from Bavaria, Luxembourg, Belgium, Saxony, and Prussia. Some had migrated to America to escape militarism at home. Most of them did not understand the momentous events swirling over the land and saw no reason why they should become involved. They recalled the promises made by the state's agents who met them in New York and presented a glowing picture of the opportunities and freedom which Wisconsin offered. Many of them had purchased small farms or city homes and were heavily in debt. They feared that enforced military service might mean missed mortgage payments and the threat of foreclosure. They feared that their families might suffer if they were drafted, for danger and death lurked on the distant battlefields. The editors of such papers as the Milwaukee *See-Bote* and the Port Washington *Ozaukee County Advertiser* encouraged the fears of these uneasy people so that they would vote Democratic and hate Republicanism. The German-Americans of Ozaukee County were especially ill at ease, for they were convinced that an anti-Catholic policy had been pursued in the naming of an army chaplain. Furthermore, the draft quotas assigned to Ozaukee and Washington counties exceeded those of larger and more populous counties.

Fearing that the public's reaction to enforced conscription might affect Republican chances to win the November, 1862, elections, the state's governor bowed to party pressure to postpone the draft lottery until after the ballots were counted. Six Wisconsin counties, all with large elements of foreign-born, witnessed various degrees of disorder when the draft was finally made. Anti-draft demonstrations occurred in Milwaukee, but troops patrolled the streets and overawed the menacing mobs. Green Bay (Brown County) and Fond du Lac witnessed hostile activities, but the authorities also kept the situation in hand. Moblike demonstrations, which featured the throwing of stones and the hurling of insults, set the stage for a riot in Sheboygan County, but the courage of the quartermaster and the plucky draft officials saved the day.

Several Washington County communities witnessed violence, and mob action forced a postponement of the lottery. In Port Washington the explosion of anti-draft sentiment produced a real riot. The draft commissioner was attacked by an angry mob and forced to flee for his life; the machinery for the draft was destroyed; and the homes of several substantial citizens (all Republicans) were sacked. Much property was destroyed. The governor ordered troops to the disaffected areas. In the presence of posted troops, the draft officials completed the process of drawing names to meet assigned quotas.[95] But anti-draft sentiment continued to be a political factor in several Wisconsin counties, and Democrats reaped a political harvest in areas heavily peopled with immigrant Americans. Some Democratic editors unabashedly expressed a sympathy for the Europeans who had left their homeland to seek peace and happiness in America. "In Heaven's name," wrote the editor of the Sheboygan *Journal*, "let us have no more of this conscription—a system which the most proscriptive monarchial government would scarce resort to."[96]

Democratic partisanship was displayed publicly in Illinois early in 1862. An election for delegates to a state constitutional convention turned into a Democratic landslide. Samuel Buckmaster, elected to preside over the august body, shamelessly stated that he wanted a partisan constitution drafted. He said that he was elected as "a square-toed Democrat" and he wanted the Democratic-controlled convention to checkmate the Republican party.[97] The partisan delegates subsequently conducted half a dozen "investigations" intended to embarrass the administration of Governor Richard Yates. The Democratic majority tried to shear the Republican governor of his military power and to check his authority on other fronts too.[98] It halved the Republican governor's four-year term. It investigated army appointments and army purchases in the hope that the state administration could be discredited. It gerrymandered brazenly when it rearranged the boundary lines for the state's legislative and congressional districts. The convention's foul partisanship and its usurpation of authority made the document it drafted an unpalpable one. The contest over ratification degenerated into a strict party fight, and the Republicans retaliated by marshaling their state organization to turn out an anti-constitution vote. Democrats fought to have the proposed constitution ratified so that they could capitalize upon the political trends evident in the Midwest—a trend that was later revealed in the fall elections of 1862. When the "new" constitution was rejected at the polls, the Democrats moaned while Republicans held victory rallies. "The result," wrote a Republican regular, "is a single rebuke to those who framed a partisan constitution for their own special benefit."[99]

Democratic efforts to turn public opinion to political advantage received an assist from the exposition of corruption in various quarters. The finger of guilt was pointed in the direction of Simon Cameron, Lincoln's choice to head the War Department. Misjudgment, influence-peddling, and fraud came to light and President Lincoln was embarrassed at the charges and the revelations. In January of 1862 Mr. Cameron vacated the war portfolio. Fraud, corruption, and extravagance also characterized General John C. Frémont's administration of the Department of the West. Fraud and corruption seemed to be the order of the day on other fronts too. Dealing in confiscated cotton became a national scandal. Crooked contractors delivered shoddy material, and dishonest quartermasters filled their pockets at public expense. The charges and countercharges left respectable men nauseated. The Democrats naturally tried to use exposures and rumors of dishonesty to political advantage. Democratic editors constantly condemned the Lincoln administration for failing to clean house. They criticized Lincoln for failing to make an example of the "birds of prey" who had been "fed and fattened upon public plunder."[100] "Even patriotism," wrote one critical editor, "cannot overleap the mountains of incompetency, corruption and political intrigue which are reared before it in Washington."[101] Democratic congressmen, too, rushed in to attack the corruptionists and to discredit the administration. John G. Davis (Kentucky), Daniel Voorhees (Indiana), and William A. Richardson (Illinois) took turns damning Cameron and Frémont. Davis said that the nation needed an Andy

Jackson to clean out the Augean stables of corruption and that Jackson would have hung Cameron and scourged Frémont. "Not one-half of the money poured into the public treasury by the people goes to defray the expenses of war," said the affluent Kentucky congressman; "it is stolen by the cormorants at Washington." He added that Lincoln was "as corrupt as those surrounding him" and merely "the smallest toad in the puddle."[102] Voorhees advocated a policy of "punishing the thieves." He suggested that the liberties of the people were in greater danger from the "corruptions and from the profligacy practiced in the various Departments of the Government" than from the enemy in the field.[103] Richardson condemned not only Frémont and Cameron, but the entire administration. Other midwestern congressmen joined the attack upon "pilfering and pelf" and tried to turn the matter into Democratic votes. They gave support to a House resolution which censured Cameron for mismanagement and misjudgment and for pursuing a policy "highly injurious to the public service."[104]

Democratic politicos also tried to turn the many defeats suffered by Northern armies into votes at election time. The list of decisive defeats for Union arms in the first two years of the war was written in blood, and there were few victories. The situation encouraged defeatism. Democratic politicians said that the war was a failure and the President was incompetent. Lincoln ineptly juggled his commanders and repeatedly bet on the wrong horses. In vain he searched for a general who could match General Lee on the battlefield. Democratic critics laid the blame for the military defeats at Lincoln's doorstep. They believed that "managerial confusion" reigned in Washington and that army appointments and removals were based more on politics than on ability. Democrats were shocked when Radical Republicans launched a campaign to remove General McClellan from command. They deplored the vicious attack upon McClellan made by Congressman John A. Gurley of Ohio and rallied to McClellan's defense. Midwestern Democrats applauded when S. S. Cox of Ohio came to McClellan's support with an effective speech in the House of Representatives. "I have read your patriotic defense of McClellan and your masterly using up of Abolition gospeler [Gurley]," wrote an Ohio constituent to Cox, "and laughed and cheered in turn."[105] After Cox had finished his attack upon the political critics of General McClellan, Daniel Voorhees entered the fray. Voorhees, called the "Tall Sycamore of the Wabash" by his friends, gave a masterly oration colored by learning as well as sarcasm. Voorhees drove the spit into Gurley and then proceeded to roast him with searing words and fiery ridicule until he had burned him to a crisp.[106]

Democratic defense of McClellan failed to prevent his removal. His failure to follow up the advantage he held after the Battle of Antietam made him vulnerable, and Radical Republicans made his dismissal a condition for giving Lincoln the support he needed. Radical Republicans were "sick" of keeping "bitter and uncompromising political enemies" in command, wrote an Illinois Republican. This Radical Republican wanted Democratic generals demoted and Republican generals ("friends that stand by his [Lincoln's] political principles") advanced.[107] Such Republican governors as Oliver P. Morton of Indiana and Samuel J. Kirkwood of Iowa believed it their duty to select military leaders from those who sympathized with the aims of the administration. Governor Richard Yates of Illinois used his appointing power to Republicanize the army.

When Zachariah Chandler took charge of the Radical Republican campaign "to get" McClellan, the general's removal became imperative. The Democratic editor of the Detroit *Free Press* labeled Chandler's anti-McClellan speech a "bastard philippic." Democrats generally regarded the "Report" of the joint Committee on the Conduct of the War as an "infamous document" and its authors as mere "political assassins."[108] When McClellan was removed from command of the army right after the November election of 1862, Democrats fumed. They claimed that the removal was made because he was a Democrat and because early in his career he had opposed abolitionism. They contended that Lincoln was more interested in appeasing the radical wing of his party than in saving the country and winning the war. Midwestern Democrats claimed that Lincoln's "bungling" and "imbecility" explained many of his acts and that incompetence and stupidity were Lincolnian traits.[109] One Democratic Congressman put "imbecility" in the "trinity of evil" fostered by Republicanism. "The way things are going," he wrote, "is enough to make angels swear if they ever indulge in that classical amusement."[110]

Democratic harping on corruption, bungling, incompetency, and on military failures did gain some votes. The Democrats, as the "outs," were anxious to collect votes wherever they could be found. It was good politics to speak of "failures" and Republican fanaticism during the political campaigns of October and November of 1862. After the votes were counted, Republicans tried to explain the cause of their defeat. One Republican analyst, trying to explain the widespread opposition to the Lincoln administration set upon "loss of confidence on the part of the people in the wisdom of the government" as the logical explanation.[111] Surely defeatism and the failure of President Lincoln to solve his military problems nurtured Copperheadism.

In certain sections of the Midwest, the Copperhead movement was flavored with religious prejudice, or religious concern. The immigrant-Americans, especially the Irish and the Low Germans, recognized that the Republican party possessed a Know-Nothing taint. To these Democrats and Catholics, the Republican party seemed to be but an omnium-gatherum for Know-Nothings, Abolitionists, and Whigs. These German-Americans and Irish-Americans mistrusted the Republican party when they saw so many former Know-Nothings waving the party banners. Prominent Republicans like Salmon P. Chase, Henry Wilson, and Schuyler Colfax had Know-Nothing backgrounds. Shelby Cullom, Republican bigwig who served as speaker of the lower house of the Illinois state legislature, was widely known for his participation in Know-Nothingism. In Indiana most of the members of the Know-Nothing movement went over to the Republican party before the war. The same was true in Ohio, Kentucky, and Missouri. One of the most prominent Detroit Republicans had acquired distinction for defending the "right" of a Protestant clergyman to give anti-Catholic tirades and sermons. Jesse Clement, editor of the Dubuque *Times*, Radical Republican organ, had previously acquired a reputation as an intemperate Know-Nothing and as a notorious Catholic baiter. Clement's attacks on the Irish Catholics were seconded by Rev. Billingsgate Smith, Republican editor of the Dubuque *Union*, who mixed religion and politics in the pulpit as well as on the editorial page.[112]

It was easy for such Democratic editors as Peter V. Deuster of the Milwaukee *See-Bote* and Mahony of the Dubuque *Herald* to weld the Irish and German Catholics into solid voting blocks for the anti-administration party. Such German-language newspapers as the Indianapolis *Indiana Volksblatt*, the Fort Wayne *Staats Zeitung*, and the Dubuque *National Demokrat* also made appeals to religious bigotry. The Fort Wayne *Sentinel*, the New Albany *Ledger*, the Cincinnati *Enquirer*, and the Detroit *Free Press* made their appeals to religious prejudice more subtle but equally effective. Catholics were warned that New England puritans wanted to make their sectional church into a national church. The prominence of Congregational clergy in the Republican party helped scare Irish and German Catholics into the Democratic party. It was also pointed out that such freethinkers as Carl Schurz and other Forty-eighters were active Republicans. Democrats also reminded the Irish- and German-Americans that Horace Greeley, the prophet of Republicanism, and his New York *Tribune* were tainted with Fourierism, socialism, "free-lovism," and communism, which were all supposedly anathema to Catholics. Therefore, it was easy for Democratic strategists to build a solid voting block out of religious prejudice, or religious fears. Religious views since the beginning of time have been a powerful motivating force. It is no accident that the German Catholics and Irish Catholics almost without exception voted the straight Democratic ticket and joined in the Copperhead movement.[113]

In a sense, the gulf between the Irish and the Republicans was more than a religious one, and religious prejudice was but one of the levers used by Democratic politicians to force Irish-Americans into the party of Douglas and Vallandigham. It was, more truly, a socioeconomic breach between the lower and higher strata of American society. In a sense, the Republican party, directed by ex-Whigs, was the party of wealth and industry; Republicans usually were both employers and exploiters. The Irish and the Low Germans, on the other hand, belonged to the "lower class" of urban society. Educationally, socially, and economically they were the inferiors who feared free Negro competition and tended toward locofocoism. As members of the laboring class, they paid a heavy price in the early years of the war. Wages lagged far behind the rising cost of living. A touring foreign correspondent noted that "labor" was "ground down to the utmost power of endurance."[114] Although opportunities for employment increased after the first year of the war because of jobs vacated by volunteers and war production, the influx of free Negroes and border-state white refugees tended to give employers a tighter control of the labor market.[115]

Republican editorial writers frequently offered evidence that a socioeconomic barrier existed between their enlightened party members and the "inferior" immigrant-Americans. The Republican editor of the Cincinnati *Commercial* condemned the "lowly" Irish and classified them as "stuffed apes."[116] The Republican editor of the Detroit *Advertiser and Tribune* regretted that the "ignorant" Irish had become "locusts" who proved their worthlessness by voting the Democratic ticket.[117] After a Chicago municipal election turned into a Democratic landslide the embittered editor of the *Western Railroad Gazette,* secured his revenge by lambasting "lowly" Irish "voting cattle" who carried "Dimmecratic tickets" in their hands at the polls. He characterized them as knaves, illiterates, and "filthy, stinking God-forsaken wretches."[118] Other Republicans, more learned and more wealthy than the unlettered Irish, also hated to see the "unwashed Dimocracy" assert itself.[119]

The lower classes of the cities had their counterpart in the "Butternut Democracy" of the rural regions, made up mainly of Southerners who crossed into Ohio, Indiana, Illinois, or Iowa to pre-empt the poorer soils of those states. Their homesteads were often below average in size and quality. They were often illiterate and uncultured, according to New England standards. They wore homespun clothing usually dyed with the bark of the butternut tree. Those ex-Southerners, usually Methodists or Baptists, recognized that Congregationalism was a bourgeois church and that the scions from New England controlled the economic lifeblood of their community. The ex-Yankees were the moneylenders, the storekeepers, the mill-owners, the land speculators, and the business promoters; the ex-Southerners were the debtors, the less learned, the small farmers who squeezed out a meager living. The religious, social, and cultural crevasses which separated the ex-Yankees and the ex-Southerners of the upper Midwest also helped produce different political loyalties. Most ex-Southerners and their sons developed an allegiance to the Democratic party, whereas the ex–New Englanders were first Whigs, then Republicans. In time and in turn, the ex-Yankees usually became the ardent unionists, while the ex-Southerners usually joined the Coppperhead ranks.[120]

The Copperhead counties of Ohio, inhabited mainly by the ex-Southerners or immigrants from Germany or Ireland, were scattered over the state. In Iowa the ex-Southerners occupied the lower tier of counties, where the soil was less fertile and less productive than in the northern part of the state. In Indiana the lower half of the state, a less fertile region, was taken over by ex-Southern residents. Lower Illinois, peopled mostly by settlers who crossed the Ohio River, possessed the state's poorer soils. Republicans derisively named that area "dark Egypt." Illiteracy, poverty, and Copperheadism were the region's distinguishing marks.[121] The Republicans should have expected the poorer sections of the Midwest to support leveling movements, to dress in butternut clothing, and to vote the Democratic ticket. One Ohio observer who watched the "Butternut Democracy" on parade recorded his contempt for the backwoods people:

I went out and saw the Copperhead demonstration today. It was large. There were a number of women in the procession on horseback. Many of their riding skirts were so old, rusty, ragged & dirty, they might have belonged to their grandmothers. It was the unterrified, unwashed Democracy.[122]

Republican contempt for the "Butternut Democracy" knew no bounds. Democratic editors, on the other hand, came to the defense of the backwoodsmen who wore jeans and linseys dyed with the "humble butternut." "Shame on the newspaper or party that would make poverty or simplicity a reproach . . . ,"[123] wrote one Democrat. The Democratic editor of the Indianapolis *State Sentinel* made his reproach stronger and longer:

The *Journal* has a great deal to say about the "butternut" Democracy, and every Shanghai office seeker and sympathizer with Giddings [Republican abolitionist congressman], who can sport a white vest and handkerchief, and keep his shirt collar from cutting his ears off, repeats the word with a sneer whenever he sees a number of honest farmers together. Those city dandies have a great contempt for people who toil, and who dress in homespun, and who occasionally soil their hands by taking hold of the plow and the shovel. Their delicate noses instinctively turn up at the dress of honest toil, and "butternut," "pokeberry," or some other slang is lisped in derision. It used to be the "barefeet" Democracy in Jackson's time—then it was the "pokeberry" Democracy, and now it is the "butternut" Democracy—and they all, as used, mean the same thing—a contempt for those who earn their bread by honest toil.[124]

Both Republicans and Democrats, it is evident, admitted that midwestern Copperheadism in some sections possessed socioeconomic aspects.

Border state residents who complained against Lincoln's acceptance of abolition, or deteriorating economic conditions, or the numerous arbitrary arrests soon learned that the greatest threat to their rights came from soldiers who camped and plundered. Residents of Kansas, Missouri, and Kentucky suffered as both Confederate and Union soldiers invaded and confiscated. "Jayhawking" became a popular pastime among soldiers stationed in Missouri. Soldiers easily convinced themselves that "confiscation" or "jayhawking" was unlike theft or robbery. A soldier campaigning in Missouri reported:

We have plenty to eat now. The Boys Jayhawk a great many things. Last night they went from our mess into the town of Springfield, broke open a cellar, and took all the canned fruit nine or ten men could carry. . . . At first I thought it was stealing to take things in that way, but a "change has come o'er the spirit of my dreams" and I consider jayhawking a legitimate trade, especially when the articles taken are food for soldiers.[125]

Soldiers in search of food and excitement failed to distinguish between the property of friends of the Union and that of Confederate sympathizers. Apples, chickens, and honey tasted the same whether taken from pro-Southern or pro-Union homes. "As an instance the other day," wrote a soldier campaigning in Missouri, "we were marching along—an old man brought water from his well to the roadside and gave it to the men to drink and while he was doing this some of the men went into his premises and actually stole and carried off thirty stands of bees and stole the honey."[126]

Kentucky residents constantly complained against thefts which were classed as confiscation. Union soldiers especially gained an unsavory reputation as midnight marauders. They raided cellars, emptied hen houses, and looted granaries. Fence rails turned into firewood and property was often wantonly destroyed. "The man on whose farm we camp for one night," wrote a seasoned campaigner, "is ruined."

These extracurricular activities of the Union soldiers turned friends of the Union into critics of the Lincoln administration. Soldier-plundering made more Kentuckians into Copperheads or rebels than newspaper propaganda and congressional acts did. Discontent became so widespread in Kentucky, Missouri, and Kansas that martial law superseded civil law. Union governors were little more than the puppets of Union generals. Arbitrary arrests were made on a wholesale basis, elections were controlled by the Union officers, and civil government backed down before government by the sword. Kentuckians, Missourians, and Kansans compiled long lists of grievances. In late 1862 the reputation of the Lincoln administration reached an all-time low.

Midwestern Copperheadism, as avid opposition to the Lincoln administration, was a complex and nearly intangible movement from the very start. It was a tangle of economic, religious, social, personal, and sectional threads. Its composition varied from state to state, locality to locality, and person to person. It was greater than the sum of its parts. It was colored by a conservatism that opposed the changes which the Civil War was slowly but surely bringing to America. To a degree it was simply Jeffersonian Democracy in revolt against the Hamiltonian principles that were triumphing in America. In a large measure, midwestern opposition to the Lincoln administration was built on the foundation of Democratic partisanship. The opposition party was struggling for survival.

The Democratic party's struggle for survival received a tremendous assist in the elections of October and November 1862. Ohio Democrats elected their slate of state officials (the governor and half of the state officials were elected in even years) won fourteen of the nineteen congressional seats, and polled 185,000 votes to the 178,000 garnered by the Republican candidates. Illinois Democrats elected nine of the fourteen members of Congress and secured control of both houses of the state legislature. Governor Yates (elected to a four-year term in 1860) was thus scheduled to face a hostile legislature during the next session. Indiana returns paralleled those of Illinois. Eight of the eleven congressional seats went to Democrats and a hostile legislature was also elected to oppose the Republican governor, Oliver P. Morton (like Yates, elected for a four-year term in 1860). Wisconsin and Minnesota trends heartened Democrats in those states. Wisconsin Democrats bragged that their party had polled nearly 20,000 more votes than in the gubernatorial election of the previous year. Although Democrats secured half of the six congressional seats, they missed getting control of the state legislature. Michigan Democrats won only one of the state's six seats in Congress, but they gave Republicans a real scare, for the incumbent Republican governor received a scant majority of 6,600 out of 131,000 votes cast. Iowa Democrats, hampered by an intra-party split, failed to realize the full benefits of the political trend.[127]

Democrats gloried in the extent of "the political revolt of

1862." Samuel Medary of the *Crisis* termed the election the great-est "revolution" since the political triumph of Andrew Jackson.[128] The elated editor of the Indianapolis *State Sentinel* made claims even more extensive, writing that it was one of the greatest revo-lutions in the history of the world.[129] These Democratic leaders viewed the election returns as a repudiation of the Lincoln ad-ministration and its many unpopular policies. Vallandigham, de-feated at the polls because of Republican gerrymandering, taunted the President: "Where are your bastiles now, your arbitrary arrests?" The triumphant Democrats read the election returns as a repudiation of Lincoln's proclamations and his "usurpation" of power. They interpreted the results as a victory for conservatism, and they hoped that the President would revoke his proclamation of emancipation and discontinue the practice of arresting citizens arbitrarily. The election results emboldened Lincoln's critics. They encouraged Democrats to practice partyism and foretold the coming of a bitter political feud in Indiana and Illinois.[130]

If Democrats expected Lincoln to retreat from the position he had taken regarding emancipation, they were mistaken. Lincoln's message to Congress of December 1, 1862, made no concession to the election returns. "The tenacity with which Mr. Lincoln holds on to his emancipation proclivities, notwithstanding the rebuke administered in the result of the election at the North of the past fall," wrote a disillusioned Kentuckian, "cannot fail . . . to alarm the friends of the Union and of Constitutional liberty throughout our broad land."[131]

Not only were conservatives alarmed over Lincoln's statements that he was moving forward upon the issue of emancipation, but they pondered the meaning of his contention that revolutionary action and revolutionary ideas were necessary to save the coun-try.[132] Conservatives were reminded of Robespierre! They feared radicalism and hoped to return to the ways of the past. They re-peated their claims that the election had repudiated radicalism and developed their slogan "The Constitution as it is, the Union as it was."

While Democrats grew bolder in their criticism of President

Lincoln and asked that the clock be turned back, word of another military disaster spread a cloud of gloom over the North. General Ambrose E. Burnside, onetime darling of the Radicals, rashly stormed Lee's impregnable position atop Marye's Heights near Fredericksburg on December 13. The Federal assault was repulsed and the Northern casualties totaled nearly 13,000. Democratic politicians placed this failure also at Lincoln's door. A wave of defeatism swept over the North and the Copperhead ranks grew in number. Some Democrats thought that Lincoln's impeachment was in order. In an almost illegible hand a Wisconsin leader of the opposition party confided his anti-Lincoln prejudices to his diary:

The President of the United States is responsible for the miserable state of things, and for this and many special and arbitrary acts which he has committed and authorized to be committed, I solemnly believe that [he] ought to be impeached and legally and constitutionally deposed from the high office of President of the United States.[133]

Samuel Medary, doughty editor of *Crisis,* also thought that Lincoln deserved to be impeached. He closed the year on a gloomy note: "The year 1862 has been a year of blood and plunder, of carnage and conflagration, . . . of falsehood and corruption, . . . of bastiles, persecutions and tears, . . . of despotism, desolation and death."[134] Republican leaders, looking back on a year in which they had failed on the battlefields and at the polls, also were discouraged. Count Adam Gurowski wrote a final notation in his diary: "Dec. 31, 1862—Midnight—Disappear! Oh year of disgraces, year of slaughter and sacrifices."[135]

II

Rampant Partyism

THE EARLY MONTHS of 1863 were days of gloom for supporters of the Lincoln administration; seldom did any ray of hope shine through. There were no military victories of any significance. Many midwesterners convinced themselves that the South could not be beaten, and war-weariness undermined Northern morale.

The midwestern malady of defeatism contributed considerably to the emergence of a peace movement. On January 14, Clement L. Vallandigham shocked Lincoln's supporters by asking that coercion cease and reunion be effected through concessions to the South. Moreover, Lincoln's critics, who viewed the January 1 Emancipation Proclamation as unconstitutional, publicly charged the chief executive with altering the objectives of the war. Many, therefore, begged to be excused from further support of the war or of any administration measure.

Partyism entered a new phase early in 1863. Encouraged by the election results of late 1862, Democrats boldly hacked at their political adversaries. The Democratic-controlled state legislatures in Indiana and Illinois engaged in knock-down, drag-out fights with Republican governors. Democratic state and local conventions waged war upon the Lincoln administration, widening the breach between the two political parties. Democratic congressmen turned their guns on the President and on administration policies. Even Democratic judges boldly gave decisions challenging the administration. Republicans were equally guilty of rank partisanship, so partyism erupted with full fury, causing irreparable damage.

President Lincoln's prayer for a decisive military victory went unanswered in the early months of 1863. The Army of the Potomac was inactive, licking wounds suffered in mid-December at Fredericksburg, where Lee gave Burnside a military lesson. General Joseph Hooker, named to succeed Burnside, spent the winter months rebuilding morale and reorganizing his army. McClellan's partisan supporters dreamed of what might have been; Burnside's blunder at Fredericksburg seemed to justify their faith in a general famed for caution on the battlefield and candor in his public statements.

While the eastern armies rested and recuperated, Federal and Confederate troops played a game of cat and mouse in central Tennessee. A major engagement took shape in the closing days of the old year between Federal troops commanded by General William S. Rosecrans and a Confederate force under General Braxton Bragg. The advantage which Bragg gained early in the contest was wiped out by events of January 2. On that day a reckless attack against the Union entrenchments cost the Confederates 2,000 men. Consequently, General Bragg withdrew southward. Both sides lost so heavily that neither was in condition to renew the fight. This encounter, known as the Battle of Murfreesboro (Stone River), could hardly be called a Union victory. Federal casualties (nearly 13,000 out of an army of 47,000) were higher than those of the enemy. Furthermore, the Confederates destroyed more than 500 wagons filled with Union provisions and supplies valued at more than a million dollars. So General Rosecrans spent the early months of 1863 counting his losses, collecting new supplies, and waiting for spring.

While the major armies lay idle, Confederate raids occurred in Kentucky and Missouri. Residents of the states north of the Ohio River became anxious when rumors or reports of Confederate raids into the Blue Grass State appeared in their newspapers. On

February 5 one of General John Morgan's raiders led a company far into Kentucky, burned South Union Depot, captured and destroyed a loaded steamer tied to a pier on the Green River, and scampered back into Tennessee. There was a fear in certain quarters that Confederate raiders might reach the soil of Indiana, Illinois, and Ohio. Governors Morton of Indiana and Yates of Illinois were somewhat jittery: each had a hostile legislature on his hands and Kentucky was nearby. Northern morale would suffer if the Confederates crossed the Ohio. This would be proof that the administration's military policy was a complete failure.

Defeatism was widespread in early 1863. Many midwesterners were convinced that the South could not be conquered and that enough blood had already been spent. On the floor of the House of Representatives on January 14, 1863, Vallandigham, then a lame-duck congressman, publicly announced his conversion to the cause of peace. Vallandigham reviewed the military failures of the North and proclaimed that the South could not be coerced or vanquished.[1] Many Democratic editors applauded Vallandigham's views and a number of them printed the bombshell in its entirety. Dennis A. Mahony of the Dubuque *Herald* called it "bold, logical, direct, and positive."[2] Samuel Medary of the *Crisis* added his indorsement of Vallandigham's noteworthy speech and warned the Lincoln administration that the West wanted the Mississippi River opened and its markets restored. The Columbus editor wrote that the West would "not wait a twelve-month longer without making an effort on its own account."[3] The editors of the Dayton *Empire* and the Hamilton *True Telegraph* admitted that they, like Vallandigham, were defeatists. Joseph J. Bingham of the Indianapolis *State Sentinel* printed all of Vallandigham's speech, but he still thought that the war could be directed toward a successful conclusion under Democratic auspices.[4] In other quarters, too, the lack of military successes and the mounting casualty lists spread discouragement, discontent, and defeatism.

The question of emancipation, debated throughout 1862, remained an emotional issue in the early months of

1863. Many Democrats had hoped against hope that President Lincoln would obey the popular will of the electorate as expressed in the fall elections of 1862 and retract his pledge to issue a final proclamation of emancipation on January 1, 1863. Even after Lincoln restated his intentions in his December 1, 1862, message to Congress, some Democrats deluded themselves that Lincoln might return to the conservative camp and leave well enough alone. Those who hoped that the President would interpret the election returns as a mandate to repudiate radicalism were taken aback on January 1. On that memorable day Lincoln "freed" the slaves of the rebels (exempting the border states), hiding his humanitarianism behind the cloak of military necessity.

No other Lincoln-penned document elicited such paeans of praise and such damning denunciation as the Emancipation Proclamation. Radical Republicans rejoiced that Lincoln had seen the light and that the mighty North now had a moral cause to stir it to action. They emitted a chorus of huzzas, labeling January 1, 1863, an "Epochal day."[5] One of President Lincoln's secretaries, pausing as he made copies of the original document, looked into the distance. He could hear the sound of clanking iron ("as of breaking and falling chains") and the shouts of joy and laughter of the "newly freed." He also heard "the anger of the fierce opposition, wrath, fury, dismay."[6]

Expressions of "wrath, fury, dismay" soon came from the ranks of the Democratic party. Editors wrote vicious editorials, orators lambasted the President and his proclamation; and pamphleteers added words of disapproval and indignation.

The newspaper editors most successfully used the Emancipation Proclamation to whip up anti-administration sentiment. Mahony of the Dubuque *Herald* directed his caustic attack against both Lincoln and the proclamation. He called the proclamation the "crowning act of Lincoln's folly" and asserted that its promulgator was "a brainless tyrant, a perjured public servant, a blundering partisan, a buffoon President."[7] Mahony sincerely believed that the document was proof that Lincoln and his party had practiced "deceit," changing the war into an abolition crusade. The Dubuque diehard also believed that the proclamation was unconstitutional and its issuance proof that Lincoln intended to become a despot or tyrant. "Abolition created the Administration, has shaped its policy, has dictated its appointments," wrote the embittered Irishman, "and must be left to furnish the material requisites of men and money."[8] In other words, he believed that Lincoln's "last unconstitutional act" excused Democrats from supporting the war in any way. He was sure that the President brazenly and brashly directed the ship of state against the current of public opinion. He shamelessly suggested that revolution was the only means left to redress grievances, and issued a challenge to all those "who love liberty":

The people who submit to the insolent fanaticism which dictated this last act, *are and deserve to be enslaved* to the class which Abraham Lincoln self-sufficiently declares free. If they possessed a tithe of the spirit which animated Rome when Cataline was expelled from its walls . . . they would hurl him into the Potomac . . . Cabinet, Congress, and all.[9]

In spite of Mahony's complete detestation of Lincoln and his immoderate statements on many occasions, the acute Iowan correctly assessed the effect of the Emancipation Proclamation on the Midwest. He believed that it would discourage enlistments in many sections, that it would breed further discontent in the border states, that it would prompt Democrats to plump for peace, and that it would unite the South to a man.[10]

Other Democratic editors restated some or all of Mahony's arguments against the Emancipation Proclamation and some even matched the Iowan's malevolence. The editor of the Ashland *Union* termed Lincoln's proclamation a "ukase" and its author a "tyrant and usurper."[11] The partisan editor of the Chatfield *Democrat* condemned Lincoln as a tyrant and added that the proclamation was "the most foolish joke ever got off by the six-foot four Commander-in-Chief."[12] The editor of the Green Bay *Advocate* defined the proclamation as "a rash act," calling it "one of a series of imbecile and disastrous steps."[13] The neighboring editor of the Oshkosh *Courier* claimed that Lincoln's "political medicine" would "kill both the patient and the doctor."[14] The anger of Samuel Medary of the *Crisis* and William T. Logan of the Dayton *Empire* knew no bounds. Similar bitterness was evident in the editorials written by Flavius J. Mills of the Sheboygan *Journal*. Mills called the Emancipation Proclamation "a youthful indiscretion" and continued to condemn it for more than a year. He was positive that Lincoln had deliberately deceived the Democrats, perverting a war to save the Union into a war to free the slaves. Dismayed and disillusioned, he expressed this partisan pronouncement:

All the support the war has ever received from the Democrats was originally obtained by a base cheat, an infamous swindle, a damnable deception. . . . The Democratic party trusted and was betrayed. "The war for the Union" was cordially supported by Democrats all over the North. It turned out to be a war of abolition, of violation of the Constitution, a war by the Eastern oligarchy.[15]

Some Democratic editors allowed their racial prejudices to color their editorials. Such papers as the Cincinnati *Enquirer*, the Hamilton *True Telegraph*, the Belleville *Democrat*, and the St. Louis *Missouri Republican* appealed to the spirit of Negrophobia. Mahony had reminded his readers that emancipation would flood the entire North with cheap labor, and the same fear was expressed by other editors. Peter V. Deuster of the Milwaukee *See-Bote* tried to convince German workmen that free Negroes might get their jobs and undermine their security.[16] Another Milwaukee German-language weekly, the *Banner & Volksfreund*, added the prediction that Lincoln's latest proclamation would reduce the Negro to "poverty, rags, and helplessness."[17] The rationale that slavery was best for both the Negro and the white man found supporters north of the Ohio River. "In my heart I believe our policy [opposing emancipation] is the best for the white race, the black race, the country, and humanity," wrote an Ohio supporter of Vallandigham, "and I can die on the scaffold if needs be, but I cannot change my faith."[18] That Ohioan's anti-Negro bias grew more intense after he became acquainted with some "contrabands" who were in trouble in Dayton. He revealed that prejudice in a letter to his brother:

I have been engaged in the Court House since Wednesday assisting Mr. Elliot in the persecution of some negroes for burglaries and petty thieving. There was a miserable nest of them . . . 5 in number . . . the heads of five households . . . living all together, having everything in common, not excepting their women, and subsisting almost entirely upon the fruits of their crimes. Four out of the five were of the class known now-a-days as contrabands . . . slaves freed by the advance of our army into Dixie. They are the advance guard of that great army which is advancing northward to take possession of our jails and penitentiaries. Ere long we will be compelled to build new ones for their accommodation.[19]

Mahony's prediction that the Emancipation Proclamation would divide the North and deepen disaffection was verified in many sections of the Midwest and was confirmed by the action taken in many editorial offices. Henry N. Walker of the Detroit *Free Press*, for example, had given the Lincoln administration qualified support before January 1, 1863. His criticism of the administration had been tempered by his devotion to the Union and his desire to defeat the South. After Lincoln issued his final proclamation of emancipation, Walker became a violent critic of the administration, a bold partisan, and a leading Michigan Copperhead. In long and severe editorials he argued that the President had no constitutional right to free the slaves and to "pervert" the objectives of the war as earlier established by Congress. He contended that the doctrine of military necessity was but an excuse used by all tyrants. He called the proclamation "a rope of sand," for it did not touch slavery in those areas where the federal government had authority, whereas it "pretended" to free slaves in those areas where Lincoln's "ordinances" had no force. Like Mahony, editor Walker argued that the document was a devious and divisive measure. It would divide the North and be used by Southern radicals to smash the last vestiges of Union sentiment in the South. "In only one quarter will there be joy over the proclamation," wrote the editor of the Detroit *Free Press*. "Jefferson Davis will seize upon it as kindling to fire the Southern heart. Every rebel in arms will grow sturdier in his hate and opposition to a government whose head thus takes pains to convince him that it is abolition-ized."[20]

The metamorphosis of the editor of the Chicago *Times* was quite like that of Walker of the Detroit *Free Press*. Wilbur F. Storey, who took over control of the Chicago *Times* shortly be-fore the start of the Civil War, followed a sane path during the first two years of the conflict. He was a mild critic of the Lincoln administration until Lincoln plunged into the sea of abolition. Then Storey cut the cord of restraint and the Chicago *Times* soon gained a reputation as an imprudent newssheet. He turned a paper which had earlier practiced moderation into the best-known Cop-perhead newspaper in the Midwest. Editor Storey regarded the Emancipation Proclamation as unnecessary and undesirable and termed its issuance "the most wicked, atrocious, and revolting deed recorded in the annals of civilization."[21]

The course of action pursued by Storey of the Chicago *Times* and Walker of the Detroit *Free Press* was similar to that followed by two other editors whose names became well known before the end of the war. Marcus Mills "Brick" Pomeroy of the La Crosse *Democrat* and Charles H. Lanphier of the Springfield *Illinois State Register* were both moderate critics before Lincoln issued the Emancipation Proclamation; they learned to hate the administra-tion in the days that followed. Pomeroy's record early in the war stamped him as a unionist. During 1862 he supported the Union party movement, repudiated the partisan "Ryan Address," and kept his criticism of President Lincoln within reasonable bounds. But aversion to abolition chilled his patriotism. He labeled Lin-coln's proclamation "indiscreet" and predicted that it would be "powerful in producing evil results." Gradually he took steps which made him a notorious and unreasonable critic.[22] Lanphier, like Pomeroy, was a mild-mannered opponent of the Lincoln ad-ministration early in the war. The conflict over the "Copperhead" constitution of 1862 turned Lanphier into a partisan editor, dis-trustful of Republicanism. The proclamation of emancipation con-vinced Lanphier that Lincoln had reversed and violated his early promises and pledges. He argued ably against Lincoln's doctrine of military necessity and claimed that the proclamation would prolong the war. He ridiculed it, designating it a "bull" and suggesting that the President use his newly acquired power to abolish smallpox by proclamation.[23] After January 1, Editor Lanphier exhibited his partisanship by assuming the leadership of the Copperhead movement in Illinois and by waging a constant war of words against both Governor Yates and President Lincoln.

The anti-emancipation and anti-Lincoln views so widely expressed in the editorial columns of Democratic newspapers were frequently restated at state and local party rallies of the opposition party. At the state-wide rally held in Springfield on January 5, 1863, Illinois Democratic leaders took turns condemning the Emancipation Proclamation. William A. Richardson, who sought the U.S. Senate seat formerly held by Stephen A. Douglas, condemned the President's proclamation and, for good measure, launched into an anti–New England tirade. Samuel S. Marshall, a rival for the Senate seat, more than matched Richardson's invectives. He spoke emotionally against Lincoln's "usurpation" of authority and insisted that the Democratic party would forcibly resist further "usurpations" of the "imbecile administration." William C. Goudy, a Chicagoan who was often carried away by his own partisanship, publicly warned Governor Yates and President Lincoln that their "unlawful" proclamations were encouraging rebellion and civil war in the Midwest. Richard S. Merrick outdid his predecessors in boldness and bombast. After he condemned the Emancipation Proclamation, he made an appeal to religious prejudice and to midwestern sectionalism. He appealed to Irish Catholic voters to oppose the proclamation, even implying that separation from the homeland of puritanism was desirable.[24]

Ohio Democrats, sponsors of a gala affair at Columbus, honored the memory of Andrew Jackson early in January and utilized that occasion to denounce the emancipation policy. Lyman R. Critchfield, the state's attorney general, listened to the toast, "The Constitution as it is, the Union as it was, and the negroes where they are," before giving a speech denouncing the course of events. Dr. Edson B. Olds, Samuel Medary, and Allen G. Thurman took turns criticizing the Lincoln administration and the plea of "military necessity." Truly, the rally was an anti-emancipation affair.[25]

A state convention, held by Michigan Democrats on February 11 to nominate candidates for judicial posts, condemned emancipation and supported a national convention to compromise the issues of the war.[26] Indiana, Iowa, and Minnesota state conventions, held later in the year, all drafted resolves opposing Lincoln's proclamations and Radical Republican idealism.

The action taken at state Democratic conventions was often repeated in county conventions and local rallies. Chicago Democrats, for example, held an "immense meeting" on January 23, 1863. They approved anti-administration resolutions and listened to table-thumping speakers denounce everything from emancipation to the tariff.[27] Nearly every county Democratic meeting in Indiana witnessed speeches and resolutions critical of the administration's surrender to "Abolition pressure." Brown County Democrats adopted a resolution categorizing Lincoln's plea of necessity as "a tyrant's plea." Carroll County members of the opposition party called the proclamation an "act of despotism." Green County members ratified a resolution which decreed that Lincoln's proclamation of January 1 earned its author "well merited oblivion and eternal infamy."[28]

Local party rallies often featured out-of-state speakers. George Francis Train, eccentric Boston financier and an avowed Lincoln critic, toured the Midwest, mixing his politics with a travelogue. In one sentence he would sing the praises of Ireland or describe the beauties of Rome; in the next he would claim that Lincoln's policy was characterized by duplicity and imbecility.[29] Henry Clay Dean, an erratic Iowa Democrat who was an oratorical attraction, toured various midwestern states, delighting his partisan audience with anecdotes and acrimony. He claimed that he "skinned" the administration and always had a collection of choice epithets denouncing the proclamation.[30] Christian Kribben of St. Louis, who could denounce administration measures in German as well as in English, was a drawing card in midwestern communities where German-Americans were numerous. Madison Y. Johnson and David Sheean, after their release from arbitrary confinement in Fort Lafayette, were in great demand for local party rallies. They denounced Lincoln's "usurpations," giving accounts of their lives as "prisoners of state" in the "Bastile."[31] John Reynolds, renowned and respected Democrat before his retirement from politics, returned to the political wars in Illinois after Lincoln issued his proclamation of January 1, 1863.[32] So did William Allen, Ohio politico of an earlier generation. Amos Kendall, loyal supporter of Jackson in the 1830's, wrote to a midwestern friend that there was need "to rescue the President from the hands and counsels of the abolitionist . . . and . . . to abandon his emancipation proclamations."[33] Truly, it seemed that the Emancipation Proclamation stirred Democrats, both old and young, to renewed political activity.

Democratic congressmen, too, assailed emancipation. Samuel Sullivan Cox, variously classed as "War Democrat" and "Copperhead," condemned emancipation bitterly.[34] Vallandigham never ceased to denounce Lincoln's role as emancipator and became more critical with each passing week.[35] David Turpie, a U.S. senator from Indiana, not only criticized the proclamation, but also spoke against the bill to provide compensated emancipation in Missouri.[36] Daniel Voorhees of Indiana and James C. Allen of Illinois spoke defiantly on the floor of the House of Representatives.[37] George H. Yeaman, a Kentuckian serving in the House of Representatives, introduced a resolution which denounced the proclamation as an ill-chosen war measure, a destroyer of peace possibilities.[38]

While Democratic congressmen voiced their opposition to emancipation in Washington, Democratic legislators in various states added their voices to the chorus of discontent. James F. Robinson, the governor of Kentucky, pronounced Lincoln's action a "base usurpation" of power and advised the state legislature to register its protest in strong language.[39] A resolution passed by the lower house labeled the Emancipation Proclamation "unwise,

Clement L. Vallandigham of Ohio. (Courtesy of the Ohio Historical Society, Columbus.)

Daniel W. Voorhees of Indiana. (Courtesy of the Indiana Division, Indiana State Library.)

Edward G. Ryan of
Wisconsin. (Courtesy of the
Wisconsin State Historical
Society.)

Charles H. Lanphier of
Illinois, editor of the
(Springfield) *Illinois State
Register*. (Courtesy of the
Illinois State Historical
Library.)

Marcus Mills "Brick" Pomeroy of Wisconsin, editor of the La Crosse *Democrat*. (Courtesy of the Wisconsin State Historical Society.)

Samuel Medary of Ohio, editor of the *Crisis*. (Courtesy of the Ohio Historical Society, Columbus.)

Dennis Mahony of Iowa,
editor of the Dubuque
Herald. (Courtesy of the
Iowa State Department of
History and Archives,
Des Moines.)

Henry Clay Dean of Iowa.
(Courtesy of the Iowa State
Department of History and
Archives, Des Moines.)

Arrest of Vallandigham at Dayton, May 5, 1863
(From *Frank Leslie's Illustrated Newspaper*, May 23, 1863)

Flyer advertising Dr. J. M. Hiatt's exposé of the Knights of the Golden Circle.
(Courtesy of the Indiana State Historical Society.)

COLUMBIA. "Where are my 15,000 Sons—murdered at Fredericksburg?" LINCOLN. "This reminds me of a little Joke—" COLUMBIA. "Go tell your Joke at SPRINGFIELD!"

(From *Harper's Weekly*, January 3, 1863)

PENNSYLVANIA BEEF CONTRACTOR. "Want Beefsteak? Good Gracious, what is the World coming to? Why, my Good Fellow, if you get Beefsteak, how on earth are Contractors to live? Tell me that."

(From *Harper's Weekly*, August 17, 1861)

LINCOLN'S DREAM; OR, THERE'S A GOOD TIME COMING.

(From *Frank Leslie's Illustrated Newspaper*, February 14, 1863)

A RARE OLD GAME OF "SHUTTLECOCK."

JEFF—"*No good sending him here. I'll have to send him back.*"
ABE—"*He's none of mine, anyhow.*"

(From *Frank Leslie's Illustrated Newspaper*, June 20, 1863)

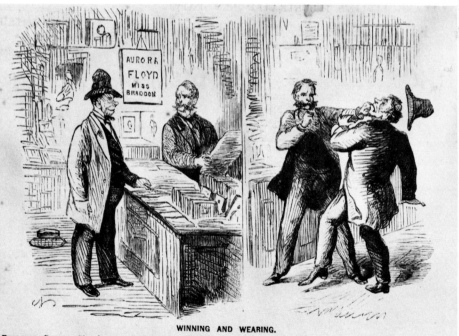

WINNING AND WEARING.

DOUBTFUL CITIZEN—*Sir, do you sell Copperhead Badges? I want one.*

PATRIOTIC STOREKEEPER—*This is the only badge you Copperheads deserve.* (Doubtful citizen wears it for some days.)

(From *Frank Leslie's Illustrated Newspaper*, May 23, 1863)

THE COPPERHEAD PLAN FOR SUBJUGATING THE SOUTH.

War and Argument—Cold Steel and Cool Reason—having failed to restore the Union, it is supposed that the South may be *bored* in coming back.

Our Picture represents the successful operation of this exceedingly humane and ingenious device.

(From *Harper's Weekly*, October 22, 1864)

THE COPPERHEAD PARTY.——IN FAVOR OF *A VIGOROUS PROSECUTION OF PEACE!*

(From *Harper's Weekly*, February 28, 1863)

MARVELOUS EQUESTRIAN PERFORMANCE ON TWO ANIMALS,

By the celebrated Artist, PROFESSOR GEORGE B. MAC, assisted by the noted Bare-back Rider, GEORGE H. PENDLETON, on his Wonderful Disunion Steed, PEACEATANYPRICE.

N.B. *The beautiful creature,* PEACEATANYPRICE, *recently imported from Europe, was sired by* JOHN BULL, *and dam'd by* AMERICA.

(From *Harper's Weekly*, October 8, 1864)

Pygmies in the Hands of a Giant. (Original cartoon by Herman Viola.)

Vanquished! Then Exiled and Disgraced. (Original cartoon by Herman Viola.)

unconstitutional, and void."[40] The Copperhead-manned legislature in Illinois adopted a resolution which declared Lincoln's proclamation "a gigantic usurpation" which would "protract the war indefinitely," and individual members took time to utter their anti-emancipation sentiment.[41] A motion introduced into the Indiana legislature declared that Indiana would "never voluntarily contribute another man or dollar" until the Emancipation Proclamation was withdrawn.[42] Wisconsin Copperhead legislators, functioning as an aggressive minority, succeeded in modifying a Republican attempt to give full and direct indorsement to the Emancipation Proclamation.[43]

The protests of the politicos permeated the ranks of the citizenry. "I am sorry," a father wrote to his soldier-son, "that you are engaged in this war, which has no other purpose but to free the negroes and enslave the whites; to overrun the free States with a negro population and place us all, who labor for a living, on an equality with d——d negroes sent on us by abolitionists, who alone are in favor of prosecuting this unholy, unconstitutional, and hellish war."[44] Countless desertions were blamed upon Lincoln's proclamation.[45] Even some moderate Republicans were disgusted with the turn of events. An Indiana doctor, previously a Republican regular and an ardent unionist, wrote of his misgivings:

I am very much tempted to resign. I am tired of the way things are going at Washington. It appears as if nothing but the nigger can engage their attention there. The proclamation and other things have demoralized this army until it is worthless for any good. You would be astonished to know the facts. Soldiers are deserting every day . . . and if the army at other places is like our own here, we may as well acknowledge the Rebel Confederacy.[46]

No one knows how many officers actually resigned because of Lincoln's proclamation. At times the proclamation was but an excuse to end an experience that had lost its glamor, an experience fraught with hardship and with danger. Some Ohio and Indiana officers resigned, publicly protesting against the proclamation.[47] A number of officers of the 90th Illinois, a predominantly Irish

regiment, resigned in protest. The regiment was immediately iso-
lated and charged with "mutiny."[48]

The emancipation issue stirred discontent anew in the Blue
Grass State. Kentucky soldiers and Kentucky citizens were taken
aback. Criticizing the Lincoln administration became the most
popular parlor game. Kentuckians, generally, regarded Lincoln
"as false to his pledges, his position, and his country."[49] Emancipation and military rule made Kentucky a recruiting ground for
Confederate soldiers and rebel sympathy.

Some emotional midwesterners living north of the Ohio River
also threatened to line up on the side of Jefferson Davis. One Illinois stay-at-home wrote to a soldier-friend that, as far as he was
concerned, "the whol damned Black army" could "go to Hell the
short way." Angrily and antagonistically he added words of treason: "We are all Jeff Davis men now. Every man that has got the
sand will throw off on the Lincoln Government now after the proclamation setting the nigger free. ILL's [Illinois] is bound to go
with the Southland. You and your party who are fighting against
slavery will have to hunt your holes."[50]

While the debate over emancipation sharpened
midwestern tempers, Democratic-controlled state legislatures met
in Indiana and Illinois. In each state a feud developed between
the legislature and the Republican governor. Both sides resorted
to questionable tactics to gain political advantage. Rivalry turned
into hatred, disagreement into detestation. The political pot boiled
to overflowing.

Even before the state legislature met in Indiana in January of
1863 the stage was set for a political dogfight. Democrats, emboldened by the election returns of late 1862, warned Governor
Oliver P. Morton that Republicanism was doomed and that his
days were numbered. Outsiders like Vallandigham and William A.
Richardson taunted the Republican governor when they spoke at
an Indianapolis rally. Exuberant Democratic editors implied that
the Democratic-dominated legislature would "hog-tie" and "horse-
whip" the Republican governor, strip him of his powers, and

strangle Republicans by gerrymandering. Some editors, intoxicated by their victory at the polls, poured brine upon Morton's
political wounds by suggesting that he resign "in obedience" to
the popular will.[51]

Governor Morton, on the other hand, led the Republican campaign to discredit the Democratic legislature even before it met.
Morton was not one to wait for the enemy to fire its guns before
he attacked. Morton and his lieutenants turned rumors to political
advantage. They reported that subversive secret societies were
active in Indiana, that Indiana "traitors" planned to free Confederate prisoners confined in nearby camps, that a move was afoot
to depose the patriotic governor, and that a plot to form a "Northwest Confederacy" was being hatched.[52] "I am advised," Morton
telegraphed to Washington, "that it is the intention of the Legislature when it meets in this State to pass a joint resolution to
acknowledge the Southern Confederacy and urge the Northwest to
dissolve all constitutional relations with the New England
States."[53]

Morton's insulting insinuations angered the Democratic legislators, who vowed that they would secure revenge. Democrats
resented the Republican governor's attempt to gild his every act
with patriotism and to depict himself as patriotism personified.
In such circumstances it is easy to see why tempers were seriously
strained even before the legislative session began in Indianapolis.

Before the organization of the two houses of the legislature was
completed, Republicans practiced partisanship by writing their
own definitions for "honor" and "patriotism" in a resolution
praising General Rosecrans' soldiers for their heroism at Murfreesboro.[54] The Democrats also wanted to praise Rosecrans' soldiers,
but they were convinced that true patriots would always oppose
unconstitutional measures. So both sides haggled over the wording
of the resolution, and the spirit of discord prevailed.

While partisan charges and countercharges were being made,
the legislature turned to the question of electing two U.S. senators.
In order to forestall the election of anyone who was not an out-
and-out unionist, the Republicans sponsored a resolution implying

that some Democratic leaders were lukewarm patriots and sympa-thized with treason. Democrats, resenting the implications, at-tempted to bury the resolution in committee. Republican members of the upper house of the legislature countered by bolting the ses-sion in order to block the Democratic proposal to proceed with the election of the U.S. senators.[55] Republicans pretended it was a question of patriotism rather than partyism; their strategists claimed that the Republicans were motivated by loyalty to their country.

The embarrassed Democrats condemned the "skedaddling tac-tics" of the Republican truants. Forgetting that they themselves had resorted to bolting practices two years earlier, Democrats pre-tended to see a similarity between the Republican "seceders" and the South Carolina secessionists.[56]

While Democrats waited for the Republican bolters to return, Governor Morton stood by ready to deliver his "message" in the usual manner. Democrats serving in the upper house claimed that they could not accept the invitation of the lower house to sit in joint session to hear the governor's "message" until the bolters returned and there was a quorum. They hoped that Governor Mor-ton might request the bolters to return. Morton, however, coun-tered by having his "message" printed. He sent separate copies to each house and released it to the press. The Democratic speaker of the lower house refused to accept the "message," contending that the governor's tactics were irregular and unconstitutional. The Democratic majority backed up the speaker, voting to return the message until it could be delivered according to accepted pro-cedure.[57] Governor Morton held his ground. Several defiant Demo-crats suggested that the legislature substitute the message earlier delivered by Governor Horatio Seymour to the New York legis-lature. They lauded "the exalted and patriotic sentiments" of the Democratic governor of New York as they prodded and insulted their own governor, chiding him for neglecting his duty and refus-ing to be co-operative.

Morton had played his cards well. The Democratic legislators finally sent committees to call on the obdurate governor to inquire when he intended to submit his "message" officially. Morton claimed that he had fulfilled his obligations and defended his course of action vigorously, pre-empting patriotism as his special province. The "message," consequently, was never read officially in either house of the legislature, although the Democrats recognized it by ordering the printing of the controversial document. They also referred portions of the "message" to appropriate committees.[58]

This petty, partisan feud over the governor's "message" presaged preposterous practices to come. The Democrats, outmaneuvered in the eyes of the watchful public, desired revenge. They were in a churlish mood, for they considered Governor Morton defiant and stubborn. Furthermore, they objected to his continuous intemperate attacks on his Democratic opponents. They sought revenge by trying to fasten charges of corruption on the governor's head and by taking steps to strip him of his constitutional authority. They sifted evidence concerning the letting of contracts and concerning Morton's financial practices. One bill provided for the creation of an executive council composed of Democratic state officials elected in the fall of 1862. This council would check or sanction the actions of the governor; he would lose the status of leader and become a servant. Another measure proposed reorganization of one of the important state boards (Board of Benevolent Institutions) so that the Democratic legislators would control appointments and policies. A third measure —the most obnoxious of all—was intended to shear the governor of his military powers. This so-called Military Bill would have wrested control of the state militia (Indiana Legion) from the hands of the Republican governor, turning over military patronage and military control to a Democratic-dominated board. With a friendly state supreme court in session, partisan Democrats did not fear to venture upon unconstitutional grounds. The revengeful Democrats also hoped to draw new boundary lines for the state's congressional and state legislative districts. They proposed to gerrymander brazenly, handicapping Republican hopefuls in future elections. The malicious and malevolent Democrats pursued a course so absurd and outlandish that they were destined to lose public faith and favor.[59]

Governor Oliver P. Morton, aggressive and possessed of strong convictions, did not intend to stand idly by while avenging Democrats threatened his power and patronage. Experienced in political warfare, he launched a powerful counteroffensive. With the aid of his brother-in-law (William R. Holloway) and with the assistance of the editor of the Indianapolis *Journal*, Morton sought to discredit the Democratic-controlled legislature. Morton's aides, who served as correspondents for the Midwest's major Republican newspapers, kept a flood of releases rolling out of Indianapolis. There were charges that the Copperhead legislature hatched a "betrayal plot," that there was a move to take Indiana into the Southern Confederacy, and that traitorous secret societies had headquarters in Indianapolis.[60]

Morton's coterie of confidants took steps to marshal public opinion against the legislature. The editors of the state's many Republican newspapers took their cues from Berry R. Sulgrove, editor of the Indianapolis *Journal*. The Republicans sponsored "Union meetings" and public rallies and heard effective speakers like Andrew Johnson of Tennessee. Twenty-five thousand listened as Johnson defined patriotism in a three-hour oration in Indianapolis. Morton organized the Loyal League and revitalized local Republican clubs. Politically minded officers, like Colonel John T. Wilder, initiated a campaign to draft regimental petitions indorsing the patriotic governor and criticizing the Copperhead legislature. Then Governor Morton spread the slogan that "the soldier views were the true views." A flood of soldier and civilian petitions poured into Indianapolis, and the energetic governor used them to advantage. Slowly and surely, Morton's extensive propaganda campaign turned the public opinion against the insolent and partisan Copperhead legislature.[61]

The Copperhead legislators, meanwhile, weakened their position with extracurricular activities. They instructed Indiana Congressmen to vote for "the Ship Canal Bill."[62] Democratic legislators pushed their scheme to gerrymander. They continued to insult the governor. They postponed action upon the governor's budget while they practiced politics. They discussed the advisability of proposing a four-state convention to discuss the "country's difficulties" and to crystallize anti-Lincoln sentiment. They wanted a national convention to restore "the old Union, the old Constitution, and the old flag."[63]

Governor Morton and Republican politicos seized the opportunity to label the legislators "peace men" and "traitors." Having turned the question of partyism into one of patriotism, Republican legislators bolted again; their objective was to block the partisan program of the Democratic-controlled legislature. On February 25 some Republican members absented themselves to prevent passage of the gerrymander bill. The next day nearly every Republican member bolted to prevent action on the so-called Military Bill. With the consent and connivance of Governor Morton, the bolters ran off to southern Indiana, ready to cross into Kentucky if the sergeant-at-arms tried to force them to return.[64]

The bolters—the Democrats called them "secessionists"—offered to return to Indianapolis if the Copperhead legislators would promise to vote appropriations, drop their reapportionment or gerrymander scheme, discard the plan to take military affairs out of the governor's hands, permit the regular board to govern the benevolent institutions, and cease sponsoring a "national convention."[65] The Democratic members, holding the appropriations bill as their trump card, were sure that Governor Morton's need for funds would eventually bring the bolters back to Indianapolis. They had delayed action on the appropriation bills in order to transform their "program of vengeance" into law.

But the Copperhead legislators underestimated both Governor Morton's determination and the bolters' devotion to all things Republican. Compromise efforts came to naught. The session came to an end on March 8, as specified in the state constitution. The biennial appropriations were unprovided for, and both Democratic and Republican legislators wondered what the next move would be. A stubborn governor and an ill-mannered legislature brought an end to constitutional government in Indiana.

Democrats hoped that Governor Morton's need for funds would compel him to call a special session of the legislature. But the governor did not want another rough-and-tumble fight with Copperhead legislators. He made up his mind to go it alone and announced his intention to a gathering of "125 Republicans," among them "nearly all the Union men of the last legt. [legislature]." They indorsed his intention in "one unanimous voice."[66]

Governor Morton subsequently took direct charge of affairs, often overstepping constitutional bounds; but he wielded power with vigor and tact, cloaking his actions with patriotism. He borrowed money from individuals, corporations, Republican-officered counties, and from the federal government.[67] His dictatorial practices drew protests from the Democrats, who ridiculed his observations that his patriotism placed him above constitutional government.[68] The winds of fortune blew favorably in Indiana, and Governor Morton took full advantage of them. Inept Democratic leadership, sordid Republican tactics, and bitter partisanship nullified the election results of 1862 in Indiana.[69] Democratic legislators lost public favor when they threw away their opportunity to pursue a positive program.

A sequel to the Indiana story of petty partisanship was written into Illinois history. The Illinois setting was similar to that in the Hoosier State. The fall elections had been Democratic victories. Therefore Governor Richard Yates faced a hostile legislature bent upon brewing political mischief. Governor Yates, like Morton, decided to remain alert and take advantage of Democratic errors. He was determined not to let the Democratic legislature gain political advantage. Democrats gloated publicly that Yates's wings would be clipped, and Yates's friends warned him to get ready for the fight. "Draw now the sword for battle," wrote one Republican, "and throw away the scabbard."[70] The Republicans feared that the Democratic-dominated legislature would pass some "rash or vicious legislation."[71]

When the Illinois state legislature convened in Springfield on January 5, 1863, the stage was set for a first-class political controversy. The Democrats proved that they placed politics above general welfare by naming Samuel Buckmaster as speaker of the lower house. Buckmaster was well known for his tobacco-chewing and his partisanship—certainly not for his knowledge of parliamentary law. Buckmaster rewarded his supporters with an intemperate speech, a harangue "in which he went out of his way to pitch into the General Government in a most savage manner."[72] The speech angered the Republicans. In a sense it proved that Buckmaster was not qualified to lead.

Radical Democrats had plunged "headlong into the whirlpool of partisan agitation" before the first week of the session had passed. Moderate Democrats feared the session would be "frittered away" by politicians "in the manufacture of political capital."[73] One Democratic proposal asked for a "special committee" to investigate "State spending" and the distribution of executive patronage, for Democrats hoped to find some irregularities in the expenditure of the war fund and the governor's contingent fund.[74] Another impatient Democrat introduced a set of resolutions which was very critical of the Lincoln administration and defined Lincoln's policy as one "calculated to bring shame, disgrace, and eternal infamy upon the hitherto unsullied flag of the Republic."[75]

Having needled the Republicans, the Democratic members next took steps to select a critic of Lincoln as the new U.S. senator. The contest was between Samuel S. Marshall and William A. Richardson. Both were well-known Copperheads and Democratic party regulars. Marshall thought that he deserved top priority because he had been his party's nominee in the previous legislature. The honor, however, went to William A. Richardson, then serving in the lower house of Congress. Richardson had gained some notoriety by helping to draft the "Address of the Democratic Members of the House of Representatives of the United States to the Democracy of the United States" in 1862 and had lined up with Vallandigham on most measures.[76]

After selecting an anti-Lincoln Democrat to represent Illinois in Washington, the Democratic legislators returned to their self-assigned task of undermining Republicanism and hamstringing

Governor Yates. One partisan measure proposed to place the distribution of all war funds in the hands of a committee of three Democrats. One of the three committeemen would be Charles H. Lanphier, titular head of the Democratic party in Illinois and editor of the Springfield *Illinois State Register*. This bill was also intended to give the three-man committee control of army appointments, of equipping troops, and of procuring supplies. It usurped Governor Yates's authority and aroused Republicans to a man. Republicans began an active war upon the "misbegotten legislature," fully aware that its outlandish partisanship would cost it the support of public opinion.[77]

The Democratic partisans added insult to injury. One bill gerrymandered the Congressional districts. A joint resolution instructed Illinois representatives in Congress to vote against the appropriation of money to help any state emancipate Negroes. One proposed law made an effort to protect freedom of speech and of the press in Illinois by requiring grand juries to investigate all arbitrary arrests already made within the state.[78] Some of the Democratic proposals proved that midwestern Copperheadism was a forerunner of postwar Grangerism. One bill proposed establishment of a state commission to check railroad abuses and to set railroad rates. The Democratic legislators blamed the "railroad monopolists and extortionists" for the defeat of the Lake Michigan–Mississippi River canal bill in Congress. They accused President Lincoln of pandering to New England capitalists and ignoring the economic needs of the Middle West.[79] One of the most controversial measures was introduced by the Hon. Charles A. Walker of Macoupin County. Walker's proposal, which contained a list of fifteen "grievances" nurtured by Democrats, asked for the appointment of state commissioners to a national convention. It included recommendations for an armistice and for the "cession of hostilities."[80]

Walker's proposal split the Democratic ranks, for most of the Copperhead legislators were still unwilling to stand on an armistice platform. Furthermore, Walker's proposal made the Democratic-dominated legislature vulnerable to Republican attack. Republicans seized the opportunity to turn the question from one of law into one of loyalty and patriotism. Governor Yates and his advisers claimed that patriotism, more than partyism, prompted the Republican attack on the legislature.

While trying to rally the soldiers and the people against the Copperhead legislators, Republican legislators resorted to parliamentary shenanigans in the legislature. Ineffective leadership prevented the Democrats from writing most of their proposals into law. Samuel Buckmaster, speaker of the lower house, was incapable of directing the various measures through the parliamentary labyrinth created by his Republican critics. The Republican legislators confused Buckmaster with a series of motions, countermotions, amendments, and amendments to amendments until only an expert in parliamentary procedure could tell where the question stood. Whenever Republicans made another motion or amendment, Buckmaster reached into his pouch for more tobacco. One member reported that Mr. Buckmaster would "take another chew of tobacco, without ejecting what he had with difficulty crammed into his mouth a moment before, and the faster the members talked, the faster Sam chewed."[81]

Republican tactics of delay and obstruction took a different turn in the upper house, where the Democrats had only a thirteen to twelve margin. Any deflection or absence of the Democratic members gave the Republicans a chance to bring the legislative cart to a halt. The serious illness of one Copperhead legislator, James M. Rodgers worked to the advantage of Governor Yates and his Republican partisans. Whenever the Democrats had a majority of their members present, Republicans used bolting tactics to check the passage of Democratic-sponsored measures. Although there was much talk by individual Democrats, the process of turning Democratic proposals into law was at a virtual standstill. At the end of the first month Democratic achievements were few, and the Republicans were thankful although still apprehensive.[82]

Failure of the investigating committee to discover any dishonesty in the state administration or to provide political fodder for the Democrats caused the Copperhead strategists to change their tactics. Convinced that abolition, military defeats, and the threat of federal conscription was turning popular sentiment against the administration, the Democrats decided to take a recess, to name delegates to a proposed national convention, and to wait for the crystallization of antiwar sentiment. Resolutions to recess from February 14 until June 2 were introduced in both houses of the Illinois state legislature.[83] Copperheads hoped that the proposed Louisville convention would give the Democrats every political advantage. They also hoped to bury the Republican party when the legislature reconvened in June.

The Republican legislators countered by opposing both the proposed Louisville convention and the resolve to recess. The parliamentary cobweb they wove confused Speaker Samuel Buckmaster. One of the editors of the Chicago *Tribune* urged the Republican members of the lower house to go home, break the quorum, and so end the session.[84] But Democratic members of the lower house, holding a fifty-two to thirty-one majority, succeeded in blocking the Republicans. They passed both the convention bill and the resolution to recess from February 14 to June 2.

Republicans recognized that the upper house held their hopes to stymie the Democratic program. The serious illness of James M. Rodgers often deprived the senate Democrats of their one-vote margin. Republican senators gave long speeches of the blood-and-thunder variety, trying to filibuster and defeat the two Democratic measures. The debates were spicy and personal. Spectators expected the exchanges to lead to fisticuffs. The Democrats finally brought the resolution to recess to a vote. Then most of the Republicans jumped across a railing and scurried out of the chamber, trying to break the quorum. The alert sergeant-at-arms and his staff chased the runaway Republican legislators, trying to round up enough of the bolters to constitute a quorum. One of the bolters—the Democratic press referred to them as "seceders" —sought refuge in the governor's room. In the nick of time, the fugitive escaped his pursuer, the assistant sergeant-at-arms, and locked the door through which he had passed. The assistant sergeant-at-arms rattled the door and, when he could not open it, notified the escapee through the keyhole that "his presence was demanded in the senate." No one answered.[85] Enough runaways to constitute a quorum, however, were rounded up and returned to the senate chamber. The doors were locked and the resolution to recess was passed.[86] That night the Republican senators met in caucus and decided to break up the session by taking trains for home, after announcing the conditions on which they would return.[87]

Hardly had the Republican skedaddlers left town when news of the death of James M. Rodgers, one of the Democratic members of the state senate, made the rounds. Most of the Republican bolters hurried back to Springfield, hopeful of passing several appropriation bills already approved by the lower house. Democratic disorganization plus the convenient arbitrary arrest of William H. Green, Democratic senator from Mt. Vernon, gave the Republicans control of the upper house. Much to the consternation of the Democrats, the Republican senators sidetracked the convention bill and hustled through several appropriation bills. Their efforts to secure a reconsideration of the appropriation bills failed because the Copperheads no longer had a majority and because the recess deadline was fast approaching. The frustrated Democrats charged Republican senators with "unscrupulous demogogism," "fraud," and "parliamentary dishonesty."[88] The Republicans, on the other hand, were jubilant; they had won the first round as the recess took effect. "All the pet measures of the democracy have been defeated," wrote the Springfield correspondent of the Chicago *Tribune*, "while the Republicans have carried nearly all they could have expected."[89]

During the legislative recess the Democrats marked time. They elected a member of their party to fill the vacancy created by the death of James M. Rodgers and planned to resurrect the various partisan measures which had been stalled in the legislature. Republicans took advantage of the recess to organize an anti-Copperhead campaign. They claimed to have a monopoly upon patriotism in Illinois and charged that Democratic legislators belonged to subversive secret societies and intended to take Illinois out of the Union. Governor Yates tried to convince the unwary that the legislators wished "to revolutionize" the state. He asked President Lincoln for authority to disperse the legislature and to declare martial law,[90] and he waged a vicious propaganda campaign against the Copperhead legislators. One of the most effective propaganda items was a printed pamphlet, *Copperheads under the Heel of an Illinois Farmer* (1863). Copperhead legislators, according to the author, "should have asses' ears to set off their heads"; they were "traitors and secessionists at heart."[91] Governor Yates also effectively collected a batch of petitions from Republican-minded regiments. The regimental petitions, which criticized the legislators and praised the governor, and many soldier-written letters were released to the Republican newspapers and proved effective in undermining public faith in the legislature.

When the legislature reconvened on June 2, the Democrats were in a revengeful mood. They again held a thirteen to twelve edge in the state senate, and Samuel Buckmaster talked of revenge and retaliation. The lower house revived the bills which set up legislative control of military affairs, established a railroad commission to govern rates and service, and took control of the penitentiary system out of the governor's hands. Democrats in the lower house also passed a soldiers'-aid bill and established a board of three members of their party to superintend spending of a $100,000 fund. They also passed a series of resolutions which denounced the suppression of the Chicago *Times* after the active sergeant-at-arms rounded up enough Republican members to make a quorum.[92]

Every partisan measure which passed the lower house floundered in the state senate. The absence of Republican members, when votes on Democratic measures were in order, checked the Copperhead program. One day when several Democratic members were absent, senate Republicans found themselves in the driver's seat. They immediately rushed through a resolution to adjourn *sine die,* and then they went into hiding. The lower house, of course, refused to go along with the *sine die* proposal and offered to set a later date. Governor Yates, in Chicago at the time, was notified that his golden opportunity had arrived, for the state constitution authorized the governor to prorogue the legislature if the two houses disagreed on an adjournment date. When Governor Yates returned to Springfield, the senate Democrats were trying to rescind the resolution to adjourn *sine die*, but no quorum could be collected by the baffled sergeant-at-arms.

Yates acted swiftly. He composed a "proclamation of adjournment" and sent it to both houses of the state legislature. The Republican lieutenant-governor, in on the scheme, adjourned the senate "in good style." Speaker Samuel Buckmaster, presiding over the lower house, was bewildered by Yates's directive to adjourn. A tumultuous scene occurred, but Buckmaster finally thought it his duty "to vacate the chair." Republican members rushed out of the building, packed their bags, and hurried home. Democratic legislators, sullen and stunned, decided to hold a party caucus to try to solve their dilemma. They returned to the legislative chambers to pass a set of resolutions and to adopt "a protest." When the sergeant-at-arms reported that the Republicans had left for home, the Copperhead legislators brought their rump session to an end. Republican alertness and Democratic incompetency had created a situation which allowed the governor to score "a resounding political triumph." By resorting to a technicality, Governor Yates got rid of a Machiavellian-minded state legislature.[93]

Democratic editors, aware that the Republican governor had bested the Democratic legislators, turned to their quills to record their dissatisfaction. The editor of the Chicago *Times* claimed that Governor Yates was guilty of an "act of despotism" and that he was suffering from *"delirium tremens."*[94] Editor Lanphier, who had served as adviser to the Democratic legislature, called the act of prorogation "wholly indefensible and but little short of infamous."[95] Another Democratic editor used stronger language. He referred to Governor Yates's *"coup d'état"* and compared the

Illinois incident with the technique which Louis Napoleon used to make himself dictator of France.[96] Truly, in Democratic circles there was weeping and the gnashing of teeth.

Meanwhile the Republicans sang a merry tune and mixed praise of Governor Yates with their words of joy. The Springfield *Illinois State Journal* defended the governor's action as "proper and constitutional," adding that it had "relieved the State of an intolerable nuisance." "He has performed an act called for and approved by the best men of all parties in the State," added the editor with tongue in cheek, "and has entitled himself to the thanks and approbation of the people."[97] Such newspapers as the Chicago *Tribune* and the Chicago *Journal* congratulated Governor Yates for besting the mischievous legislators.[98] The Republican-minded editor of the Chicago *Western Railroad Gazette* described the Springfield incident in a humorous vein:

The brilliant coup d'état of Gov. Yates proroguing the Copperhead swell mob known as the Illinois Legislature created as much dismay (in that body) as Oliver Cromwell when he dissolved the Long Parliament. It was regular "cut throat" awful in its effects on the "yellow boys," altogether rich, racy, and irresistably funny to outsiders. The Speaker turned black in the face as an African, while Wabash Fuller, in the middle of a roaring speech, was so affected that he suddenly collapsed in his chair ("struck all a heap") with such violence that the seat of his mental facilities it was feared was seriously impaired.[99]

In spite of the state-wide approval which Illinois Republicans gave to the act of prorogation, an aura of illegality hung over Yates's parliamentary strategy, although it was later sanctioned by the state Supreme Court.[100] Realistic Democrats, of course, recognized that the feud between the "Copperhead" legislature and the Republicans had ended in Yates's favor. Alertness had scored over stolidity, and firmness had triumphed over Democratic indecision. By exploiting partyism the Democrats hoped to reap a crop of political fodder. Their plan boomeranged, and the fruits of their labors were dissatisfaction and disgrace.

The Democrats, outmaneuvered in Illinois and Indiana, could hope for little in the states of Ohio, Michigan, Iowa, Wisconsin,

and Minnesota. In those states the Republican-controlled legislatures kept things in hand. The Copperhead minorities in these
state legislatures possessed only a nuisance value. Neither could
Missouri or Kentucky Democrats expect to have their way, for in
the border states general orders drafted by military commanders
took the place of statute law. Midwestern Democrats who had
expected Illinois and Indiana to give them leadership and a positive program were sorely disappointed. Midwestern Democrats
had a chance to prove their worth in the early months of 1863 but
were found wanting.

       While the Copperhead legislators and the Repub-
lican governors were sparring in Indiana and Illinois, some Democrats turned to the courts to check the Lincoln administration.
The decision in *Ex parte Merryman* (1861) by Chief Justice
Roger B. Taney encouraged anti-Lincoln critics to use the courts
to protect themselves. President Lincoln and his generals, however, ignored Taney's momentous decision, and Democrats sang
the Chief Justice's praises in vain.

A court decision, strikingly similar to *Ex parte Merryman*,
came out of Wisconsin in January of 1863. The case had its
origin in the Wisconsin draft riots of 1862. Wisconsin's Republican governor used the state militia to arrest a large number of
the Ozaukee County rioters. Under orders of the governor, the
prisoners were turned over to Federal army authorities to be
tried by court-martial in accordance with a presidential order subjecting persons resisting military draft to martial law and suspending the writ of habeas corpus.

Edward G. Ryan, author of the "Ryan Address" of 1862 and
chieftain of the Wisconsin Copperhead clan, volunteered his
services in behalf of the defendants. Before the state Supreme
Court, Ryan argued that Lincoln's suspension of the writ of
habeas corpus was unconstitutional, that Congress alone possessed
such authority, which could only be exercised in limited cases.
He claimed that a dictatorship would envelop the country if military law could function where the courts were open. "I want to see

the Court have the courage to set the brute law of the sword at defiance!" he shouted as he closed his plea with an oratorical flourish.[101]

The august panel of jurists accepted Ryan's line of reasoning. In their decision (the so-called Kemp case) the judges declared that Lincoln's proclamation suspending habeas corpus was unconstitutional and that suspension of habeas corpus was purely a legislative prerogative.[102]

Ryan's personal victory over the Lincoln administration via *In re Kemp* jolted the President like a bolt from the blue. One of Wisconsin's U.S. senators, Timothy Howe, rushed home from Washington to secure a transcript of the case record in order to procure a speedy review by the U.S. Supreme Court. There was fear in some Republican circles that Taney's court might welcome the opportunity to reprimand the Lincoln administration again. Edward Bates, Lincoln's attorney-general, advised against an appeal. Both Bates and President Lincoln feared that an adverse decision by Taney's court would "do more to paralyze the Executive . . . than the worst defeat our armies have yet sustained."[103] The administration, therefore, decided not to bring *In re Kemp* to Washington and to ignore the decision as best they could.

Flushed with victory, Ryan argued another "Copperhead case" before the Wisconsin Supreme Court in February, 1863. He sought a writ of habeas corpus for some draft evaders. He argued that the federal draft law of 1862, which authorized states to draft into the state militia to meet their quotas, was unconstitutional. Ryan's chief argument was that Congress had illegally and unconstitutionally delegated legislative power to the President. The judges of the state's highest court brushed aside Ryan's arguments and their decision (*In re Griner*) gave support to the Lincoln administration.[104] As far as Ryan's personal war with the administration was concerned, the count stood at one victory and one defeat.

Another habeas corpus case had its setting in neighboring Illinois. Judge Charles H. Constable of the fourth judicial district of Illinois became the central figure in a bizarre story. Judge

Constable was well known for his Democratic leanings and his detestation of military encroachment on civil authority. He already had several anti-administration decisions to his credit and Republicans condemned him as a Copperhead.

Early in 1863 a series of events again put Judge Constable in the limelight. Colonel Henry B. Carrington, whose jurisdiction was limited to Indiana, exceeded his authority when he sent two sergeants into Illinois to arrest four "deserters"—one supposedly absent without leave from an Indiana regiment and the other three from the 130th Illinois. Carrington's two sergeants crossed into Illinois and arrived in Marshall, where they arrested the four "deserters." Marshall's residents, mostly Democrats, were infuriated and resented the "invasion from Indiana." The Clark County sheriff then arrested Colonel Carrington's two sergeants as "kidnappers," and Judge Constable was called upon to solve the problem of what to do with the "deserters" and the "kidnappers." After listening to the charges, countercharges, and the evidence, Judge Constable discharged the four "deserters," and ordered the two "kidnappers" imprisoned. He set bail at $500 and laid down the condition that they appear before a grand jury to answer the charge of "kidnapping" Illinois citizens.[105]

Enmeshed in Illinois law and embarrassed because his agents had been caught trespassing outside of his district, Colonel Carrington called upon his friend and confidant, Governor Oliver P. Morton, to save him. Governor Richard Yates of Illinois expressed sympathy for Colonel Carrington after he gave a strange excuse for his action, and Yates implied that a subversive secret society was really responsible for Judge Constable's decision.[106] Governor Morton was anxious to extricate Carrington from his predicament, for Carrington had been both loyal and friendly. Morton, accompanied by Carrington, called on General Horatio Wright to secure the release of the two sergeants still imprisoned in the Marshall jail. General Wright, commanding the Department of the Ohio, had Illinois as well as Indiana within his jurisdiction. General Wright, indignant that civil judges should assert control over military personnel, gave Colonel Carrington authority to send an expedition into Illinois to "free" the two sergeants, to rearrest the four "deserters," and to arrest Judge Constable for "harboring and protecting deserters."[107]

Colonel Carrington's love of drama prompted him to commandeer a train, organize a "motley army," and invade Illinois. He dressed forty of his troopers in "butternut jeans," while the other half of the command wore their regular military outfits. He himself led the expedition in its midnight excursion across the Illinois border and into Marshall. The case of the two sergeants, charged with "kidnapping" Illinois citizens, was scheduled for a morning court session. Carrington and his "butternut-brigade" occupied most of the courtroom seats. After the court convened and the two sergeant-prisoners were brought in, the remainder of Carrington's force took its place outside the courthouse. Carrington and his soldiers sat sternly as the case proceeded. Judge Constable rose to give the jury final instructions. Then Colonel Carrington—he had reserved the lead role for himself—dramatically announced his presence. He ordered the release of the two sergeants and the arrest of Judge Constable. Carrington's soldiery executed the orders in the midst of intense excitement. Judge Constable calmly acquiesced, considering himself a martyr to the cause of civil rights, and the special train chugged back into Indiana with jubilant soldiers and a sullen judge-prisoner aboard.

The Republican press suppressed news of the Constable affair. Nevertheless, the effort of an Illinois judge to challenge the rights of the military ended in favor of Colonel Carrington and Governor Morton. No reprimands came from Washington. Judge Constable was examined before Judge Samuel H. Treat of the Southern District of Illinois. The charge was "encouraging soldiers to desert." A full examination indicated that Colonel Carrington's sergeants were outside of the district in which they had jurisdiction and that Judge Constable had acted "properly" in releasing the "deserters" and in holding the sergeants to bail. Accordingly Judge Constable was discharged from custody and he returned to Marshall to reopen his court.

While Judge Constable was feuding with Colonel Carrington, another habeas corpus case took shape in the Midwest. Judge

Samuel E. Perkins, whom Democrats considered a defender of civil liberties and individual rights, became the central figure in this controversy over the role of military law in a democracy. The provost marshal of Indiana issued a proclamation which forbade the sale of liquor to soldiers. Joseph Griffin, a licensed liquor dealer, was arrested for violating this military order. Griffin claimed that military orders could not restrict the activities of civilians and that military rules applied only to soldiers in service. Consequently Mr. Griffin sued for damages. The case reached the Indiana Supreme Court as *Griffin* v. *Wilcox* early in 1863. The court under the leadership of Judge Perkins gave a decision in favor of Joseph Griffin and against the army authorities. The judges admonished the military authorities, stating that military law did not pertain to citizens in areas where the courts were open. The judges even went out of their way to slap President Lincoln's hands. They opined that Lincoln's proclamation suspending the writ of habeas corpus was unlawful and unconstitutional.[108] The court's decision was naturally praised by the Democrats and condemned by the Republicans. Democratic editors lauded Judge Perkins for defying military force and staying the hand of tyranny. Republicans condemned Perkins as a Copperhead and called the action of the court "traitorous." Republicans pretended that the decision in *Griffin* v. *Wilcox* gave aid and comfort to the enemy. Many of them wished to substitute military necessity for civil law.[109]

In addition to defending civilian rights against military authority, the Indiana Supreme Court made an effort to stymie Governor Morton's high-handed tactics. The failure of the Copperhead legislature to appropriate funds did not handcuff the energetic governor. In violation of the state constitution, Governor Morton raised funds from private individuals, from corporations, and from Republican-controlled counties. Since the state treasurer was a Democrat, Governor Morton established an extralegal "financial department" which he placed under supervision of his military secretary. He operated the state arsenal as if it were his own private company. He paid for state purchases and continued to borrow from the federal government. When Governor Morton ordered his "financial department" to pay the interest on the state debt, the Democratic state treasurer erected legal barriers and the issue came before the Indiana Supreme Court. Judge Perkins, directing the court's course, rendered a decision unfavorable to Governor Morton. The Supreme Court declared that lack of a specific legislative appropriation to pay the interest upon the state debt made it illegal for the governor to do so with other moneys. The court, of course, had no means to enforce its ruling. Governor Morton denounced the "Copperhead Court" and ignored the decision. He continued his irregular rule, following the principle of expediency and cloaking his actions with patriotism. Constitutional government had collapsed in Indiana and the courts could not force the strong-minded governor to obey their decisions or follow the constitutional path.[110]

Neither Democratic-minded judges nor Democratic-controlled state legislatures could check the course of events in early 1863. Both the Democrats and the Republicans seemed anxious to place party welfare before the welfare of the nation. Partisan Republicans were anxious to utilize the war setting to crush the Democrats, while they cloaked their own actions with righteousness. Such Republicans judged their political opponents harshly:

The sole objects of the Democrats, now constituting the disloyal northern opposition, is to regain political power. . . . The present leaders of the Democratic party are men purely politicians and of the immoral kind. They have thrown away all principles whatever, and have the advantages which utter recklessness gives to wicked men.[111]

It was the familiar story of the pot calling the kettle black. Events in Springfield and Indianapolis, where Democratic-dominated legislatures quarreled with Republican governors, proved that no one party had a monopoly on Machiavellian methods or rank partisanship. The Republicans would have destroyed the two-party system, which had become part of the American political tradition, if they could have benefited thereby. The early months of 1863 witnessed the triumph of partyism. Partisanship in the Midwest took no recess even in the darkest hours of the Civil War.

I I I

The High Tide
of Midwestern Copperheadism

THE MONTHS immediately preceding the battles of Vicksburg and Gettysburg saw the Copperhead movement reach high tide. Discontent was rampant, and despair made inroads. These months tested the mettle of the Lincoln administration, and there was a question whether the President's policies or those of his political adversaries would triumph. The administration was in dire need of a decisive military victory, but none was forthcoming.

War weariness undermined civilian morale. In March of 1863, Congress wrote the principle of federal conscription into law, and by May and June the machinery of enrolment was in operation. Western sectionalists expressed concern over the National Bank Act, which they interpreted as a capitalists' measure. Westerners were shocked at the tactical errors committed by General Ambrose E. Burnside as Commander of the Department of the Ohio. His arrest of Vallandigham and his suppression of the Chicago *Times* brought on a wave of Copperhead indignation and antagonism.

A Democratic propaganda agency, organized in New York, took measures to "diffuse political knowledge" and to convince the public that the Lincoln administration was a failure. Dennis A. Mahony and "Brick" Pomeroy gained national notoriety for their roles as administration critics. In April, May, and June of 1863, there was fear that civil war within a civil war might visit the upper Mississippi Valley.

Those who prayed for victory in these crucial months of 1863 found their prayers and pleas unanswered. General Joseph Hooker, commanding the Army of the Potomac, tried pincer tactics against Lee's forces in Virginia. The movement turned into a disaster for the Union forces. The Confederates inflicted more than 17,000 casualties on Hooker's troops at the Battle of Chancellorsville, from May 2 to May 4. It was another disheartening defeat for the North, and President Lincoln again juggled generals in that sector.

The war also went badly in the Midwest. General Rosecrans' army lay inactive in central Tennessee, still recuperating from its earlier encounter with General Bragg's Confederate forces around Murfreesboro. Meanwhile General U. S. Grant's forces suffered two disheartening reversals near Vicksburg. Confederate General Earl Van Doren destroyed the Federal base at Holly Springs and captured or burned large supplies stored there. Then the Confederate cavalry wrecked the railroad nearly to Paducah, Kentucky. Grant sent General William T. Sherman down the Mississippi to effect a breakthrough to Vicksburg. The Confederates easily repulsed Sherman's forces at Chickasaw Bayou and the Northern army suffered heavy casualties. Grant was under fire from several quarters and there was considerable pressure on Lincoln to have him replaced.

In late June of 1863 the Confederates added insult to injury by making a raid across the Ohio River. Captain Thomas Hines, one of General John Morgan's raiders, led a company of cavalry on a horse-stealing expedition into Indiana. Hines's raiders were able to elude the Indiana state troops for several days, but eventually most of the invaders were trapped. Captain Hines and a handful of his men, however, escaped across the Ohio River without either honor or the stolen horses. The raid had more than nuisance value. It furnished the Confederates with propaganda to boost the morale of civilians and soldiers. Conversely, midwestern governors rested less easily and the inhabitants of southern Indiana, Ohio, and Illinois worried about their homes and possessions.

The absence of Northern victories in these crucial months

caused Union morale to dip to an all-time low. "Our reverses have been so frequent and so uncalled for," wrote one of Governor Morton's advisers, "[that] the people have become tired and discouraged."[1] There was some fear that the Copperheads might take desperate measures. "If this cursed Rebellion don't get some crushing blows soon," wrote an Illinois Republican, "the once United North may get to be like 'the Kingdom divided against itself.' "[2] Midwestern Copperheads capitalized on the situation, and their ranks grew in size and in strength.

As civilian morale declined, so did army morale. Criticizing army life became a favorite pastime around the campfires, and desertions were common. The harshness of field experience often crushed the patriotism so noticeable at volunteering headquarters. General Joseph Hooker reported that desertions averaged several hundred daily in his command, and over-all desertions averaged close to 5,000 per month early in 1863.[3] An Illinois surgeon reported from Memphis that the 130th Illinois lost "25 men in one night," and that one company in the regiment was "reduced to 19 men."[4] The soldiers of one regiment of General Grant's army refused to embark for a down-river destination; they swore they would not go and stacked their arms.[5]

Army desertions had many different causes: the ague, dysentery, incompetent officers, delinquent pay, homesickness, solicitude for the family, inadequate equipment and provisions, and cowardice. The sentiments and views of the folks back home were all-important. Sometimes homefolks encouraged their soldier-sons to desert. His family might assure the soldier that he would be "protected" if he deserted and returned home.[6]

The deterioration of soldier and civilian morale affected volunteering adversely. Realists recognized that the method of raising troops needed to be overhauled drastically. President Lincoln labeled the volunteer system "inadequate," saying he did not wish to "waste time" to "re-experiment" with it. He wanted some system of federal conscription instituted.[7] Republican governors, cognizant of the political dynamite in the state draft system, welcomed the idea of federal conscription.

Republican businessmen, as taxpayers, frowned upon the bounty-enlistment system. They paid the taxes or made the donations which enabled local governments to offer tempting bounties to a community raising its quota. These businessmen, aware that the bounty-enlistment system touched their pocketbooks, supported federal conscription as a desirable alternative. Republican congressmen, determined to crush the South, suggested that federal conscription was necessary.

The debate over the desirability of compulsory conscription came to a head in March, 1863. Democrats generally opposed the institution of federal conscription; they wanted the bounty system retained, improved, and extended. Samuel Sullivan Cox, a Copperhead congressman from Ohio, chided his Republican colleagues for "admitting" that patriotism was dead. He claimed that the volunteer-bounty system had not really failed. "Repeal the confiscation act, the emancipation proclamation, and other unconstitutional measures—withdraw the negro entirely," he advised the administration, "and a conscription bill will not be necessary to reinvigorate the country."[8] The editor of the Dayton *Empire* also laid the blame for the absence of volunteering at the doorstep of the administration. He was convinced that imbecility, corruption, and pro-Negro measures had dampened the spirit of patriotism so evident in the early days of the war.[9] Prominent Democrats were aware that their political supporters (the "butternuts" in the country and the laborers in the cities) preferred a volunteer system dependent on large bounties to a conscription system which offered none. The conscription bill, however, was railroaded through Congress, and the politicians made little effort to create a democratic and efficient system. Their act of March 3, 1863, enabled a draftee to buy his way out of service by furnishing a suitable substitute or by paying $300 in commutation money.

The $300 exemption clause was bitterly assailed by most Democrats; they claimed that the provision was neither democratic nor fair. The astute editor of the Hamilton *True Telegraph* stated the position of the Democrats. "As a general thing," he editorialized, "the Abolitionists are in office or in a condition to buy themselves free. Not so with the Democracy. They are the yeomanry of the country. They live by labor and are the tillers of the earth; and [they are] not in a condition to buy their freedom of the Administration."[10] The editor of the Indianapolis *State Sentinel* expressed similar views. "Senator [Henry] Wilson," wrote that Democratic scribe, "inserted the $300 exemption in the conscript law to save the sons of the Abolition aristocracy of New England from the necessity of shouldering a musket. . . ."[11] Some Copperheads objected to the measure because it implied that a man's life was "valued at $300."[12] Chicagoans who belonged to the German Workingman's Association held a special meeting to put their anticonscription views on record. These German-Americans expressed their opposition to the $300 exemption clause which "favored the rich and discriminated against the poor." More than a thousand voted for the resolution which asserted that the conscription measure was "subversive to the fundamental principle of the republic, in which all must have equal rights and duties."[13]

That section of the conscription act which established the provost marshal system also drew the attention of Democratic orators and editors. The elaborate machinery of enforcement included a provost marshal general in Washington, an assistant provost marshal general in each state, and provost marshals, enrolment officers, and boards of enrolment for each congressional district. The long hand of Washington thus reached down into the counties. Those wary of centralized government were suspicious of the provost marshal system. The editors of the Chatfield *Democrat* claimed that the corps of provost marshals would "obliterate state lines," adding, "No despot in the world today wields a greater power over the persons of his subjects than does King Abraham the First."[14] "Brick" Pomeroy of La Crosse, Wisconsin's bitterest critic of the administration, argued that the conscription act would elevate President Lincoln to the "position of *MILITARY DICTATOR*," crush the last semblance of states rights, and threaten all of the traditional civil liberties.[15]

The editor of the Dayton *Empire* expressed the same fears. He wrote that the rights of the states and the liberties of the people were "at the caprices of folly and tyranny." "The fate of the Republic," he added with alarm, "may now be said to be fixed."[16] The editor of the Milwaukee *See-Bote* conducted a continuous campaign against the conscription act. He pretended to fear a "czarist-like despotism" and claimed there was a similarity between the "Polish forcing act" (the drafting of the Poles by the Russian czar) and "Mr. Lincoln's law" which would sacrifice German-Americans at the whims of New England. He added that the provost marshal system was instituted to keep Republicans in power and predicted that the provost marshals would use Negro troops to keep white men under their thumbs.[17]

The coming of conscription contributed to the popularity of Copperheadism from March to June of 1863. Wives who feared that the federal draft might take their husbands faced the future with less faith and more fear. Mothers who loved their sons more than their country shuddered at the thought of losing children to the draft. Filial devotion, especially in families which did not understand the causes and objectives of the war, often expressed itself more strongly than patriotism. The draft naturally threatened the unity of family groups, and to many the war seemed so needless, futile, and faraway.

Enrolment for the draft under the direction of the provost marshals proceeded slowly and surely. Instances of violence or resistance, as expected, were reported in nearly every midwestern state. There were outbreaks in various parts of Kentucky, and it was necessary to send military details to give protection to the enrolling officers.[18] Ohio, the home state of Vallandigham, accepted enrolment passively. Only three counties reported resistance and Federal troops were sent to assist enrolling officers there.

In Indiana, where the political feud between Governor Morton and the Democratic-controlled legislature revived partisanship, numerous cases of violence were reported. General Burnside, who supervised military affairs in the states north of the Ohio River, feared that martial law might have to be instituted in order to enrol Hoosiers for the draft. Governor Morton led him to believe that a secret society to resist enrolment was organized in Indiana and that the Hoosier State was on the verge of rebellion.[19] Attacks on enrolling officers in Putnam, Owen, Fulton, and Boone counties necessitated the use of Federal troops, but enrolment was then completed without further incident.[20] In Sullivan County an enrolling officer was shot to death, and a squad of "50 soldiers" was detailed to help his successor complete his assignment.[21] In Rush County a deputy provost marshal was ambushed and two of his assistants were wounded. But order was quickly restored and the enrolment was completed.[22]

Governor Yates of Illinois thought that martial law might be necessary to carry out the enrolment in his state. His joust with the Democratic-dominated legislature left him uneasy, and rumor-mongers added to his uneasiness by reporting anti-draft men arming and organizing in Douglas, Sangamon, and Christian counties.[23] Actual violence, however, occurred in only two Illinois counties. An anti-draft riot occurred in Chicago (Lake County) as several hundred Irish citizens assaulted a U.S. marshal and his deputies. The Federal officers had arrested two Irishmen for refusing to give their names to an enrolling official. The Fulton County incident was largely the fault of an arrogant enrolling officer. An "unduly alarmed" provost marshal called for Federal troops to overawe malcontents after backwoods Democrats chased him out of their community. Republican propagandists labeled the incident the "Fulton County War" and blamed a subversive secret society for the disorders. Republican newsmen, anxious to use the incident to benefit their party, made mountains out of molehills, and so gave birth to another Civil War legend.[24]

Two incidents cast a shadow over enrolment in Wisconsin. Unknown persons killed an enrolling officer in Dodge County. Milwaukee County exhibited considerable unrest and a deputy engaged in registering citizens was manhandled and threatened. The civic officials, however, handled the situation in both Dodge and Milwaukee counties and issued no requests for Federal troops. State officials feared that violence might erupt in Washington and

Ozaukee counties, scenes of rioting and resentment the previous fall, but the enrolment was carried out without trouble.[25]

The states of Michigan, Minnesota, and Iowa reported no major incidents during the enrolment. Things were not pleasant for the enrolling officers, but the registration was carried to completion without trouble. Enrolling officers sometimes called on the sheriff to give them aid and encouragement. "The Copperheads were so unfavorably disposed," reported an Iowa official, "that I employed the Sheriff at my own expense to attend the sittings [cases where exemptions were claimed] to aid in preserving order."[26]

All in all, enrolment proceeded much more peacefully and rapidly than most state and federal authorities believed possible. Governors Morton of Indiana and Yates of Illinois erred in mistaking vocal opposition for disloyalty. "Their threats were loud," wrote Governor Morton's adjutant general, "but never carried into effect."[27] Some of the credit for the negligible violence and the successful completion of the enrolment should have gone to midwestern Democratic leaders. Such prominent midwestern Copperheads as Vallandigham, Daniel Voorhees, George H. Pendleton, and Chilton A. White had voted against the conscription bill in Congress, yet they later exerted influence in behalf of peaceful enrolment in April, May, and June of 1863. Daniel Voorhees went into Sullivan County, after incidents of violence had occurred, to urge his constituents to co-operate with provost marshals and to avoid violence. Vallandigham, too, urged obedience to the law. These Copperheads urged their Democratic followers to acquiesce, pointing out that the Democratic party was traditionally the party of law and order. They said that the ballot box and the courts were the mediums through which to redress grievances.[28]

An Illinois jurist, proud of his Democratic leanings, asked his friends "to allay the public excitement and not aggravate it." He recorded his sentiments as advice when he wrote, "Neither individuals nor communities can act wisely when under the influence of excitement, and now of all times when the national existence . . . is involved, it is the duty of everyone to try to calm his neighbor and not excite him."[29] Verily, the eloquent jurist stated the Democratic position:

The conscript law will be carefully examined and if legal it will be submitted to, if not it will be met in a legal mode through judicial tribunals and not through unlawful violence. . . . We should not follow the teachings of the abolitionists who have for so many years been teaching the right of individuals to resist and oppose the laws which they believe to be wrong. This they have taught their followers in regard to the fugitive slave law, even after it had been held unconstitutional by the proper legal tribunal. Let us not follow their wicked teachings. . . . In this way we can preserve peace at home and restore the Union in which the Northwest is so much more deeply interested than any other portion of the country.[30]

Advice of moderation from many Democratic mouths—for the Democratic party was essentially conservative—helped to keep the less learned and more emotional within bounds. Governors Morton and Yates, anxious to squeeze the last ounce of political sap out of everything, failed to give such Copperheads as Richardson, Voorhees, or Vallandigham any credit for their contributions to the cause of law and order.

The record shows that some citizens "skedaddled" to Canada to avoid the draft and that a few who had been regarded as full-fledged citizens claimed exemptions as aliens. Some citizens of both parties paid "premiums" to clubs organized to procure substitutes when the name of a club-member was drawn in the draft lottery. Members of such clubs, however, were more apt to be Republicans than Democrats. "Butternuts" of the backwoods and Irish workers of the cities were the substitutes which the clubs were apt to procure. The "Butternuts" and the Irish-Americans usually lacked the know-how to organize such a club and the money to make it work.[31]

Those Democratic congressmen who had voted against the conscription bill went on record as opposing another controversial measure. This was the habeas corpus act of March 3, 1863—a measure intended to indemnify the President by authorizing him "to suspend the privilege of the writ of *habeas corpus* in any case throughout the United States, or any part thereof."[32] During the wrangling over the measure, Democratic spokesmen put themselves on record as defenders of civil liberties and individual rights. Two Kentucky congressmen led the opposition to Thad Stevens' efforts to indemnify the President and to place additional authority in his lap. The Hon. Charles A. Wickliffe, a member of the House of Representatives, feared that Lincoln might set himself up as "a military dictator" and made an eloquent plea in behalf of civil rights and the constitutional guarantees.[33] United States Senator Lazarus W. Powell combined a personal attack on President Lincoln with his arguments against the habeas corpus bill and the efforts to give official sanction to measures which the President had already justified as necessary. Senator Powell asserted that Lincoln had violated the U.S. Constitution more in his two years in office than Charles I and James II together had violated the English Constitution in twenty-two years. The outspoken senator insisted that American liberties were disappearing and that indignant citizens were alarmed and restless. Public opinion, smoldering like a volcano, might erupt and overflow if further "usurpations" occurred.[34]

The most famous of the Democratic speeches in behalf of constitutional government was that delivered by Daniel Voorhees, the "Tall Sycamore of the Wabash," and later published under the title of "The Liberty of the Citizen." Voorhees prepared his declamation with care and blended history and logic with classical quotations to strike some telling blows in behalf of conservatism and constitutionalism. Voorhees traced the historical development of civil and individual rights and wove a flowery wreath of praise about them. He pounded the podium with dramatic effect. He sounded a warning against many actions taken in the name of necessity by the administration.[35] Voorhees' superb effort was cheered by many of his Democratic colleagues. It won widespread acclaim in Democratic circles, and many editors printed it. The editor of the Dayton *Empire*, for example, used such adjectives as "powerful," "eloquent," and "forceful" to describe it, adding: "It ought to be in the hands of every man in the country. We trust its circulation among the people may reach millions."[36] Democrats generally recognized that the habeas corpus and conscription acts, both dated March 3, 1863, were in conflict with American tradition. In the hands of an unscrupulous President, they could be used to turn a republic into a dictatorship.

Congressional Copperheads objected to more than the habeas corpus bill and the conscription measure. They viewed the creation of the state of West Virginia as a violation of both the spirit and letter of the Constitution. They questioned the partisan course pursued by the Committee on the Conduct of the War and recognized that it was an instrument in the hands of the Radical Republicans.[37] They reserved choice epithets for the proposal to raise and use Negro troops. Such capable congressmen as John J. Crittenden of Kentucky and S. S. Cox of Kentucky led the Copperhead attack upon this Radical Republican measure. Cox said that the proposal was an attempt "to place the African soldier upon a perfect equality in every regard with the white soldier."[38] Crittenden warned the administration that the use of Negro troops would deepen unrest in the Bluegrass State.[39]

Western Copperheads argued against two other laws, both of which aroused the western sectionalists to action. One measure levied excise taxes on manufactured spirits; the other proposed to establish a national bank system. Vallandigham and Voorhees ably argued against the "bank monopoly" and the "centralization of power." They used the same arguments Jackson's friends had used against the recharter bill a generation earlier. Two other Copperhead congressmen, James C. Allen and William A. Richardson, led the forces which secured postponement of the tax on state bank notes and "the granting of the money monopoly" to the nationally chartered banks.[40]

Most Democratic editors of the upper Mississippi Valley also criticized the establishment of a national bank system, although patriotic preachments, wartime confusion, wartime need, and widespread antipathy to wildcat banking all paved the way for its acceptance in some quarters. Samuel Medary of the *Crisis*, for example, warned eastern capitalists: "The West will not bleed at every pore because well-preserved and fanatical New England declares that such is her patriotic duty." Medary contended that he was a Jacksonian Democrat and that the "monstrous Bank Bill" violated the principles which "Old Hickory" had advocated.[41] Michael Faran, co-editor of the Cincinnati *Enquirer*, followed the same line of argumentation: "The enormity of this bill is sufficient to make General Jackson, who killed the old Bank of the United States, turn in his coffin. . . . The design is to destroy the fixed institutions of the States, and build up a central moneyed despotism."[42] Other editors joined in the attack.[43] Western Democrats generally believed that the passage of the National Bank Act symbolized the defeat of Jeffersonian-Jacksonian doctrine, the resurrection of Whig "heresies," and the triumph of eastern capital.[44]

When the third session of the Thirty-seventh Congress came to an end, many administration critics heaved a sigh of relief. They believed that personal animosities, extralegal measures, and partisan practices put this Congress in the "disgraceful" category. Copperheads and conservatives were alarmed that such proposals as compulsory conscription, the habeas corpus act, and the National Bank Act had become law. One of Vallandigham's supporters recorded his views in an editorial:

The Thirty-Seventh Congress closed its term yesterday at 12 o'clock. Its acts will live in history to the humiliation and disgrace of the American people. A more reckless and unscrupulous set of fanatics and agitators never disgraced the halls of the American Congress, than the abolition members of that body whose term of office has just closed. We hope never again to be compelled to endure like infliction.[45]

While the controversy over conscription and the National Bank Act continued in many sectors, three midwestern Democrats gained a measure of notoriety. They were "Brick" Pomeroy, Clement L. Vallandigham, and Wilbur F. Storey. Vallandigham was already a well-known figure. The other two were newspapermen, caught in the swirl of events, who gained a reputation during the months when Copperheadism reached high tide.

Marcus Mills "Brick" Pomeroy was a small-town newspaperman, unknown outside his state in the early years of the war. He was a mild critic of the administration until Lincoln's Emancipation Proclamation indicated that abolition had become official policy.[46] Pomeroy's aversion to abolition chilled his patriotism. Trips to army headquarters at St. Louis and Helena proved soul-stirring experiences that helped convert him to immoderate Copperheadism.

The trip to St. Louis was a revealing experience. Friends provided him with first-hand information about army frauds, favoritism, disorganization, and incompetence, and about sagging soldier morale and morals as well. He saw army contractors and quartermasters "making money by the cord." He saw hordes of "unlawful wives and prostitutes" in camp and watched liquor shipments unloaded at army bases. He noted that army authorities and soldiers called stealing "confiscation" and gained the impression that soldiering was "rotten business." Stacks of pine coffins and visits to army hospitals affected him deeply. "These rough, brown, cheap, worm-eaten coffins, piled up there like oyster cans, silently waiting to fold their wooden arms about our sons, brothers, and fathers," he wrote with deep feeling, "rather took the poetry out of the soldier straps and goldcovered cord to be seen strutting around, giving orders to the glory hunters in plain blue."[47]

His sojourn at Helena, headquarters of the Army of the Southwest, was an even more unhappy experience. Pomeroy accompanied the troops when they chased guerrillas, foraged for food, and raided plantations to confiscate cotton and to free the slaves. Dealing in confiscated cotton seemed to be the primary army activity. Watching the army in action caused him to lose all respect for the Lincoln administration. "If the enemy is to be conquered," he wrote, "why in God's great name do we not march troops to battle, instead of cotton fields?"[48] He became infuriated when he saw army contractors and cotton agents, like a flock of vultures at a carrion feast, descend on the army, lining their pockets and helping to demoralize the soldiery. When he was not slushing through the Arkansas mud or playing poker and listening to gossip or comments, he wrote editorials and exposés for several newspapers. His disclosures and intemperate letters were published in such newspapers as the Chicago *Times*, the Milwaukee *Evening News*, and the La Crosse *Democrat*.[49]

Pomeroy's racy "reports" cursed the "devilish vandalism" of the soldiery, for he was critical of the army policy of scouring the countryside for provisions. "When God has forgotten us, and men rule but to plunder," he wrote, "the people may well begin to pause and tremble." With the ardency of a reformer he put his disdain and despair into words:

The war is not being carried on to preserve the Union. Such talk is all bosh. Once in the country simplicity of our heart, we thought so; but the truth has dawned upon our vision full and clear. Were there no presidents to make—did there not exist parties in the North and South which appeal to the passions and prejudices rather than reason —were there no cotton in the South—no chance to *steal* in one day more than a man can *earn* in a lifetime—were there no rich speculators and moneyed men, as selfish and unprincipled as the devil himself, now controlling this crusade, there would be peace today over the land.[50]

A close look at war turned him toward the idea of peace. He wrote of a hospital ship as "a boat load of pain and agony." He thought of amputated arms and legs as the "true trophies of war." He described the war as "a waste of men, blood, and treasure." "The more I see of this war," Pomeroy wrote in one of his editorials, "the more I feel like swearing at the fanatical fire-eaters and abolitionists who brought it on." The more Pomeroy wrote and editorialized, the more he convinced himself that the South could not be whipped, that dishonesty dominated the army, and that the Lincoln administration was corrupt and incompetent. He believed that the war had degenerated into a "murderous crusade for cotton and niggers." The angry editor rained malediction upon the head of General Benjamin N. Prentiss, commanding the Arkansas sector; he referred to Helena as "a second Golgotha." He theorized that generals were changed frequently in that theater of war so that many generals' pockets would be filled—all indebted to the Lincoln administration for their "pelf."[51] Each week's revelations were longer, more disparaging, and more insulting to the general whose hospitality he enjoyed.

When copies of the Chicago *Times* bearing Pomeroy's reports were shown to General Prentiss, the commander was furious. He ordered Pomeroy arrested and brought to his office. There General Prentiss gave Pomeroy a tongue lashing and dictated an order commanding the La Crosse editor to leave the army lines immediately. Pomeroy was warned that, if he returned, he would be arrested as "a spy."[52]

Embittered and impudent, "Brick" Pomeroy returned to La Crosse and to the editorial sacrarium of the La Crosse *Democrat*. There he dipped his quill in more poisonous ink, writing scathing denunciations of President Lincoln and composing vitriolic verse. He wrote of "the imbecility of the Administration," and he slandered the President. He said that Lincoln was a "fool," a "blockhead," "a flat-boat tyrant," and an "imbecile." Pomeroy made anti-Lincoln diatribe a specialty and malevolence an art. Lincoln became "hell's vice-agent on earth," "a usurper," and "fanatic." Pomeroy's blatancy and boldness earned him a kind of national notoriety. His audacity and acridity brought him the attention he craved. Democratic and Republican editors clipped his editorial comments and spread his reputation as a curmudgeon and a Copperhead. Democrats clipped to prove that Lincoln was unworthy and that criticism was bold. Republicans clipped to prove that Pomeroy was "mad" and that traitors sat in editorial offices.

While "Brick" Pomeroy waged war upon the Lincoln administration in his editorial columns, an Ohioan used oratory to gain converts to the Copperhead cause. Vallandigham had won both praise and condemnation for his pro-peace speech of January 15 in the House of Representatives. After Congress adjourned, Vallandigham returned to Ohio to continue his crusade for compromise. He was somewhat embittered. He had suffered defeat in the October, 1862, elections only because the Republicans had brazenly gerrymandered to prevent his re-election. The tart and insulting comments made by Radical Republicans in Washington were still ringing in his ears. Vallandigham had the stuff of which martyrs are made, and the midwestern setting provided him with the opportunity.

General Ambrose E. Burnside was assigned to command the Department of the Ohio in March of 1863, about the time Vallandigham returned to Dayton from Congress. Burnside had faith in force and in the threat of force.[53] Burnside could not understand that there are two sides to most controversies. He interpreted criticism of the administration as sympathy for the rebels, and naïvely believed the treason charges bandied about by Republican propagandists. The wrecking of the office of the *Crisis* by a crowd of soldiers and civilians—an incident followed by a series of charges, threats, and inflammatory utterances—worried General Burnside. Democratic leaders were bitter and angry; some of them wished to make the property of Republican rivals security for the safety of their own. "For every Democratic printing office destroyed by a mob, let an abolition one be destroyed in turn," suggested the editor of the Dayton *Empire*. Then Editor William T. Logan added, "For every drop of Democratic blood spilled by Abolition mobites, let theirs flow in retaliation."[54]

A defiant editor, at a later day, put Democratic thoughts into words when he said, "When they ignite the match, let us apply the torch." His advice was a blending of defiance and retaliation:

Matches are cheap. If fanatics and fools seek mob law and anarchy, by all means let them have it. Burn down and destroy theirs as they have or may destroy yours. By dark or by daylight—by fire or by powder—feed those who may injure you the dish they prepare. . . . For every dime of your property destroyed by political opponents, destroy a dollar's worth in return. Stores, houses, barns, offices, and churches burn.[55]

Republicans were warned that if they tried to "mob" Democratic newspaper offices they would be "welcomed with bloody hands to hospitable graves."⁵⁶ The threats and counterthreats caused General Burnside to suppose that martial law was necessary, for he had slight regard for the civil processes.⁵⁷

A second cause of uneasiness to Burnside centered around the treason tales and secret society charges which Colonel Henry B. Carrington provided for his superiors. Colonel Carrington, commanding the subordinate District of Indiana, concocted an assortment of cock-and-bull stories and related them to Burnside with a straight face. Governor Morton's support of the tales convinced Burnside of their veracity, and he made ready to defend the arsenals and prison camps within his jurisdiction.

A third worry for Burnside was the situation at Dayton, scarcely sixty miles from the general's headquarters in Cincinnati. The "tremendous ovation" accorded to Vallandigham on his return to Dayton in March of 1863 carried down to Cincinnati. The "homecoming celebration" was one of the grandest ovations ever given to any man in Ohio.⁵⁸ This "gala event" featured two bands, thirty-four rounds from a booming cannon, "deafening cheers," a noisy parade, and much speechmaking. The speechmakers abused President Lincoln and his Ohio supporters. Vallandigham's response and appreciation put the frosting on the cake.

Reports of the Dayton "homecoming" reached Burnside in short order. He regarded all criticism of the President as unpatriotic and traitorous. Burnside, furthermore, was acquainted with the choice epithets which Radical Republicans hurled at Vallandigham. One had called him a "hyena" and suggested they hang him first and "apologize if necessary afterward."⁵⁹ Since Burnside believed that Copperhead speeches and editorials gave encouragement to the enemy, he issued his well-known "General Orders, No. 38" on April 13, 1863. That proclamation announced that those who committed 'acts for the benefit of our enemies" would be "tried as spies or traitors." The order stated that "the habit of declaring sympathy for the enemy" would no longer be tolerated and that individuals arrested would be subject to military procedure.⁶⁰

Midwestern Democrats raised a chorus of protest against Burnside's "General Orders, No. 38." It implied that critics of administration policy were traitors and struck a heavy blow at freedom of speech and of the press. Furthermore, it disregarded the existence of civil law and civil authority, and put interpretation of military orders in the hands of the military. Democrats regarded its application as a defiant and open violation of the Constitution. One wrote that the Constitution guaranteed *"a trial by an impartial jury"* to "every person charged with crime."[61]

No midwesterner was more disturbed by General Burnside's challenge than Clement L. Vallandigham. The outspoken Ohioan had long since convinced himself that he was the spokesman for rights and liberties. In 1862, when arbitrary arrests were being made, Vallandigham recorded his protest against public apathy: "Yes, it is amazing that our people—Americans, proud, boastful, free—should have submitted to usurpation and despotism which would have roused Greece even to resistance after two thousand years of servitude." Then Vallandigham added: "Yet I think often of the scornful exclamation of Tiberius as day by day he went out from the presence of a degraded and servile Senate. *O Homines ad Servitutem paratos.*"[62]

Vallandigham convinced himself that despotism was enveloping the country and that the Radical Republicans had much in common with the Robespierre faction during the French Revolution. He feared that state lines would be obliterated and that civil rights were dying. He was willing to prove his devotion to "The Constitution as it is, the Union as it was." Vallandigham also supposed that General Burnside had him in mind when he wrote "General Orders, No. 38."

Since Vallandigham had nothing but contempt for General Burnside and nothing but scorn for "General Orders, No. 38," the doughty Daytonian spoke out defiantly almost at once. At a Democratic mass meeting in Mt. Vernon, on May 1, 1863, Vallandigham made his bid for martyrdom. The presence of one of General Burnside's agents, leaning against the speaker's platform and scribbling in a little black book,[63] encouraged Vallandigham to blast away with both barrels. Vallandigham declared that the administration had deceived the people as to its objectives. He believed that the war was a medium to free the blacks and to enslave the whites. He insisted that it was his constitutional right to speak, express his views, and criticize the administration. He labeled General Burnside's "General Orders, No. 38" a base usurpation of authority. He could spit upon it and stamp it under foot. His right to speak, he said, was based upon "General Order No. 1," the Constitution of the United States.

Vallandigham propounded the thesis that oppression occurred in direct proportion to a people's servility. People were free if and when they were determined to be so. He invited his hearers to defy arbitrary orders. "The sooner the people," he declared in ringing tones, "inform the minions of usurped power that they will not submit to such restrictions upon their liberties, the better."[64]

General Burnside, informed of Vallandigham's defiance, ordered the fiery Daytonian arrested. Several days later a detail of 150 soldiers moved into Dayton at night. They aroused Vallandigham from his bed at three o'clock in the morning and escorted their political prisoner to Cincinnati.

After Vallandigham's friends put the pieces of the puzzle together, they realized that an arbitrary arrest had occurred while they slept. Several prominent Daytonians hurried to Cincinnati to consult with Vallandigham and to find out what course of action they should pursue. The less prominent spread word of Vallandigham's arrest and gathered on street corners. Everywhere there were "crowds of excited men."[65] Republican leaders of Dayton went into hiding, lest they become targets of the indignation everywhere evident. The afternoon edition of the Dayton *Empire* fanned the flames of discontent; its feature editorial bore the headlines:

VALLANDIGHAM KIDNAPPED

A dastardly Outrage!!
Will free men submit?
The hour for action has arrived.[66]

That editorial feature mixed curses and innuendo intending to stir up partisan readers. It blamed the city's Republicans, whom it labeled "cowardly, scoundrelly abolitionists," for Vallandigham's arrest—"a hellish outrage." It suggested that "blood and carnage" were necessary to rescue "endangered liberties."[67]

Liquor from the grog shops and the inflammatory editorial of the Dayton *Empire* helped stir up the mob. A crowd of nearly 200 indignant citizens gathered in front of the *Empire* building, as if seeking inspiration from that bastion of Democratic dogma. Across the street stood the office and printing plant of the Dayton *Journal,* the Republican newspaper which had been very critical of Vallandigham. The mobsters, milling in front of the *Empire* office, thought of the *Journal* building as a symbol of despotism, of *lettres de cachet,* and of Vallandigham's arrest. Members of the mob hurled insulting epithets in the direction of the *Journal* building. The throwers of those verbal darts were joined by bolder spirits. Some threw stones to show off their marksmanship and their contempt. A few drew their pistols and fired at the windows. Several made balls of pitch, applied the match, and tossed the flaming missiles across the street. One such "turpentine ball" landed among papers stacked in the editorial office. Flames and smoke poured out of the *Journal* building and "in an incredibly short space of time flames burst from the roof." Some misguided malcontents cheered; another bastile was being destroyed![68]

Someone, fearful that a riot was taking shape, had earlier requested General Burnside to rush troops to Dayton. By the time the troops arrived, the fire was out of hand, for the mobsters had interfered with the work of the Dayton Fire Department. After a soldier killed a rioter who was cutting a water hose, the mob quickly dispersed. Half a block of the city was reduced to ashes— a sacrifice to the god of vengeance. Dayton hotheads had given a fiery answer to Burnside's arrest of Vallandigham.

No sane Dayton Democrat indorsed the action of the mob. Several of them took steps to quiet the excitement and remove its taint from the Democratic party. Young Thomas O. Lowe, a devoted Democrat and an enthusiastic follower of Vallandigham, used an "open letter" to express the views held by most Dayton Copperheads:

I am a believer in the right of revolution. Whenever a people are crushed beneath the heel of despotism, and have no other means left them of obtaining the inalienable rights of men, it is their sacred right after long suffering to arise in their might against their oppressors. The circumstances justifying revolution do not exist in our country now. Although in my judgment, there have been many unwise, arbitrary, and cruel things done by the present administration towards their political opponents in the North, we have still left us the great remedy for all political wrongs, the ballot-box.[69]

Blame for the riot rested equally upon Vallandigham, General Burnside, and William T. Logan, editor of the Dayton *Empire*. Vallandigham had implied that resistance to oppression and arbitrary arrest was expected of people who would be free.[70] Logan had written a fiery editorial, a "crazy article [which] did more mischief than anything else."[71] Burnside's rashness, arbitrariness, and "General Orders, No. 38" jostled the Dayton beehive. Imprudent acts produced unfortunate results.

General Burnside used the Dayton riot of May 5 as an excuse to institute martial law throughout Montgomery County, Ohio. Bluecoats carrying guns and bayonets paraded in the streets of Vallandigham's home town. An uneasy peace existed in Dayton.

While Burnside's troops occupied Dayton, the general convened a military commission in Cincinnati. Vallandigham was charged with expressing sympathy for the enemy, "declaring disloyal sentiments," and violating "General Orders, No. 38." Vallandigham in turn denied that a military commission had any right to try him in a state where the courts were open. The military commission brusquely denied Vallandigham's contention and ordered a plea of "not guilty" entered in the prisoner's behalf. Samuel Sullivan Cox, who had shared the Mt. Vernon speaker's platform with Vallandigham on May 1, acted as the prisoner's counsel and testified in his favor. Cox insisted that Vallandigham had advised resistance only through the ballot box. He denied that Vallandigham had applied "epithets" to Burnside, claiming that "honor" for himself. Cox's contentions were given in vain. The die had been cast. The military commission found Vallandigham guilty and sentenced him to close confinement in a Federal prison for the duration of the war. General Burnside approved the findings of his commission and selected Fort Warren (Boston) as the Federal prison where Vallandigham would be confined.[72]

Vallandigham's friends sought to free their "martyr" via a writ of habeas corpus. Judge Humphrey H. Leavitt of the U.S. Circuit Court at Cincinnati denied the application for habeas corpus, sidestepping the question of the military commission's jurisdiction. Judge Leavitt's decision was carefully calculated to avoid a clash of the military and civil authorities.

President Lincoln, as well as the members of his cabinet, "regretted" that General Burnside had acted so brazenly; cabinet members "wished he [Vallandigham] had been sent over the lines to the Rebels."[73] Exile to the Confederacy, rather than imprisonment in some Northern penitentiary, could serve a twofold purpose: (a) it would negate Vallandigham's bid for martyrdom, and (b) it would stigmatize all criticism of the administration as "pro-Southern" or "traitorous." Lincoln, therefore, changed Vallandigham's sentence to banishment to the Confederacy. General Burnside was instructed to send Vallandigham to the headquarters of General Rosecrans, "to be put by him beyond our military lines."

The job of conducting Vallandigham to the enemy lines General Rosecrans assigned to his provost marshal general, Major William N. Wiles. The major took Vallandigham to Murfreesboro during the night. There he was put in a light wagon with some officers and conducted to the inner line of pickets before daybreak. A small squad of cavalry led the way; nearly a company followed the wagon. Early in the morning the officer in charge proceeded to the enemy's lines with a flag of truce, to see whether or not the enemy would accept Vallandigham.[74] The Confederate officer in charge refused to receive Mr. Vallandigham under a flag of truce, "or in any official manner," and the discussions continued for several hours. Vallandigham complicated the negotiations by insisting that he be classified as a prisoner of war when ushered into the Confederate lines. Somehow or other, Major Wiles got Vallandigham off his hands. Whether he was turned over to the Confederates or merely "dumped down" between the lines and left still seems a debatable question.[75] The exiled Daytonian, nevertheless, took steps to get off Southern soil as soon as he could. After a short stay in Richmond, where he was interrogated by Confederate officials (Vallandigham continued to insist that he was a prisoner of war), he hurried to Wilmington, North Carolina. At that port he took a fast blockade-runner for Bermuda, arriving there June 22, and some time later he boarded a British ship bound for Halifax and Canada.

While Vallandigham and Pomeroy were the subjects of discussion and speculation, a third midwesterner was adding to his reputation as a critic and a Copperhead. He was Wilbur F. Storey, editor of the Chicago *Times*. Storey had moved to Chicago early in 1861, when he acquired the Chicago *Times*. He gained a reputation as a mild but persistent critic during the first year of the war. The arbitrary arrests of 1862 alarmed Storey, and Lincoln's proclamations of emancipation angered him. The influential editors of the Chicago *Tribune* conducted a constant and scurrilous attack on Mr. Storey, and he soon found the doors of society barred and double-locked. Such persecution made him a more resolute and dim-sighted critic of all things Republican. Early in 1863, he deserted mildness for madness and the Chicago *Times* soon gained a reputation as the Midwest's best-known Copperhead newspaper. Storey's editorials became known for their violent tone—a historian somewhat later described the *Times* as a "foul and damnable reservoir which supplied the lesser sewers with political filth, falsehood, and treason."[76]

Republican generals took steps to exclude the Chicago *Times* from their military districts. Storey interpreted such arbitrary action as a violation of the principle of freedom of the press. Consequently, the editor of the Chicago *Times* became even more bitter and more abusive of the powers that be. Storey's harsh criticism of General Burnside's handling of Vallandigham galled the thin-skinned Commander of the Department of the Ohio. Burnside countered with "General Orders, No. 84." "On account of the repeated expression of disloyal and incendiary sentiments," the military edict stated, "the publication of the newspaper known as the Chicago *Times* is hereby suppressed."[77] General Burnside then ordered his subordinate, who commanded the District of Illinois, to carry out the order of suppression. On June 3, a squad of soldiers from Camp Douglas occupied the offices of the Chicago *Times*, stopped the presses, and destroyed most of that day's edition. General Burnside, thus, made the name of Wilbur F. Storey known from Maine to California.

Actual suppression of the Chicago *Times* lasted only a few days. Editor-proprietor Wilbur F. Storey applied to the federal circuit court judge in Chicago for an injunction restraining Captain James S. Putnam and his troops from interfering with the publication of the newspaper.[78] The federal judge immediately issued a restraining order while weighing the question of a permanent injunction. Before the courts took further action, President Lincoln interceded in behalf of the Chicago *Times*. The President revoked General Burnside's instructions suppressing the *Times*. Storey's newspaper resumed publication on June 5, and its circulation sharply increased as a result of the incident. General Burnside, chastened and reproved, revoked "General Orders, No. 84" and offered to resign his command because he had embarrassed the President.[79]

General Burnside's arbitrary action in regard to Vallandigham and the Chicago *Times* watered the roots of midwestern Copperheadism. The Lincoln administration suffered because of Burnside's imprudence, for the public reaction to the high-handed action of the Commander of the Department of the Ohio strengthened and increased Cooperhead ranks.

Vallandigham's arrest, of course, stirred midwestern Democrats to action. Emboldened editors, some seeking martyrdom, denounced Burnside in vile language. They defended Vallandigham's right to criticize and reprimanded the administration for trampling traditional rights underfoot. The Dubuque *Herald,* long associated with Dennis A. Mahony, called Vallandigham's arrest "a cowardly and despotic act of the reigning oligarchy." The defiant editor wondered whether people desired and deserved their rights. "They only deserve liberty who prize its blessings," wrote the scribe, "and they tyranny who couch [*sic*] before its blows." He recorded his sentiments in strong language:

A crime has been committed against the most vital right of the poor and the rich, the humble and the exalted—the right to think, to speak, to live. When this thing is consummated, then plainly before the American people does Abraham Lincoln stand—the murderer of the nation. The plea of military or governmental necessity is a flimsy screen which will command no respect. No necessity can justify the monstrous outrage.[80]

Most of the Democratic protesters did not agree with the radical position which Vallandigham held on the question of peace or compromise, but all of them insisted that it was his constitutional right to speak out upon the issues of the day. All believed that the doctrine of necessity was a threat to man's rights and freedom, and that such a doctrine was a threat to democratic government. They feared that General Burnside's substitution of military trials for civil processes was a dangerous practice. Many Democratic protesters, therefore, depicted Vallandigham as a martyr to the cause of civil liberties. The editor of the Iowa City *State Press* believed that Vallandigham was a martyr whom time and history would eventually vindicate:

Noble Vallandigham! Doubly noble in your imprisonment! When this wild storm of fanaticism shall have spent itself, the people—chastized into the exercise of their "sober second thought"—will do justice alike to your motives and your actions.[81]

Many of the carping editors got a measure of revenge by lambasting President Lincoln and by denouncing the administration. They claimed that the President was using General Burnside and other "satraps" to establish despotism. They depicted Lincoln as a ruthless dictator who trampled upon civil rights. The editor of the Hamilton *True Telegraph*, for example, termed Burnside's measures "the act of a desperate and mad administration," and "the most atrocious outrage ever perpetrated in any civilized land."[82] Lincoln was depicted as "a usurper," "a tyrant," "a demagogue," and "a despot."[83]

Democratic orators joined the party's editors in condemning the administration. Democratic-sponsored mass meetings and party conventions featured prominent politicos who played on the Vallandigham theme. The largest of the May meetings was held in Indianapolis on May 20; approximately 20,000 of the party faithful congregated to listen to orators condemn President Lincoln, General Burnside, and General Milo S. Hascall. Hascall, newly named commander of the District at Indiana, had brought Hoosier Democrats to the verge of rebellion with an order which threatened all administration critics with arrest and imprisonment.[84]

Daniel Voorhees presided over the vast assemblage. He set the pace with an eloquent address denouncing General Hascall's arbitrary order and praising Vallandigham—"fallen a little sooner, perhaps, than the rest of us, a victim of base usurpation."[85] Voorhees, too, was willing to be a martyr to the cause of civil rights. "A man can die for a cause like this without grief or sorrow," shouted the defiant orator, "but to prolong life at the expense of liberty, is what a proud race can not and will not do."[86] Other speakers followed, and the interruption of the program by armed soldiers threatened to turn the affair into a first-class riot. Democrats and soldiers engaged in fisticuffs, and a number of arrests were made, some for carrying concealed weapons and others for uttering "disloyal" opinions. When some of the homeward-bound Democrats fired pistols in the air as their special trains were pulling out, soldiers stopped the trains, searched the passengers, and confiscated some small arms. Republican propagandists later built the incident into the "Battle of Pogue's Run."[87] While Indiana Democrats deserved some of the blame for bringing the state to the verge of revolution, they deserved some of the credit for keeping the cup from overflowing.

The largest of the June meetings of the midwestern Democracy

—"the most tremendous gathering of the people ever witnessed in Illinois"[88]—took place in Springfield. Partisan Democrats estimated that between 75,000 and 100,000 attended that party parley. Six different speaker stands were set up, and a parade of anti-administration orators occupied them. Christian Kribben of St. Louis, S. S. Cox of Ohio, and Daniel Voorhees of Indiana were the featured speakers, and they were followed by a dozen prominent Illini. Vallandigham's arrest was bitterly assailed, the suppression of the Chicago *Times* was viciously denounced, and administration incompetency was deplored. Resolutions reprimanding the Lincoln administration for violating the Bill of Rights and ignoring constitutional guarantees were introduced and adopted. The Springfield rally was proof that General Burnside inadvertently aided the Copperhead cause. It also indicated that midwestern Copperheadism was in its heyday.[89]

Another of the more interesting Democratic rallies was held in Milwaukee, Wisconsin, on June 25. Again Vallandigham was depicted as a "martyr" to the cause of constitutional rights, and again the suppression of the Chicago *Times* was condemned. The chief speaker of the day—15,000 supposedly attended—was Edward G. Ryan. Ryan, who wove Jeffersonian quotations into his speech, lit into the Lincoln administration with a vengeance. He accused the President of trying to establish "a military despotism," and he denounced Lincoln's advisers as "fools" and "Knaves." Ryan had no respect for Lincoln:

I will say here in the outset that I do not regard the President of the United States as a monster. I regard him simply as a weak, inefficient, unfortunate man, thrown by hazard, by some inscrutable destiny which Divine Providence may understand, into the highest position on earth, which he is totally unfit by original endowments or political education to fill, and when he will go down through all history, like Richard Cromwell, a weak, vain, amiable man; ridiculous for the sin of the world; ridiculous because he was thrown by accident into a place for which he was wholly unfitted.[90]

Ryan thought that Lincoln was a puppet in the hands of unscrupulous manipulators—"a mere doll, worked by strings."[91]

While Copperhead critics flayed the administration, Vallandigham's friends took steps to have him nominated as the Democratic party's gubernatorial candidate. Before his arrest, he had no chance for the nomination.[92] But soon after his arrest, the editor of the Hamilton *True Telegraph* hoisted a Vallandigham-for-Governor banner.[93] Samuel Medary of the *Crisis* used his influence to promote Vallandigham's candidacy,[94] and other extremists fell into line. The Democrats wanted to hand the Lincoln administration a rebuke that would reverberate from Maine to Missouri.[95] Conservative Ohio Democrats were powerless to head off the Vallandigham-for-Governor boom. The exiled Ohioan was nominated by acclamation at the party convention held on June 11 in Columbus. Party hotheads cheered. They were in the mood to chide the administration, for they viewed Vallandigham's nomination as a strike against "tyranny and usurpation."[96] Party conservatives feared that the Ohio Democrats had taken lethal medicine and had substituted spite for good sense.

The period which saw such Copperheads as Vallandigham, "Brick" Pomeroy, and Wilbur F. Storey occupy the midwestern spotlight also witnessed an outpouring of anti-administration propaganda. Some of the pamphlets, circulars, and books were published for use in the political campaigns of 1863. Most of the items were the work of individual Democrats, willing to invest their money to vindicate themselves or to undermine the Republican party's hold on the state and national governments.

Vallandigham himself made a contribution to Copperhead literature. A full month before his arrest he had helped to compile a collection of his speeches and pronouncements. That 250-page book, entitled *The Record of Hon. C. L. Vallandigham on Abolition, the Union, and the Civil War,* was intended to aid him in achieving his gubernatorial ambition.[97] Vallandigham did gain the Democratic nomination for governor in June of 1863, not because of his book but because of General Burnside's "blunder." Nevertheless, the book was widely circulated in Ohio to give some support to Vallandigham's candidacy.[98]

No other midwestern Copperhead worked in the area of publication-propaganda more zealously than Dennis A. Mahony of the Dubuque *Herald*. Mahony, who had been confined in Fort La-fayette as a "guest" of the government the last four months of 1862, wanted revenge, and he turned to writing and publication to achieve it. Early in 1863 the Dubuque editor began an exposé of the arbitrary arrests. It was his way of vindicating himself be-fore the country. Mahony selected *The Prisoner of State* as the title for his manuscript and journeyed to New York to complete the text and supervise its publication. The 414-page book came off the press in April of 1863 and the author distributed his handi-work in many quarters.

The Prisoner of State was dedicated to "Edwin M. Stanton, Secretary of War, U.S.A." The carefully composed dedication was "a savage piece of writing"; the editor of the New York *Herald* called it "a dedication with a devil in it."[99] Mahony claimed that Stanton's responsibility for many arbitrary arrests, his disregard of constitutional guarantees, and his many acts of "outrage, tyr-anny, and despotism" earned him "infamy"—and the honor of having the book dedicated to him. "I am, sir," wrote Mahony as he addressed the Secretary of War, "one of the many hundred victims of the despotism of the arbitrary power of which you have become the willing, servile, and pensioned tyrant."[100]

The first portion of *The Prisoner of State* included a dozen or more critical essays on Lincoln's "assumption of arbitrary power." Most of the essays had previously appeared as editorials in the Dubuque *Herald*. Mahony argued that the administration's "cir-cumvention of judicial rights" was pure effrontery—"a reproach upon Americans as a sovereign and free people." He contended that the principle of self-government had been repeatedly violated by the President and Stanton. He argued that it was a question of precedent plus constitutionality versus political expediency and executive despotism. It was not a question of patriotism, he wrote, but one of law and principle! The Dubuque editor, functioning as a propagandist, charged that Lincoln was transforming a democ-racy into a despotism. The various essays, probing into the area of practical politics, analyzed the "many unconstitutional acts" of the President. Mahony called upon history to justify his role as critic and Copperhead.

The second portion of the book related in detail the story of Mahony's dramatic arrest and his strange experiences in "Old Capitol" prison. This autobiographical account bid for the readers' sympathy and was written in a charming and readable style. The final section reported on some other "prisoners of state," and it briefly related the story of Mahony's release.

The Prisoner of State, replete with many historical inaccuracies and inappropriate analogies, was praised by Iowa Copperheads. They regarded the book as an excellent exposition of the "despotism" engulfing the country. The acting editor of the Dubuque *Herald* lauded Mahony's book in a three-column review; excerpts were ably woven into the review. The reviewer ended his evaluation with a brief paragraph:

> Take it all in all, it is of engrossing interest. Several defects are noticeable, but the main object of the work is accomplished—an exposé of one of the most damnable, despotic dynasties that has been permitted to exist in the 19th Century.[101]

While midwestern Democrats and Republicans debated the merits of *The Prisoner of State*, Mr. Mahony stayed on in New York to write a second anti-Lincoln book. This second volume, a 160-page paper-bound work, was entitled *The Four Acts of Despotism* and was published in late May. Mahony treated "the Tax Bill, the Finance Bill, the Conscription Bill, and the Indemnity Act" as the four measures which were especially "onerous to the American people."[102] *The Four Acts of Despotism* proved that Mahony was a western sectionalist, a Jeffersonian Democrat, and a prophet of postwar Greenbackism.

Mahony was not the only former "prisoner of state" who put his anti-administration prejudices into print. Judge Andrew D. Duff of Illinois told his story in an eighteen-page pamphlet entitled *Letter of Judge A. D. Duff of Franklin County to the Public of South Illinois, Relative to His Arrest and Imprisonment by the Abolition Despotism*. Judge Duff's treatise mixed a bid for public sympathy with stinging censure of the Lincoln administration,[103] and it circulated as a campaign document in the various election contests. Dr. Edson B. Olds's story also took the form of a political pamphlet. While Dr. Olds had been confined as a political prisoner, his Democratic supporters elected him to the state legislature. After his release he was the "lion of the occasion." The speeches which he gave at his home-coming celebration and as a member of the state legislature were printed in full in the Lancaster *Ohio Eagle* and in the *Crisis*. Those speeches were included in the Olds pamphlet entitled *Arbitrary Arrests*. Dr. Olds had severely chastised the Lincoln administration for its violation of civil rights, and the speeches were a mixture of personal experiences, history, and Copperhead criticism. The aging doctor told of heart-rending scenes which he had witnessed in the "bastiles" and stated and restated his stand against arbitrary arrests.[104]

The personal attacks on the administration through books and pamphlets were supplemented by a number of party "addresses," or printed political speeches. A notable speech which S. S. Cox made in New York City, for example, was printed and distributed as a political tract. That document, entitled *Puritanism in Politics*,[105] appealed to the sectional prejudices of many midwestern Democrats. Cox had attacked New England for its egotism, intolerance, and greed; he exposed puritans as "wolves in sheep's clothing." Cox's Ohio disciples shouted "Amen!"[106]

The Democratic party "addresses" drafted in Iowa and Michigan exemplify that type of political literature. They were written before the April elections and were given state-wide circulation. The Michigan document had been prepared by William V. Morrison for the Michigan State Central Committee. It soon was known as the "Morrison Address" and became the political platform of the Michigan Democrats. A learned and readable "statement of faith," it rained heavy blows upon the Lincoln administration.[107] The Iowa-based address was the handiwork of LeGrand Byington, an embittered Democrat who had previously lost a two-year effort to obtain a contested congressional seat. The Byington-drafted document, entitled *Address of the Democratic State*

Central Committee to the People of Iowa, called for a political reformation. Byington wanted to "rescue" the government from "a merciless *consolidated despotism*" and from the hands of an "abolition-minded, sectional party." He wanted the government to return to a position in which law and the Constitution would dominate. Mr. Byington condemned the many arbitrary arrests of "Lincoln & Company," and claimed that the "higher law theories" were a tyrant's plea of necessity. The outspoken Iowan believed that Lincoln and the war situation were affecting the government adversely, changing a federal union into a strongly centralized system. The shadow of Jacobinism and the French Revolution darkened the land![108]

Midwestern Democrats, acting as individuals, could not match the flood of Republican propaganda which deluged their section. They were also familiar with many Republican documents produced and distributed by the Loyal Publication Society, and some midwestern Democrats thought that their party should also have a national agency to "educate" the public and to counteract Republican efforts.[109]

Samuel F. B. Morse, inventor of the telegraph and an outspoken Peace Democrat, became leader of the movement to establish a national Democratic propaganda agency. He claimed that an agency was needed for the "purpose of *diffusing useful political knowledge,*"[110] and named his organization the Society for Diffusion of Political Knowledge. Professor Morse pre-empted the office of president for himself, but he added several midwestern Democrats to the society's executive committee.

The Society for the Diffusion of Political Knowledge began its publication program in mid-February of 1863. Its first document was a speech which S. S. Cox had delivered in the House of Representatives a month earlier. Five thousand copies of that speech-pamphlet were printed and distributed. The printing was done in the plant of the New York *Era,* and that newspaper contributed office space for the society's headquarters.

The approach of the April elections served as an incentive to speed up the publication program. A speech of George E. Pugh of Ohio was turned into a political pamphlet and a large number of copies of Cox's *Puritanism in Politics* were printed. Professor Morse revealed his anti-Negro prejudices in a bulletin entitled *Results of Emancipation*. Midwesterners were also interested in some of the items which were published or distributed by the society: Charles Mason's *Address to the People of Iowa*, four German-language tracts intended to keep Germans within the Democratic party, a biblical justification of slavery, and a document simply entitled *Argument*, written by Morse.

Democrats believed that these documents helped to win the April elections in the Midwest. Chicago "Dimmycrats" elected their complete Copperhead slate in spite of Republican efforts to hide themselves behind the "Union Party" label. Toledo, St. Paul, and Detroit voters threw out Republican incumbents. Springfield, home of President Lincoln, rebuked the administration by giving an increased majority to Democratic candidates. Democratic contentions that their party was enjoying a "real revival" were also borne out by reports from Milwaukee, Louisville, Columbus, and Dubuque. The editor of the Dubuque *Herald* reported on the spring election returns: "Old Dubuque never falters. She is Copperheaded, copper bottomed, and copper fastened. She is in short, the white man's country, and we glory in it and will labor to keep her so."[111]

Vallandigham's home town, Dayton, also flew Democratic colors after election day. The editor of the Dayton *Empire* gloried in the election returns, viewing the results as "a victory for Vallandigham."[112] The editor of the nearby Hamilton *True Telegraph* also celebrated the Democratic victories throughout Ohio and the Midwest. He believed that the April election results rejected Republicanism, repudiated the Lincoln administration, and pushed the Copperhead tide to a new high. "Democrats," he wrote, "keep the ball rolling. . . . Keep the old liberty fires burning brightly till next fall, till we sink the disunionists below the water mark."[113]

The months preceding July of 1863 were, indeed, the darkest experienced by the Lincoln administration. The election returns of April, 1863, and of the previous fall revealed widespread opposition to the administration and encouraged Copperheads to be bolder. The high-handed and maladroit tactics of General Burnside and his subordinates stirred the Copperhead beehive. The threat of military conscription created a feeling of uneasiness everywhere. The absence of any significant military victories helped to develop defeatism and to weaken faith in the administration. The people had not yet learned to trust the sad-faced occupant of the White House.

There was a genuine fear in some quarters that a showdown over the question of civil rights and free elections lay in the offing. "Resistance to tyrants," wrote one Iowa editor, "is obedience to God."[114] Bold Democrats threw down the gauntlet. "Brick" Pomeroy, boldest of the bold, warned the President bluntly: "If Lincoln will abide by the Constitution there will be no rows—no riots, nor civil war in the North. If he does not—if he drives with reckless hand the remainder of his term farther from Law and Constitution, the people will not follow and blood will flow."[115]

Two other events proved that the months immediately preceding the Union victories at Gettysburg and Vicksburg witnessed the Copperhead high tide. Some disillusioned and dejected Democrats launched a peace movement. Then, at the same time, some organized the Sons of Liberty as a secret political society. The fate of the Lincoln administration hung in the balance.

I V

Formation of the Peace Movement

THERE WERE SEVERAL WAYS in which 1863 was a critical year: the Confederate cause reached its zenith and the midwestern peace movement took on definite shape. Clement L. Vallandigham made his contribution to the cause of peace in this fateful year. Requests for an armistice and resolutions begging for an honorable peace were numerous. Some of the "peace men" sponsored the calling of a national convention. The peace movement became inseparably linked to Vallandigham's campaign for the governorship of Ohio. His defeat in October of 1863 was a jolt to those who looked to him to lead the country down the path of peace.

The peace movement of 1863 had its roots in the efforts to reconcile the North and South which preceded the war. Most midwestern Democrats had favored the Crittenden compromise proposals and conciliation at the Washington Peace Convention of 1861.[1] Some who favored compromise believed that the economic ties binding the South and the West should not be broken. Some midwestern manufacturing, financial, and commercial interests feared the coming of a war, for they thought it would invite economic hardship as well as bloodshed. One of the co-editors of the Cincinnati *Enquirer*, for example, wanted compromise and peace because he had invested heavily in a boiler-plate business dependent on the Ohio-Mississippi river trade.[2] Cyrus H. McCormick, too, feared that a civil war might prove disastrous for his firm, because Southern sales and credits loomed large in his company's plans.[3] Cities like Cincinnati, Cairo, and Louisville looked southward for their trade and prosperity. Farmers who knew that the down-river markets consumed their surplus crops also hated to see the avenues of trade closed and blamed extremists of both North and South for the crisis.

Western sectionalists like Vallandigham and Lambdin P. Milligan recognized that the effects of coercion and war would be far-reaching. The failure of compromise efforts would isolate their section, putting it at the mercy of the Northeast. They feared that the Northeast would seize the opportunity which a war would bring to impose its commercial and industrial interests on the Northwest. The Midwest, furthermore, would lose the balance of power it had held in the political arena. As a section it had played the Northeast against the South, gaining a weight in affairs far beyond its numerical strength. Civil conflict, then, would adversely affect the political power of the West and its prosperity as well.

Democratic realists also gauged the effect compromise would have on the opposition party. The no-slavery-in-the-territories policy held the Republican platform and party together. If this issue should be settled by constitutional amendment, Lincoln's party might fall apart. Democrats whose chief concern was annihilating the Republican party, therefore, were generous in offering to surrender Republican principles. Lincoln's supporters also recognized that their party would die if it sold its birthright. "For God's sake," wrote a Republican party realist, "don't let our men lower the standard . . . [or] Lincoln will be the last, as he is the first, of the Republican presidents."[4] "I hope from the bottom of my soul no pro-slavery concessions will be made," wrote another, explaining his reason: "It will ruin the Republican party if they do."[5]

Some farsighted Democrats opposed war and favored compromise for other than party, economic, or sectional reasons. There was a genuine fear that sectional strife might bring an end to the American experiment in democracy. European civil wars had often ended in dictatorship, and the same thing could happen in America. Then there were those who detested war as a means to an end. These men recognized that orphans and widows, death and desolation, and suffering and despair were inevitable in war. "War is the great uncivilizer of the age," one such critic wrote, and "it sucks up the life-blood of a nation, saps the foundations of public virtue and private morality, and hangs a dark cloud over the future of humanity."[6]

Democratic spokesmen believed that in early 1861 a majority of the people preferred compromise to war, conciliation to coercion. State and local resolutions indorsing an honorable compromise flooded the Midwest. Almost without exception, Democratic editors wanted a peaceful solution to the crisis.

After the Fort Sumter affair unleased a flood of patriotic fervor, Democrats who had argued for compromise went their separate ways. Some took their cue from Stephen A. Douglas: "There can be but two parties, the party of patriots and the party of traitors. We [the Democrats] belong to the former."[7] "Let blood flow," suggested one of Douglas' supporters, "until the past is atoned, and a long future secured to peace, prosperity, happiness, and honor."[8] Some party stalwarts, like John A. Logan and John A. McClernand, offered their services to the country and marched off to war. Other party stalwarts were less war minded. Charles Mason and Dennis A. Mahony of Iowa, James C. Robinson of Illinois, and Samuel Medary and Vallandigham of Ohio refused to surrender their pro-peace and pro-compromise views even after the South Carolina rebels had fired upon the American flag. "I am all the while hoping," wrote Mason, "that no very bloody encounter will take place until further and sufficient time is given to cool the passions now raging on both sides, sufficiently to lead to some peaceful measures."[9] Mahony warned his readers that war might destroy both slavery and the Union, and consistently prayed for peace and compromise.[10] Robinson condemned Lincoln less violently than Mahony, but he still hoped the Democrats would agree on a "peace policy."[11] Vallandigham believed that the South could not be conquered, that "civilized people" always preferred conciliation to bloodshed, and that a prolonged war could only mean the death of civil liberties.[12] He hoped that "the sober second thought of the people" would force the administration to accept compromise. If Ohio were invaded, he would "aid in defending her to the last extremity," and he expected the people of Virginia, Kentucky, and Missouri to do likewise.[13] Medary, sitting in the office of the *Crisis*, saw the Republican party as the "masked face" of abolition. In almost every issue of his weekly newspaper he advocated peace.[14] The editor of the Indianapolis *State Sentinel* also thought that a silver lining might be found in the war clouds, especially if time tempered the emotions. "Let one more effort be made for conciliation," he editorialized, "before the blow is struck which will make us bear towards each other a brother's hate."[15]

While these conservative Democrats prayed for peace and stressed moderation, the guns boomed at Bull Run. Compromise, a faint and futile hope before the battle, had less chance and fewer champions afterward. John A. Logan, who earlier damned Douglas for supporting the war, joined the war party after a harassing experience at Bull Run, where he had gone as an observer.[16] McClernand became a brigadier general and asked for field service. Mason offered his services but Iowa Republicans found them unacceptable. "Brick" Pomeroy tried to raise a company of La Crosse "Tigers" to fight Marion-style, but the company failed to materialize. David Tod of Ohio, earlier an opponent of coercion and an advocate of compromise, became a War Democrat. Republicans were pleased that pro-compromise sentiment seemed to evaporate. "There is no longer a peace party," wrote one Republican observer. "It is as hard to find a peace man now as it was to find a Tory after the Revolutionary War had ended in the independence of America."[17]

That Republican observer failed to understand the midwestern setting and the disposition of such Democrats as Mahony and Medary. Three factors helped to revive peace and compromise sentiment in the fall of 1861: the depression, the specter of abolition, and the approach of the fall elections. Some Democrats blamed Republicans for the "dismal state of affairs," and they talked vaguely of peace and compromise as a bid for votes. Others straddled the fence, giving support to the war while they talked of "honorable peace."

A midwestern Democrat played his peace cards boldly in the House of Representatives in Washington. S. S. Cox introduced a resolution suggesting the establishment of a national peace commission. Cox suggested that a committee composed of one member from each of the states still in the Union should recommend amendments to the Constitution to "assuage all grievances and bring about a reconstruction of the National Union."[18] The committee then would select a seven-member commission of "prominent men."[19] Cox supposed that the Southern states would take similar steps. Then the commissioners, meeting at Louisville on "the first Monday of September," would retain contact with their "congressional committees," work out compromise agreements, and agree on several desirable amendments to the Constitution. Such prominent midwestern Democrats as Voorhees and Vallandigham supported Cox's plan. The proposal was defeated, however, by a strict party vote (85 to 41), and the "peace offering" was made in vain.[20] Less than a month later, an Indiana congressman, John G. Davis, renewed the request for a national convention to meet at Louisville or Lexington. He even suggested an "immediate armistice."[21] But the nation was in no mood to compromise, and when Davis or Vallandigham talked of peace they represented the minority opinion in their congressional districts. "There is no denying the fact now," wrote a supporter of Vallandigham in August of 1861, "that he is the most unpopular man in the north, and that here in his own district he has but a minority of the people with him. . . ."[22]

As they bid for votes, Democratic partisans often made ridiculous assertions. They pretended that peace and compromise were easy to attain and that only the abolitionists stood in the way. The imprudent editor of the Louisville *Democrat* claimed that peace and conciliation would be realized if the Republicans disbanded their party in the interests of patriotism.[23] The editor of the Crawfordsville *Review* advised voters to "give the Democracy the reins of government," and he promised that "in less than sixty days, peace and a Union of all the States" would "take place."[24] The editor of the Detroit *Free Press* suggested that the surest way to restore the Union was for Congress to adjourn and for Northerners "to bury abolitionism."[25] One Indiana editor offered a novel, if impractical, proposal to bring about reunion. ". . . if I had the power I would hang about one thousand Northern fanatics and an even number of Southern fire-eaters as high as Haman," he wrote, "and then give the people a chance at the ballot box to settle the matter, and peace would once more hover over our land and nation, and 'brotherly love prevail and every moral and social virtue cement us.' "[26] There seemed to exist a widespread belief that Southern unionists would mysteriously arise and oust the secessionists if Northern conservatives won the elections and backed compromise measures.[27]

As the April elections of 1862 approached, Democratic talk about an "honorable peace" became more widespread in the upper Mississippi Valley. The full effects of the economic depression of 1861–62 dampened some of the war enthusiasm. Midwestern sectionalists were anxious to restore their beloved section to its prewar economic and political level. Conservative Kentuckians were convinced that they had most to gain from a compromise which would restore the nation to its prewar status and eliminate their state as a battleground. Lazarus W. Powell, a conservative senator in Congress, claimed that he represented the views of the majority of Kentuckians when he talked of compromise and hoped for peace.[28]

Powell, like many other midwestern Democrats, believed that the trend toward abolition in the North adversely affected the prospect of restoring the Union to its prewar status. Mahony stated this belief repeatedly, arguing that the trend toward abolition tended to crush the Union movement in the South, providing Southern radicals with propaganda material and widening the breach between the two sections.[29] Some self-deluded Democrats even claimed that the Union victories at Fort Henry and Fort

Donelson opened the door to compromise, provided Lincoln proclaimed that Southern institutions would be "untouched."[30] "Give the Southerners the rights guaranteed by the Constitution, and let them know *authoritatively* that such is our intention," wrote a prominent Detroit Democrat, "and in ninety days we are reunited."[31]

Democrats generally interpreted the election results of April, 1862, as a victory for conservatism and compromise. They viewed the election returns as a mandate to "sustain the integrity of the Union through the Constitution." They attacked abolition with renewed vigor, believing it endangered the hope for compromise. "The real strength of the rebels," wrote the editor of the Detroit *Free Press*, "consists in their being able to quote from the northern secession journals, sailing under the black flag of abolition, such language and sentiments as excites the South to frenzied madness."[32] If Northern conservatives could crush abolition and Southern conservatives repudiate their section's radicals, rationalized a prominent Illinois Democrat, then "patriots" of the two warring sections could agree on a restoration of the Union "by way of a negotiated peace."[33]

When Lincoln bowed to the pressure of the Radical Republicans in September of 1862, the conservatives were disheartened and dismayed. "Stop him! Hold him! is all I can say by way of advice to you as a friend of the President," wrote a St. Louis citizen to one of Lincoln's advisers. "Beg him to write no more letters to newspapers, and never to publish a proclamation. Suggest to him that a dignified retreat from his present position is the only road to a restoration of peace and quiet."[34] Conservative Democrats who had talked of an "honorable peace" recognized that the administration's acceptance of abolition as official policy scuttled and endangered their dreams of conciliation and compromise.[35] Such prominent politicos as William Allen of Ohio and John Reynolds of Illinois came out of political retirement to speak in behalf of constitutionalism and compromise.[36] Some embittered critics of the administration suggested that the Democratic party openly and officially withdraw its support of the war. One angry critic asked that the President be arrested for issuing his preliminary proclamation of emancipation and tried for treason.[37] Another thought that Lincoln deserved to be impeached and removed from his high office so that constitutionalism, reunion, and peace might become the order of the day.[38]

Conservative Democrats looked to the fall elections of 1862 to check the course of Radicalism. If the conservatives were to restore "the Union as it was," they needed to control the machinery of government. "Congress and the Administration," wrote one Northern conservative, "have gone so far in the Abolition movement that they cannot ever submit themselves to the South *any* propositions which the South could accept."[39] Democrats, on the other hand, might "emancipate President Lincoln from Abolition thralldom" and make peaceful reunion possible.[40] Democratic victories would be a repudiation of abolitionism and might encourage unionism below the Mason-Dixon line. Mahony argued that peace would be possible if Democrats won the elections handily. Lincoln then could recall or revoke his proclamation of emancipation. If abolition were thus repudiated, Mahony argued, secession would fall in the South "without the loss of life or treasure to put it down."[41] One of Mahony's Democratic friends even invented an appropriate epitaph for abolitionism: *"Here sleeps the murderer of its country's peace; the convicted enemy of constitutional free government."*[42]

An "honorable peace" seemed more probable after the elections. Radicalism had been repudiated. Midwestern Democrats hoped that President Lincoln would adjust his policy to the election results and return to a moderate course. Some wishful conservatives thought that Lincoln might be prevailed upon to withdraw his preliminary proclamation of emancipation. He would thus encourage the Southern states to return to the Union, restoring "the Union as it was."[43]

Peace sentiment flourished after the fall elections were over. Advocates of peace became bolder and more numerous. Pro-compromise Democrats argued that the election returns were a mandate to push the cause of conciliation. But the advocates of peace had no practical program. The extreme view continued to be voiced by Medary of the *Crisis*. He claimed that the Union was "gone," that the war was "hopeless," and that the sensible course was to withdraw Northern troops and cease fighting[44]—claims which even Vallandigham was not ready to make in 1862. Some midwestern sectionalists like Lambdin P. Milligan thought that the best way to force New England to give heed to the "message of peace" was to threaten to establish a separate western confederacy.[45] Some Democrats talked of a national convention which could take action to restore "the old Union." "We can see nothing disloyal in holding such a Convention," wrote the editor of an Ohio newspaper. "Its representatives would be fresh from the people."[46]

But most of those who talked of an "honorable peace" had no formula to achieve it. They did not favor a "dishonorable peace" —one which recognized Southern independence. "Whatever peace they [Democrats] countenance," wrote the editor of the Detroit *Free Press*, "must be an *honorable peace, and must preserve every star in the flag.*"[47] Those Democratic dreamers could claim that the war was "unnecessary and destructive," but they refused to clarify their peace program further. The ability of Democrats to carry water on both shoulders was well illustrated by the vague utterances of such Democratic spokesmen as William A. Richardson. The Illinois politician was more interested in votes than in clarity. "This Government cannot be restored by the sword alone," said the Illinois conservative. "You must carry with it the olive branch."[48]

While Democrats discussed the meaning of the election returns and debated the possibility of peace, President Lincoln issued his formal and definite Emancipation Proclamation. Democrats reacted violently. Some turned to denunciation to express their sentiments. Several bold Democrats bluntly stated that Lincoln's refusal to retreat on the question of emancipation excused their party from further support of the war.[49] A few western sectionalists, like Milligan, gave the turn of events a deeper meaning. They interpreted Lincoln's proclamation of January 1, 1863, as proof that the President was a tool in the hands of New Englanders bent on extending the Industrial Revolution. Milligan believed that continuance of the war would but break down the influence of agriculture, increasing the power of the moneyed and manufacturing interests. Milligan and other Jeffersonian Democrats wanted to stay the course of the Industrial Revolution in America. They saw peace and reunion as a means to that end. Then the plantation South and the agricultural West could co-operate to turn the clock back.[50]

While Democrats tried to chart their course and set their compass, Vallandigham dropped a "peace bomb" in Congress. Vallandigham was somewhat embittered because of the Republican-engineered gerrymander that had defeated his bid for re-election. Furthermore, he was convinced that the administration had changed the objectives of the war: the war for the Union had been changed into one to free the slaves. The wishes and wants of the West were blandly ignored while New England and revived Whiggery rode herd. The tide of patriotism was ebbing. Union defeats far outnumbered Union victories. The conviction grew that the war would be long and costly. Midwesterners talked of a national convention; the Copperhead-controlled legislatures in Indiana and Illinois were ready to suggest a national convention as the means to restore the Union and end the war. Vallandigham possessed the convictions and the courage to take the lead in advocating the cause of conciliation and compromise.

On January 14, 1863, Vallandigham stated his convictions concerning war and peace in a well-prepared speech upon the floor of the House of Representatives. He started mildly enough. He reviewed the events leading to the failure of compromise. He blamed the Republicans for scuttling the compromise proposals and insisting upon coercion as official policy. He interpreted the South's rebellion as a deliberate and "wicked" answer to Northern fanatical abolitionism. Vallandigham did not believe it feasible or morally right to whip Southerners "back into fellowship and love at the point of the bayonet." Twenty months had passed since the war had begun. The President's unconstitutional acts multiplied, and traditional freedoms stood in jeopardy. He spoke of millions of dollars expended and thousands of soldiers added to the casualty lists—"three hundred thousand lives lost or bodies mangled." With all the resources of money, men, "enthusiasm," "confidence," and "credit," the administration had failed to conquer the South—failed "disastrously" and "ignominiously." Turning the war into an abolition crusade was an error, a perversion of objectives that solidified rebel resistance and drove Democrats into anti-administration ranks. Westerners were chagrined at the turn of events, especially the President's acceptance of abolition and his homage to New England. Those eastern "disunionists" might force the West to break away too! "The people of the West want peace," he asserted, "and they begin to more than suspect that New England is in the way."[51]

He did not believe that the South could be conquered or coerced back into the Union. He spoke out for "the Union as it was." "The sole question today," Vallandigham bluntly affirmed, "is between Union with slavery, or final disunion. . . ." He feared that anarchy and despotism might engulf the North, for civil liberties had been trampled on and basic rights violated. A "reign of terror," more violent than that which occurred during the French Revolution might become a part of the American Civil War. So he hoped that a friendly foreign power might be accepted as a mediator and the issues settled amicably. He wanted the fighting to cease as a first step toward ultimate reunion; "let passions have time to cool and reason to resume sway." So Vallandigham proposed an "informal, practical recognition" as the means to conciliation, compromise, and reunion. Time would heal. He stated his case:

But why speak of ways or terms of reunion now? The will is yet wanting in both sections. Union is consent and good will and fraternal affection. War is force, hate, revenge. Is the country tired at last of war? Has the experiment been tried long enough? Has sufficient blood been shed, treasure expended, and misery inflicted in both the North and the South? What then? Stop fighting! Make an armistice—no formal treaty. Withdraw your armies from the seceded States. Reduce both armies to a fair and sufficient peace establishment. Declare absolute free trade between the North and the South. Buy and sell. Agree upon a Zollverein. Recall your fleets. Break up your blockade. Reduce your navy. Restore travel. Open up railroads. Re-establish the telegraph. Reunite your express companies. No more monitors and iron-clads, but set your friendly steamers and steamships again in motion. Visit the North and West. Visit the South. Exchange newspapers. Migrate. Intermarry. Let slavery alone. Hold elections at the appointed time. Let us choose a new President in sixty-four. And when the gospel of peace shall have descended again from heaven into their hearts, and the gospel of abolition and hate expelled, let your churches meet again in Christian intercourse, North and South. Let the secret orders and voluntary everywhere reunite as brethren once more. In short, give all the natural and all the artificial causes which impel us together, their fullest sway. Let time do his office—drying tears, dispelling sorrows, mellowing passion, and making herb and grass and tree to grow again upon the hundred battlefields of this terrible war.[52]

Vallandigham's "peace bomb" shook the country. It shocked the Republicans and startled the Democrats. A few of the bolder Democratic editors printed it in entirety.[53] Some heartily indorsed it; others expressed no editorial opinions. Mahony applauded Vallandigham's boldness, indorsed his sentiments, and called it a "Great Speech." "It is bold, logical, direct and positive," wrote Mahony. "The people think with him and were he prepared to lead, would act with him at the word. We must and will have a speedy peace."[54] The editors of the Dayton *Empire* and Hamilton *True Telegraph*, constituents of Vallandigham and close personal friends, wrote in a like vein. " 'Peace' is on a million lips," read an editorial in the *True Telegraph*, "and it will thunder, ere long, in the ears of our rulers like an Alpine storm."[55]

Most midwestern Democrats were unwilling to accept Vallandigham's unrealistic program. They might want "peace" or an "honorable compromise," but they were opposed to an armistice. Talking of peace and reconciliation was one thing; giving up the fight and admitting defeat was another. Logically, then, midwestern Democrats again turned to a national convention as an instrument to end the war and reunite the country.

Kentucky Democrats took the lead in suggesting that midwesterners partake in a regional convention where the peace bubble
could be blown to balloon size. The Kentucky peace men suggested
Louisville as a suitable site for their regional peace powwow.
Illinois, Indiana, Ohio, and Missouri might send delegates. The
Kentuckians looked hopefully in the direction of Illinois and Indiana, for Democratic-controlled legislatures were in session in
those two states. The regional convention might be the prelude to
a national convention and the peaceful solution to the nation's
ills.[56]

Peace men who indorsed the idea of a meeting in Louisville put
pressure upon the Illinois state legislature to give support to the
convention idea. Local mass meetings and county party rallies
frequently adopted pro-peace petitions or resolutions. A Union
County resolution, for example, indorsed both "peace" and "the
supremacy of the Constitution of the Union."[57] The Coles County
resolves asked for "peace" and "the Union as it was."[58] A Han-
cock County mass meeting declared in favor of an "armistice"
until "a convention of all the states" could settle "the matters in
dispute." That resolution called upon the "legislators" to name a
slate of convention delegates and urge Lincoln to co-operate in
the peace movement.[59] A Macoupin County rally called upon the
state legislature to take the initiative in promoting the cause of
peace and compromise.[60]

The Hon. Charles A. Walker, Macoupin County's representative
in the lower house of the Illinois state legislature, took steps to
carry out the pro-peace wishes of his constituents. He introduced
a resolution which listed "fifteen grievances," patterned after
those of the Declaration of Independence. The resolution then
instructed the state legislature to appoint commissioners "to meet
in national convention" at Louisville on "the first Tuesday in the
month of April, 1862." The resolution called on Congress to support an "armistice" and the "cessation of hostilities."[61]

The Walker-sponsored resolution was heatedly debated in the
lower house of the Illinois state legislature. Republicans con-

demned it, and the hesitant Democrats felt compelled to support the controversial resolution. Charles A. Keyes gave his reason for his support of the convention bill:

We must go to the people of the South with the "sword in one hand and the constitution in the other, the one for war, the other for conciliation." . . . I am willing to make peace with the people of the south upon fair and honorable terms. I am in favor of compromise. I desire an armistice, and a convention of all the states for the purpose of bringing about a settlement of our troubles, and bringing this terrible war to an end. I believe the people in convention can fix an honorable peace. It is for the people of the north and the south to make peace. The leaders will never do it. . . . Let us hope that the "nation may arise out of this crisis," chastened by misfortune, educated by sorrow, one, indivisible and eternal.[62]

The Walker-sponsored resolution passed the lower house, and the speaker immediately named six "commissioners" to the proposed Louisville convention.

Republican members of the upper house built a parliamentary maze around the convention resolution introduced in that body. Furthermore, the defection of two Democrats—the Democrats held a meager thirteen to twelve edge in the state senate—held back the convention bill.[63] Confident that they could force the bill through in short order, the Peace Democrats played their trump card—a legislative recess from February 14 until early in June. The proponents of peace had every reason to believe that a legislative recess would give them every advantage. Republicanism seemed to be withering on the vine. Reaction to the Emancipation Proclamation dampened the war enthusiasm. War weariness was spreading and pro-peace sentiment permeated the national temper.

As February 14 approached, senate Democrats tried to force through both the convention bill and the bill to recess. Republican strategists permitted the recess bill to pass but they outmaneuvered their pro-peace opponents on the convention measure. The Peace Democrats had put the cart before the horse. When the hour for recess came, the convention bill was still on the docket. The pro-convention Democrats went home muttering to themselves and cursing their Republican rivals.[64]

The effort to foist a pro-peace and pro-convention measure down the throat of Indiana legislators ended more ignobly. The legislature's Committee on Federal Relations had become a depository for petitions and memorials drafted by local citizens. Some of the petitions asked for an immediate armistice, some hoped for "peace and prosperity," and others suggested that a national convention bring the Union back together. The Committee on Federal Relations prepared a report which was a distinct disappointment to the peace men. The report denounced secession and indorsed coercion rather than an armistice: "The Union of the States is a necessity; and under no consideration or circumstances will we ever consent to surrender it. We must be one people, under one government and one flag."[65]

The supporters of a national convention had trouble gaining a hearing for their plans as the Copperhead-controlled legislature and the adamant governor dueled. Rank partisanship and petty politics prevented the wheels of legislation from turning. The Democratic-dominated legislature tried to usurp the governor's powers and prerogatives. In turn, Governor Morton tried to discredit the legislators.[66] Republican members bolted and broke quorums to prevent passage of Democratic-sponsored bills. The statutory date for adjournment passed. The Democratic program evaporated into nothingness. Convention bills died in committee. Indiana's failure to support the proposed Louisville convention helped to turn it into a fiasco. The trial balloon of the Peace Democrats never left the ground. Ohio, despite the "peace bomb" of Vallandigham, held back. Iowa, Wisconsin, Minnesota, and Michigan contributed little more than empty phrases, for those states were firmly controlled by Republican governors and Republican legislatures.

The failure of the Peace Democrats to bring about a national convention left the peace movement in a disorganized status. Military failures, suffered early in 1863, helped to convince the war-weary that conciliation could be more successful than coercion in reuniting the nation. Those who were especially fearful that a despotism was enveloping the government were alarmed by such events as Vallandigham's arrest, the suppression of the Chicago *Times*, and the mobbing of Democratic newspaper offices; they consequently turned toward compromise or conciliation as a means of saving democratic government. Individual Democrats scattered over the Midwest raised their voices in behalf of peace or compromise. "Brick" Pomeroy posed as a humanitarian as he advocated peace:

The people do not want this war. Tax payers do not wish it. Widows, orphans, and over-taxed working men do not ask or need this waste of men, blood, and treasure. There is no glory to be won in a civil war, no more than in a family quarrel. If politicians would let this matter come before the people, there would be an honorable peace within sixty days. But so long as blind leaders govern and fanaticism rules the day, so long will there be war, tears, and desolation.[67]

Henry Clay Dean, an Iowa preacher who lost his minister's license because he criticized the Lincoln administration and spoke out for peace, toured the Midwest as a lecturer and politician. He claimed that the biblical admonition, "blessed are the peacemakers," should be heeded. He claimed that war was not the best means to achieve the nation's objectives. "To create wars upon moral pretense," he wrote in condemnation of the abolitionists, "is to overturn the moral law, the source and foundation of all laws, and Christianity, the standard by which every good must be measured."[68]

William T. Logan, editor of the Dayton *Empire* and friend of Vallandigham, spoke out for peace as boldly as anyone. He thought of war in terms of widows and crepe, death and desolation. He was tired of war and bloodshed:

The earth is crimson with the blood of brave men. Desolation, ruin, and suffering follows the march of contending armies. . . . In almost every household there is a mourner, and, in almost every heart a vacant place. The ferryman on the river Styx has done a heavy freighting business during the past twelve-month. . . [69]

Other editors exhibited the same sentiments of war weariness. They were tired of war; they hoped for peace. "When will the hideous moloch who holds the press and sword of this nation," asked a lesser-known newsman, "call off his dogs of war and suffer peace once more to bless our bleeding country?"[70]

Some Democrats were convinced that "Lincoln and Company" no longer represented the true wishes of the people. They cited the election results of 1862 and 1863 in support of their contention. They were sure that the popular reaction to the Emancipation Proclamation and toward the arbitrary arrests offered further proof that the administration was out of step with the times. "Go among the farmers, the laborers, the mechanics, the bone and sinew of society, who suffer the most severely from the shocking condition of public affairs," wrote Editor R. H. Sylvester of the Iowa City *State Press*, "and there will be found a swelling undercurrent of hostility to the war. . . ."[71] That editor was convinced that the country was tired of war and that coercion as policy had failed miserably. He thought that only blind Republicans, dishonest contractors, and officeholders wanted war to the bitter end, howling "Stand by the Government!" and "No peace with the Rebels!" Dipping his pen in partisan ink, he wrote:

It is impossible to deceive the people with this sort of clap-trap any longer. They have eyes to see the lowering future which daily darkens before them. They have ears to hear the ominous reverberations of the earthquake. They have wisdom to discern that a restoration of the Union is impossible to accomplish by force of arms. . . . They want the war to stop. They protest that its miseries, fruitful only to new miseries, have accumulated to a horrible magnitude enough already. . . . They ask for peaceful councils and will insist upon them until they prevail and until the truth be ascertained whether there is not sense enough, Christian intelligence enough, and good statesmanship enough in the United States to bring about an honourable settlement of a ruinous war. . . .[72]

When midwesterners mixed talk of peace with their criticism of the Lincoln administration and of New England, they gained the ear of General P. G. T. Beauregard, a Confederate commander charged with the defense of Charleston harbor. Beauregard, who had once commanded Confederate forces in Tennessee before he gained the displeasure of Jefferson Davis, naïvely believed that midwestern Copperheads were pro-Southern in their sympathies;

he mistook Democratic disaffection for disloyalty. He took western sectionalists at their word when they threatened to set up a separate confederacy.

In the fall of 1862, when General Braxton Bragg had taken his Confederate army on an offensive into Kentucky, Beauregard proposed that Southern and western governors meet in Memphis under a flag of truce. He thought that they might agree on peace terms quite favorable to the South. In turn, the governors' recommendations would be submitted to both Confederate and Union governments.[73] General Beauregard urged such diplomacy in addition to campaigns in the field.

The failure of General Bragg's campaign caused Beauregard to discard the "Memphis convention" idea. Beauregard, however, had another grandiose scheme. He wanted the South to help the West establish its own confederacy. He wanted Southern governors to issue a joint address urging midwesterners to withdraw from the war and to set up their own government. The Southern governors could guarantee free use of the Mississippi River and promise full friendship.[74] No Southerners of importance took Beauregard's proposal seriously, partly because the conceited general bypassed his president and partly because they were better judges of the midwestern situation.

In May of 1863 Beauregard was at it again. He thought that the western reaction to Vallandigham's arrest and the pro-peace pleas emanating from that section gave the South an opportunity to win the war and get the Lincoln administration to beg for terms of peace. Beauregard's "master plan" called for General Lee to assume the defensive and send ample reinforcements to General Bragg in the West. Bragg's forces could then destroy the Union armies in Tennessee and Kentucky. Victorious Confederate troops would then move up into Ohio, secure the assistance of Vallandigham's "friends," and help midwesterners to establish their own confederacy. Beauregard believed that Lincoln and the Northeast, "brought to their senses," would then sue for peace.[75]

Beauregard's belief that midwestern Copperheads were friendly to the South was found to be a mistake a short time later. Six weeks after Beauregard proposed his plan to win the war, General John Morgan and his raiders crossed from Kentucky into Indiana to steal horses and test Northern tempers. Vallandigham's political supporters and Democratic partisans living in southern Indiana and Ohio fought vigorously against the invaders. Several of Morgan's raiders later testified that the " 'Copperheads' and 'Vallandighamers' fought harder than the others."[76] Democrats and Republicans who lived in the counties through which Morgan's men passed viewed the invaders as "horse-thieves," "extortionists," and "blackmailers." The unfriendly reception accorded to the raiders should have convinced General Beauregard that his "grand design" was impractical and that he had badly misjudged midwestern Copperheads.

Democrats like Editor R. H. Sylvester and Dennis A. Mahony, who argued that the South could not be conquered, had their reputations as prophets badly tarnished by events at Gettysburg and Vicksburg. These Union victories brought hope to Northern hearts and gave a much-needed lift to civilian morale. Unrealistic Democrats, however, refused to give up their hopes for a negotiated peace and for concession and conciliation. These partisans and peacemakers supposed that the South would now be more receptive to suggestions that compromise should replace coercion in reuniting the nation. Charles H. Lanphier, editor of the *Illinois State Register*, was one of many Copperheads who thought that Union victories of early July, 1863, presented the North with "a golden opportunity." "Let us," he advised the administration, "extend the olive branch from our station of victory."[77] Lanphier claimed that a presidential proclamation of general amnesty to "the masses in the rebellious states upon return to their allegiance" would set the stage for reunion and peace.[78] Other Democrats also indorsed the idea of presidential amnesty in order to revive unionism in the South and to lay the groundwork for a compromise between the warring sections.[79] Most of the advocates of peace and reunion were much more vague and indefinite. They merely advocated that the North march to battle with a sword in one hand and an olive branch in the other.[80]

While midwestern Copperheads blandly discussed the future of the war and the possibilities of peace, two peace proposals were carried by self-styled emissaries. Both occurred in July, 1863, and both were unknown to western advocates of peace and compromise. The first peace pipe was carried by Alexander H. Stephens, who served as vice-president of the Confederacy but was a critic of Jefferson Davis. Stephens thought that the South would lose a prolonged war and he believed that a despotism was taking shape in the South. He offered his services to the Confederate government as an emissary to go to Washington and resolve the controversy over the treatment and exchange of prisoners. He hoped that the discussion would then turn to the more important questions of conciliation and peace. Stephens possessed some strange faith in the possibilities of peace and was willing to serve as the agent of the "God of Peace."[81] ". . . I am not without hope," Stephens wrote, "that indirectly I could . . . turn attention to a general adjustment upon such basis as might ultimately be acceptable to both parties and stop the further effusion of blood in a contest so irrational, unchristian, and so inconsistent with all recognized American principles."[82]

To pacify some of his critics, Jefferson Davis permitted Stephens to go on his strange mission. He spelled out requests concerning the question of prisoner treatment and exchange in detail, but failed to make any commitment to Stephens on the question of peace or compromise. Thus Stephens, in effect, was an unauthorized ambassador of peace who approached his task with uncalled-for optimism. Davis' insistence upon Southern independence—no promises were to be made unless they preserved "the equal rights of the Confederacy"—helped doom the peace mission even before it began. As far as peace was concerned, Stephens was on his own.

The Confederate emissary journeyed to Fort Monroe and requested permission to proceed to Washington, D.C. Lincoln and the members of his cabinet could not decide what action to take.

The President was inclined to send a representative to Fort Monroe to find out what Stephens' proposed visit was all about. Most of the cabinet members, including William H. Seward and Edwin M. Stanton, objected to recognizing Stephens as either an official or unofficial emissary of the Confederacy.[83] Union victories at Gettysburg and Vicksburg were being celebrated at the same time, so some cabinet members viewed Stephens' proposal as the last gasp of a drowning man. On July 6 the Lincoln administration shut the door on Stephens' wish to come to Washington,[84] and the Stephens peace bubble burst abruptly. A dejected and dispirited peace agent returned to Richmond. Chastened, he kept his disappointment to himself. Midwestern Copperheads never heard of his strange mission.

The second peace pipe of July, 1863, was carried by Dr. Issachor Zacharie, a New Yorker who had been a chiropodist, speculator, and spy. In 1862 he had accompanied Major General Nathaniel P. Banks to New Orleans. There, he served as a personal agent for both Lincoln and Banks, winning the favor of some of the finest New Orleans families and gaining the indebtedness of a member of the Confederate cabinet. He thought that his contacts with Southern men of influence would enable him to undertake effectively a peace mission to Richmond. Dr. Zacharie thought it possible to make "Peace with *Honor* to the *North* and *without humiliation to the South*."[85] President Lincoln appeared sympathetic to Zacharie's mission, yet he refused to give the self-appointed emissary any official status or any commitment. Dr. Zacharie, nevertheless, visited Richmond in late July of 1863 and met with Judah P. Benjamin and other Confederate cabinet members. The peace mission accomplished nothing. Lincoln recognized that the wheel of change had turned too far to restore the nation to its prewar status, so he lent no support to any conciliation schemes. In later days Dr. Zacharie blamed Lincoln more than Davis for sabotaging peace hopes of July, 1863. He was convinced that the Lincoln administration did not wish to stop the war and the bloodshed.[86] Many midwestern Copperheads held the same views.

Republicans and Democrats readied themselves for the fall elections of 1863 while still celebrating the Union triumphs at Gettysburg and Vicksburg. Democrats who still hoped for peace and compromise looked toward the ballot box as a way to convince the Lincoln administration that it was out of tune with the times.

If the Peace Democrats could win the August, 1863, elections in Kentucky it might be possible to start the peace ball rolling again. The Kentucky contest was between two factions of Democrats, each claiming to be Union Democrats. Most ex-Whigs and friends of Lincoln indorsed the gubernatorial aspirations of Thomas E. Bramlette, who had previously held a commission in the Federal army. Critics of administration policy favored the candidacy of Charles A. Wickliffe. Some Kentuckians were critical of the administration because abolition had become official policy. Many were anxious for peace and compromise—a restoration of "the Union as it was." Wickliffe and his supporters contended that Thomas E. Bramlette was "too subservient to Lincoln." They claimed that a military regime had displaced civil government in the Bluegrass State. They were critical of the many political arrests, of the intimidation of prominent Democrats, and of the dissolution of party rallies.

The vote in early August was an overwhelming defeat for the Democratic faction headed by Wickliffe as well as a rebuff to the cause of peace and compromise. Bramlette, Lincoln's candidate, polled 68,000 votes to Wickliffe's 18,000. The defeated candidate claimed that Federal soldiers stationed at the polls screened the voters, burned Wickliffe ballots, and directed citizens how to vote. Lincoln's personal popularity in Kentucky and the victories at Gettysburg and Vicksburg, however, had far more to do with Wickliffe's defeat than the presence, in places, of Federal bayonets. President Lincoln, naturally elated over the election results in Kentucky, wrote, "The election in Kentucky has gone very strongly right." Then he added, "Old Mr. Wickliffe got ugly, as you know, ran for Governor, and is terribly beaten."[87] Both Wickliffe and the peace movement were crushed in Kentucky.

After the Kentucky elections were over all eyes turned toward Ohio. Ohio Democrats had named Vallandigham as their party's gubernatorial candidate after his arrest and banishment in May and June of 1863. The platform which Vallandigham's supporters had drafted for their candidate contained a cautious advocacy of conciliation and compromise.[88] To many Democrats, Vallandigham symbolized the peace crusade. They recalled his notable speech of January 14 in which he had asked for an armistice and had pleaded for peace. Yet Vallandigham, from exile in Canada, trimmed the sails of the peace pronouncements he had made six weeks earlier. The victories for Union armies at Vicksburg and Gettysburg were, perhaps, accountable for that. *An Address to the People,* issued on July 15 from the Canadian side of Niagara Falls, made a bid for votes and sympathy. That address emphasized that Vallandigham's arrest and civil liberties were the chief issue in the October election; he condemned the "weak despots in Washington." He was still convinced that the aroused South could not be crushed or conquered. He argued that only the Democratic party possessed the qualifications to reunite and rebuild the nation. He claimed that the vindictive policy of the Radical Republicans prolonged the war and that only the Democratic party commanded any respect from Southern unionists.[89]

Democratic supporters of Vallandigham's candidacy made appeals for votes in every possible direction. They spoke of the dangers of a military despotism. They presented "Val" as the apostle of peace. They appealed to racism and Negrophobia and to midwestern mistrust of puritanism and eastern capital. They warned that railroad monopolists endangered the livelihood of all Ohioans. They sought votes over the widespread antipathy to conscription. And they tried to stir up sympathy for the man they designated "martyr."[90] They pretended that the election of Vallandigham as governor of Ohio would be a triumph of principle over power, liberty over force.[91] Samuel Medary was the most bitter and caustic of all of Lincoln's critics. He fulminated against the "Prince of Rails" while he gave full support to Vallandigham's campaign and the cause of compromise. Medary entitled an editorial "Abraham Lincoln More of a Traitor than Jefferson Davis" and he blamed the occupant of the White House for all the nation's ills. Vallandigham's election, on the other hand, might be an important step in the direction of peace and reunion.[92]

Daytonian Democrats sponsored an immense rally on the eve of the election; one Vallandigham supporter estimated that 35,000 attended.[93] They paraded. They displayed banners, "Vallandigham: the People's friend, the tyrant's foe"; "The Constitution as it is, the Union as it was"; and "Vallandigham, Peace, and Prosperity." They sang songs from a *Vallandigham Song Book*.[94] They listened to speakers praise the exile and vowed that if Vallandigham were elected 100,000 Democrats would journey to Canada to escort their hero home in triumph.

The Republicans did not let the election go by default. They recognized that Vallandigham's election to the governorship of Ohio would enhance the cause of peace and weaken the war effort. He had become a symbol, so they turned all their energies and ingenuity toward defeating him. They eased General Ambrose E. Burnside out of Ohio and made him the scapegoat for Vallandigham's arrest. They organized the Union party as a vote-getting device behind which they could hide their partyism and patriotism. They named a War Democrat, "Honest Johnny" Brough, as their nominee to oppose Vallandigham and to bid for the independent vote. Union victories at Gettysburg and Vicksburg aided their cause. They launched a treason campaign against Vallandigham, trying to depict the issue as one of treason versus patriotism. Some Republican editors labeled Vallandigham "a sympathizer with the rebels" and "a convicted traitor." The editor of the Detroit *Advertiser and Tribune* published a forged "Vallandigham letter," an epistle supposedly addressed to a Confederate officer and expressing the wish that Southern arms might triumph. Although Vallandigham and Democratic leaders immediately labeled the letter a hoax and a fraud, the damaging document continued to make the rounds of the Republican press.[95] The editor of the Cincinnati *Gazette* linked Vallandigham with "treason." "Vallandigham is put in nomination by the Confederates ... and by means of secret organization instituted by the Secessionists," wrote the

slanderer, "he contrives to seize the machinery of the party. . . ."[96]
Republican rascals chanted:

> Hurrah for Brough and Abraham,
> And a rope to hang Vallandigham[97]

The Republican State Central Committee of Ohio printed and
circulated a number of campaign pamphlets and anti-Vallandigham tracts. One, *The Peace Democracy, Alias Copperheads*, depicted Vallandigham as a man of "morbid prejudices" and "ex-
cess vanity." It was claimed that Vallandigham had assured Jefferson Davis that the Northwest was ready to rebel. Vallandigham
betrayed the Union; he would live in infamy like Judas Iscariot![98]
The Loyal Publication Society, with headquarters in New York,
prepared several campaign pamphlets for Ohio Republicans. *A
Savory Dish for Loyal Men* not only condemned Vallandigham as
a "traitor," but also included a letter from General William S.
Rosecrans which thanked the Ohio legislature for its resolution denouncing peace "on any terms." Outsiders, mainly Republicans,
invaded Ohio by the score to orate in behalf of Brough and the
Union. Oliver P. Morton, governor of neighboring Indiana, even
visited Vallandigham's home town to condemn the Democratic
gubernatorial candidate and to speak in behalf of union and liberty.[99] In addition, Republicans convinced Lincoln and Secretary of
War Edwin M. Stanton that it was necessary to furlough Ohio
soldiers and send them back home to vote. Republican strategists
left no stone unturned in their efforts to whip Vallandigham at the
polls.

While campaigning against Vallandigham, the Republicans also
undermined the peace crusade. They argued that anyone who advocated peace and compromise gave encouragement to the rebels
and divided the North. They devised a strange syllogism and circulated it widely in their partisan press: "Benedict Arnold was for
peace; the Copperheads are for peace; therefore the Copperheads
are Benedict Arnolds."[100] Governor Morton, campaigning for
Brough in Ohio, told Democrats that it was impossible to turn
back the clock. The time had long since passed when it was prac-

tical to restore "the Union as it was." He stated that premise bold-ly: "You may as well attempt to raise the dead. Slavery has cut its own throat, and there is no surgery in the reach of Providence to close the wound."[101]

Election day dawned bright and clear. But October 13 was an unlucky day for Vallandigham. Brough whipped the exiled Ohioan by more than 100,000 votes. Even if the 43,000 soldier votes had not been cast, it would have been considered a resounding defeat for the Peace Democrats of Ohio. The crushing defeat of Vallan-digham cheered Republicans everywhere.[102] "Count every ballot a bullet fairly aimed at the heart of the rebellion,"[103] shouted Sal-mon P. Chase. While Republicans toasted their Ohio victory, they took steps to maintain their hold upon the machinery of govern-ment in states like Michigan, Wisconsin, and Illinois. The polit-ical wind was again blowing in their direction, and they let out the sails to take advantage of it.

Republicans interpreted their widespread election victories as a repudiation of the peace movement; one viewed them as "a pro-test of the country against the insanity or crime that, under the name of peace, would divide the nation and destroy its name forever."[104] Democrats, seeking a scapegoat for the nationwide Republican trend, blamed Vallandigham for all their party's ills. Some set about reorganizing their party, purging the Vallandig-ham element. Vallandigham's devoted followers recognized that the cause of peace and compromise had been dealt a staggering blow. They had always emphasized that the will of the populace should be heeded, and that argument now haunted them. The people of the Midwest—the voters of Ohio especially—had spoken through the ballot boxes. The people had endorsed administration policy; they had repudiated the wishes of the peacemakers. So Vallandigham's friends could do little more than acquiesce in the election returns. "The people have voted in favor of the war and the way it is at present conducted," wrote one chastised Copper-head, "and it has to go on of course. The case went to the jury and they have rendered their verdict and I am not disposed to move for a new trial."[105]

Crushed at the polls, the peace movement was ineffective and badly disorganized in late 1863. Scattered voices advocating peace and compromise still whispered its message occasionally. James S. Rollins, a Missouri congressman, futilely sought to revive the Crittenden resolutions in the House of Representatives and to breathe life into the peace movement.[106] Sidney Breese, an Illinois jurist with presidential ambitions, justified restoring "fraternal relations" and advocated seven amendments to the Constitution to help reunite the two sections and to publicize his political aspirations.[107] James A. McMaster, editor of the New York *Freeman's Journal* and advocate of peace, toured the Midwest to convince the Democrats not to desert the cause of peace; his theme was a biblical and historical justification of conciliation and peace.[108] The approach of the Christmas season gave the discredited Democrats a chance to talk of "peace on earth, good will to men." Only a few used that opportunity. The editor of the Indianapolis *State Sentinel,* for example, entitled an editorial the "Prince of Peace" in his Christmas Day issue. "If we were Christians in deed as well as in theory and profession," he wrote, "this anniversary of the birth of the Prince of Peace would not find a Christian nation embroiled in contention, in strife, in war."[109]

At Windsor, Canada, Vallandigham spent a lonely Christmas. The halo of the martyr had lost some of its glow. Ohioans had rejected him and what he had come to represent. The prestige of the Lincoln administration grew with each passing day. Midwestern Copperheadism, so popular in early 1863, had begun to fade. Mars again hurled his thunderbolts and the fickle public applauded vigorously.

V

Knights of the Golden Circle
and Sons of Liberty

DURING THE EARLY MONTHS OF 1863, when midwestern Copperheadism reached high tide, rumors and reports concerning the Knights of the Golden Circle flew thick and fast. Astute Republican governors like Oliver P. Morton and Richard Yates made an effort to discredit both Copperheads and Democrats by linking them to the Knights of the Golden Circle. Their aides gave publicity to old exposés and concocted new ones. Like midwestern Copperheadism, KGC rumors were popular in 1863.

While rumors made the rounds and the peace movement was strong, some Democrats took steps to create a secret auxiliary to their political party. They named this inner-chamber organization the Sons of Liberty and hoped it would serve the Democratic party as effectively as the Union Leagues had served their political rivals. They hoped that the Sons of Liberty could help win elections, give support to weak-kneed Democrats, infuse new life into the party, and counteract the effective work of the Union Leagues.

The Republican propagandists contended that the Sons of Liberty were the descendants of the Knights of the Golden Circle and that both were traitorous. They developed myths to frighten voters into voting for Republican candidates. The legends which they foisted on an unwary populace were believed even after the war.[1]

The KGC story of 1863 had its historical beginnings in Ohio during the 1850's. In its earliest days it revolved around the name of George Washington Lamb Bickley, a rover, promoter, and charlatan. He had a glib tongue and facile pen and worked in Cincinnati as a lawyer, lecturer, writer, doctor, and teacher. Bickley developed the faculty of deluding himself as well as others. He married a widow, mismanaged her estate, and tried to organize the Continental Union, a secret society intended to be the successor of the dying Know-Nothing movement. All "worshippers of the Pope" and all "disunionists" were excluded from membership in Bickley's strange society. Public indifference to his organization forced Bickley to change his plan. He revised the ritual, devised a "great seal," and christened his new organization "Knights of the Golden Circle." He assumed the title of "General" and tried to make a fortune from ten-dollar membership fees.[2] A Bickley-written pamphlet invited support for a vague scheme to superimpose the "superior Anglo-American civilization" on the "inferior" Latin Americans.[3] "We are," wrote Bickley, "only the tools in God's hands to regenerate Spanish America."[4] The spurious general envisioned the Golden Circle as a means "to colonize and finally annex northern Mexico to the Domain of the United States as in the case of Texas."[5]

When the Ohio charlatan could no longer delude his wife and elude his creditors, he left Cincinnati and sought his ten-dollar memberships elsewhere. He transferred "headquarters"—his suitcase—to Washington, pretending that members were numerous and that wealth and honor awaited those who joined his "filibustering fantasy." While touring the South, Bickley's plans took more definite shape and he tailored them to suit the Southern temper. He suggested that Southerners gain revenge against the abolitionists by joining his secret order and "colonizing" Mexico. "The K.G.C.," he assured Southerners in a printed address, "would fight the battles of the South on Mexican soil."[6] He urged a "colonists'" rendezvous "near Fort Ewen, on the south bank of the Rio Nueces" in Texas "by the fifteenth of September, 1860."[7] This bizarre scheme failed for lack of followers and funds; the Golden Circle existed more in Bickley's imagination than in fact.

As secession fever seized the South, the garrulous pretender tried to transform his secret society into a military organization capable of repelling invasion and guaranteeing Southern rights. But there was no magic in Bickley's wand, and the Golden Circle continued to exist only in his fancy. He wandered into central Tennessee, married a backwoods belle, though he had a wife in Cincinnati, and settled down near Tullahoma.

While Bickley lived quietly in central Tennessee, Washington was a beehive of activity. South Carolina's secession brought a flood of excitement to the nation's capital. There were rumors that secessionists might seize Washington. There were also rumors that a secret Southern-based society might take over Washington and prevent Lincoln's inauguration. Reports reached Washington that the Knights of the Golden Circle were organizing in the Midwest. A member of President Buchanan's cabinet received an anonymous letter saying that "a secret band of avengers" would strike down all "foes of the South" when the war came.[8] Congressmen took cognizance of these rumors, setting up a committee to investigate. The special committee's report, dated February 14, 1861, discredited the rumors and tall tales. "The Committee is unanimously of the opinion," read a section of the report, "that the evidence produced does not prove the existence of a secret organization here or elsewhere hostile to the government, that has for its object an attack on the United States Capitol."[9] Jittery Washingtonians, however, preferred their fears to congressional reports. Lincoln's mysterious entry into Washington at midnight and in disguise played into the hands of the rumor-mongers. Unreliable reports concerning the Golden Circle and traitorous secret societies continued to circulate in the capital city.[10]

Rumors concerning a secessionists' secret society also circulated in Kentucky and Cincinnati, giving the Golden Circle free publicity. The editor of the Louisville *Journal* charged that a secret order, dedicated to promoting secession, existed in Kentucky. He wanted the order exposed and discredited, and he believed its members desired to plunge the state into civil war.[11] As the rumors flew thicker and faster, the Kentucky legislature launched an inquiry into the activity of subversive organizations, seeking to ascertain the objectives and extent of the Knights of the Golden

Circle.[12] Mr. George W. L. Bickley, delighted with free publicity, called on his imagination again. In an "open letter" he claimed a state-wide membership of eight thousand. Although no evidence was unearthed to substantiate the self-styled general's fantastic allegation, the foundation for building a KGC phantasm was well laid. One Kentucky lady, for example, warned her brother in Washington that she had heard that the Knights of the Golden Circle intended "to shoot all the influential men in the cabinet."[13] Circulating old wives' tales about the Golden Circle became a favorite parlor game.

The KGC tales were too good to be confined to Kentucky. Cincinnati newspaper editors took note of the stories and speculations, and rumors spread over the Midwest. When a steamboat exploded on the Ohio River, a KGC plot rather than a defective boiler was blamed. When a frame shop building of the Illinois Central Railroad Company burned in southern Illinois, officials took pains to blame a "secession villain" rather than carelessness. Perhaps the Golden Circle had tried "to prevent the company from taking troops to the south."[14] When Canada-bound Confederate agents were arrested in the Midwest, editors suspected that the agents were members of the Golden Circle. The rumors usually improved with retelling.

Two midwesterners fabricated exposés to take advantage of the sentiment of the times. The first disclosure bore a Cincinnati copyright—perhaps coming from the press of the Cincinnati *Gazette*—and its author claimed to have been "Governor-General" of the Golden Circle in Kentucky.[15] The second "authentic exposition" came from the pen of Dr. J. M. Hiatt, an Indianapolis Democrat who rushed his "astounding disclosure" into print when he noted the widespread sales of the Cincinnati exposé.[16] Dr. Hiatt's venture into the field of fiction proved very profitable, as "large orders" were received by the publisher from "all parts of the country."[17] Little did the Democratic doctor realize that he was helping to create a Frankenstein which would one day haunt his party and threaten its existence.[18]

The two published exposés also contributed materially to the building of the KGC legend. Bickley's mental delusion was gradually turning into a midwestern apparition.

Other locales contributed to the KGC hysteria, and wily politicians blackened their opponents with tar from the KGC barrel. A Kentucky supporter of a congressional candidate, for example, publicly circulated the rumor that General Bickley was "drilling his men and secretly scattering circulars" to defeat his friend.[19] John C. Brain unwittingly aided gossipers through his strange activities in La Porte, Indiana. His case illustrates how KGC headlines were made. Brain, a swindler from Pittsburgh and Chicago, tried to ply his trade in La Porte. He publicly claimed to be an agent of the Golden Circle, boasted of his spying activities, and tried to hire a woman to deliver revolvers to the South. He tried to post a handbill inviting people to join the Southern army and argued in behalf of secession whenever he found someone who would take him seriously. He wanted to establish a new government—"like in France"—and he asked for contributions for his various enterprises.[20] Excited La Porte citizens, unable to distinguish between a fool and a traitor, appealed to the public officials, and a federal marshal arrested the self-styled KGC agent and recruiter.[21] Investigators found Brain to be an "unmitigated scoundrel" and an idle babbler—a man of a moronic nature and mischievous bent.[22] The KGC rumors which the Brain case set in motion were never publicly repudiated by Republican officials, and his arrest was offered for years as proof that agents of the Golden Circle were active in the Midwest.

More KGC reports came from the home of a wealthy Indiana banker. After hearing that his son was being held as a Confederate prisoner of war, the banker was visited by three different scamps, each claiming KGC connections. Each of the three suggested that for a handsome fee the Golden Circle would secure the son's release.[23] The banker mistrusted his callers and passed the information about their KGC claims on to Governor Oliver P. Morton.

The first KGC exposé used for political purposes had an Ohio setting. Republicans tried to influence voters with KGC tales on the eve of the October, 1861, elections. Thomas H. Hodder, defiant editor of the Marion *Democratic Mirror,* and Dr. J. M. Christian, Democratic leader of Marion County, were the victims of the Republican-concocted smear. The bizarre story had its setting in a personal and newspaper feud which Hodder carried on with his political and business rival. Hodder's cutting editorials, aimed at his rival and at "Black Republican fanaticism," angered the editor of the Marion *Republican,* who suggested vigilante action to deal with Hodder. A Republican clergyman also encouraged his followers to persecute and intimidate the editor of the *Democratic Mirror.* Unknown persons threatened Hodder's life and suggested burning down his printing plant. In retaliation, Hodder and his friends organized an informal mutual protection society.[24] They agreed on a specific signal to be used if one of the Democratic members needed help or if the office of the Democratic newspaper was mobbed.

Republicans suggested that the Democratic mutual protection society was a branch of the Golden Circle. On the eve of the October elections, five young Republican rogues fabricated evidence linking Hodder and Marion Democrats to the Golden Circle. Their evidence included forged letters, ambiguous affidavits, and bogus oaths, which they turned over to a federal marshal and to Republican newspapers.

The federal marshal arrested Hodder and Christian, the two most prominent Democrats of Marion. The Republican press seized on the story and used it to influence the voters. The Marion *Republican* issued an extra, presenting the questionable evidence as a grand exposé. Other Republican editors copied the story, publishing the affidavits, bogus oaths, and forged letters. Richland and Crawford County editors got into the act, claiming that the Golden Circle was active in their communities too. The editor of the Columbus *Ohio State Journal* embroidered on the tale, adding the name of Samuel Medary to the list of suspects. Columbus alone had nine hundred members, it was claimed, as the Marion County story snowballed. Cincinnati Republican editors supposed that a statewide KGC organization existed. The exposé made the rounds of the Republican press of the Midwest. Even the St. Louis papers gave publicity to the story. Slowly and surely legend was taking shape.[25]

Democratic editors and politicians rushed their denials and their words of disbelief into print to try to keep the political scale from swinging toward the Republicans. "We believe that this secret organization has no existence in reality," stated Medary, of the Columbus *Crisis*, "and it is our conviction that the whole affair was concocted by a few dishonest politicians to influence well-meaning men to vote against the Democratic party nominees."[26] George W. Manypenny, the Democratic editor of the *Ohio States-man*, ridiculed the exposé and the KGC charges. He believed that a politically minded federal marshal managed "the show," and was sure the bogus oaths came from the same press as the Marion *Republican*.[27] Later events proved Medary and Manypenny right. Messrs. Hodder and Christian regained their freedom in a post-election trial in which it was revealed that no link tied their mutual aid society to the Golden Circle and that fraud and forgeries made up the evidence.[28] The grand jury of Crawford County called in twenty-five witnesses to chase down the rumors, sifted the hearsay and political gossip presented as evidence, and then reported: ". . . we are forced to the conclusion that the Knights of the Golden Circle exist in this county in imagination alone."[29] A grand jury, sitting in Richland County also found the KGC charges to be a "roorback of huge dimension"[30]—simply "a diabolical electioneering scheme."[31] Lincoln's political supporters in Ohio were caught promoting humbug and playing "a very silly game."[32] Pre-election KGC accusations and post-election evidence contradicted each other. Dishonest politicians were caught engaging in "disgraceful deviltry," and reputable Republicans hung their heads in shame. Apparently a lesson was learned, for in later years Ohio was remarkably free from KGC exposés and stories of subversive secret societies.

The KGC bogeyman next put in his appearance in Detroit. The fantastic treason tale which Republicans concocted in Michigan was based on former President Franklin Pierce's visit to Detroit and a hoax letter written by a Democrat to trap Republican editors. Pierce visited relatives and a former member of his cabinet in September, 1861. The hoax letter was writen by Dr. Guy S. Hopkins, a young man who had learned to hate Republicans. Dr. Hopkins had refused the "unconditional loyalty," demanded by some Republicans, and was abused and vilified. His files were searched for proof of pro-Southern sympathies. Vandals smashed his office. He was assaulted at night. Unknown Republicans suggested that Dr. Hopkins belonged to the Golden Circle, and the editors of the Detroit *Tribune* and the Detroit *Advocate* charged that a subversive secret society existed in Michigan. Instead of offering proof to support their charges, the editors defied the Democrats to disprove them. When Franklin Pierce visited North Branch and Detroit, the Republican editors were guilty of slander and character assassination. They devised rumors that his midwestern tour was treasonable and that it was somehow related to KGC activity in Michigan. "Our opinion," wrote the uninhibited editor of the Detroit *Tribune*, "is that Franklin Pierce is a prowling traitor spy."[33]

The slander heaped upon Franklin Pierce angered Dr. Hopkins. Intimidation and persecution only made him more defiant. He sought a measure of revenge by "composing" a letter which could serve as "evidence" that a secret league existed in Michigan. Dr. Hopkins planned to get the letter into the hands of Detroit's Republican editors. He hoped they would publish the letter and build KGC castles. Then he planned to expose the humbug, publicly proving the gullibility of the Republicans. "My fartherest expectation," Dr. Hopkins later wrote, "was that it [the hoax letter] would be sent to one of the treason-shrieking presses and when exploded would produce much 'fun.' I fancied such a 'sell' would be apt to quiet their howls."[34]

The hoax letter fell into the hands of the federal marshal stationed in Detroit. He showed the letter to the Republican editors of the *Tribune* and the *Advertiser* and then arrested Dr. Hopkins, shipping him off to Fort Lafayette and forwarding the Hopkins letter to the State Department. Dr. Hopkins, confined arbitrarily in prison, had no chance to make a public explanation.[35] Secretary of State William H. Seward suppressed the letters which Hopkins wrote to him from his cell.

The Detroit Republicans, meanwhile, planned an exposé built around the Hopkins letter. In March of 1862, as the spring elections approached and the intensity of political campaigning increased, the city's Republican editors laid down a barrage of supposition and piled one accusation on top of another. They charged that Democratic secret societies functioned "to prevent enlistments" and to develop *"open resistance to the government."*[36] Former President Pierce's Detroit host had treason charges laid at his doorstep in a feature editorial entitled "A Traitor amongst Us." Pierce's patriotism was again impugned.

Detroit Democrats ridiculed the charges emanating from the Republican editorial rooms. "The charge that I ever belonged to the Knights of the Golden Circle, or lacked loyalty," wrote Pierce's Detroit host, "is base and malicious."[37] The Detroit *Free Press* accused Republicans of "sheer slander" and deliberate dishonesty. He challenged his rivals to substantiate their vague accusations and their treason charges.[38]

The Republicans then lowered the boom. They published the Hopkins letter in full and added a new batch of accusations that a "secret league" existed in Michigan and that prominent Democrats were its agents and abettors. The Hon. Zachariah Chandler, misinformed by his Detroit tipster, used the floor of the U.S. Senate to charge that a "most treasonable and infamous" secret society existed in the Midwest, even permeating the U.S. Army.[39] The Detroit-based exposé made the rounds of the Republican newspapers. Dr. Hopkins, in prison, could not get his side of the story into print. The hoax letter, intended to reveal Republican credulity, backfired badly. It aided the Republican cause and it helped them to build a bigger and better KGC bogeyman.

Illinois Republicans also tried to play the game of rattling KGC skeletons to serve political ends. The chief performers in Illinois were Governor Yates and a Republican newsman named Joseph K. C. Forrest. Early in 1862, Governor Yates found himself with a Democratic-dominated constitutional convention on his hands.

The Democratic delegates mixed Jeffersonian principles and political muck in their partisan cauldron. They halved Governor Yates's term of office, sheared the chief executive of his military powers, embarrassed the state administration with diverse investigations, and dirtied their hands by gerrymandering. The harassed governor turned to his political friends for help and advice. Joseph K. C. Forrest, a confidant of the governor and Springfield correspondent for the Chicago *Tribune*, hurried to Yates's aid. He grabbed the KGC skeleton out of the Republican-kept closet and launched treason charges with an explosive report to the Chicago *Tribune*:

It has been rumored for some days, that there were many Knights of the Golden Circle and members of mutual protection societies in the convention. I have forborne to allude to them before, but they come so thick upon me, that I can so no longer. The number of K.G.C.'s has been placed so high, as to come within a few votes of a majority of the convention.[40]

The editorial writer for the Chicago *Tribune* took note of Forrest's allegations and added his own warning. "There are people in that convention," he wrote, "who would not hesitate to involve our people in anarchy—who wait only the favorable moment to seize the military power of the state, and to turn the arms of Illinois upon the flag of our common country."[41]

The Democratic delegates at the state constitutional convention promptly took steps to challenge the Forrest-fabricated allegations. One, holding a copy of the Chicago *Tribune*, from which he read Forrest's charges, demanded an immediate investigation and proposed that a special committee be appointed to look into the matter. William J. Allen, prominent Democrat and delegate from downstate Illinois, indorsed an investigation but he was sure that no KGC evidence could be unearthed. "I know of no such organization myself," stated the Hon. Mr. Allen, "nor do I believe that any member here belongs to such an organization."[42] "I think there is nobody at Chicago, or anyplace else," added another Democratic delegate, "who believes there is a single Knight of the Golden Circle anywhere in this state."[43] Even some Republican delegates, unaware of the game which Yates and Forrest were playing, added their disbeliefs as to the KGC allegations.[44]

The Democrat who presided as chairman of the constitutional convention wisely named three Republicans to the six-man special committee, so that Governor Yates's suporters could not make whitewash charges at a later date. The special committee examined Forrest's vague charges, which the Republican newspapers had broadcast over the state, and called on Mr. Forrest to substantiate them. Forrest meekly admitted, when under oath, that he had no tangible evidence to offer and that he had compounded his story from vague rumors, unfounded reports, and gossip that had reached the governor's desk.

Having chased every rumor down a dead-end street, the special committee concluded its investigation and issued its report. That report, signed by all six members of the special committee, concluded that all the KGC rumors were without foundation. The report also censured Forrest for circulating fables and giving dignity to gossip.[45] Chastised and humiliated, Forrest held his tongue while the constitutional convention finished its work. His first effort to rattle the KGC skeleton ended ignobly, and Democrats rejoiced in his disgrace. "The only question left is, where next will these unscrupulous Republican editors attempt another game on the K.G.C. humbug?" asked the editor of the Detroit *Free Press*. "They have tried it three times, and each time failed," he added, "so we think it is time it was 'three times and out.' "[46]

But the KGC rumors refused to die. Illinois Republicans again made vague charges and insinuations as they marshaled their party voters to prevent ratification of the "Copperhead Constitution." The editor of the Chicago *Tribune* took the lead in linking the "Copperhead Constitution" and the Knights of the Golden Circle. He made it appear that traitorous members of the Golden Circle rather than partisan Democratic delegates had framed the constitution. He labeled the proposed constitution a "secession swindle" and he termed it the handiwork of "mousing politicians, many of them Knights of the Golden Circle."[47] Illinois Republicans celebrated with parties and parades when the "Copperhead

Constitution" failed its ratification test. The editor of the Chicago *Tribune* credited the adverse vote to an enlightened electorate which recognized the imprint of the "cloven hoof of the K.G.C." on the proposed constitution. The editor added that he had heard that every lodge of the Golden Circle from Cairo to Chicago had circulated pamphlets in behalf of ratification. A feature editorial carried the headline : "Illinois Saved from the Grasp of Traitors."[48] The editor of the *Illinois Gazette*, taking his cue from the *Tribune*, wrote in like manner, thanking the voters for defeating both the Knights and the "Copperhead Constitution." He was sure that the convention proceedings "pointed with unerring certainty to the presence of the K.G.C."[49]

Democratic denials failed to stop the spread of the KGC rumors. War hysteria encouraged the legend that a subversive, secret, pro-Southern society had castles and agents scattered over the entire Midwest. Knaves had given the KGC snowball an extra nudge in Ohio, Michigan, and Illinois. In 1862 Republicans in Kentucky and Indiana also got into the act.

Kentucky unionists badly needed a bogeyman in 1862. The widespread arrests of prominent Kentuckians built up anti-Lincoln feeling. Martial law in most of Kentucky needed constant justification. There were elections to be won and voters to be screened. Sympathy for the Confederacy existed everywhere.[50] Furthermore, ardent unionists planed to organize a secret patriotic league to keep Kentucky in the Union and on the side of the Lincoln administration. To justify the establishment of the secret Union League, the patriots needed a bogeyman. The KGC scarecrow, talked of in early 1861, was dressed in new clothes and again placed on duty.

The Kentucky exposé of 1862 took the form of a pamphlet, circulated for the benefit of the newly organized Union League. The anonymous pamphlet came from "the pen of one who knows," and claimed that KGC agents were busy organizing a nationwide "string of castles" with secret degrees and passwords. The unknown author warned readers that the "knights of treason" wanted to seize control of the government, to assassinate unionists, and to promote defeatism and treason. He classed the Cincinnati *Enquir-*

er, Milwaukee *News*, Detroit *Free Press*, and the Chicago *Times* as "auxiliaries" of the subversive society. The exposé specialized in vagaries, suppositions, and generalities. Its intent was twofold: (*a*) to link the Democratic party of Kentucky to treason and (*b*) to serve as an incentive or excuse to organize the Union League. If Lincoln's Kentucky supporters pretended that a pro-Southern secret society existed in their state, they could justify the establishment of the Union League as a counter–secret society.[51]

The state of Indiana also contributed considerably to building KGC aircastles in 1862 through Berry R. Sulgrove, editor of the Indianapolis *Journal*, and Governor Morton. Three incidents furnished the factual basis: a railroad accident, a judge's letter, and a grand jury report. Again war hysteria and Republican propaganda helped to transform molehills into mountains.

Editor Sulgrove and Governor Morton laid the foundation for their tales of treason with charges that pro-Southern Hoosiers had organized a mutual protection society. The gritty governor and his subservient editor claimed that Copperheads had organized the society for the "purpose of opposing the war and defeating all attempts to sustain it by taxation."[52] Although Morton and Sulgrove could offer no evidence to support their charges, they did not hesitate to restate them. When Democrats challenged them, Messrs. Morton and Sulgrove offered as evidence the KGC or secret league rumors and reports which had been aired in Kentucky, Illinois, Ohio, and Michigan.

In May of 1862, when Governor Morton was involved in a minor railroad accident, Editor Sulgrove had an excuse to give his imagination full play. The accident occurred in Sullivan County, choice Copperhead country. Editor Sulgrove had previously stated that the MPS—Mutual Protection Society—was strongest in Sullivan County. It was easy for Editor Sulgrove to build the train accident into an assassination attempt by the MPS members. "It was but murder," concluded the editor of the Indianapolis *Journal*, "going hand-in-hand with treason."[53] Editor Sulgrove's pen transformed a minor train accident into a major

KGC plot. Other Republican editors of the Hoosier State echoed his charges.

As the date of the Republican state convention approached, Editor Sulgrove and Governor Morton took steps to revive and repeat their oft-made KGC and treason charges. They received an assist from Judge James Hughes, a former Democrat. Judge Hughes visited Indianapolis on the eve of the Republican party convention and made a number of patriotic speeches. He met privately with Governor Morton and he agreed to play the governor's game. After Judge Hughes returned to Bloomington he wrote the letter which he had promised, claiming that a subversive secret society existed in Indiana. The strange letter, addressed to Governor Morton, was full of unsubstantiated charges. The letter claimed that a serpentine society, "understood to be hostile to the payment of direct taxes to support the war," existed in Brown County and other counties. The traitorous order, Judge Hughes wrote, was "rapidly spreading throughout the State."[54]

Governor Morton read Judge Hughes's letter to the delegates attending the Republican state convention and delivered an impassioned patriotic speech. The "Judge Hughes Letter" was published in every Republican newspaper in the state. The vagueness of the charges was covered over by the reputation of the writer. It was assumed that the Judge's contentions were true. Republicans everywhere offered the "Judge Hughes Letter" as proof that their earlier KGC and MPS charges were correct.

Indiana Democrats were somewhat stunned by Judge Hughes's strange letter. They wondered what price Governor Morton had paid. They countered with claims that the letter was written at the Governor's invitation for "base political purposes." They supposed that Judge Hughes was busy counting his thirty pieces of silver. Editor Joseph J. Bingham of the Indianapolis *State Sentinel* criticized Judge Hughes for making charges without evidence. A prominent Democrat of Brown County, aware that the "Judge Hughes Letter" was written to serve partisan motives, offered to pay for an investigation by an "investigating committee of competent gentlemen." Democrats believed that the "Judge Hughes Letter" was intended to awaken lethargic Republicans and to link the Democratic party with treason.[55]

Judge Hughes's strange letter gave a federal grand jury in Indiana an excuse to chase KGC rumors down a side road. The grand jury, meeting in July of 1862, functioned more as a partisan than a judicial body. An active Republican directed the probe; a politically minded federal marshal impaneled the jury; all fourteen jurors were Republican voters.[56] Even Governor Morton took a hand, trying futilely to recruit witnesses who could offer evidence about secret societies.[57] As a part of its regular work, the grand jury returned a number of indictments. Its side-road excursion resulted in an interesting by-product, a brief report on subversive societies in Indiana. The report[58] stated that a "secret and oath-bound organization" (the Golden Circle) existed in Indiana and that "some fifteen thousand" Hoosiers were affiliated with it. It stated that the secret order was strongest in those Indiana counties wherein volunteering lagged. It labeled the Golden Circle "a place where treason was concocted—the nest where traitors are hatched." Confederate prisoners confined in Camp Morton, outside Indianapolis, were "believed" to belong to that society. The report also repeated the outworn rumor that Confederate and Union soldier-members "shot over each other's head." Those who compiled or composed the report explained the absence of tangible evidence simply: it was impossible to obtain information from members, for they regarded their KGC oath as superior to a civil oath. They thus used the absence of evidence as proof that the Golden Circle existed.

Democrats believed that the appearance of the grand jury's report during the state convention of the Democratic party was more than a coincidence. They believed that the report was a partisan document prepared for partisan purposes. Joseph J. Bingham, Democratic spokesman and editor of the Indianapolis *State Sentinel*, wrote that the grand jury had been "humbugged" for partisan purposes and that the report was "a Munchausen presentment."[59] Editor Bingham believed that Republicans had visited the land of fiction. Other Democratic editors also debunked the strange grand jury report. Some believed that its chief purpose was to conjure up Republican votes in the fall political campaigns. Others charged that Lincoln's party was guilty of cultivating "war hysteria" for political gain. Democrats pointed out that secret society scares and exposés had become a Republican mania. They feared that the witchcraft craze of old New England might be re-enacted upon Indiana soil.[60] All were sure that the grand jury report was a silly and shallow document, compounded of suspicion and speculation. The Democrats who ridiculed or condemned the document failed to guess why Republican strategists badly needed a bogeyman in Indiana. Lincoln's supporters were trying to organize the Union League and had encountered little enthusiasm and much apathy. The grand jury's report provided both a stimulus and a justification for their efforts.

Illinois Republicans watched Governor Morton of Indiana carry on his personal war against Democrats and the Golden Circle. Illinois newspapers reported on his activities; they reprinted the "Judge Hughes Letter" and the grand jury report which gave dignity to gossip about the Golden Circle. Republican editors of Illinois also circulated the KGC tales which had their origin in Kentucky and Michigan. They prepared their readers for other stories yet to come. With a jittery governor heading the Republican organization, Illinois was ready for a major exposé.

In August of 1862, Illinois Republicans needed a KGC revelation. Republicanism was on the run. The depression of 1861–62, military failures, and the trend toward abolitionism undermined the reputation of the party in power. Yates and his party realized that a Democratic revival threatened their hold upon the machinery of government. The fall elections were six weeks away and Republican prophets made gloomy predictions. Furthermore, the Union League movement was floundering and needed a shot in the army.[61] Then too, an overly zealous federal marshal in southern Illinois had made a number of political arrests, with more arrests planned, and the popular reaction to arbitrary arrests scared the Republican chieftains. They were desperate. In their hour of need, Joseph K. C. Forrest stepped forward.

Forrest was no stranger on the Illinois scene. He had won recognition as a newspaperman in Chicago in 1840, serving an apprenticeship on the staff of the *Evening Journal* and the *Gem of the Prairie*. He was one of the founders of the Chicago *Tribune* and served as managing editor of the Chicago *Democrat*. In the 1850's he read law in the office of J. Young Scammon, and Forrest followed Scammon into both Swedenborgianism and the Republican party. Forrest worked for Yates in the gubernatorial contest of 1860 in Illinois, and after Yates's election the bold newsman-lawyer begged for a slice of patronage pie. Governor Yates named Forrest a state agent in the early months of the war. After Forrest returned to Springfield, he mixed law, newspaper work, and politics, serving as the Springfield correspondent of both the Chicago *Tribune* and the St. Louis *Missouri Democrat*.[62] Forrest recognized that his newspaper connections were invaluable to Governor Yates. He became a confidant of the governor and sought a position on Yates's staff.[63] It was then that he wrote the KGC exposé that filled four columns of fine print in the Chicago *Tribune* of August 26, 1862.

Forrest collected his materials from four sources: (*a*) his imagination, (*b*) letters and rumors which reached the governor's desk, (*c*) four affidavits, each signed with an "X," and (*d*) a report by a federal agent who toured southern Illinois. Six months earlier, Forrest had proved his ability as a fabricator of KGC tales. During the meeting of the Illinois state constitutional convention, Forrest had set a slanderous story in motion, but the delegates collared the unscrupulous newsman and forced him to admit that he had based his yarn upon fancy rather than fact. Forrest's imagination provided the material which transformed questionable evidence into an elaborate KGC exposé.

The letters and reports which reached Governor Yates's desk provided much of the matter which Forrest used. Usually the gullible letter-writers reported upon what they had heard rather than what they had seen. Usually the rumor-mongers reported on what was "happening" in neighboring counties rather than their own. Usually the letter-writers were the uneducated and the credulous. One worried writer, for example, reported that he had heard that the "nights of the Golden Sircul" drilled every moonlight night, and that every "bunch" was "giting his orders for his portian [*sic*] of the work to do."[64] Another letter-writer said that he feared an uprising when the Knights got "more forse."[65] A near-illiterate farmer who failed to get along with his Democratic neighbors wrote that he was sure that the "Goldon Circle" was active nearby.[66] Another wrote that it was reported that a "ministre of the gospel" had organized a KGC "lodge."[67] Other letters passed through Forrest's hands and he freely culled "evidence" from them for his exposé.[68]

The four affidavits came from the files of David W. Phillips, U.S. marshal for the Southern District of Illinois. Each was given by an illiterate—one was a deserter interested in escaping a court-martial.[69] Two of the deponents imagined an open Democratic rally, the Williamson County barbecue, to be a meeting of the Knights of the Golden Circle.[70] The third mistook a Democratic party caucus for a secret session of Knights.[71] The fourth claimed that he had been initiated into the Golden Circle, on which he gave contradictory information.[72] When Forrest incorporated the four affidavits into his exposé, he did not reveal the names of the deponents. When David W. Phillips, the federal marshal who mixed cotton-dealing and politics with this work, reported that the evidence clearly linked those Democrats whom he had arrested to the Golden Circle, he stretched the truth. The four affidavits which he offered as documentary evidence failed to bear out his contentions.[73]

Federal agent Albert P. Davis contributed the fourth ingredient which Forrest mixed in his cauldron. Davis' report on subversive activities in southern Illinois accused some prominent downstate Democrats of membership in the Golden Circle, and that document passed through Phillips' and Yates's hands before it was forwarded to Washington, D.C. The report was long on supposition and accusations, short on proof. Nevertheless, it was an important ingredient of Forrest's exposé.[74]

Most Republican newspapers of Illinois republished Forrest's fantastic tale. The editor of the Carbondale *Times* claimed that 30,000 members of the Knights of the Golden Circle could be found in southern Illinois.[75] Republican newspapers elsewhere picked up the *Tribune*-published exposé and gave it national publicity. The New York *Evening Post* featured Forrest's exposé, and its editor added his own suppositions. "It is thought in Washington and Springfield," he wrote, "that there are in Illinois not less than seven hundred treasonable societies based upon some modification of the plan upon which the Knights of the Golden Circle build."[76] Forrest's fabrication of August, 1862, became the basis for the myth that Illinois was the center of KGC and treasonable society activity and that Illinois had more KGC members and a more closely knit KGC organization than any other state in the country.

Forrest's KGC allegations angered Illinois Democrats. Charles H. Lanphier, editor of the *Illinois State Register* and keeper of the Democratic party conscience, called the exposé sheer "political hokum." He called Forrest "an unscrupulous hireling pimp" and he viewed the exposé as a bold lie intended "to affect the elections."[77] Editors of such papers as the Jonesboro *Gazette* and the Chicago *Times* wrote in like vein, predicting that time would prove KGC charges groundless.[78] Those downstate Democrats who were arrested or charged with Golden Circle activity were infuriated and indignant. William J. Allen wrote that all the affidavits which implicated him were "false in every particular."[79] Judge Andrew D. Duff asked for an opportunity to prove the affidavits an "unmitigated falsehood." He offered to pay the expenses of the deponents ("the falsifiers"), so accused and accusers could stand face to face.[80] Others heaped denial on denial and piled disbelief on dissent.[81] But their denials and protests could not keep the story from spreading or immunize the gullible. The KGC bogeyman continued to haunt Illinois citizens throughout the war.

Both Illinois and Indiana Republicans had a reason to revive KGC charges and to hatch new revelations early in 1863. Those two states were the scenes of Democratic land-slides in the fall elections of 1862, and the legislatures scheduled to meet in January of 1863 were in Democratic hands. Rumors were widespread that the Democratic-controlled legislatures would hog-tie the governors, shear them of their powers, and wage war upon the Lincoln administration.[82] To keep their advantage, Indiana and Illinois Republicans took their KGC bogeymen out of mothballs and tried to scare the voters. Governors Morton and Yates, jittery and desperate, needed help to stay in the driver's seat. Both were willing to play upon the credulity and fears of the people to achieve their ends.

Henry B. Carrington helped Governor Morton pull his chestnuts out of the fire. Carrington, a Republican politician whom Governor Morton had appointed to superintend the recruiting and train-ing of Indiana troops, gradually became Morton's man Friday. Whenever Governor Morton publicly condemned Knights of the Golden Circle or denounced Democrats for their pro-Southern proclivities, Carrington echoed the Governor's words and beat the bushes for non-existent evidence.[83] Carrington wore a colonel's insignia and had his eye upon a general's star. His penchant for bungling caused Secretary of War Stanton considerable concern, but Carrington's intrepidity and loyalty caught Governor Mor-ton's fancy.[84] When federal authorities took measures to assign Colonel Carrington to field service, Morton intervened in order to keep the colonel in Indianapolis.[85] At Morton's insistence, a special District of Indiana was created as Colonel Carrington's jurisdiction. Then Governor Morton made Carrington doubly in-debted by securing a brigadier general's commission for him. It was Carrington who became the creator of all Indiana KGC ex-posés and who repaid his political debt by trying to link Indiana Copperheads to the Golden Circle.

Carrington started the KGC snowball rolling in Indiana late in 1862. After the fall elections, Governor Morton charged pub-licly that a secret political-military order existed in Indiana. He said that the society's purpose was to establish a northwest confederacy and to hinder the war effort.[86] Morton evidently felt he needed a KGC scarecrow in order to revive a political party which had been badly beaten and battered at the polls and to have a reasonable excuse to organize and arm Republican zealots into a "Loyal Legion." Carrington came to Morton's aid with a report to Secretary of War Stanton. That report contended that a subversive and dangerous secret society had mushroomed in Indiana. Carrington listed five objectives for the traitorous organization: (a) "to incite desertion of soldiers with their arms," (b) "to resist arrest of deserters," (c) "to stop enlistments," (d) "to disorganize the army," and (e) "to prevent further drafting."[87] Carrington pretended that treason and subversion were most prominent in the Democratic counties and that discontent was widespread, requiring strong countermeasures.

Governor Morton never missed an opportunity to keep the Golden Circle in the headlines. On January 14, 1863, he blasted the Knights in a patriotic Indianapolis address. Ten days later at Shelbyville he repeated his charges and enlarged on them. The KGC fears were aired at other places by other Republicans.[88] Berry R. Sulgrove, editor of the Indianapolis *Journal*, gave publicity to Carrington's fears and Morton's charges. In the Indianapolis *Journal* of January 19, 1863, Sulgrove gave two columns to exposing and condemning the Golden Circle. He mixed insinuations, innuendos, and misrepresentations. He condemned the Copperhead secret society and the plot to establish a northwestern confederacy.[89] Less than two weeks later, Editor Berry R. Sulgrove again warned his Republican readers to beware. He circulated rumors that the Golden Circle, with the aid of dissatisfied Democrats, intended to attack the state arsenal in Indianapolis.[90] When a deserter gave garbled and contradictory information about the Golden Circle in his efforts to escape punishment, Editor Sulgrove sifted the evidence and offered it as testimony that the Golden Circle was active in Indiana.[91] He accepted rumors as facts and exaggerated for effect. By late February, Editor Sulgrove was ready to claim that a session of a county Democratic club was in reality a meeting of the KGC.[92]

Carrington, with the assistance of Editor Sulgrove and Governor Morton, was soon ready to give the KGC snowball another push. In January of 1863, Carrington prepared a special report which he forwarded directly to President Lincoln. He repeated the suspicions and assertions regarding a subversive secret society which he had earlier made to Lincoln's Secretary of War. He wrote that subversives were trying to effect "national ruin" in Indiana. For good measure, Carrington added four pages on the "condition of the times" in Indiana.[93] Carrington's exposition and assertions received a timely assist from Asher and Company, a publishing firm in Indianapolis. That company published an exposé of the Knights of the Golden Circle in pamphlet form.[94] Priced to sell at twenty-five cents, the exposé-pamphlet became an important item in building the KGC legend in Indiana. Carrington and Morton were active in circulating the pamphlet, and the Union Leagues became an agency for its distribution.[95] Asher and Company published more copies, and the state was soon flooded with them.

Carrington continued to shadowbox with the KGC bogeyman. Whenever deserters evaded a posse, Carrington claimed that Knights had given the fugitive secret aid and timely assistance.[96] Whenever a squad of soldiers seeking to arrest a deserter clashed with the deserter's family or friends, Carrington assumed that KGC members were involved.[97] When soldiers, tired of campaigning or dissatisfied with incompetent officers, expressed a desire to be back home, Carrington was sure that the Golden Circle was exercising its insidious influence.[98] When volunteering lagged, Carrington blamed the subversive secret society.[99] When a Greencastle gunsmith reported that robbers had broken into his shop and stolen his rifles and revolvers, Carrington concluded that Golden Circle members were responsible.[100] When Democrats met in secret caucus, Carrington's imagination turned the session into a KGC meeting.[101] In fact, Carrington saw Knights under every bed and in every closet. His pen transformed backwoods violence into Golden Circle activity. His duty, as Governor Morton's aid, was to convince Hoosiers that the KGC was active and extensive in Indiana and that Democrats toyed with treason. In March, 1863, Carrington composed a lengthy memorandum on affairs in Indiana. He sent separate copies to Secretary of War Stanton and to President Lincoln. "The fact is," he wrote with a flourish, "that the *order* has *grown faster* than the party leaders wished and has assumed a shape and bitterness that may not be controlled if it breaks forth, even by them."[102] Carrington pretended that Governor Morton sat on a powderkeg and that high-handed measures were needed to keep the situation under control.[103]

In need of a KGC specter to retain his Indianapolis assignment and Morton's good will, and to cloak his bungling, Carrington assiduously hunted for evidence to substantiate his secret-society charges. He interviewed all deserters who were under arrest, promising immunity to those who would offer testimony on KGC activity and offering rewards to those who had KGC revelations for sale.[104] Governor Morton encouraged Carrington. Morton needed a KGC bogeyman even more than Carrington. He had more at stake. He was anxious to arm the Union Leagues, buoy up Indiana's war effort, discredit the Copperheads, and justify his dictatorial tactics. Morton's marriage to the KGC legend was one of convenience and practicality. Carrington was the chief witness.

Two events of July, 1863, played into the busy hands of Morton and Carrington. One was Morgan's raid into Indiana and Ohio. Governor Morton feared that General John H. Morgan and his raiders might seize the Indianapolis arsenal, free the Confederate prisoners in nearby Camp Morton, and gain control of the entire state. Morton pretended that Morgan's raiders had been invited to invade Indiana by KGC members and domestic traitors and that the invasion was a signal for a KGC-led uprising. Even after Morgan was captured on his horse-stealing expedition in Ohio, Governor Morton insisted that the abortive raid was linked to KGC schemes. Brigadier General Carrington, who became intoxicated during the chase, repeated and elaborated on his governor's

KGC contentions. Their propaganda helped give birth to a legend that refused to die in postwar years.[105]

The second event which gave the Morton-Carrington duo grist for their propaganda mill was the arrest of George W. L. Bickley in New Albany, Indiana. Bickley had lived a quiet existence in south central Tennessee after the collapse of his Mexican filibustering scheme. In July of 1863 Bickley found himself within the Union lines, living in territory ruled by martial law. Foolishly and fearlessly, Bickley presented himself to the commanding officer at Tullahoma to ask for a pass for himself and his family. Bickley even asked for that pass in his own name. The commanding officer, knowing the name Bickley had been associated with the Knights of the Golden Circle, asked a series of leading questions.[106] Bickley brazenly denied any knowledge of the secret order and gave the name of a Cincinnati banker as a reference. The alert commanding officer relayed his suspicions to his superior, Major General William S. Rosecrans. Rosecrans in turn checked several Cincinnati residents by telegraph about Bickley. The replies from Cincinnati revealed that the man seeking a pass was the creator of the Knights of the Golden Circle, that he had abandoned a wife before he headed southward, and that the woman who was his companion was not his lawful wife.[107] General Rosecrans then directed that Bickley be given a pass, but he also instructed the provost marshal to trail the garrulous fellow and to arrest him if he deviated from a prescribed route.[108]

George W. L. Bickley, in keeping with his character, violated his parole and his instructions. He veered from the prescribed route and was soon thereafter arrested in New Albany.[109] Again Bickley denied any knowledge of the Golden Circle. Agents seized his baggage, searched his trunk, and found ample evidence that Bickley was the creator and the head of the Golden Circle. The evidence also indicated that Bickley was a liar, braggart, and idle dreamer. The astounded agents sorted the items they confiscated: newspaper clippings, letters, three mysterious packages of powder (later analyzed as gum gambage, opium, and rhubarb), the great seal of the KGC, pamphlets, printed addresses, and miscellaneous material.[110]

Bickley was handcuffed and taken to Louisville. Federal officials accused him of being a Confederate spy and head of a traitorous secret society with branches north and south. He was held for a time in the military prison and was heavily guarded, as if the federal authorities expected Knights to free their leader.[111] Federal authorities released news of Bickley's arrest to the press, and imaginative Republican editors made the most of the opportunity.[112] Governor Morton and Brigadier General Carrington offered news of Bickley's arrest as proof that their KGC tales were worth retelling. Hoosiers watched attentively while Morton and other Republicans launched a new attack on Copperheads and the Golden Circle. So the legend that a subversive secret society functioned actively in the Midwest gained stature and respectability. Bickley inadvertently did Morton and Carrington a favor when he set foot on Indiana soil.

The Bickley story possessed a stranger ending. Federal authorities transferred him to the state penitentiary at Columbus, Ohio, and debated the advisability of a public trial. They investigated Bickley's reputation and examined the seeds from which his Golden Circle had grown. Then they dropped the question of giving him a hearing or a trial. A public trial would explode the KGC myths so widely circulated and the reputation of the tellers of tall KGC tales would be tarnished. Their investigation revealed that Bickley was an "utterly untrustworthy individual,"[113] and they did not want the public to know that his every word was worthless and suspect. So they allowed the KGC legends to circulate and kept the impostor in solitary confinement.[114]

Bickley tried to obtain a hearing. He wrote letters to General Jere T. Boyle, General William S. Rosecrans, Secretary of War Stanton, Secretary of State Seward, Governor David Tod of Ohio, and President Lincoln. He wrote to Lincoln in a begging vein, appealing to his sympathy and for his assistance:

I am now in a cell seven by three and a half feet, which contains besides myself a bed, a stool, and water and urinal buckets. . . . In this living tomb, days, weeks, and long months pass, and I know nothing of what is taking place in my country, I hear no word of my business or family. I hear the sound of no human voice save the whisperings of convicts—fellons [*sic*] and murderers—who surround me. I am not allowed to write to my family or friends, to converse with any one. . . . In a word, sir, I am buried alive.[115]

Bickley, of course, vigorously denied that there was any connection between the prewar organization he had founded and the subversive society supposedly existing in the Midwest during the war. If such a wartime organization existed, it had stolen the name he had devised. If the wartime organization was subversive, it had altered its prewar objectives. Bickley denied any treasonable intent and asked for an opportunity to free himself.[116] His requests fell on deaf ears. Administration bigwigs were disappointed that evidence linking Bickley to the wartime Golden Circle was lacking. They realized that a public trial would undermine the KGC legend which they were building. So they kept Bickley "buried alive" during the remaining years of the war. His arrest in Indiana in July of 1863, however, had served Governor Morton and his man Friday to good purpose. Inadvertently, both Bickley and General Morgan played into the hands of Morton and Carrington.

The smear campaign which Morton and Carrington conducted against Democrats and the Golden Circle in Indiana attracted considerable attention throughout the Midwest. Illinois Republicans were especially interested, for their state also had been the scene of a Democratic resurgence. The Copperhead legislators inaugurated the year's activities with a series of acts which smacked of rank partisanship. They tried to shear Governor Yates of his constitutional authority, conducted embarrassing and unnecessary investigations, and practiced political chicanery.

Governor Yates soon launched a political counteroffensive. He called on Forrest, whom he appointed a private secretary, to direct a smear campaign against the Copperhead legislature and against the Illinois Democrats. Forrest's newspaper connections enabled him to publicize each KGC rumor that he heard and each tale that he invented. When panicky citizens wrote to Governor Yates, telling KGC rumors which they had heard, Mr. Forrest passed that information on to the Chicago *Tribune* and to other Republican newspapers. When a mutinous Illinois regiment stacked its arms, Forrest claimed that those soldiers were all members of a KGC circle.[117] Forrest hinted that the Golden Circle was again active in Springfield, and he predicted that the Copperhead legislators would take "revolutionary action."[118] When the state legislature continued its partisan practices, Forrest fabricated a report that the Illinois council of the KGC had sent "a delegation of peacemakers" to Richmond and he pretended that only Golden Circle members favored peace. Forrest reported that the Knights had established a "grand castle" in Washington, and that the subversives sought to establish a "Northwestern Confederacy" and to force President Lincoln "to abdicate."[119] It was even charged that the *Illinois State Register*, the Democratic organ in Springfield, was the mouthpiece of the state Golden Circle and that the Springfield "castle" had burned its records to hide KGC secrets.[120]

Illinois Democrats denied Forrest's charges as fast as he made them. Editor Charles H. Lanphier of the *Illinois State Register* cautioned readers to discount all of Forrest's claims or reports. He reminded Democrats that Forrest had choked on his KGC allegations the previous year.[121] Editor Lanphier insisted that Forrest had a reputation as a liar and fabricator of fanciful fiction. When Forrest continued to revive old rumors and make new KGC charges, Lanphier lost his patience. He labeled Forrest a "foul-mouthed calumniator." He said that Governor Yates's aide was "a born toady and a chronic devotee of power" who vomited out his aspersions faster than they could be denied.[122] "The indefatigable Joe Forrest," wrote Editor Lanphier, "has discovered another mare's nest. He has made the study of the habits and customs of the K.G.C. his specialty, and is *au fait* with the genuine specimen as Aggassiz [*sic*] with antediluvian birds and fishes."[123] Not until Forrest left for Washington to accept a federal appointment did Illinois have a respite from KGC tales and secret society charges which Yates's loyal aide produced with his pen and his imagination.

When Forrest returned to Springfield in August of 1863 to help Republicans win the fall elections, KGC rumors again flew thick and fast. Forrest set in motion reports that Charles Quantrill, Missouri bushwhacker, had attended the Illinois Democratic convention.[124] He imported KGC tales from Missouri and Indiana and embellished them.[125] He transformed the Democratic state convention into a KGC assemblage with a stroke of his pen. He wrote that "rascally copperheads" were "meditating a St. Bartholomew massacre of the innocent and helpless loyal leaguers in Illinois."[126] He blamed the "Fulton County War" (resistance to the arrest of several deserters) upon secret society members.[127] The imaginative propagandist also claimed that seventy-one "castles" of the Golden Circle functioned in Illinois and that the state's "grand castle" met surreptitiously in Chicago. Editor Lanphier, who denied each of Forrest's KGC charges, explained why the Knights again made the headlines:

Governor Yates and Joe Forrest have got back. As a natural consequence the Chicago *Tribune* and the St. Louis *Democrat* once more teem with accounts of K.G.C. assemblages, of treasonable manifestations, and the like, of which the country had heard nothing for the past month. As there seem to be no K.G.C.'s in the state except when Forrest is here, we advise Governor Yates to take him away once more. . . .[128]

After the elections were over and Forrest returned to Washington, Illinois had another vacation from KGC rumors and Forrest-fabricated treason tales.

While Forrest and Carrington waged a war of words against the Knights of the Golden Circle in Illinois and Indiana, midwestern Democrats discussed the desirability of organizing a secret association as an adjunct of their political party. The Union Leagues, the secret and militant arm of the Republican party, functioned effectively, and some Democrats advocated fighting fire with fire. Furthermore, the course of events in 1863 convinced many Democrats that they needed a mutual protection society dedicated to preserving constitutional government and guaranteeing civil rights to Democratic party members. The wrecking of newspaper offices by mob action gave an impetus to the mutual protection idea—the Belleville *Volksblatt*, the Richmond *Jeffersonian*, and the Columbus *Crisis* were attacked by mobs in March, 1863. Loyal Democrats became even more alarmed when another wave of arbitrary arrests occurred in early 1863. They resented the summary treatment accorded to Vallandigham. Democratic party rallies were sometimes broken up by Republican rowdies or by soldiers-on-leave who took the law into their own hands. Democratic leaders were sometimes attacked by unknown assailants at night or accosted by blackguards during the day. Democratic election workers were sometimes mistreated and party stalwarts were shunned or intimidated. To some it seemed that law and order had given way to "reign of terror."[129]

The institution of conscription with its accompanying provost-marshal system seemed to be a threat to man's freedom and independence. Copperheads viewed the forced draft as a violation of the democratic tradition. The high-handed tactics of military men like Burnside, Hascall, and Carrington added to the uneasiness. When Governors Yates and Morton started to arm the Union Leaguers, some Democrats were convinced that a "creeping dictatorship" was displacing democratic government.[130] In some circles, a fear existed that free elections were in danger, for if freedom of speech and press were crushed, the right to vote was a farce.[131] "These encroachments upon the rights of the people," wrote the editor of the Dayton *Empire*, "will, if tamely submitted to, end in our complete degradation."[132]

Worried Democrats, therefore, wondered whether a secret Democratic society might not be the best guarantor of their rights, liberty, and property. At the same time it could counteract the work which the Union League was doing in behalf of the Lincoln administration and the Republican party. There was a genuine desire to secure the "floating population [which] the Opposition were obtaining."[133]

Democrats who favored organizing a secret society to aid them in winning elections and maintaining constitutional government received no encouragement at party headquarters. Editor Lanphier of the *Illinois State Register* advised his Democratic readers to frown upon all secret political organizations. "True democracy," he wrote, "works in the light of day."[134] Wilbur F. Storey, aggressive editor of the Chicago *Times,* denied the necessity of any Democratic dark lantern society.[135] Joseph J. Bingham, executive secretary of the Democratic party in Indiana and outspoken editor of the Indianapolis *State Sentinel,* had gone on record as opposing all organizations which hid behind the mask of secrecy. "We are now, as we have ever been," he had written in 1862, "opposed to all secret political societies."[136] Some of Bingham's party members in the Jackson County convention put their opposition to secret societies into plain English: "*Resolved,* That we are opposed to Know-Nothingism, the Knights of the Golden Circle, the Wide Awakes, and *all* other secret political organizations as anti-Democratic in their tendencies, and nurseries and hotbeds of treason."[137] Democratic party leaders, almost without exception, wished to keep their opposition to the Lincoln administration out in the open. Secrecy and back-chamber activities ran counter to their principles.

An Indiana Democratic politician named Harrison H. Dodd refused to take the advice of his political superiors. He believed that a secret Democratic society could serve a useful purpose by advancing the party's political fortunes, guaranteeing civil rights to members of the Democratic party, and offering "mutual protection." He wanted a society which could fight the Union League on its own ground and according to its own methods.

Dodd was a well-known Indianapolis figure. He and his brother were partners in a publishing firm; the Indianapolis city directory came off their press in 1862. He had gained considerable recognition in Democratic party circles. He was active in the Marion County Democratic club, presided at the Sixth District congressional convention, and appeared as a speaker at a Hendricks County Democratic celebration. In 1862 he served as a marshal at the

Democratic state convention. When he was elected president of his county's Democratic club in January, 1863, he publicly criticized Governor Morton, and he talked of organizing a "devoted Union order" which might neutralize Governor Morton's dictatorial aspirations.

Dodd had seen his fellow Democrats intimidated and insulted. He was present when John R. Elder, fellow publisher and elderly Democrat, suffered humiliation for challenging the votes of nonresident soldiers. Elder pointed out, as a challenger at the polls, that some soldiers who insisted upon voting did not have their names on the poll list. Some twenty soldiers, indignant because the election judge upheld Elder's protest, turned on the Democratic challenger, attacked him with clubs and fists, and made him flee for his life.[138] Governor Morton's failure to denounce the incident and Carrington's failure to discipline the offending soldiers upset Dodd. He feared that free elections in Indiana would suffer the same fate that had befallen them in Kentucky. Dodd himself was a victim of the hysteria of the times. It was no longer safe to swim against the current of public opinion, whipped to fever pitch by the patriotic harangues of Governor Morton.

The political campaign of fall, 1862, was bad enough, but conditions preceding the April, 1863, elections were intolerable. While Dodd was on his way to attend a Democratic rally at Danville, he was threatened and abused while changing trains at Cartersville. His experiences in Danville were most unpleasant. In the first place, Danville Democrats were denied the use of the county courthouse, and their party rally was rescheduled out-of-doors. Then, while the Democratic meeting was in session, armed Union Leaguers drilled nearby. When Dodd was speaking and criticized the state of affairs, Republican rowdies and Union Leaguers interrupted the program. Dodd, naturally, wondered whether civil rights and free elections might not disappear entirely in Indiana.

The return trip from Danville to Indianapolis added insult to injury. While Dodd was changing trains at Cartersville he was seized by a mob of soldiers and Union League members. They jostled him, insulted him, and called him a "traitor." Some of the mobsters suggested that their prisoner be hung from the nearest tree. A few of the roisterers held out for a tar-and-feathers party. Dodd was sure that his life was in jeopardy. Moderates, however, obtained the upper hand and Dodd gained his freedom. He always credited the "intervention of Providence" for his life. When Dodd arrived back home, considerably shaken, he shared his experiences with his Democratic friends.[139] Dodd thought that Democrats had no alternative but to organize secretly to protect themselves and their rights.

The April elections in Indianapolis helped convince Dodd that Democrats must create a partisan society patterned after the Union Leagues. The polls witnessed many unsavory incidents and acts of violence. Scuffles were numerous. Soldiers voted illegally. Democratic voters were intimidated. Timid Democrats stayed at home on election day. In protest, the entire slate of Democratic nominees withdrew from the May election contest, implying that free elections no longer existed in the state's capital.[140] Realistic members of the Democratic party recognized that only abuse and defeat confronted them at the polls. Dodd again urged the establishment of a secret Democratic society to save the party and guarantee free elections.

Dodd's arguments seemed sensible in view of the news and rumors that drifted into Indianapolis. Vallandigham's arrest and his trial by a military court aroused Indiana Democrats. There were rumors that Negro troops were being used in Kentucky. The destruction of Democratic newspaper plants by mobs also added to the uneasiness of Lincoln's political enemies. The Republican resurgence in the spring elections of 1863 added to Democratic apprehensions.[141]

Dodd and some friends, therefore, decided to organize a secret branch of the Democratic party. They selected the name "Sons of Liberty" for their organization, hoping that it would be as "patriotic" and successful as its Revolutionary War namesake. It's aims were to "defend" the Constitution, to preserve civil and individual rights, to win elections, and to serve as the militant arm of the Democratic party. It could, furthermore, serve as a mutual protection society and counteract the successful activities and influence of the Union Leagues. If President Lincoln and Republican governors knew that Democrats were secretly and effectively organized to protect their rights, Dodd and others argued, there would be no Republican effort to interfere in the elections, suppress freedom of speech and press, and arrest Democrats arbitrarily.[142] Dodd's order, the Sons of Liberty, was related in no way or fashion to the Knights of the Golden Circle.[143]

When Dodd drafted the plans for his secret Democratic society, he provided that the order would be headed by a "Supreme Grand Commander" and that the organization in each state would have a "state council" headed by a "Grand Commander." In turn, there would be county councils and local units. Dodd devised an impressive ritual and he provided for membership by "degrees." He published a seven-page booklet, *S.L.*, to be distributed to interested members and to impress Republicans. Dodd took the title of "Grand Commander" in his state and divided Indiana into four military districts.[144] Three of the "commanders" selected for the "military districts" never accepted their appointments and never served as members.

Dodd prevailed upon S. Corning Judd to accept the leadership of the Illinois Sons of Liberty. Judd was a reputable and respected citizen of Illinois. He had a long record of activity in the Democratic party and knew Lincoln personally. He had served as a presidential elector (Douglas ticket) in 1860. He had campaigned actively in 1862 for ratification of the "Copperhead Constitution." In 1863 he served as chairman of his county's central committee. He had ability and courage and he believed that a military despotism was enveloping the country. It was "criminal and cowardly," he thought, for citizens to stand by while the rights of free men were trampled under foot.[145] Judd helped to establish the "Illinois Council" in Springfield on June 17, 1863, on the same day that the state Democratic convention was in session. Its supporters viewed it as a Democratic "union league"—similar in organization and purpose.

Judd and Dodd found few recruits for their secret society in Illinois and Indiana. It existed more on paper than in practice. At times Dodd drew the cloak of the Sons of Liberty over a local Democratic club, and there was a pretense that the two were one. Dodd and a few others brazenly boasted that they belonged to a secret society and exaggerated in order to arouse Republican apprehension. Dodd and Judd wanted Republicans to fear the Sons of Liberty and to believe that it was a powerful organization.

Prominent Democrats shunned the Dodd-sponsored society. The party machinery avoided giving any encouragement to the Sons of Liberty. The Chicago *Times* warned its readers to avoid all secret societies. Republican newspapers published the ritual of the Sons of Liberty and pretended that its members were traitors. The order languished. Dodd inadvertently played into the hands of such propagandists as Forrest and Carrington. They might confuse the Knights of the Golden Circle and the Sons of Liberty, misrepresenting the latter, but Republican readers believed the charges and the stories. Dodd's organization seemed to be drifting into oblivion.

In Missouri, meanwhile, a man named Phineas C. Wright dusted off a scheme he had earlier advocated. When Wright had lived in New Orleans before the war (1856–57), he had drawn up plans for a fraternal order which he named the Order of American Knights. Its projects included the promotion of states rights and a Central American colonial scheme.[146] In 1859 Wright moved to St. Louis, and there he mixed politics and law. When President Lincoln espoused the cause of emancipation, Wright stepped forth as a critic of the government. He wrote treatises on politics, glorifying states' rights, and critiques of the Lincoln administration. He believed that Lincoln wished to wreck the Constitution and feared that the president was building "a strong, irresponsible, central despotism." He believed that the administration was corrupt and that the nation was heading down the road of ruin.[147]

Wright watched conditions in Missouri deteriorate during 1863. Smuggling developed into a major industry. Cotton agents built up ill will as they lined their pockets with gold. Guerrillas raided for private gain. Republican leaders waged acrimonious war on each other.[148] Lincoln's proclamation of emancipation built up a reservoir of anti-administration sentiment. Wright feared that civil rights and free elections might disappear in Missouri.

In December of 1863, Wright revived the Order of American Knights. He published a pamphlet and a call-to-arms. The call-to-arms assumed the form of an "Occasional Address of Supreme Commander," a strange document compounded of states' rights sentiments and an abhorrence of "Black Republicanism." It set forth a list of objectives: (a) to educate members to be straight-line Democrats, (b) to counteract the designs of the other secret orders (Union Leagues, Knights of the Golden Circle, and Know-Nothings), (c) to promote friendship and fellowship, and (d) to provide a place of refuge in Central America for the multitudes which the war was making homeless and destitute.[149] The self-styled "Supreme Commander" did not put his own name to the "Occasional Address." He used the pseudonym P. Caius Urbanus.

Wright drew Charles L. Hunt of Missouri into his confidence and interested him in the work of the Order of American Knights. Hunt, who mixed farming, land speculation, and politics, envisioned the American Knights as a militant organization of Peace Democrats—an organization that might write a peace plank into the Democratic party platform and nominate a "peace man" as the party's representative in 1864.[150]

Wright carried on speechmaking, politics, and OAK promotion in several midwestern states, but his strange secret order received rebuff and ridicule in Illinois and Indiana.[151] Even in Missouri, Supreme Commander Wright failed to build a following. Wright was an impractical man, without the ability to make his dreams come true.

As 1863 came to an end, the Democrats were dejected and disorganized. Inept leadership had hampered them; no one of stature had stepped forward to don the mantle worn so gracefully by Stephen A. Douglas. The year had started out hopefully enough; the roots of discontent were planted firmly. But the

Democrats were divided over policy and practice. Victories at Gettysburg and Vicksburg helped Republicanism become respectable again. President Lincoln began to gain the confidence of the masses; his persistence, patience, and humility appealed to them. They envisioned the nobler aspects of the struggle; they were swept along in the stream of history.

Vallandigham's defeat in the Ohio gubernatorial contest offered proof that Democrats were sliding downhill. They knew that such sideroads as the Sons of Liberty or the Order of American Knights would not stop their slide. They did not like to be pelted with mud by Forrest and Carrington, but had no defense against such tactics.

Politicians looked ahead to the 1864 presidential elections. Copperheads lost the edge they had earlier held in Illinois and Indiana. The Democrats looked apprehensively to the future, as if they were dimly aware of coming events.

V I

Exposés
and Treason Trials

As THE WAR progressed into 1864, President Lincoln grew in stature and popularity. Emancipation, opposed by so many mid-westerners in 1863, gained respectability. Realists recognized that time was on the side of the North. The tide had turned at Vicksburg and Gettysburg. Early in 1864, Lincoln summoned General U. S. Grant to Washington and placed the unassuming general in command of all federal troops. This was Grant's reward for the successful campaigns of Donelson, Vicksburg, and Chattanooga. The General took personal command of the Army of the Potomac, and named General William T. Sherman to take charge of western operations. The two commanders set out to bind the Confederacy with a ring of steel. Early in May, Grant and his army moved into the "Wilderness." Sherman and his western army moved toward Georgia. Both began a series of flank movements which were destined to bring the military phase of the war to an end.

Having put all his military eggs in Grant's basket, Lincoln was free to turn his attention to politics. National nominating conventions would occur during the summer. Then would come another presidential campaign. Lincoln wished for another term; it would give him a chance to carry his program to its completion. Some of the Radical Republicans, however, tried to sidetrack Lincoln. The President's friends, therefore, set about building political fences, soliciting support, and taking necessary measures to secure the renomination and the re-election of their candidate.

The Democratic party was also a divided one. Peace Democrats were adamant, desiring to push their program regardless of the consequences. Some of the confirmed peace men took steps to resurrect the Sons of Liberty to give them control of the party machinery and help bring about an armistice. H. H. Dodd and his cohorts bungled and fumbled. They gave the Republicans "evidence" which was pyramided into exposés and treason trials. The series of exposés and the treason charges helped to re-elect Lincoln and doom the Copperhead cause.

Dodd and other midwestern Peace Democrats were alarmed when McClellan's stock as a nominee rose sharply early in 1864.[1] They recognized that co-operative action was necessary to head off the McClellan boom. So a considerable number of midwestern Peace Democrats accepted the invitation of several New York Democrats to meet in their city and map their strategy.[2] Dodd and several of his friends tried to use the occasion to revise and revitalize the Sons of Liberty, as a pro-peace as well as a secret partisan organization.

Several of the midwestern Peace Democrats detoured by way of Windsor on their way to New York City. They wanted to meet with Vallandigham and get his suggestions and advice, for the exiled Ohioan was a symbol of the peace crusade. Dodd, Amos Green, and James A. Barret had another reason for meeting with Vallandigham. They developed the theory that, if Vallandigham would accept the leadership of the Sons of Liberty, both the peace movement and the peace society might prosper.

Dodd was convinced more than ever that peace and compromise were the only alternatives to despotism. He had been the victim of several more unhappy experiences and believed that Lincoln was slowly but surely establishing a dictatorship in America. In September, 1863, local authorities had seized him and thrown him in jail when he addressed a rally of Jasper and Newton county Democrats.[3] After his release, he seethed with indignation. He returned to Indianapolis to condemn the "despotism" which he imagined had taken over America. Governor Morton's dictatorial tactics added to Dodd's uneasiness. He convinced himself that compromise and peace must become the basic planks of the Democratic platform. In January, Dodd sought election as a Democratic delegate to the party's national convention. He defined his program in a single word and spelled it with capital letters—"PEACE." He predicted that bayonets would control the next presidential election and vowed that no man elected by force, fraud, or violence would be inaugurated.[4]

Dr. Barret and Amos Green, like Dodd, were passionate peace men, and they were equally disgruntled and disillusioned. Dr. James H. Barret had served briefly in the army, but resigned in disgust.[5] After President Lincoln made emancipation an official policy, Dr. Barret became an embittered critic of the administration. He had great admiration for Vallandigham and became an advocate of peace and compromise. Amos Green, also of Illinois, had gained a reputation as a vicious critic of the Lincoln administration. His editorials had revealed his hatred of Lincoln and occasionally exceeded the bounds of propriety. He had twice been arrested and twice freed. He, like Barret and Dodd, was convinced that civil rights were slipping away and that a dictatorship was taking shape.

Green and Barret, in their interview with Vallandigham, discussed the possibility of peace men capturing the Democratic convention, writing an appropriate platform, and naming a pro-peace candidate. Then they discussed the advisability of organizing and promoting a secret Democratic league to help promote the program of peace and win elections. They could take the framework of the Sons of Liberty and of the Order of American Knights and weld the two into one. Both of these organizations existed more in theory than in fact. Messrs. Green and Barret assured Vallandigham that the society would possess only "pure" ideals and objectives. It would be patriotic and political and nothing more. Then they suggested that Vallandigham lend his name to the organization and accept leadership of the order. They argued that his name had a magic quality, and that he could help to insure the society's success by becoming the "Supreme Grand Commander." Vallandigham hedged. In principle he was opposed to secret political societies. The Republicans, however, had the Union League, and it had proved to be an effective political and educational force. Reluctantly Vallandigham agreed to serve.[6] Amos Green and Dr. James A. Barret then left for New York City. There they would meet with other Peace Democrats and plan to stop the McClellan landslide. They might also sell the secret society outline to other Democrats.

Although the February 22 conference of Peace Democrats in New York City was a distinct disappointment in many ways, several of the informal discussions concerned with the establishment of a revitalized secret society bore fruit. Dodd, anxious to make the Sons of Liberty into a powerful political force, had to act with caution. Phineas C. Wright, creator of the Order of American Knights, still hoped that his society might take root. Wright had recently joined the New York *Daily News,* and he overrated his influence as an editor and an organizer. Dodd promised to incorporate portions of Wright's organization into his own.

On his return trip to Indianapolis, Dodd stopped to visit with Vallandigham in Windsor. He was accompanied by Dr. Thomas C. Massey of Ohio, who had decided to lend a hand in creating a society which might help him, the peace movement, and Ohio Democrats. Dodd and Massey informed Vallandigham that he had been elected head of the "new" Sons of Liberty. They added that a new constitution for the order was partially prepared and a new ritual partially devised. Vallandigham gave the proposed constitution a cursory examination. He eliminated much of the hocus-pocus which made up the ritual and added selections from the Virginia and Kentucky resolutions as lessons of the "Inner Temple." He then agreed to serve as "Supreme Commander" for a year.[7] Dodd and Massey bade Vallandigham farewell and returned to their homes, each bearing the self-selected title of "Grand Commander" for his state.

Dodd and Massey again visited Windsor in mid-April. A handful of other Peace Democrats also came to meet with Vallandigham. Their chief concern seemed to be with the forthcoming national convention of their party. McClellan's political star was rising, and the Peace Democrats groped blindly for ways to impose their views on the party. They wanted a peace plank nailed to their party's platform and a peace man as their party's nominee. Vallandigham agreed to write an open letter. By discussing the issues of the day he could emphasize the need for peace and the need for Democrats to nominate a peace man.

Some of the Peace Democrats who met with Vallandigham also discussed the welfare of the Sons of Liberty. S. Corning Judd, being promoted as gubernatorial timber by some Peace Democrats in his state,[8] reported on conditions in Illinois. He pretended that Illinois was well organized and had a "military organization." Judd asserted that Illinois Democrats would not give up their rights without a struggle and would insist on free elections and on their constitutional rights.[9] Dodd reported on affairs in Indiana. He was optimistic about the future of the Sons of Liberty; he was bitter about President Lincoln's and Governor Morton's dictatorial practices. If the Sons of Liberty were effectively organized, they could insure free elections and challenge the government's usurpations.

Dr. Thomas Massey reported upon conditions in Ohio. That state's Peace Democrats had not yet recovered from the resounding defeat in the gubernatorial contest the previous fall. Alexander Long, in Congress, and Samuel Medary, in the *Crisis*, argued in favor of an armistice and an end to the "unconstitutional war,"[10] but neither the Sons of Liberty nor the Peace Democrats made gains in the Buckeye State. Charles L. Hunt, being solicited to head the Sons of Liberty in Missouri, added sour seasonings to the proceedings. He was a friend of Wright, creator of the Order of American Knights. He argued that the dissatisfied Democrats in his state preferred the more pro-Southern Order of American Knights to the Sons of Liberty. Not only did he favor an immediate armistice, but he believed it advisable to give aid to the Southern rebels. Vallandigham rudely interrupted. Visibly angry, he gave Hunt a severe castigation.[11] He would have nothing to do with the Missouri "Outfit"! He might be a critic, but he was no traitor!

More sour sauce was added by James A. McMaster, the "annoyingly frank" editor of the New York *Freeman's Journal.* McMaster, whom Dodd and Vallandigham wished to designate "Grand Commander" for the state of New York, had no respect for Lincoln or faith in his administration. McMaster had been arrested arbitrarily early in the war and released after spending seven months in Fort Lafayette. When he returned to the editorial desk of the *Freeman's Journal,* he was critical and outspoken as before, glorying in the role of martyr to a free press. McMaster shocked Vallandigham with some of his forthright statements justifying the principle of secession. Vallandigham again dissented and another disagreement took place. Hunt of Missouri came to McMaster's defense, while Judd of Illinois supported Vallandigham.

The clash of words and the heated controversy cast the pallor of death over the Sons of Liberty. The Democratic dissenters could not agree upon co-operative action. So the order of the Sons of Liberty began to collapse even before it was officially launched, and again became a paper organization. As "Supreme Commander," Vallandigham never issued an order or called a meeting.[12] He held a title, not an office. The Windsor meeting at which an infant could have been baptized turned into a funeral service. The self-styled "Grand Commanders" returned home disgusted and disillusioned.

The order found no takers in Michigan, Wisconsin, Minnesota, or Iowa; no evidence exists that an effort was made to extend it into those states. Even in Kentucky, where discontent was widespread owing to the high-handed tactics of General Stephen G. Burbridge and the recruitment of Negro troops, no members were enrolled. Dodd's dream of an effective and extensive secret society slowly and surely faded away.

While Dodd's strange and secret order disintegrated, an army colonel took steps to investigate and expose the "subversive societies" in Missouri. The colonel's name was John

P. Sanderson. He served as provost marshal general under General William S. Rosecrans, commanding the Department of the Missouri with headquarters in St. Louis.

John P. Sanderson had had a checkered career. In Pennsylvania before the Civil War he had dabbled in law, politics, newspaper work, and Know-Nothingism. By tugging at Simon Cameron's coat-tails he managed to obtain the post of chief clerk in the War Department when Lincoln and the Republicans took over on March 4, 1861. After the debacle at First Bull Run, Sanderson resigned his clerkship in favor of a colonelcy. He was shuffled from one assignment to another. When General Lovell H. Rousseau bid for an independent command in the Kentucky-Tennessee sector, he offered Sanderson the position of chief of staff. Secretary of War Stanton quashed the hopes which General Rousseau and Colonel Sanderson held. Sanderson was tempted to resign, and prominent Louisville unionists urged him to purchase and edit the Louisville *Journal*. Sanderson was in Louisville when news of George W. L. Bickley's capture made the headlines and when reports and rumors about Golden Circle activity were on every tongue. While debating the advisability of taking up an editorial quill rather than a colonel's sword, he accompanied General Rosecrans' army on its ill-fated invasion of Georgia. He was with Rosecrans when the Confederates swept his right flank off the field at Chickamauga. Sanderson consoled the disconsolate general and helped Rosecrans write his official report on the battle. When Rosecrans was deposed from command of the Army of the Cumberland, Sanderson tagged along. While Rosecrans waited for a new assignment in Cincinnati, Sanderson bided his time at Newport Barracks nearby. They read the Cincinnati *Gazette* and became acquainted with the tall tales of KGC treason which it spread. *Gazette* editors seemed to specialize in inventing fanciful tales whenever Carrington or Forrest ran out of ammunition.

When Major General Rosecrans received the St. Louis assignment as commander of the Department of the Missouri, he invited Sanderson to come along. He offered him the post of provost marshal general in his jurisdiction. Sanderson coveted the position, but the appointment needed the approval of the Secretary of War. Stanton deferred the appointment, for there were reports that Sanderson had been guilty of flight and cowardice on the battle-field of Chickamauga.

General Rosecrans wondered why Sanderson's appointment was delayed. He became impatient, and sent an emissary, a major serving on Rosecrans' staff, to Washington to find out who originated the cowardice charges and why the appointment was being held up. Secretary Stanton, who had no love for Rosecrans, countered by arresting the emissary for trespassing outside his jurisdiction. Rebuked again, Rosecrans felt that Stanton was rubbing salt into his wounds. Finally Sanderson's assignment cleared War Department hurdles. The chastised general and his dejected aide moved to St. Louis and assumed their new duties in March, 1864.[13]

Conditions in Missouri had deteriorated to a point where plundering, smuggling, and "rascality" made affairs "pitiable."[14] Furthermore, the unionists were divided into two camps—radicals and conservatives—and members of the two factions seemed to hate each other nearly as much as they hated the Confederates. Each side had influence in Washington, and the situation was loaded with dynamite.[15] Previous army administrators had failed to please both factions. Truly Rosecrans and Sanderson had jumped from the frying pan into the fire.

Sanderson made an effort to bring order out of chaos. He arrested smugglers, deserters, and Confederate sympathizers. A strange assortment of callers filed past his desk—petitioners, beggars, accusers, and suspects. Colonel Sanderson interviewed them all. One of the callers was "a lady smuggler of rebel mails." Another had tried to recruit for the Confederacy in Missouri. Still another claimed to hold "a high position in the Organization of the Knights of the Golden Circle."[16]

While some informers talked about the activity of the Knights of the Golden Circle, others reported on the Corps de Belgique or the Paw Paws—both were purported to be pro-Confederate organizations active within Sanderson's jurisdiction. The evidence was vague, confusing, and unreliable. Several copies of the

"Occasional Address . . ." which were intended for members of the Order of American Knights and written and published by Phineas C. Wright, attracted the most attention.[17] Another interesting item was a letter written by Christian Kribben, a prominent Peace Democrat of St. Louis. The Kribben letter, confiscated by an Illinois provost marshal, indicated that the writer had participated in conferences in Windsor, Canada, and in New York.[18] Sanderson suspected the worst. The pieces in the puzzle were many, and Sanderson was unable to put them together. He decided, however, that he would gather material for an exposé of the Knights of the Golden Circle. His decision to bring forth a gigantic exposé was made before he had been in St. Louis a week and before any reliable evidence had come his way.[19]

Sanderson's decision to investigate subversive societies came after a long interview with a jailbird who used the name of G. Byron Jones. He claimed to have once recruited for the Confederate army, and seems to have expressed Union and Confederate sympathies alternately. While in jail in St. Joseph, he wrote a letter to the St. Joseph *Tribune* "exposing the Paw Paw organization."[20] After Jones was transferred to the Gratiot Street Prison, Sanderson periodically visited and interviewed the loquacious scoundrel. Jones claimed that the majority of the Paw Paws belonged to the Golden Circle. He offered to exchange information about the Knights in Missouri for his "freedom" and a position as Sanderson's agent. Desperate for information about the Golden Circle, Sanderson hired Jones as a spy to ferret out "the leading spirits and all the operations of the Knights of the Golden Circle." Sanderson argued that "it takes a thief to catch a thief."[21]

Colonel Sanderson soon added seven more "detectives" to his staff. Several of them claimed to be "paroled rebel officers." One claimed membership in the Golden Circle; another claimed that he was an active member of the Order of American Knights. Sanderson briefed several of the agents on his fears and sent them to look for the needles in the KGC haystacks. Not only did the agents scour Missouri for rumors and information, but they were also sent into Illinois, Kentucky, Michigan, Indiana, and Ohio—to such cities as Louisville, Indianapolis, Cincinnati, Detroit, and Chicago.[22] Sanderson exceeded his authority when he sent his agents outside of the Department of the Missouri, but he was playing for big stakes.

While Sanderson's agents toured the Midwest in search of information, chance brought many rumors to St. Louis. Sanderson took notes on all of them. An Iowa congressman charged that the Golden Circle hampered the draft in his state.[23] A federal marshal, more interested in the welfare of the Republican party than in defending civil rights, said that a subversive secret society existed in Iowa and that its true aim was to bind the states of the upper Mississippi Valley to the Southern Confederacy.[24] The editor of the Paris, Illinois, *Times* blamed the "Mattoon Incident" on Copperheads belonging to a subversive secret society.[25] The imaginative editor of the Quincy *Whig* charged that Quantrill's Missouri guerrillas and Quincy's members of the Golden Circle had hatched a "bloody programme" of "plunder, robbery, and murder."[26] Republican newspaper editors blamed the Edgar County riots in Illinois on members of a Copperhead secret society, calling the incident the "Edgar County Insurrection."[27] The federal officer commanding in Cairo offered the supposition that the Order of American Knights had absorbed and superseded the Golden Circle.[28] The same officer also came across an "informer" willing to produce a revelation if the price were right.[29] Another would-be informer, confined in an Illinois hospital, offered to give "a true exposition of the Knites of the Golden Circle."[30]

The rumors which drifted into Sanderson's headquarters from Iowa and Illinois possessed less substance than those originating in Indiana. Carrington and Governor Morton shadowboxed with Copperheads in the Hoosier State, claiming that such prominent Indiana Democrats as Judge Samuel E. Perkins, Lambdin P. Milligan, and Harrison H. Dodd belonged to a secret and subversive Copperhead organization. Judge Perkins entered Governor Morton's doghouse after the jurist held military arrests to be illegal when the civil courts were open and in operation.[31] Milligan brazenly advocated an armistice and argued that Democrats should maintain their constitutional rights "at all costs"—some argued that they should use "arms if necessary."[32] Dodd caused consternation in Republican circles by publishing and circulating a pamphlet purporting to relate the proceedings of a state meeting of the Sons of Liberty in Indiana. Dodd pretended that members of the Copperhead secret society were as numerous as the leaves on the trees.

Governor Morton publicly denounced all who refused to support his partisan and patriotic policies. He gave dignity to rumors that a "Northwest Conspiracy" was being hatched in Democratic quarters and claimed that a "treasonable" secret society existed with the indorsement of Democratic leadership. He insisted that there was "a circle within a circle in the Democratic party."[33] One Republican editor reported that Daniel W. Voorhees, prominent Indiana congressman and Copperhead, had visited Horatio Seymour of New York "to bring pressure upon him [Seymour] to lead in a Northern uprising. . . ." Although Governor Seymour labeled the charges "untrue and absurd," and Congressman Voorhees protested that the scandalous charges injured his "life, liberty, and honor," other Republican editors copied and circulated the calumny.[34] Sanderson, in St. Louis, soaked up the Indiana miscellany like a sponge, later incorporating some of the rumors and charges into his exposé.

Even Ohio contributed. The winds of rumor carried reports that Vallandigham, impatiently waiting in Windsor, had been named head of the Sons of Liberty and that a national conclave had been held in New York City. It was said that Vallandigham was planning to return to Ohio and that his return would be a signal for a midwestern uprising. It was reported that Canadian-based Confederates planned to invade Ohio to free prisoners confined in the barracks on Johnson's Island in Lake Erie, near Sandusky.[35] Governor John Brough of Ohio also aired his fears that another Confederate raid might attempt to free rebel prisoners held in the state penitentiary at Columbus.[36] An Ohio congressman, James A. Garfield, added to Brough's disquietude by producing "treason letters" on the floor of the House of Representatives and charging that prominent Buckeye State Democrats had helped recruit Confederate soldiers in the state. Although Garfield was later embarrassed when it was proved that the "treason letters" were simple forgeries, Republican newspapers, like the Cincinnati *Gazette* and the Columbus *Ohio State Journal,* continued to spread vicious rumors linking prominent Ohio Democrats with the South.[37]

Garfield's contributions to Civil War mythology were far exceeded by those of Byron H. Robb. Robb was a blackguard and vagabond, wanted in St. Louis for violation of parole and for perjury,[38] who unblushingly approached Governor Brough to say that he could deliver information concerning a boat-burning organization active in midwestern waters. Robb, an inveterate liar, claimed that he knew a "Colonel Vayden," the supervisor of a network of 150 agents who booked passage on western steamboats and then set them afire, receiving "25 per cent of the valuation of every boat" as pay for their dangerous work. Robb promised that he "could get" the "whole crew" if he were put on the payroll as a detective and permitted to go to Canada to mix with Confederate agents there.[39] Both Congressman Garfield and Governor Brough had faith in Robb's revelations and channeled the "Colonel Vayden" and "boat-burning conspiracy" stories into the Republican press, contributing to the subversive-society myth already so popular in some circles. In Republican hands a perjurer's effort to milk the government became a "Copperhead conspiracy." Sanderson, in St. Louis, swallowed the revelations of Robb whole. He could find a place for them in the exposé which was in the making.

Sanderson imported one interesting story from the state of Michigan. The story centered on Phineas C. Wright, creator of the Order of the American Knights. Wright visited the Midwest early in April of 1864, lecturing in St. Clair and other Michigan cities. He was arrested at Grand Rapids on April 27, 1864, and hustled off to Fort Lafayette without explanation. Federal officials knew that they had no damaging evidence concerning the former St. Louis resident and would not risk a trial. They solved their dilemma by keeping Wright behind bars without publicity or fanfare.[40]

Both Colonel Sanderson and Major General Rosecrans were also interested in a conference which General Samuel P. Heintzelman[41] held with several midwestern governors in Indianapolis in mid-April. Governors Morton and Yates talked at length on the unrest in their states because of the activity of "Copperhead organizations" and traitorous secret societies. One of Governor Morton's detectives reported that a subversive order had "a large enrollment" in Canada, Illinois, and Indiana and "some members" in Ohio, Iowa, and Missouri.[42] Unknown to General Heintzelman, Morton and Yates exaggerated the unrest and the secret societies in order to keep more of their states' volunteers assigned to camp duty within their jurisdiction.

Sanderson studied the basketful of material he had already collected. He was quite confused by the conflicting information which his eight agents had garnered. Their reports were long on supposition, short on proof. He was more puzzled by the maze of contradictory "evidence" which had come to his desk: letters confiscated in the mails, clippings from various midwestern newspapers, items seized in raids, rumors and tittle-tattle, accusations of Republican partisans, and "confessions" or "revelations" of prisoners willing to say anything to gain their freedom. Nevertheless, Sanderson set to work with scissors and paste to prepare a report for his military superior. He wilfully and mistakenly attributed to Vallandigham the "Occasional Address . . ." composed by Wright. Sanderson concluded that the Order of American Knights was the descendant of the Golden Circle and that Vallandigham was the order's "Supreme Commander." He reported that the Order of American Knights was the right arm of General Sterling Price, the Confederate commander then threatening Missouri. He noted that the Order of American Knights had a sinister objective: "the overthrow of the Federal Government, and the creation of a Northwestern Confederacy."[43]

While Sanderson worked on his lengthy OAK canard, he frequently discussed his "evidence" and his exposé with his immediate superior, Major General Rosecrans. The trusting general swallowed the tale, hook, line, and sinker. To make the story more convincing, Colonel Sanderson ordered the arrest of three St.

Louis citizens whom he considered the chief OAK men in Missouri.[44]

General Rosecrans reported on Sanderson's "discoveries" to General Heintzelman, commander of the Northern Department, with headquarters in Cincinnati, and to Congressman James A. Garfield and President Lincoln.[45] Rosecrans pretended that the documents and the evidence were too valuable to be intrusted to the mails. He sought to find an excuse to send Sanderson to Washington with the OAK materials. Rosecrans was anxious to find out what Washington forces were responsible for holding up Colonel Sanderson's bid for a brigadier general's star.[46] Under the prompting of General Rosecrans, Governor Yates of Illinois also asked President Lincoln to invite Sanderson to Washington to make certain secret-society "revelations."[47]

President Lincoln was aware of the existence of a War Department order forbidding the sending of staff officers to Washington on errands. Furthermore, Lincoln was aware of the animosity between Secretary Stanton and General Rosecrans. Lincoln convinced himself that Rosecrans was trying to bring on a conflict between the President and his Secretary of War. Lincoln resolved the problem by sending his personal secretary, John Hay, to St. Louis to interview Rosecrans and Sanderson and to secure the "extraordinary evidence."[48]

When John Hay, emissary extraordinary, arrived in St. Louis, Colonel Sanderson failed to have his report finished or the miscellaneous evidence classified. Sanderson promised, however, that it would be ready in a couple of days. Hay took a trip into Illinois to visit friends for several days. On his return to St. Louis, Rosecrans and Sanderson briefed him on their "findings" and their belief in an OAK "conspiracy." Sanderson gave Hay a 6,600-word exposé as well as the one hundred pages of "evidence" which he had collected.[49] Hay, with tongue in cheek, politely accepted the stack of material and took it back to Washington.

Both Rosecrans and Sanderson realized that Lincoln's secretary-emissary was unimpressed. They had staked their reputations on the exposé which Sanderson had fabricated. They refused to accept Hay's indifference as a defeat. They had invested too much to turn back. Sanderson, therefore, feverishly collected more "evidence" to substantiate his OAK revelations. General Rosecrans turned to letter-writing to sell the bill of goods which Sanderson had prepared.

Suddenly the roof fell in on the Rosecrans-Sanderson duo. Sanderson's bid for a raise in rank received a rebuff in the War Department. Even President Lincoln expressed a lack of faith in the ability and integrity of Rosecrans' aide.[50] Stanton added insult to injury by disallowing Colonel Sanderson's application for a remittance from the contingent fund to defray the expenses of his corps of detectives. Stanton had no faith in Sanderson or in the mare's-nest he was building. Rosecrans then by-passed the Secretary of War and wrote directly to Lincoln begging the President to interfere and approve the application for money which Sanderson had already spent.[51] The Secretary of War again rebuffed Rosecrans and Sanderson. He ordered the release of the principals whom Sanderson had arrested in St. Louis. Not only did the Secretary of War order the release of Charles L. Hunt, but he also directed Sanderson to return immediately "the archives and papers" which had been seized.[52] General Grant also intervened in behalf of Dr. James A. Barret, another of the St. Louis residents whom Sanderson had arrested.[53] Grant refused to believe that Sanderson had nipped a conspiracy in the bud and did not believe that Dr. James A. Barret, a former friend, was a traitor and conspirator. The doors in Washington seemed to be tightly locked; Rosecrans and Sanderson stood outside in the cold.

The St. Louis team was discouraged but not yet defeated. Sanderson collected more evidence, including eyewitness accounts of the detective who was present in Dayton and Hamilton when Vallandigham returned to Ohio and made public appearances at Democratic rallies. He prepared a supplementary report and placed it in Rosecrans' hands with a sheaf of documents and evidence.[54] General Rosecrans, meanwhile, tried to help vindicate his disgraced provost marshal general. He deluged President Lincoln with letters, insisting that those whom Sanderson had arrested were guilty and that the OAK conspiracy was a reality and not a dream. He claimed that Vallandigham was untrustworthy and familiar with all movements made by federal troops. He wrote that the "McClellan Minutemen," active Democrats who wanted McClellan nominated and elected, were linked to the Order of American Knights and that the complotters had 140,000 active members in Illinois alone. He protested against the Secretary of War's orders to release Charles L. Hunt and Dr. James A. Barret, writing that the release of "the leaders" would "endanger the public safety and defeat the ends of justice."[55] General Rosecrans wrote to others too. One letter to General Heintzelman begged for "proof" which Sanderson could incorporate in his exposé. Rosecrans also solicited "evidence" from Carrington, who had several agents in his employ, and from Governor Yates of Illinois. Rosecrans naïvely believed that a "Northwest conspiracy" endangered the country, and he was anxious to help his aide, who was dejected and disgraced.

The situation in Missouri deteriorated meanwhile, and there was criticism directed at General Rosecrans and Colonel Sanderson. Charges of maladministration threatened Sanderson's reputation as an officer and administrator.[56] Furthermore, Sanderson hoped that a well-publicized OAK exposé might give him a chance to exchange his colonel's insignia for a general's star. He was anxious to redeem himself and remove the tarnish linked with his name in Washington. Having failed to gain the ear or affection of federal officials in Washington, Sanderson decided to turn to old friends and Republican newspapermen to get his story before the people. He burned the midnight oil preparing a lengthy press release and OAK exposé. He assured friends that he was preparing some startling revelations and entitled his OAK report and press release "Conspiracy to establish a Northwestern Confederacy."[57] He gave his friend, the editor of the St. Louis *Missouri Democrat* —a Radical Republican newspaper despite its name—first chance to print the story. If the public would buy his story, the OAK exposé would wash away his past sins.

The Sanderson exposé appeared in the July 28, 1864, issue of the *Missouri Democrat*[58] and soon found its way into many Republican newspapers all over the country.[59] The Cincinnati *Gazette*, the Springfield *Illinois State Journal*, and the Chicago *Tribune* generously gave space to the Sanderson exposé.[60] The New York *Tribune* gave publicity to Sanderson and his OAK tale. With tongue in cheek the editor not only found Vallandigham guilty, but suggested that the 200,000 "McClellan Minute Men" in New York were a part of the conspiracy.[61] The editor of the New York *Commercial Advertiser* matched the *Tribune*'s banter with salient sarcasm. "Mr. Clement Vallandigham," wrote the editor, "sits like a fiend sipping cobblers with George Sanders [a Confederate agent] . . . and if he fails to be nominated at Chicago, will quietly drop a spark from his cigar on the train of this subterranean battery, and blow us all into chaos and black night."[62] Even some Confederate newspapers published portions of the OAK exposé which was published in the Chicago *Tribune*.[63]

General Rosecrans and Colonel Sanderson actively circulated the OAK exposé. Sanderson sent a copy to his political patron in Pennsylvania and asked others to give it publicity.[64] He also wrote to Governor Yates, urging him to broadcast the exposures "until the Presidential election is over" and to use the exposé to stir the Union Leagues to action.[65]

Midwestern Democrats, of course, debunked Sanderson's OAK contentions as they had earlier refuted the KGC tales which Republicans regularly circulated before elections. The Democratic newspaper in St. Louis ridiculed Sanderson. Its partisan editor classed the "astounding disclosures" as pure "humbuggery" and pointed out that Sanderson's exposé was "full of contradictions and inconsistencies." He pointed out, for example, that Sanderson credited Illinois with having "fifty thousand more Knights" (OAK members) than there were "members of the Democratic party."[66] The editor of the New York *Journal of Commerce* viciously criticized both Colonel Sanderson and his exposé:

Some stupid or wily agent, of the radicals out West, has discovered a mare's nest, and sent on recently a long rigmarole about a Northwest conspiracy. The agent of the press in St. Louis, who was victimized by the scamp, deserves sharp censure. A greater lot of trash and falsehood was never concocted for the telegraph wires. It is one of the old "Lincoln dodges" to affect the Chicago Convention [the national Democratic convention] and elevate the falling stock of the administration party; but is so weak an invention as not even to command contempt this hot weather. . . . Will some one ascertain the name of the incorrigible stupid who sent this long story over the wires.[67]

The editor of the Chicago *Times* refused to believe the OAK "fantasy," and resented the implication that he was involved in it or in the "Northwest Conspiracy."[68] The editor of the Detroit *Free Press* added words of disbelief too. He wrote that "the purported Northwestern Conspiracy," discovered by an "obscure Provost-Marshal in St. Louis" was an attempt "to direct public attention from the misdeeds of the party in power."[69] Charles H. Lanphier, editor of the Springfield *Illinois State Register*, gave no credence to the Sanderson "sensation." He wrote long and lively rebuttals, claiming that Republican "rapscallions" had cried "Wolf! Wolf!" so often that respectable persons no longer believed their fanciful tales. Previous Republican-manufactured exposés had evaporated into thin air. Lanphier, like other Democrats, believed that the story was untrue in its entirety and that Republicans were circulating the "revelations" so that the Lincoln administration would have an excuse for introducing martial law to control the elections.[70] But Democratic rebuttal or denial could not stop the OAK and the "Northwestern conspiracy" myths from gaining an acceptance in the stream of history.

As a teller of tall tales, Sanderson had a plucky competitor in Henry B. Carrington, Governor Morton's devoted protégé. The Indiana governor scuttled the efforts of the Secretary of War to assign Carrington to field service and when Carrington was arrested by his immediate superior, General Orlando B. Willcox, for drunkenness and neglect of duty, Governor Morton again helped his aide, having Willcox transferred to another sector, and restoring Carrington to command of the District of Indiana.

Carrington had his work cut out for him. Anxious to refurbish his reputation, he also needed to repay Governor Morton. He wanted Governor Morton to win re-election in the fall as a vindication of Morton's dictatorial policies. Governor Morton was on the spot. The Indiana State Supreme Court, in Democratic hands, was preparing a decision damaging to the Governor. Morton's friends on the court had informed him that a decision, being prepared by Chief Justice Samuel E. Perkins, would invalidate the Governor's financial methods. Furthermore, Vallandigham's surprise return to Ohio upset Governor Morton. Morton wanted Vallandigham rearrested.[71] Prominent Indiana Democrats like H. H. Dodd, Lafe Develin, and Lambdin P. Milligan praised Vallandigham and talked of peace and compromise. Another Morgan raid into Kentucky added to the uneasiness of Morton and his associates.

Carrington rushed to Governor Morton's defense with a series of charges and countercharges, pretending that Vallandigham's return to Ohio and General Morgan's raid into Kentucky were related events, the signal for a Copperhead revolt.[72] Then Carrington charged that the burning of steamers "loaded with Government stores" was a Copperhead activity; Northern "devils" were in league with the rebels. When General Morgan retreated from Kentucky and no "Copperhead uprising" materialized, Carrington worked out an explanation. Morgan's ineffectual timing had upset the plans of the Copperhead conspirators. Carrington linked the names of such Democrats as Dodd, Develin, and William A. Bowles to the "treason plot."[73]

Carrington hired a detective, S. P. Coffin, to find out something about serpentine societies supposedly existent in the Midwest. He also appealed to General Stephen G. Burbridge, who kept a firm hand upon "disloyal elements" in Kentucky, for information and assistance. The name of Judge Joshua Bullitt of Louisville was linked to the activities of midwestern Peace Democrats. Since Judge Bullitt criticized both General Burbridge and President Lincoln and had occasionally called on Indiana Copperheads, Carrington suspected that he was guilty of treasonable activities. General Burbridge, Carrington's political kin, planted a detective in the Democratic party headquarters in Louisville.[74] This spy, named Felix G. Stidger—destined to win fame for his sleuthing—reported periodically to General Burbridge. The gritty Burbridge soon arrested Judge Bullitt "for inviting civil war to Kentucky" and "for favoring the cause of secession," but the jurist was soon released for lack of evidence.

On June 28, 1864, Carrington played his trump card, a document known later as the "Carrington Report." Carrington obtained his information for the extraordinary document from three sources: (*a*) an interchange of knowledge and supposition with Colonel Sanderson of St. Louis, (*b*) information furnished by detectives S. P. Coffin and Felix G. Stidger, and (*c*) rumors, wishful thinking, and political prejudice. Carrington claimed that midwestern Copperheads were planning to overthrow the government through a subversive secret society. He claimed that the Knights of the Golden Circle had changed the name and ritual in late 1863, becoming the Order of American Knights, and that a further reorganization in February of 1864 transformed the OAK into the Sons of Liberty. Carrington reported that Vallandigham was the titular head of the Sons of Liberty and claimed that H. H. Dodd headed the subversive order in Indiana, and that Horace Heffren and William H. Harrison served as "deputy grand commander" and "grand secretary," respectively. He contended that Indiana was divided into four military divisions, each headed by a "major general" and listed Milligan, Bowles, James C. Walker, and Andrew Humphreys as the four "major generals." Carrington claimed that the order was a "secret, oath-bound, despotic, and absolute" society with both a civil and a military division. He added that its members favored states' rights, justified the Southern rebellion, proposed to stop the war, and held "revolution against the Lincoln Administration" both a duty and a right. Carrington contended that the "subversive order" was well organized in twelve states and that Indiana alone had 30,000 active members. In addition, Carrington gave another public airing to the passwords, signs, oaths, degrees, and ritual "associated" with the Sons of Liberty.[75]

The "Carrington Report" was published in full in the Indianapolis *Journal* of June 29, 1864. The editor selected telling headlines: "REBELLION IN THE NORTH!! Extraordinary Disclosure! Val's Plan to Overthrow the Government! Peace Party Plot!" etc.[76] Other Republican editors, in and out of Indiana, picked up the story. The document served its purpose, drawing attention from the adverse decision which the Indiana State Supreme Court gave against Governor Morton and his financing methods. The report justified Morton's dictatorial tactics. It cast a stigma on Indiana Democrats who criticized the Lincoln administration and who charted an independent course for their party. It took some of the wind out of Vallandigham's sails and cast a cloud over the Peace Democrats of Kentucky who had assembled in Louisville to select delegates to the Democratic national convention. Thus Carrington repaid Governor Morton for many favors.

The publication of the "Carrington Report" and Sanderson's OAK exposé helped to give a deathblow to the Sons of Liberty. S. Corning Judd, head of the order in Illinois, let the Sons of Liberty in his state die by default. Judd had presided over the last meeting of the Illinois council in March of 1864, although on two subsequent occasions—"the last on the 5th or 6th of July" —an "indifferent sprinkling of members met."[77] Judd realized that the Carrington and Sanderson exposés had helped to end the order's usefulness.[78] The situation was quite similar in Indiana, although Dodd, creator of the order, was more reluctant to bury the corpse. "Carrington's Report" made the secret passwords and the ritual of the Sons of Liberty public property and the order evaporated into nothingness.[79] It had been as ineffective in Indiana as in Illinois. The hand-picked state officers and district commanders never attended meetings. Dodd, Judd, and Vallandigham were anxious to give the Republicans the impression that the secret Democratic society was extensive and important, so that critics of the Lincoln administration would *"have their Constitutional rights at all hazards."*[80] They pretended that the Sons of Liberty was an agency to effect such guarantees. They wanted a

Democratic bogeyman which would scare Republicans away from trespassing on their constitutional rights. There was a genuine fear that the Lincoln administration would invent "an excuse to declare martial law and invest the election precincts with bayonets sufficient to patrol the elections as they had done in other states," notably in nearby Kentucky.[81]

A Democratic secret society, though its aims were honorable, could be very vulnerable. War hysteria readily turns a partisan vine into poison ivy. An administration which can control public opinion readily blackens the reputation of its critics. Democratic secret societies could not keep their secrets. It was easy for Republican governors or army officers to honeycomb such secret societies with spies, as Judd and Joseph J. Bingham, Democratic chieftain and editor of the Indianapolis *State Sentinel,* soon realized. Detectives and agents swarmed over the Midwest; some were in the employ of provost marshals, others were hired by district commanders, or governors, or Washington officials. They hunted for elusive "Sons" or "Knights" in all corners of the country, even in Canada. Often the agents stepped on one another's toes, and sometimes they initiated one another into the dark-lantern society. In Indianapolis, for example, one government agent revealed "the secrets" to another soon after he had secured them from a third.[82] Democrats like Dodd and Judd pretended that the Sons of Liberty existed; the detectives and agents did most of the initiating. The ephemeral society, naturally, died ignobly after Carrington and Sanderson published their exposés.

Carrington had another opportunity in the fall of 1864 to repay Governor Morton for past favors. Morton desperately needed help because the October state elections were approaching. Morton sought re-election and needed a Republican-dominated legislature. He could interpret his re-election as popular indorsement of his four-year "reign," and a Republican-dominated legislature could indemnify his unconstitutional acts and negate several anti-Morton decisions of the state Supreme Court. The political forecast, however, was not favorable for Republicanism.

President Lincoln could claim no telling victories on the military front. In fact, there seemed to be a public reaction to the slaughter before Richmond. The Copperhead cry of "Peace and Compromise" again proved popular. This time Morton needed more than a paper exposé; arrests and treason trials could be more convincing.

Morton asked for the arrest of leading members of the Sons of Liberty. "The Governor," Carrington later wrote, "urged the arrest of the Indiana members as essential to the success of the National cause in the autumn elections."[83] But General Heintzelman questioned the validity of the limited evidence at hand. Heintzelman, therefore, refused to sanction the arrest of Dodd and other leading Democrats associated with the Sons of Liberty, although he did acquiesce in General Burbridge's request to place Judge Joshua F. Bullitt of Louisville behind bars.[84]

Carrington doubled his efforts to link leading Democrats to treason. He borrowed Felix G. Stidger as a detective, having the former clerk transferred to his employ from General Burbridge's staff. Stidger started out as secretary of the Lousville Democratic club and there gained the confidence of Judge Bullitt. Stidger pretended that the meetings of Judge Bullitt's political junta were really meetings of the Golden Circle.[85] Somewhere he picked up the rumor that Captain Thomas H. Hines, one of General John Morgan's raiders, was a member of Vallandigham's staff, and Stidger faithfully reported that rumor as a fact.[86] A trip into several Indiana communities failed to turn up any interesting information. Stidger could find no tangible evidence of treason, nor any secrets of the subversive society he sought to expose. After Stidger came upon a copy of the "Carrington Report" of June 28, 1864, and a copy of the Sanderson exposé of July 27, 1864, the quality of his revelations improved. He culled generously from both and incorporated their suppositions into his own reports. An interview with Colonel Carrington laid down the direction Stidger would go.[87] Stidger's reports now took on the appearance of authenticity. They contained "damaging evidence," and Stidger wrote at length.

While Stidger made the acquaintance of Indiana Democrats, Carrington collected rumors as evidence. There were rumors that Vallandigham and his followers would take the upper Mississippi Valley by force. There were rumors that some prominent midwestern Democrats were on General Morgan's payroll. There were reports that Canadian-based rebels planned to free Confederate prisoners in Northern prisons.[88] One of the more convincing storytellers used the name of Green B. Smith; he was later proved to be a parolee and scoundrel. Smith's revelations were published in the Cincinnati *Gazette,* and attracted the attention of Carrington. Smith claimed that he was an officer of a subversive society dedicated to bringing civil war to the Midwest. He claimed that the subversive society had 90,000 members in Indiana. No one knows the price Green B. Smith received for his fairy tale. The Democratic editor of the Indianapolis *State Sentinel* called the revelation a humbug—a Munchausen tale—and Green B. Smith "a black liar."[89] Governor Morton, on the other hand, pointed to Smith's exposé as proof that treason ran rampant in Indiana. Having filed Smith's revelation on his desk, Carrington looked elsewhere for evidence. A search of Daniel Voorhees' office turned up a batch of evidence—rituals and other material of the Sons of Liberty.[90]

While Carrington tried to unravel the Sons of Liberty puzzle, Dodd was also busy. He and his friends banded together to build a new order on the foundations of the old. They christened their new society the "Order of American Cincinnatus," and viewed it as "a defensive organization" to repel force with force. They established the order "to maintain the Constitution and the laws of the United States in their purity."[91] If the Lincoln administration used arms at the polls, the members of the Cincinnatus would fight for their rights. Dodd pretended that most of the officers in the defunct Sons of Liberty held similar posts in the new organization.

On the evening of August 6, 1864, at a "council meeting" of the Order of the American Cincinnatus, Dodd shocked the assembled few with the question of sponsoring open resistance to the programs of Governor Morton and President Lincoln. Those present pronounced the proposition of the self-styled grand commander to be monstrous[92] and immediately set to work to prevent Dodd from carrying out "any ambitions or criminal projects of his own." They confided their concern to Joseph J. Bingham, editor of the Indianapolis *State Sentinel* and chairman of the Democratic state central committee.[93] Bingham took immediate steps to bury Dodd's scheme, for the editor knew that Dodd had furnished Governor Morton with enough dynamite to blast the Democratic party into slivers. Bingham called a special meeting of Indianapolis Democratic leaders who convinced Dodd to discard his plan. At a special meeting of the Democratic state central committee on August 11, Dodd again gave assurances that his project had been shelved. The membership agreed that an address to the people, urging them not to resist the draft and to seek redress at the polls, should be immediately prepared and circulated.[94] "To all these acts," wrote one of the Democratic members, "Dodd was made a party and expressed himself as satisfied."[95]

Bingham and other Democratic leaders breathed a sigh of relief when the Dodd "scheme" was safely shelved. Yet they remained uneasy, for in trying to protect the welfare of their party they were "hiding" a treasonable proposition. They were playing with loaded dice. If Dodd's suggestion came to light, all of them would be implicated. They were hiding a treasonable suggestion which they should have exposed. Someone in the inner Democratic council, inadvertently or otherwise, relayed the Dodd episode to Governor Morton.[96] The astute governor, a crass opportunist, realized that he had obtained information that could injure the Democratic party and brighten his own political future.

Governor Morton and Carrington again asked for Dodd's arrest. Carrington deluged his military superior, General Heintzelman, with letters intimating that Indiana rested upon a volcano, that prominent Democrats were guilty of a secret society conspiracy, and that an armed uprising was scheduled for August 16, 1864. General Heintzelman feared that a wave of arbitrary arrests might bring on an open revolt and so was reluctant to arrest Dodd and some of the state's leading Democrats unless the evidence was reliable and conclusive.[97] Carrington and Morton arranged to watch Dodd's every move, hoping that he would give them an excuse to take definite action.

The arrival of several boxes of arms and ammunition, addressed to Dodd's partner in a publishing firm, gave federal officials the looked-for excuse. They raided Dodd's premises and made several arrests.[98] Dodd was out of town at the time of the raid and believed to be in New York City, from whence the arms shipment had come.[99]

Republican newspapers told the story of seizing "material concerning the Sons of Liberty," ammunition, and four hundred revolvers in boxes labeled "tracts." They linked the Democratic party to the secret society "conspiracy."[100] Such prominent Democrats as Joseph J. Bingham and Joseph Ristine, state auditor, were charged with membership in the Sons of Liberty and were linked to the "conspiracy." "The signs of revolution have been visible about us for many months," wrote the editor of the Indianapolis *Journal,* "and today we find ourselves standing on its very brink."[101] The raiders claimed that they had obtained the membership rolls of the Sons of Liberty, the ritual and the grand seal of the order, a "strange banner," and a lot of "treasonable correspondence."[102]

Governor Morton and Republican strategists sponsored an indignation meeting the next day. Morton gave the principal address. Again he pictured himself as patriotism personified. He hammered home the message that the turn of events substantiated his oft-made charges of domestic treason. He bore down heavily on the Democratic leadership, claiming Dodd was but their tool. "It is all one thing to Jeff Davis," he shouted, "whether he shall fall by means of a defeat at the coming elections or by the overthrow of the Union armies in the field."[103]

Most of the prominent Indianapolis Democrats were in Chicago, attending their party's national convention. Dodd himself was there, as a delegate from Indiana. When Dodd did return to Indianapolis after the Chicago convention, he was immediately arrested and put behind bars.

Dodd registered his protests and denials through the columns of the Indianapolis *State Sentinel*.[104] He denied most of Carrington's allegations and explained many of the mysteries surrounding the seized materials. The "roll of members of the Sons of Liberty" proved to be the membership list of the Marion County Democratic Club.[105] The "roll of 400 rebel prisoners," supposedly held in Camp Morton near Indianapolis, turned out to be a souvenir of one Democrat's military service. He once had charge of some Confederate prisoners captured at Fort Donelson. The "strange banner" seized in Dodd's office turned out to be a regimental banner captured by a Republican colonel on a Civil War battlefield and intrusted to Dodd for safekeeping.[106] The "treasonable correspondence" contained no hint of disloyalty or of a conspiracy, and the publication of excerpts failed to convince the skeptics who had learned to mistrust Carrington.

"We can find more treason in speeches in Congress, some by Republicans," opined the editor of the Louisville *Democrat*, "than there is to be found in these productions."[107] John C. Walker, an old-line Democrat who had feuded with Governor Morton, endeavored to help Dodd out of his dilemma. Walker, serving in New York City as a state agent of Indiana, claimed ownership of the confiscated revolvers. He wrote to Governor Morton, asking him to return the confiscated arms and ammunition and denying having violated any law.[108]

The wanton charges which Carrington made and to which Morton gave publicity cast a dark cloud over the Democratic party in Indiana. Charges of treason and conspiracy emanated from a thousand Republican lips. Democrats could not successfully explain away the charges and the insinuations against Dodd and some party leaders. Joseph E. McDonald, Democratic nominee for the governor's post, was embarrassed. Public opinion turned against the Democrats. "The exposure of the Sons of Liberty," wrote Morton's adjutant general, "is tearing the ranks of the Democracy all to flinders. McClellan stock is not quoted at all. McDonald stock is fast going down."[109]

Since Governor Morton feared that a civil trial might fail to bring conviction, he wanted Dodd tried before a military commission. He also wanted the trial to take place before the important state elections of October, 1864. General Alvin P. Hovey, a Republican-minded general and a friend of Governor Morton, was imported as military commander of the District of Indiana to direct the trial of the "conspirators." General Hovey had stumped the state for Morton's party in the elections of 1862. A couple of days before the military court was to be convened, Hovey assured a Republican assemblage that the Democrats would not carry the elections if he could help it.[110] General Hovey was as good as his word. He set the wheels of the court-martial in motion two weeks before the October elections.

In vain did Democrats try to discredit the summary proceedings. "Why introduce witnesses in prosecution only, and no rebuttal testimony?" asked one of Dodd's friends.[111] The judge advocate contributed leading questions in an effort to parlay the rumors, hearsay, and suppositions into evidence. One witness unwittingly admitted that a government agent had promised him immunity from the draft if he would testify. Felix G. Stidger, self-styled "the Spy Complete" and the chief witness of the prosecution, admitted getting his price in order to appear on the stand. Stidger said that he sought to be "provided with a sufficiency to live hereafter." He received $14,000 for his detective services.[112]

Dr. D. T. Yeakel, a reputable Indianapolis dentist who belonged to the Order of the American Cincinnatus, regarded the evidence presented at the military proceedings as a maze of conjecture and contradiction. He believed that Governor Morton instituted them in order to manufacture political capital. "These trials," he wrote, "are a mockery and a sham, for base political purposes, so conducted as to conceal their own base objects and ignominy, and to prejudice the light of all parties against the Democratic party and the Order [of the American Cincinnatus]."[113] Dr. Yeakel noticed that the government's witnesses did not know the difference between the Knights of the Golden Circle, the Order of American Knights, and the Sons of Liberty. They used the names interchangeably and thought all were cut from the same cloth. Even Stidger didn't know anything about the Order of the American Cincinnatus. He still talked about the Sons of Liberty as if it were an active rather than a discarded society. Dr. Yeakel realized that Morton's strategy was to link treason to Dodd, link Dodd to the Sons of Liberty, and link the Sons of Liberty to the Democratic party. Small wonder then, that Dr. Yeakel viewed the military proceedings as an effort to perpetrate a falsehood and to develop treason as a campaign issue.[114]

When the military trial of Dodd had gone into its eleventh day —four days before the state elections of October 11—Dodd mysteriously disappeared. The word spread that he had fled to Canada. Governor Morton and General Hovey interpreted the flight as an admission of guilt. The judge advocate moved the court to proceed at once to judgment in the prisoner's absence and the military commission convicted Dodd on all the charges and specifications. The commission sentenced him to be hanged at such time and place as the commanding general of the district should designate.[115]

Governor Morton needed more meat for his political repast. General Hovey, therefore, arrested six more prominent Democrats: Joseph J. Bingham, Lambdin P. Milligan, Dr. William A. Bowles, Horace Heffren, Andrew Humphreys, and Stephen Horsey. Governor Morton, the Union Leagues, and Republican leaders campaigned vigorously on their "anti-conspiracy" issue. The election turned into a decisive victory for the Republicans.

The new trials were begun in late October, intended to grind grist for the political campaign preceding the presidential election of November 7. They continued into early December. Joseph J. Bingham and Horace Heffren were soon freed; no charges ever were filed against the editor of the Indianapolis *State Sentinel*. The military commission found the four other principals guilty of the various charges brought against them. Milligan, Bowles, and Horsey were sentenced to be hanged, and Humphreys was ordered imprisoned at hard labor. Eventually each of the four won reprieve and freedom, partially because their guilt was in question and partially because political expediency so dictated. "From the political point of view," wrote a Republican adviser and prophet, "it can do our party no good to shed more blood; but on the contrary if we are merciful, the child is not yet born who will see the defeat of the Republican party."[116]

Morton's success in exposing a "conspiracy" and using the exposition effectively to win the October elections attracted the interest of Illinois Republicans. On the eve of the November elections, Illinois Republicans also uncovered a "conspiracy."

The central figure in the Illinois exposé, which developed the myth of a Camp Douglas "conspiracy," was a strange character named I(saiah) Winslow Ayer. He had a shady reputation and a shadowy past.[117] He claimed to be a graduate of Harvard University and to hold two diplomas from the Eclectic Medical College of Cincinnati. Later evidence proved him to be both liar and imposter. Ayer hunted up Congressman Isaac N. Arnold and tried to interest him in "a most fearful conspiracy." Ayer claimed he held the "key" which would "unlock" the conspiracy, if he were paid generously as a detective. Congressman Arnold knew that Ayer was unreliable and believed that no such conspiracy existed. Arnold therefore ignored Ayer's pleas. Ayer found someone in the office of the Chicago *Tribune* who saw the possibilities of an exposé, and that unknown patron directed Ayer to write to Governor Richard Yates.[118] Ayer, who expected to collect $5,000 for his sleuthing, assured Governor Yates that he could explode a "gigantic scheme of treason to aid Southern Rebels, to create a further secession and to establish a Northwestern Confederacy, and to carry the election by arms."[119]

Governor Yates and Joseph K. C. Forrest, who had returned to Illinois to aid in the election campaign, secured an agent's appointment for Dr. Ayer, and the imposter hurried off to Chicago to fulfil his promises. He posed as a pro-Southern fugitive from Kentucky, doing his best to convince some Chicago Copperheads that he possessed their political views. He tried, unsuccessfully, to establish a castle of the Sons of Liberty in Chicago but could find no takers. He then organized an anti-Lincoln club, and he set

the pace in denouncing the government and in talking up treasonable projects. He encouraged the collection of a cache of arms,
adding several more "detectives" to his staff, who became the
anti-government core in Ayer's secret club.

Ayer tried to trap two well-known Democrats, Judge Buckner
S. Morris and S. Corning Judd. Judd, former head of the Sons of
Liberty in Illinois, had been nominated to run for lieutenant-
governor against the Republican nominee. An Ayer-appointed
agent pretended that he was an escaped Confederate prisoner from
Camp Douglas and he begged Judd to give him food, money, or
shelter. Judd expressed indignation and threatened to call the
authorities. Having failed to frame Judd and Morris, Ayer looked
for smaller fish, talking up a "Camp Douglas Conspiracy" to co-
operate with Confederates in Canada in freeing rebel prisoners
confined in a camp outside of Chicago.[120]

Some Confederate agents based in Canada took seriously the
charges of a "Northwest Confederacy" made by such Republicans
as Governor Morton and Colonel Sanderson. These agents mistook
the vocal protests of midwestern Copperheads for disloyalty. They
dreamed of sowing the seeds of rebellion and talked of freeing
prisoners wherever they might be held. Johnson's Island and
Camp Douglas were two of the favorite targets of their schemes.
Mystery still surrounds their activities. They seem to have burned
their fingers. In postwar years, however, they brought their claims
in line with those of the exposés that Republicans concocted for
political ends.[121]

On the eve of the November elections, the Chicago *Tribune*
exposed the "Camp Douglas Conspiracy." A series of arrests
was made to give substance to the *Tribune*'s claims. Judge Morris
was seized on the afternoon of November 6 and taken to Camp
Douglas so that no civil action to effect his release could be under-
taken.[122] That evening Dr. Ayer called a meeting of his "club"
and advocated "rescue by violence" and tried to lead others into
the trap he had set.[123] The next day Colonel Benjamin J. Sweet,
commandant at Camp Douglas, made several more arrests. The

principals included Charles Walsh, who had sold some sugar to the Confederacy.[124] Several were reported to be Confederate agents.[125]

Only the credulous accepted the *Tribune* exposé at face value. It was a revelation made possible by the perfidious practices of Dr. Ayer, the co-operation of Colonel Sweet, and the machinations of several *Tribune* employees. Democrats, of course, threw cold water on the Republican coals. The editor of the Detroit *Free Press* thought the story "too ridiculous to be given a moment's credit."[126] The editor of the Louisville *Democrat* wondered how many Republican greenbacks were spent "to make" the "Camp Douglas Conspiracy." "Preposterous as it is," wrote the skeptical editor, "there are fools enough to believe it."[127] Even the editor of the conservative Chicago *Post* refused to buy the fairy tale.[128] Even respectable Republicans rejected the Camp Douglas Conspiracy story; Lincoln, for example, expressed disbelief.[129]

The principals arrested for complicity in the "Camp Douglas Conspiracy" were transported to Cincinnati for a trial before a military commission. On January 11, 1865, the military commission began to hear the evidence and Judd was called before the court to answer the questions about the Sons of Liberty, which authorities tried to link to the "Camp Douglas Conspiracy." Judd insisted that most of the evidence which the prosecution's witnesses had given was mere conjecture—"*suppositions* and *understandings* and *guesses* and *loose generalities*."[130] He defended the objectives of the organization which he once headed in Illnois. "We only desired," he said, "to act on the defensive under the constitution and the law."[131] In a letter to Lincoln, Judd reported that "such a matter as to attempt to release rebel prisoners at Camp Douglas or elsewhere . . . was never proposed."[132] Vallandigham also tried to vindicate himself and to defend the Sons of Liberty before the Cincinnati military tribunal. He told the panel of military officers that the Sons of Liberty was a mutual protection society interested in safeguarding civil liberties and inherent rights. He said its purposes were to elect Democrats to office and to counteract the activities of the Union Leagues. He emphasized that he had spoken publicly of the honorable objectives of the Sons of Liberty.[133]

Of the seven brought to trial at Cincinnati, only three were found guilty by the military commission. The three guilty ones were neither prominent Democrats nor well-known individuals. They were led into the web by Ayer. Then Dr. Ayer collected his thirty pieces of silver and set about writing a vindication of his questionable acts. He entitled his fabulous story "The Great Northwest Conspiracy in All Its Startling Details. . . ." Truly, Dr. Ayer contributed considerably to the building of the great Civil War myth of conspiracies and subversive secret societies.[134]

Although the hands of midwestern politicos gave shape to and created the secret society scarecrow, it took a Washingtonian to dress the phantom in finery and add the element of respectability. Under pressure of governors like Yates, Morton, and Andrew G. Curtain—Colonel Sanderson's patron—of Pennsylvania, Lincoln's Secretary of War instructed Judge Advocate General Holt to prepare an official report on the serpentine societies. The Judge Advocate General accepted the assignment and, in turn, called upon Colonel Sanderson, Brigadier General Carrington, and Lafayette C. Baker, the provost marshal of the War Department, to contribute evidence and information. Baker promptly responded with a brief report which added little to the hearsay concerning the Knights of the Golden Circle and the Sons of Liberty.[135] Both Carrington and Sanderson, however, procrastinated, arousing some resentment in Washington circles. Carrington, having but little documentary evidence, begged his chief detective to give his assistance and permitted Washington's deadlines to pass. Finally, after some prodding by the Secretary of War, Carrington explained the purpose and the "activities" of the Sons of Liberty.[136] The Judge Advocate General found it necessary to take a hurried trip to St. Louis to pick up the basketful of evidence and materials which Sanderson had collected.

At his desk in Washington, the Judge Advocate General studied and sifted the confusing and contradictory reports. He noticed that the three reports differed as to the names of the secret societies— the Knights of the Golden Circle, the Order of American Knights, and the Sons of Liberty—yet all listed the same members and officers as principals. Sanderson's material seemed most reliable,[137] and in the end the Judge Advocate General relied on the St. Louis data almost entirely.

Judge Advocate General Holt finished his 14,000-word report early in October and turned it over to his superior.[138] The "Holt Report" depicted the Copperhead secret societies as treasonable in nature, extensive in membership, and revolutionary in character. Holt claimed that the Order of American Knights was the descendant of the Knights of the Golden Circle and that in some areas the Order of American Knights had turned into the Sons of Liberty. He claimed that Vallandigham commanded the northern division of the subversive society and that General Sterling Price, a Confederate commander in the trans-Mississippi sector, commanded the southern half. Holt estimated the total northern membership at half a million and even assigned most midwestern states a quota: Indiana, 75,000 to 125,000; Illinois, 100,000 to 140,000; Ohio 40,000 to 70,000; Missouri, 20,000 to 40,000; and Michigan, 20,000. Holt listed eleven "specific purposes and operations" of the order: (1) aiding soldiers to desert and harboring and protecting deserters, (2) discouraging enlistments and resisting the draft, (3) circulating disloyal and treasonable publications, (4) communicating with and giving intelligence to the enemy, (5) aiding the enemy by recruiting for them, or assisting them to recruit, within Federal lines, (6) furnishing the rebels with arms, ammunition, etc., (7) co-operating with the enemy in raids and invasions, (8) destroying government property, (9) destroying personal property and persecuting loyal men, (10) assassinating and murdering, and (11) establishing a northwestern confederacy.

Holt blamed the Charleston, Illinois, riots on secret society members, credited the Illinois membership with being "unusually well armed," and linked the subversive societies to the peace movement. He repeated the legend of the boat-burning conspiracy. He closed the report with a literary flourish: "Judea produced but one Judas Iscariot, and Rome, from the sinks of her demoralization, produced but one Cataline; and yet, as events prove, there has arisen in our land an entire brood of traitors, all animated by the same parricidal spirit, and all struggling with the same ruthless malignity for the dismemberment of the Union."[139]

Holt's handiwork turned into an effective piece of campaign propaganda. It was rushed to the printers and emerged as a pamphlet entitled, *Report of the Judge Advocate General on the Order of American Knights alias the Sons of Liberty: A Western Conspiracy in Aid of the Southern Rebellion.*[140] Republican congressmen circulated the pamphlet in their districts and the Republican congressional election committee helped to distribute the document.[141] The Union Leagues, too, distributed Holt's report and reported that it was an effective medium for converting the unwary.[142]

Dissenting Democrats, meanwhile, gave vent to their wrath upon Judge Advocate General Holt and his "partisan electioneering document."[143] Editor Charles H. Lanphier of the Springfield *Illinois State Register* called Holt "a deliberate and atrocious liar" and "a modern Titus Oates." He claimed the report was no more than "a conglomeration of falsehoods"—"a precious pottage cooked in the cauldron of his imagination." He suggested that Holt was anxious for an appointment to the U.S. Supreme Court and that the "Report" was a bid for a judgeship.[144] Editor Henry N. Walker of the Detroit *Free Press* was as vindictive as Lanphier. Walker labeled Holt's handiwork "a foolish and wicked report" and he wrote that Holt had stamped himself as "a man who is ready to commit any folly to please his employer."[145] Some Democrats advanced the thesis that the "Report" was concocted to serve as an excuse for the introduction of martial law in the Midwest so that the Republicans could screen voters and elect their candidates.[146] Democrats generally regarded the "Holt Report" as a political document and questioned Republican campaign techniques.

Vallandigham, maligned by Holt in the "Report," denounced the document. "I have only to say that, as far as I am concerned," he wrote, "they [the charges] are absolute falsehoods and fabrications from beginning to end. They are false in the aggregate and they are false in detail."[147] Phineas C. Wright, linked with the Order of American Knights and with treason in "Holt's Report," also sought to vindicate himself. From his cell in Fort Lafayette he begged for a chance to clear his name and brush away the conspiracy web which Holt had woven. "You have," he wrote to the Judge Advocate General, "brought me before the public in a character that is not *mine*. In the name of Justice let me be heard and then let that Public judge me."[148] Wright wanted a jury trial, but he could not get a hearing from any federal official. Discouraged, he wrote to a friend:

Of these matters which have been ventilated in Indiana, Illinois, and Missouri, I know nothing whatever save through the public press. I deny that the organization with which I am connected has had any part in plots or conspiracies. Why then am I denied the opportunity to exculpate myself?[149]

Republican strategists were not interested in hearing the other side of the OAK story. By keeping Wright in Fort Lafayette and by keeping George W. Bickley in Fort Warren, the authorities prevented the prisoners from exploding the subversive society myth.

The "Holt Report" contributed to the re-election of Lincoln. "I supposed," wrote a friend of the Judge Advocate General, "[that] the discovery of the conspiracy will go far to accounting for the great majority with which the West voted for the Union."[150]

The Republican-constructed myths about Copperhead secret societies served their purposes well. It was a political apparition which appeared on the eve of elections. It was a figment of Republican imagination. Lincoln's supporters had succeeded in stigmatizing the opposition party, and at the same time they made a contribution to American mythology.

VII

The Collapse
of Copperheadism

VALLANDIGHAM'S DEFEAT in the October, 1863, gubernatorial race in Ohio showed how the political winds were blowing. By 1864 the Republican breeze had turned into a hurricane and midwestern Copperheadism bowed before its force. Unable to gain the support of the public, some Copperheads became more bitter and outspoken.

Lincoln's growing popularity with the masses hampered the Copperhead program. The turning of the military tide at Gettysburg and Vicksburg gave the administration an edge over its opposition. Reasonable men knew that the military conflict would end in a Northern victory, as Federal troops slowly strangled the Confederacy. Bloody battles might occur before Richmond and Atlanta, but time favored the side with more manpower, production, and money.

Disorganization in Democratic ranks also helped the Republicans. The Democrats were split and each faction blamed the other for the party's ineptness. Republican politicians added to Democratic discomfort, devising political stratagems which undermined Copperheadism. The Republicans stirred up nationalism and claimed patriotism as their exclusive property. They stigmatized the opposition and linked the Democratic party to treason. Their control of the governorships in midwestern states and their control of the White House and Congress stacked the cards against their critics. Sweeping Republican election victories in the October and November elections of 1864 proved that Republicans were efficient and Republicanism popular. Copperheadism had receded before the tide.

The peace movement suffered a similar fate in 1864. It failed to capture the support of the public and helped divide the party of the opposition. Under the leadership of Alexander Long and Vallandigham the movement slowly died.

The emergence of an active opposition party during the Civil War posed a threat to the Republican leadership. Republican strategists were interested in getting the Democrats to fight for the Union, but they did not want them to dictate policy.[1] The majority-party leaders were anxious to win elections and remain in the driver's seat; for only by directing the government could they hope to achieve their objectives. Professional politicians are always interested in party welfare, and some Republicans were equally interested in quashing Copperheadism and winning the war.

To stay in control of affairs the Republicans employed a variety of tactics, some new to the American scene. They organized and subsidized the Union party movement and organized the Union Leagues. They developed a system of soldier-voting-in-the-field, which they controlled. They recruited organized religion and conducted an effective and extensive propaganda campaign. They used arbitrary arrests, intimidation, and public opinion to advantage and were in a position to back up their program with power, patronage, and money. War prosperity aided the administration throughout 1864, and Copperheadism naturally gave way. Republican measures, as well as Copperhead errors, shoved the opposition party to the brink of defeat.

The Union party movement served the Lincoln administration well. The earliest "War meetings" or "Union meetings" saw both Democrats and Republicans sharing the speechmaking and the cheering. As the fall elections of 1861 approached, the Republican strategists usurped the "Union" label for their party conventions and pulled the strings backstage.[2] Partisan Democrats cautioned their membership not to fall into the Republican trap. "They are trying to grease us," wrote an Illinois Democrat, "and swallow us."[3]

Governor Oliver P. Morton made the Union party movement in Indiana a personal possession. The editor of the Indianapolis *Journal*, Morton's mouthpiece, invited all "loyal" Democrats to join the "great Union organization." "It will be time enough to revive the Republican and Democratic parties," wrote that editor, "when we know that we have a government."[4] But a leading spokesman for Indiana Democrats warned his party's members against the Republican cloven foot and the "fake disguise":

The Republicans, big and little, are singing a common song, pitched to the same key and set to the same tune, and it is "give up party to save the Government." There is quite a show of patriotism in those loud professions of "no partyism," but unfortunately it is only skin deep, not deep enough at any rate to conceal the motives which lay at the bottom of the movement. It will be noticed that all their appeals are made to Democrats. . . . this "no party" business is a one-sided game, in which the Democrats are asked to surrender everything, and the Republicans do not propose to yield anything.[5]

Although most partisan Democrats argued against the Union party movement, nationalism and patriotism were Republican allies. The Union-party strategy helped save Ohio and Wisconsin for Lincoln's party in 1861. In Ohio the stratagem put David Tod in the executive mansion and gave Republicans control of both houses of the state legislature. In Wisconsin, "where the Republican cat was well concealed under the Union meal," the Republicans learned an invaluable political lesson.[6]

In later years Republicans followed a rule of thumb. In those states where they were firmly in the saddle, they retained their party name and organization.[7] In those states where the political contests were in doubt, the Republican organization indorsed the Union party or "fusion" movement. Timothy O. Howe, U.S. senator from Wisconsin, candidly asked his Republican brethren to hide behind the Union party label in order to get more votes.

He suggested that Republicans adopt "Union and Administration" as their battle-cry. He argued that it was politically expedient to seek support from Democrats and warned his party's leaders that Republicanism was associated in the public mind with abolitionism and Know-Nothingism. The Union party label could serve the party well.[8]

The Union party "device" served the Republican party in two notable cases in the later war years. Ohio Republicans resurrected the Union movement to turn back Vallandigham's political bid in October of 1863. There was too much at stake to risk a purely partisan contest. Republicans arranged for a "Union Convention" and used the Union party label with good effect. To give some substance to their bipartisan claims they named an ex-Democrat, John Brough, to head the Union ticket. The strategy paid dividends. Democrats who disagreed with Vallandigham's extreme stand could give support to a Union ticket; it would have been bitter medicine to accept a straight Republican set of candidates.

Lincoln's supporters again turned to fusion in 1864. In some states they sponsored "Union party" conventions even though all of the participants were Republicans. They also used "Unionism" on the national level. They organized the "National Union Convention" and pretended they had shelved partisanship. At the Baltimore convention they organized the "National Union party" and named ex-Democrat Andrew Johnson as Lincoln's running mate on the fusion ticket. They hoped that Johnson's name on the ticket would attract the attention and votes of some Democrats. But zealous Democratic workers warned the public that the wolf had donned grandmother's bonnet. The editor of the Detroit *Free Press,* for example, warned his readers that the "Union party label" was

merely a cloak with which they hope to hide past wickedness and corruption from the eyes of the people. It is in reality like stealing the livery of heaven to serve the devil in. . . . For that party is in no sense entitled to the name "Union." Its leaders have for years advocated disunion. . . . They might appropriately be styled abolitionists, destructives, obliterationists, disunionists, amalgamationists. . . . That modesty which has led them to arrogate to themselves all the honesty, virtue and patriotism of the country, may have a little to do with claiming all the unionism too.[9]

Despite Democratic protests the stratagem of "unionism" helped the Republicans stay in power. It was a political lever which put the Democrats at a disadvantage and helped to discredit Copperheadism.

Republican-sponsored Union Leagues or Loyal Leagues were even more effective in checking Copperheadism than the Union-party stratagem. The Union Leagues became an effective and secret arm of the Republican party. Democratic denunciation of the Union League movement attests to its effectual usage.

The roots of the Union League movement in the Midwest extended into eastern Tennessee. Patriots or pro-Union men countered the pro-secession agitation by organizing a secret society which pre-empted the name "Union League." The success of the Union Leagues in Tennessee and Kentucky and the emigration of some Union League members to Illinois and Indiana gave the movement a start north of the Ohio River. Republican politicians recognized the Union Leagues as potential tools, especially after the April elections of 1862 indicated a Democratic trend. Illinois Republicans set up a state-wide organization in the last half of 1862, and Joseph Medill, the influential editor of the Chicago *Tribune*, served as chairman of the "executive committee." Illinois Republicans also launched a "Union League of America."[10] Indiana Republicans adopted the Union Leagues as an adjunct of their party, but they shaped the instrument to suit their tastes. The state was divided into two halves, with each section having its own organization, including a cryptographic alphabet.[11]

About the same time, an eastern Union League emerged.[12] President Lincoln favored the creation of a national Union League "to afford an effective framework to the political forces which were sustaining the Administration."[13] Lincoln, of course, wanted an organization he could control, not one that would become an instrument of the Radical Republicans. A coterie of Lincoln's friends established a "Grand Council" in the summer of 1862, handpicking the twelve members of the executive committee. With army contractors furnishing the funds, the League spread "with feverish activity all over the North."[14]

The Union Leagues were too new and too skeletal in organization to check the Copperhead tide in the October and November elections of 1862. But such astute midwestern politicians as Morton and Yates recognized the possibilities. After the elections of 1862, Morton and Yates gave the Leagues their personal blessing and took steps to make them a more effective political instrument.[15] Governors Morton and Yates visualized the Union Leagues as serving three purposes: (*a*) under the guise of nonpartisanship they could serve as an "educative agency" for "multitudes of loyal Democrats," (*b*) they could counteract the work of the Copperhead legislatures in session in Indiana and Illinois, and (*c*) they might become military organizations, prepared for "domestic emergencies."[16]

Backed by governors and patronage, the Union Leagues grew in size and influence. The organization which Joseph Medill directed had 404 councils in fifty-two Illinois counties by April of 1863.[17] Organizations and state councils were established in every midwestern state. The revitalized Union Leagues were "tested" in the April, 1863, elections. Republicans were jubilant. "Our *Union* organization is perfect," wrote an Iowa member, "and we have good reason to be proud of the result of our first effort."[18]

Rooted in Republicanism and patriotism, the Union Leagues flourished. The "floating portion" of the population fell under their spell. The council rooms were used to "educate" citizens and win support for the administration. Union Leaguers circulated campaign propaganda as patriotic literature. "You can hardly go into a public office or store," wrote a Democratic dissenter, "but you will see such documents on the tables, counters, and even *posted* up on billboards."[19]

Copperheads realized that the Union Leagues were effective antidotes to their efforts to win the support of the populace. They

labeled the Union Leagues a "Republican K. G. C. organization"
and they pretended that the letters "U. L. A." stood for "Uncle
Lincoln's Asses."[20] They misstated the objectives of the Leagues
in an effort to discredit them. The partisan editor of the Hamilton *True Telegraph* insisted that the Union Leagues were really
a new form for "old Know-Nothingism." "They hope to overthrow the institution of slavery," wrote that unabashed editor,
"and then turn their attention to the Irish and Germans, with the
hope of disfranchising them."[21] Democratic spokesmen begged
party members to boycott the Union Leagues. "It is not necessary for Democrats," wrote Charles H. Lanphier of the *Illinois
State Register*, "to prove their loyalty, to herd with abolitionists
who, under cover of sophomoric truisms, would hide their sinister
purposes."[22]

Despite Democratic protests, the Union Leagues grew in size
and number and became more effective with each passing month,
helping Republicans to win the fall elections of 1863 and to re-
elect Lincoln in 1864. The Leagues undermined Copperheadism
effectively and helped check the opposition party in the last two
years of the war.[23]

When Republican strategists established the Un-
ion party and the Union Leagues to attract independent voters,
they also organized a propaganda campaign to control public
opinion. That propaganda campaign was waged mainly through
"publication societies." A Boston merchant-financier directed the
establishment of the New England Loyal Publication Society in
1863, and New York unionists soon thereafter set up the Loyal
Publication Society of New York. Both agencies had ample
funds, able writers, and imaginative secretaries. They had patriotism on their side and enjoyed the blessings of the Lincoln administration. They waged a pamphlet war against the Copperheads. One tract, entitled *The Echo from the Army*, depicted
Copperhead views in a treasonable light. Another pamphlet, *No
Party Now but All for One Country*, espoused the thesis that the
Lincoln administration and the government were one and the

same. Several pamphlets borrowed heavily from Judge Advocate General Holt's report on subversive secret societies.[24]

The New York "publication society" printed nearly a million copies of ninety different pamphlets. Its Boston counterpart was equally active and effective. The Boston-based agency distributed tracts and pamphlets to 649 Union Leagues, 474 ladies' associations, 744 newspaper editors, 21,160 private individuals, and to the reading rooms maintained in army posts and in hospitals. Both the New York and Boston "publication societies" used the Union Leagues to distribute their pamphlets. The "publication societies" helped convince the public that Republican views were the true views. They also helped to undermine the Copperhead movement in the last half of the war.

The Republicans extended their propaganda campaign to the soldiers. Midwestern Republican governors and Republican political strategists were most anxious to convert the army to their political point of view. Republican governors appointed state agents to accompany state troops and to report on their needs. These agents served as a liaison between the governors and the soldiers and were often equally interested in the soldiers' political and physical needs. Democrats sometimes dubbed the agents "political commissars" and charged Republicans with trying to protect the soldiers' political conscience from Democratic contamination.[25] The state agents helped to distribute the welfare and relief funds provided by the state legislatures and local communities. The activity of the state agents enabled such governors as Morton and Yates to pose as "the soldiers' friend." The state agents helped to Republicanize the army.

The state agents usually had the full assistance and co-operation of the colonels and brigadier generals in their effort to mold soldier opinion. Since Republicans monopolized the governorships in the upper Midwest, most of the colonels whom they appointed were Republicans. Many Republicans insisted that party loyalty was a proper test of a man's military qualifications.[26] When Governor Morton deviated from his usual practice and named a Democrat to a colonelcy, his Republican friends put their protest into the record:

We cannot see why broken down Democratic politicians should be placed at the head of regiments. . . . when we recollect that we have contributed liberally of time, money, and whatever influence we possess to gain the political ascendancy in this district and victory, after a hard fought battle having been won, to see all the good results, as we think, not only lost but given in preference to those who have cursed *you* and the whole Republican party time and again, is so utterly suicidal that we are both surprised and chagrined.[27]

The Republican colonels and the Republican state agents helped to shape the political views of the soldiers. They sought "to educate" the soldiers "by a distribution of proper journals and documents among them."[28] Republican newspapers and tracts or pamphlets published by the Loyal Publication Society were distributed free of charge. They flooded the camps, especially on the eve of elections.[29] Democratic newspapers, on the other hand, often failed to reach their soldier-subscribers, and Democratic pamphlets and campaign propaganda were often burned or buried. Generals sometimes excluded Copperhead newspapers from their jurisdiction and took an active hand in shaping soldier opinion. General Robert H. Milroy, a zealous Republican and close personal friend of Governor Morton, was proud that he had abolitionized his troops. "I am succeeding admirably," wrote Milroy of his efforts to abolitionize his army, "and will have them the best abolitionists in the U.S."[30]

Influenced by abolition-minded officers, exposed to Republican newspapers and pamphlets, and enchanted by the stirring strains of "John Brown's Body," the typical soldier readily accepted the abolition creed. By learning to hate the rebels, he learned to hate what they stood for. So soldiers became emancipationists and enemies of slavery. ". . . there is a universal desire among the soldiery," wrote an Indiana colonel, "to take the negro from the Secesh master because they think it hurts him just so many dollars, and spite him to boot. . . ."[31] "The army makes men Union and anti-slavery," wrote an observant general. "No soldier is afraid of hurting slavery."[32] The metamorphosis of a soldier is revealed in the letter of Eli R. Pickett:

I have never been in favor of abolition of slavery until since this war has detirmend [*sic*] me in the conviction that it is a greater sin than our Government is able to stand—and now I go in for a war of emancipation and I am ready to do my share of the work. I am satesfied [*sic*] that slavery is . . . an institution that belonged to the dark ages and that it ill becomes a nation of our standing to perpetuate the barbarous practice. It is opposed to the spirit of the age—and in my opinion this Rebelion [*sic*] is but the death struggle of the overgrown monster.[33]

Republican propagandists then tried to use the "army views" to combat the views of Copperheads at home. They drove a wedge between the army and the home-based Democrats. Soldiers, as individuals and via petition, supported Governors Morton and Yates in their partisan controversy with Copperhead-dominated legislatures.

Governor Morton solicited the active support of the soldiers in an effort to turn public opinion against the Copperhead legislature of 1863. Through his military aides, he solicited soldier petitions praising him and condemning the legislators. Colonel John T. Wilder directed the pro-Morton campaign in the Army of the Cumberland, and other loyal Republicans extended it to other sectors.[34] A flood of regimental petitions poured into Indianapolis, putting the Copperhead legislators at a disadvantage. All petitions were quite alike in form and in meaning, indicating that some master hand pulled the strings.[35] By February 1, 1863, more than fifty regimental "protests" reached the governor's desk, and he used them judiciously to checkmate the legislature and cast doubt on the patriotism of the legislators.[36]

Governor Yates also used soldier petitions to advantage. He collected a stack of regimental resolves and turned them over to newspapers like the Chicago *Tribune* and the Springfield *Illinois State Journal*. The soldier resolutions lauded the "patriotic" governor and criticized the "traitorous" legislatures. Those petitions gave Yates a chance to argue that the soldier views should be followed by the people at home.[37]

Republican editors also solicited letters from their soldier-friends and published these "loyal" letters. Under Republican tutelage, the soldiery learned to hate and detest the Copperheads and wrote insulting letters to old friends threatening revenge when the soldiers came home:[38]

> Then will the soldier come, who in the past,
> Stood in the front, and met the canon's blast,
>
> . . . .
>
> Seek out the friends who, in our absence, dare
> With their foul breath, pollute the sacred air
> Of our domestic peace. It will be vain
> For you to plead—forgiveness to obtain. . . . [39]

Soldiers viewed Copperheads as a "vile reptile crew," unworthy of any favor. They named them "Benedict Arnolds" or "Judases"—"loathsome creatures" who ought to hang themselves.[40]

Democrats, of course, protested against the abolitionizing of the army and against the efforts of Republican governors to use it as a propaganda agency. Democrats complained that soldiers were being deceived about the true conditions at home. They contended that the "propaganda" which Republicans circulated among the soldiers did an injustice to the critics of the Lincoln administration. "The uninformed masses," protested the editor of the Dayton *Empire*, "were made to believe that the Democracy was leagued in dark and infernal conspiracy, not only to subvert the Governments, but to massacre the poor innocent Black Republicans in their beds."[41]

Since Republicans recognized that they could control "soldier opinion," they were anxious to extend the vote to soldiers in the field. Missouri unionists experimented with voting-in-the-field, because they needed the soldiers' ballots as well as their bullets to keep the state in the Union and loyal to the Republican party. Several Republican governors saw the potential of voting-in-the-field schemes and asked their legislators to extend the vote to soldiers along the fighting front.[42] Iowa, Wisconsin, and Minnesota passed laws which provided that state agents would visit regiments in the field, open polling places, and take the soldiers' vote.[43] The responsibility for execution of the scheme was put squarely in the hands of the colonels and many of them used the opportunity to pay off political debts.

The voting-in-the-field stratagem had its first test in the fall elections of 1862, and the experiment proved its worth. In Iowa and Minnesota it helped to turn out Democratic congressmen, giving their posts to Republicans.[44] In Wisconsin the soldier vote prevented Democrats from gaining control of the state legislature.

Democrats in Wisconsin, Iowa, and Minnesota were chagrined and dismayed. "The whole thing of this army voting," wrote one Democratic editor, "is a most consummate humbug. . . . The scheme is like a jug handle—on one side."[45] Democratic critics of the voting-in-the-field procedure collected instances of intimidation, fraud, and corruption. They charged that Republican colonels disposed of Democratic tickets by burning them, burying them, or discarding them.[46] One Republican soldier wrote that he proudly watched hissing soldiers burn and bury Democratic ballots.[47] Democrats charged that regiments recruited in "Democratic country" were not allowed to vote in the 1862 elections. They also criticized the political activities of the various state agents and politically minded colonels. Since voting was done openly and the officers knew how each man voted, politically minded colonels were able to exert direct pressure to bring about a favorable ballot. Sometimes the colonels made political speeches in behalf of their party or their candidates the evening before the election.[48] Small wonder, then, that bolder Democrats called voting-in-the-field "a cheat—a humbug—a fraud."[49]

Republicans, on the other hand, were jubilant with the results of the voting-in-the-field experiment in 1862. "We are much pleased with the vote," wrote the confidant of a midwestern Republican governor, "knowing as we do the former political sentiments of the men."[50] Republicans tried to extend the voting-in-the-field plan into other states. The Copperhead legislatures of 1863 in Indiana and Illinois successfully sidetracked all voting-in-the-field proposals, but Michigan Republicans passed a voting-in-the-field act openly contradicting a clause of the state constitution.[51] The Michigan soldier voting law helped Michigan Republicans sweep the 1864 elections. Several months later the state Supreme Court declared the law unconstitutional. Wisconsin's voting-in-the-field law also faced a constitutional test, and the state's Copperheads hoped that the state Supreme Court would invalidate it. Republican bigwigs in the Badger State insured a favorable court decision by amending the act to cover the election of judges. Then they nominated the incumbent chief justice as their party's choice for that office. The chief justice directed the court to rule favorably on the soldier voting act and was re-elected by the soldier vote.[52]

With the passage of time, the soldier vote became more Republican and better controlled. Colonels vied with each other in producing desirable vote results. Some regiments turned in votes that were 100 per cent for the Republican ticket. Some Republican-minded colonels reported to their governors that their regiments had given "a unanimous vote" for the "war candidates." Some felt that their ability to manufacture Republican votes merited raises in rank or pay. The vote cast by Wisconsin soldiers illustrated Republican efficiency. In 1862 voting-in-the-field soldiers gave a four to one majority to the Republican candidates for the state legislature. In 1864 the ratio was fourteen to one. Voting-in-the-field helped to keep Republicanism in control of the state governments. It was an effective political device which Republican governors used to check the Copperhead challenge.

In those states, like Indiana and Illinois, in which Copperhead legislatures refused to pass voting-in-the-field laws, the Republicans resorted to a simpler strategy. Furloughs were given to soldiers up front so that they could go home to cast Republican ballots.

As early as June and July of 1864, Governors Morton and Yates took steps to get state troops home for the fall elections. They exerted pressure upon President Lincoln and Secretary of

War Stanton to permit Illinois and Indiana regiments to go home to vote. Morton, worried about both his own and Lincoln's re-election, bluntly requested such a favor. "It is my opinion," Morton said in a telegram to the President, "that the vote of every soldiers [*sic*] in Indiana will be required to carry this state for Mr. Lincoln in November."[53] The Union Executive Congressional Committee rushed to the support of Governors Morton and Yates.[54] Lincoln and Stanton bowed to the pressure. Troops which could be spared were sent home to help the administration win the elections. "We have made arrangements with Stanton," wrote a jubilant supporter of Governor Morton, "to get our soldiers furloughed home to vote."[55]

Morton and Yates were also insistent on furloughing convalescents as well as soldiers up front. Supporters of Morton were especially anxious to collect the votes of soldiers in hospitals. One supporter wrote to the Judge Advocate General:

Be kind enough to ask the Secretary of War to keep an eye out for furloughing Indiana convalescents or sick home. We can give Morton from 20 to 25,000 in this honest way. Shumard [chief of surgeons] is thorough, posted in the matter, and has inspected this part of the business thoroughly. The defeat of Morton would be a national calamity.[56]

Soon afterward, Secretary Stanton gave his indorsement to the idea, suggesting that soldiers in hospitals be furloughed "until after election."[57] A straw vote taken in a Jefferson Barracks hospital indicated that Lincoln was a ten to one favorite over McClellan, and Republicans everywhere wanted furloughs for every convalescent "able to travel."[58]

Although the votes of the soldiers on furlough were invaluable, there was another important angle. The very presence of soldiers at the polls had an adverse effect on the Copperhead turnout at the polls. Defiant soldiers loitered around some polling places and embarrassed those who carried Democratic tickets. Occasionally they intimidated Copperheads and prevented them from voting. Soldiers as voters or "poll watchers" were convinced that their views were the true views. They felt it was their patriotic duty to keep Copperheadism in check.[59]

The widespread circulation of "soldier views," coupled with the propaganda activities of the Union Leagues and the Republican-sponsored publication societies, helped to shape public opinion. The intensification of nationalism, a natural course in time of war, also helped develop a climate of opinion hostile to Copperheadism. Patriotic Republicans wanted all to share their ideals and their enthusiasm for the war. They waved the flag vigorously, mouthed emotional phrases, and pointed scornfully at all nonconformists. These superpatriots encouraged intimidation and even mob action.

Every prominent midwestern Copperhead felt the wrath of the superpatriots who placed themselves above the law. Wilbur F. Storey, editor of the outspoken Chicago *Times*, was felled several times by unknown assailants who questioned his "loyalty." Samuel Medary, constant critic of President Lincoln and editor of the Columbus *Crisis*, was repeatedly threatened, and one day a mob wrecked his printing plant. Arsonists set fire to the farm buildings of James W. Singleton, Illinois Copperhead, while he was attending a Springfield "peace" rally. Dennis Mahony of the Dubuque *Herald* was repeatedly insulted, abused, and threatened. A Dubuque Republican superpatriot, Rev. Billingsgate Smith, publicly suggested that Mahony be hanged from a lamppost and the *Herald* office destroyed. Mahony's helpers also felt the wrath of superpatriots. Stilson Hutchins, who took over as editor when Mahony took an extended trip to New York, suffered many harrowing experiences. An army lieutenant, home on leave, beat him, leaving his face covered with blood.[60] Soldiers home on leave seized an agent of the Dubuque *Herald* in Waterloo and ducked him repeatedly in the river.[61] Republican businessmen boycotted Mahony and the *Herald* and turned to legal trickery to stop the publication of his well-known Copperhead sheet.[62]

The lesser-known Copperheads also suffered intimidation and persecution as patriotism swept the Midwest. One young Illinois lady wrote of her fears to her uncle:

I do not know what we are coming to. We are in danger of our lives all the time. They are threatening to hang every democrat there is in the country. Please write and advise me what you think best for us to do.[63]

When an Indiana legislator refused to swim with the current, a "Vigilance Committee" warned him that "the people might" declare themselves *above the law*."[64] A La Crosse resident who refused to blame the South for all of the nation's ills was seized by "patriots" and led around town with a rope around his neck. He was finally released and told to get out of town.[65] Timothy P. Murphy, a student at the State University of Iowa, was dismissed from school for wearing a Copperhead badge.[66] A young college student at Georgetown College, Kentucky, was denied a diploma because he refused to alter his speech entitled "Freedom Knows No Compromise."[67]

Republican celebrants sometimes mixed patriotism and whiskey in unknown portions. Springfield, Ohio, supporters of Lincoln celebrated Brough's victory over Vallandigham with bonfires, cheers, and liquid refreshments. A Springfield Copperhead reported:

The Abolish had an illumination here last night. Such a time! I never want to see the like [of it] again. The *negroes and whites* together visited the houses of prominent Democrats—hissed, groaned, and throwed stones thro [*sic*] the windows. They broke all the large windows in Dr. Wallace's Drug Store, and many others. . . . Their conduct would have shamed devils out of hell.[68]

Sometimes children suffered for the political sins of their fathers. One young Dayton girl was tormented by her Republican playmates, who tried to get her to repeat the popular Republican verse: "Hurrah for Brough and Abraham! And a rope to hang Vallandigham." When she refused, they pulled her hair and finally locked her in an empty outbuilding. When her father finally rescued his defiant daughter, her first words were: "I stood up for our side."[69]

The emphasis on conformity extended into churches, and some religious organizations gloried in their "loyalty" to the Republican cause. Congregationalist clergymen gen-

221

erally viewed the war as a moral crusade.[70] The patriotic preachments of Henry Ward Beecher, the well-known New York clergyman, were matched by those of Rev. W. W. Patton of the First Congregational Church of Chicago. Both viewed the war as a God-ordained means to destroy slavery.[71]

The support which the Congregationalists gave the war and the Lincoln administration was matched by the bishops of the Methodist Episcopal Church. The six bishops of that denomination gave vigorous support to the war from the very beginning of the conflict. Bishop Matthew Simpson of Chicago set the patriotic pace; he held conferences throughout the North and waved the flag vigorously. Proudly he proclaimed: "We will take our glorious flag—the flag of our country—and nail it just below *the Flag*."[72] Bishop Thomas A. Morris of Springfield, Illinois, and Bishop Edward R. Ames of Indianapolis joined Bishop Simpson in pledging the clergy to an "uncompromising and unconditional devotion to the Administration and the Union."[73] The hierarchy allowed no deviation from the line of patriotism. Henry Clay Dean, an Iowan who had mixed preaching and politics with considerable success, lost his license as a Methodist minister because of his Copperhead sympathies. Two Illinois clergymen, who spoke at Democratic meetings and were accused of Copperhead leanings, were reprimanded by the Methodist Episcopal Conference at Springfield, on October 13, 1863.[74] "Our ministers were true to the National cause," a prominent Methodist Episcopal cleric wrote in later years; "no one would have been tolerated if he had shown any sympathy" to Copperheadism.[75]

Other denominations clambered aboard the administration bandwagon. The Methodist Protestant church defined "loyalty" according to the Republican dictionary. Presbyterian general assemblies sometimes adopted resolutions putting their membership upon the side of the administration and the war. Baptist assemblies and Lutheran synods also espoused the aims of the Lincoln administration and took stands which undermined Copperheadism.

The official action of the church assemblies encouraged local

pastors to speak up for the cause of God and country. Nonconformists suffered humiliation and censure. In Monroe County,
Ohio, a patriotic minister asked all "Butternuts" in his congrega-
tion to rise and be ridiculed. When one bold "Butternut" arose,
the clergyman gave him a lecture "on sin and patriotism."[76] In
Illinois a deacon was "expelled" from his parish because he had
actively circulated the Chicago *Times* and the Cincinnati *Enquirer* in his neighborhood.[77] Another deacon suffered a similar
fate because he preferred the Chicago *Times*'s politics to that of
the editor of the *Central Christian Advocate*.[78] A Bloomington,
Indiana, elder lost his church standing because he admitted that
he approved of the Democratic national platform of 1864.[79] Cyrus H. McCormick, prominent Peace Democrat and Presbyterian,
withdrew from North Church, Chicago, because his political
views were at variance with those of the patriotic preacher. The
McCormicks protested that Presbyterianism "bent itself" in order
"to suit the prejudices, the fanaticism, and the bad temper of its
votaries."[80]

The situation within the Catholic church was strange. Most of
the German Catholics and the Irish Americans voted the Democratic ticket and espoused the Copperhead cause; they feared
both emancipation and the draft. Their views were shaped by
such Copperhead newspapers as the Dubuque *Herald,* the Cincinnati *Enquirer*, the Chicago *Times*, the Detroit *Free Press* and
the Milwaukee *See-Bote*. The views of Mahony of the *Herald,*
Peter V. Deuster of the *See-Bote*, and Michael Faran of the *Enquirer* contradicted the public pronouncements of such members
of the Catholic hierarchy as Archbishop John Hughes or Bishop
Clement Smyth of Dubuque and Bishop Sylvester Rosecrans of
Cincinnati. Archibishop Hughes tried to set an example for his
fellow clerics by his public acts. Archbishop John B. Purcell and
his co-adjutor, Bishop Rosecrans, openly supported the Union
ticket and tried to discourage Cincinnati Catholics from supporting the Copperhead movement. Bishop Rosecrans, especially,
waved the flag energetically, undermining Cincinnati Copperheadism through his sermons, his writings, and public speeches.

The Catholic bishop of Chicago also took a strong prowar stand although most Catholics of that archdiocese had Copperhead leanings.[81]

The active support which Bishop Rosecrans and Archbishop Purcell gave to the Lincoln administration proved somewhat embarrassing for Copperhead editors. Mahony's personal and professional rival, the editor of the Dubuque *Times*, suggested that Mahony and Dubuque Catholics could well follow the "patriotic action" of Bishop Rosecrans and Archbishop Purcell. The editor of the Dubuque *Herald*, in turn, took issue with his rival and criticized the partisanship of the Cincinnati prelates in an editorial. Bishop Clement Smyth of Dubuque took pen in hand and wrote a letter in defense of his fellow prelates from Cincinnati; it was signed "C., Dubuque" and published in the Dubuque *Times*. The editor of the *Herald* suspected that the letter signed "C., Dubuque" was composed in the *Times* editorial office. So he led with his chin:

The abolition concern of this city comes to the defense of Bishops Purcell and Rosecrans. A correspondent who pretends to be a Catholic, assists the *Times*. If he will give his real name, we will brand a number of his statements and insinuations with the designation they deserve.[82]

The editor of the Dubuque *Times* retaliated with a right cross that all but floored his rival. He revealed that the letter-writer was Bishop Clement Smyth, and the prelate nodded his assent. The editor of the *Herald* retreated, embarrassed and humiliated.[83] Bishop Smyth subtly undermined Copperheadism in the months that followed, even accepting a Union League award. Without doubt, the activities of the Catholic hierarchy helped to stigmatize Copperheadism. By securing the assistance of organized religion, the Lincoln administration possessed some advantages.

The ability of Lincoln's supporters to stigmatize the Democrats and impugn the loyalty of the opposition helped keep Republicanism in power.

Partisan controversy over the meaning of the term "loyalty" dated back to the early years of the war. Republicans, contending that the Lincoln administration was the government, insisted upon indorsement of its every act—even the issuance of the Emancipation Proclamation. "If a Democrat expresses an opinion against Mr. Lincoln's war policy," complained an Ohioan, "the Republicans forthwith denounce him as a 'traitor.' " And he added bitterly: "Praise Abolitionism and you are a patriot; support the Constitution in a consistent, truthful way and you are a traitor—so say these Republican judges."[84] Editor Joseph J. Bingham stated the Democratic position outspokenly:

We hold that we should be false to our trust if we fail to hold to a strict accountability those who are temporarily in power, administering the Executive Department of the Government. *These men are not the Government; they are not the country.* They are, for a brief period, the instruments of conducting the affairs of the Government and the country. The power of the sovereign people is only partially delegated for special purposes. How absurd and preposterous, then, is the clamor, that when we venture to censure these agents of the people, we are arraying ourselves against the country.[85]

As the war continued and patriotism ran rampant, critics of the Lincoln administration winced as Republicans condemned them. Republicans never ceased to point out that William L. Yancey and Jefferson Davis were Democrats and rebels; all Northern Democrats were therefore suspect.[86] Republicans contended that Democrats who criticized the administration gave comfort and aid to the enemy. For political gain they labeled their critics "traitors," "secessionists," "Southern sympathizers," and "rebel apologists."[87] A Dayton superpatriot called the Dayton *Empire* a "filthy traitorous sheet" and advised his grandson: ". . . if any dirty puppy should intrude the thing upon your presence, spit upon it and return it whence it came."[88] When Mahony wrote to Horace Greeley to point out that he, Mahony, was not a "traitor" and that no charges of "treason" had been proved against him, the editor of the New York *Tribune* countered: "I am not a lawyer, and cannot say that all this makes you legally, technically a traitor. That you are morally one, essentially one, I have no matter of doubt."[89]

The controversy between Democrats and Republicans over the

meaning of the word "loyalty" became more intense in the early months of 1863. Democratic victories in the fall elections of 1862 bore fruit in early 1863. Governors Morton and Yates feuded with Democratic legislatures, and each side tried to link loyalty to its course of action. Each side also tried to give its own meaning to terms like "Copperhead" and "Butternut." Republicans capitalized on the incompetency of the Democrats and on their lack of leadership, rank partisanship, and tactical errors.

As the year passed, Lincoln's critics lost face. Gettysburg and Vicksburg helped. Lincoln's qualities of leadership helped. The intensification of nationalism also helped. When Ohio Democrats bet on Vallandigham in the state's gubernatorial contest in October of 1863, they ignored the advice of party moderates. Times were changing, but Democratic conservatives refused to admit it.

Realistic Democrats recognized that the cards were stacked against them when they made their plans for 1864. Some threw in the towel and admitted defeat.[90] Thomas O. Lowe, a disciple of Vallandigham, decided to take a prolonged visit to Europe and to return when "Republican fanaticism" and "public madness" had run its course. Lesser-known Copperheads moved west—to Colorado, California, or Montana. They decided that the hardships of pioneering were preferable to Republican-encouraged intimidation. An Illinois Republican reported:

Collins has sold out and leaves for "Idaho"— a glorious riddance. Some men of the Copperhead stripe will be on their travels before the 1st of July. A few days since the children in Martha Edding's school commenced snowballing Shissler, and the girls in Emma's school cheered them on by shouting "That's right, give [it] to the traitor." They followed him down the main street and then left him. Copperhead stock is rapidly declining. . . . they begin to see the handwriting on the wall.[91]

Some Democrats, tired of swimming against the poltical current, decided to quit politics for the duration. The price they paid in social and economic fields was more than they could afford. So they "padlocked" their lips and retired from the political wars.[92] Intimidation, persecution, boycotts, and slander were all endured by opponents of the administration. It was more than many were willing to pay.

        In the one-sided contest in 1864, not only did the Republicans hold all the aces, but they also stacked the deck. The Copperheads held the losing hands. Democrats lost the contest, in part, because of the ability of the Republicans and President Lincoln, and in part because they played the political game ineptly and failed to gauge the temper of the times. The Democrats were divided at the time they needed unity. They were leaderless in the last year of the war.

The death of Stephen A. Douglas early in the war robbed the northwestern Democrats of their outstanding leader. No one stepped forward to take his place. Vallandigham failed, because he was too outspoken, uncompromising, and temperamental.

Democratic views on the question of peace were as varied in early 1864 as they had ever been. Some still talked of carrying the sword in one hand and the olive branch in the other. They still thought it was possible to restore the old Union as it had existed *before* the Civil War. Some talked of peace without any plan to attain it. These hoped that lip service to peace might pick up the votes of the war weary. The extreme views were represented by such Democrats as William M. Corry of Ohio and U.S. Senator Garrett Davis of Kentucky.

Corry and Davis were models of consistency. They favored peace and compromise in 1861; they favored peace and compromise in 1864. Corry argued for peace in various sections of Ohio; Davis argued for peace in Washington. At a Jackson Day dinner, held in Columbus, Ohio, on January 8, 1864, Corry contended that peace and reunion were still possible. He insisted that it was the duty of Democrats to give "a peace plank" priority over such issues as "personal liberty" and "conduct of the war."[93] Davis, meanwhile, argued the cause of peace on the floor of the Senate of the United States.

Davis launched his January "peace offensive" with a series of eighteen resolutions. Those resolutions condemned President Lincoln for his "misuse of presidential power." They labeled Lincoln and the Radical Republicans as "the destructives." Soldier lives, civil rights, and constitutional government had been lost. The policy of war, carnage, and destruction had failed to reunite the country.[94]

The Radical Republicans countered Davis' intemperate action with the threat of expulsion. Henry Wilson of Massachusetts shook his fist at Davis and suggested that the adamant Kentuckian be expelled. Davis was unafraid. He was willing to be a political martyr for his cause. He answered the Radicals by offering a series of "peace resolves." The last of the series read:

Resolved, That the President of the United States be and he is hereby authorized to propose a cessation of arms and an amnesty to the authorities of the Confederate States of America, with a view to hold a convention of the people of all the States to reconstruct the Union; and if that cannot be effected then the said convention agree upon the terms of separation of the States, without the further effusion of blood and of a lasting peace among them.[95]

The radical Republicans would have expelled Davis from the Senate, but they were afraid that they might drive Kentucky out of the Union. They buried his resolutions in committee and ignored Davis as best they could. No other Democrats spoke in behalf of Davis or his peace proposal. Even Copperheads like Daniel Voorhees and William A. Richardson sat silent. They wanted peace *and* reunion.

Lincoln was much more realistic than Copperheads who talked vaguely of peace and compromise. When the President was approached by James W. Singleton and Phineas C. Wright to lead in reuniting the country through compromise, he gave a negative answer. He did not favor an armisice, "with the unending evils of permanent separation disguised by empty results of a temporary peace staring them in the face."[96] He favored "the continuance of the war until a permanent peace shall be established by suppressing the rebellion."[97] Lincoln, like most Republicans, believed that reunion by amnesty or compromise would be no more than "utter degradation and dishonor."[98]

The role of "incorrigible" which Garrett Davis assumed in the Senate was played by Alexander Long in the House of Representatives. Long was as outspoken as Davis, and he too could throw caution to the winds. While debating the proposal to prohibit slavery by constitutional amendment, Long got a chance to put in a word for armistice and compromise. He was convinced that the war was destroying constitutional liberties and degrading the nation's morals. In an April, 1864, speech on the floor of the House, Long suggested that the "slaughter" cease and he suggested that the Democratic party become an antiwar party. "If the time ever was when the Union could have been restored by war," he declared, "it has long since been dispelled by emancipation, confiscation, amnesty, and like proclamations."[99] He said that only the Peace Democrats could restore the Union. He proposed that a congressional committee call upon President Lincoln to stop the draft until the people had a chance to decide on the question of war and peace.[100]

Republicans thought that Long was expendable. They retaliated with a resolution to expel the Ohio congressman and showered him with invective and abuse. Schuyler Colfax, speaker of the House, vacated his chair to lead the Republican assault on Long. Colfax's voice trembled with emotion as he introduced a resolution of expulsion. Congressman James A. Garfield indorsed Colfax' resolution and compared his fellow Ohioan to Benedict Arnold. The flames of anger seared others, too.

Long's Democratic colleagues rose to his defense, although they did not necessarily agree with his support of an armistice. Chaos reigned as rivals tried to outshout each other. Finally Benjamin G. Harris, a Peace Democrat from Maryland, got the floor. Republicans thought that Harris might censure Long, but he shocked them by defending Long's views and proposals. Confusion reigned anew as a dozen Republicans tried to gain the floor. They were "shouting to the Speaker and endeavoring to be recognized."[101] In a stentorian voice, heard above the din, Elihu B. Washburne of Illinois moved to expel Harris as well as Long.

After order was restored, Fernando Wood of New York suggested that he too deserved to be expelled, for his views on peace were like those of Long and Harris. Another uproar occurred and the acting speaker pounded for order. Washburne, outshouting other Republicans, suggested that Fernando Wood also be expelled and sent home in disgrace.

In time Alexander Long, whose anti-Lincoln and pro-peace speech had touched off the fireworks, received an opportunity to defend himself and his views. Thaddeus Stevens, arising from a sickbed, wobbled into the House to apply the whip. He mixed vituperation and grandiloquence as he fought for Republicanism and the Union cause. But Stevens could not convince Democrats that Long was a traitor or that he merited expulsion. The motion to expel Alexander Long and Benjamin G. Harris failed for want of the two-thirds majority necessary for passage. Republicans then settled for a vote of censure, which required only a bare majority.[102]

The extreme pro-peace views of Alexander Long and Garrett Davis were shared by a few other midwestern Democrats. Samuel Medary of the *Crisis* and Dr. John McElwee of the Hamilton *True Telegraph* favored peace at any price. McElwee, for example, entitled an editorial "Stop the War." "This murderous crusade," he wrote in despair, "has gone on long enough."[103] George W. Morgan, another of the lesser-known Copperheads of Ohio, also advocated an armistice. "Reason," he said, "is the attribute of the gods—carnage is the festival of fiends." Morgan thought that the contestants in the Civil War could well learn from the American Indians. "Let us assemble around the council fire," he suggested, "and for once imitate our brothers of the forest and smoke the calumet of peace."[104] Such Copperheads as Hunt of Missouri, Dodd and Milligan of Indiana, James M. Corry and Dr. Thomas Massey of Ohio, and LeGrand Byington and Henry Clay Dean of Iowa added their thunderous "Amens!"

In a sense the independence and individualism which turned certain Democrats into Copperheads helped to negate the Copperhead movement. They could not agree with the administration and could not agree among themselves. They were unable to unite behind a single Copperhead as their choice for the presidency in the election of 1864.

They had proved their ineffectiveness as early as February when they tried to check the movement which would place the name of General McClellan at the head of the national ticket. Some of the Midwest's most outspoken advocates of armistice and compromise took a trip to Albany and New York City at the invitation of the Wood-McMaster antiwar clique.[105] Some of the midwestern malcontents like Dodd of Indiana, Green of Illinois, and Barret of Missouri made the pilgrimage via Windsor, Canada, in order to meet with Vallandigham. The exiled Ohioan, long a symbol of the peace movement, hoped that the Peace Democrats might be able to stop the McClellan boom. Dodd suggested that the Peace Democrats might achieve some of their objectives by organizing a secret society.

Any hopes that Horatio Seymour might become the Moses of the armistice-and-peace movement were shattered when the midwesterners arrived in New York City. Dean Richmond, proctor of the party in the Empire State, had McClellan's bandwagon rolling downhill, and Horatio Seymour had no wish to turn his back on his patron. The disconcerted participants in the New York peace powwow cast about for other presidential possibilities. Thomas Seymour of Connecticut was suggested, but he was relatively unknown. The Peace Democrats were nearly bankrupt in leadership. The self-styled delegates straggled homeward without a candidate or practical program. Their New York pilgrimage depressed rather than buoyed their spirits.

Vallandigham, meanwhile, grew uneasy and restive at his Canadian retreat. Confederate agents were as thick as flies and as distracting as buzzing bumblebees. There were rumors that Vallandigham was tired of inaction and exile. Word came from New Lisbon, Ohio, that his mother was on her deathbed, and he wished to see her again before her death.[106]

Some of his Ohio friends urged him to return to the States. His rearrest might stir some sympathy for the cause he had come to symbolize. Butler County Democrats planned a huge rally at Hamilton, twenty miles north of Cincinnati. Two of the sponsors, Dr. John McElwee of the Hamilton *True Telegraph* and David W. Brant, a prominent Hamilton businessman, went to Windsor to convince Vallandigham to return. They offered to escort the exiled Ohioan back to his home. Vallandigham acquiesced.

The return trip was uneventful. Federal officials made no attempt to arrest him. President Lincoln without doubt recognized that Vallandigham could be a millstone around the neck of the Democrats. Vallandigham made his public appearance at the Hamilton mass meeting on June 15, 1864. Rumors had made the rounds that he had returned and his platform appearance was electrifying. "He came unheralded from his exile," wrote a Dayton devotee, "and his sudden appearance was like an apparition from the clouds."[107]

Vallandigham delivered a carefully planned speech. It was characterized by moderation and restraint. Federal agents scribbled down his statements in little black books.[108] President Lincoln wisely left well enough alone. The taint of treason linked to Vallandigham would rub off on the Democratic party. So Vallandigham returned to his home in Dayton. He intended to use his influence to sidetrack the McClellan bandwagon and direct his party down the path of peace.

A bewildered and disorganized Democratic party readied itself for the national convention which had been postponed from July to August. Members hoped that Grant's failures before Richmond might shake public faith in President Lincoln and Republicanism. The failure of Grant and Sherman to score decisively in the summer of 1864 undermined the morale of the North. Grant had been ambushed by Lee in the Wilderness; Union casualties were more than 17,000. At Spotsylvania Court House, Grant lost another 13,500 men.

These losses stunned the North, but Grant continued his war of attrition. At Cold Harbor, six miles east of Richmond, Grant lost another 7,000 men and another 15,000 after crossing the James River and attacking Petersburg. Meanwhile, Generals

Hunter and Sigel were driven out of the Shenandoah Valley and the victorious Confederate general, Jubal Early, conducted incursions into Maryland and Pennsylvania. Although General Sherman pushed the Confederate troops back to Atlanta in a series of brilliant flanking movements, his losses ran to 10,000 by the end of July. Total Federal losses for the first seven months of 1864—through "Bloody July"—were close to 75,000 men.

Small wonder, then, that the dormant peace movement experienced a rebirth. Some Northerners began to wonder whether the Union could be re-established "by blood and slaughter and force of arms."[109] The outspoken editor of the La Crosse *Democrat* claimed that Grant's failures before Richmond left no alternative but "peace and concessions." With a heavy heart he wrote: "Patriotism is played out. . . . all are tired of this damnable tragedy. . . . Each hour is but sinking us deeper into bankruptcy and desolation."[110] Such "peace men" as Long and Mahony argued that time had proved them right. They believed that public opinion was swinging in favor of peace and compromise. Lincoln stock dwindled. He had been renominated by his party in June, but many of the Radical Republicans were dissatisfied with the ticket. The "peace men" also hoped that the turn of events would permit them to sidetrack McClellan and to name a genuine peace man as the Democratic presidential nominee. Some of the unconditional peace men boomed Thomas Seymour of Connecticut; others tried to push Franklin Pierce to the fore.[111] The editor of the *Crisis* wrote: "As the winds are blowing favorably to the Peace Party it is best not to nominate McClellan or any man who has any *war* in him. . . . I just hear that a new call has been made for 500,000 men. If so, Lincoln is *deader* than dead."[112]

While some Copperheads clamored for peace, Horace Greeley played into Lincoln's hands. Greeley, who could blend vindictiveness with pacifistic idealism, called the President's attention to the peace sentiment and offered to don the mantle of the peacemaker. Greeley had heard that "two ambassadors of Davis & Co." were in Canada with "full and complete powers for peace." Nudging the President, Greeley wrote: "I venture to remind you that our bleeding, bankrupt, almost dying country also longs for peace, shudders at the prospect of fresh conscriptions, or further wholesale devastations, and of new rivers of human blood." He reminded Lincoln that a widespread conviction that the administration was "not anxious for peace" existed in the country—to the discredit of the Republican party.[113]

Lincoln seized upon the situation to discredit the peace movement. He immediately asked Greeley to be his "personal witness" to go to Canada and deal with the Confederate commissioners. He attached a condition—the "abandonment of slavery" by the Southern states.[114] Caught in the web of his own weaving, Greeley had to accept the assignment to pull the chestnut out of the fire. Greeley, then, journeyed to Niagara Falls with conditions unacceptable to the South. Furthermore, the Confederate "commissioners" had no credentials. They were evidently more interested in developing peace sentiment in the North than in giving up the Southern dream of independence.[115]

After the Niagara Falls fiasco, President Lincoln issued a pronouncement which put the Southerners and the midwestern peace men at a disadvantage. The failure of the attempt was put at the door of the South, and the Republican press used it to stigmatize the Copperhead movement. In the eyes of Greeley, Lincoln, and the Radical Republicans, "Human Slavery" was to blame.[116] Two other abortive attempts to negotiate peace followed—the Jacques-Gilmore mission to Richmond and the Jacob Thompson–Gilmore parley at Toronto. They too served to discredit the peace movement and midwestern Copperheadism. Lincoln added to his stature as champion in the game of political chess.

While speculation as to peace policies and possibilities stirred the credulous, the Democrats prepared for their national nominating convention. McClellan's supporters conducted an aggressive campaign to secure his nomination. They named S. S. Cox of Ohio as their "chief manager," and he gave the McClellan bandwagon a downhill push. Some of the Peace Democrats denounced Cox for "selling-out" to the McClellan crowd, and one described

Cox as "selfish and tricky . . . always looking out for his own interests, regardless of principle."[117]

A motley group of Democratic delegates assembled in Chicago on August 29. Some were proud of the "War Democrat" label they bore. Others, like Dodd and Vallandigham had publicly declared for peace. The professional politicians effected a compromise. They named General McClellan as their presidential nominee and allowed Vallandigham and Dr. John McElwee, editor of the Hamilton *True Telegraph,* to shape the peace plank in the platform.[118]

The peace plank was a far cry from the peace-at-any-price position of such Democrats as Long and Dodd. "It proclaimed reunion as the condition of peace." McClellan, nevertheless, regarded it as a millstone around his neck and at variance with his principles. ". . . the Convention has damaged him [McClellan]," wrote an astute observer, "more than Lincoln speeches could in a whole campaign."[119] McClellan boldly repudiated the peace plank in the same letter in which he accepted the nomination of the Chicago Convention. McClellan insisted that the object of the war was the preservation of the Union. He, thus, went before the people as a war leader. He and Lincoln could well have stood on the same platform.

Peace Democrats like Benjamin Wood of the New York *News* and Long denounced McClellan and sought to unite upon another candidate. They wanted to cast their vote for someone who shared their peace-at-any-price views. They met in convention in Cincinnati to show their displeasure with McClellan and his pronouncements. Such midwestern Copperheads as Lafe Develin of Indiana, James W. Singleton of Illinois, and Long attended. William M. Corry, a disciple of Vallandigham, presided over the splinter session. The *Crisis,* as independent as ever, gave the assemblage its blessing, and others watched the proceedings with interest.[120]

The dissident Democrats, meeting in Cincinnati, drafted resolutions which repudiated McClellan, defended slavery as an institution, and declared the war to be "wholly unconstitutional." They proved themselves to be true western sectionalists by objecting to the ascendancy of manufacturing over agriculture and by objecting to the transformation of the federal Union into a truly centralized government.[121] The bolters then tried to persuade Long to be their presidential nominee, but he declined the honor. Unable to find a suitable standard bearer, the convention recessed and then adjourned. The dissidents returned home empty-handed. Many of them decided to gain their revenge by boycotting the polls. They would vote for neither McClellan nor Lincoln.

The cauldron of politics boiled vigorously in the months preceding the election of November, 1864. Democrats waved a hundred different banners. Some still read "The Constitution as it is, the Union as it was," but that slogan was out of date in 1864. Some implied that McClellan was the remedy for all of the nation's ills. In some magic way his election would restore "peace, plenty, and happiness." Others argued that reunion could be secured only under Democratic direction. They tried to sell a conflicting collection of principles to the unwary.

Democrats proved themselves more adept in condemning Lincoln than in lauding their own candidate. They condemned the Lincoln administration as a colossal failure. They circulated pamphlets like *Corruptions and Frauds of Lincoln's Administration* and *Mr. Lincoln's Arbitrary Arrests*.[122] Editors tried to outdo each other in criticizing the President and in heaping abuse on his head. In that contest of vilification, the editor of the La Crosse *Democrat* captured top honors—no other Democrat could match the malignity and malevolence of "Brick" Pomeroy.

"May God Almighty," wrote the disconcerted Pomeroy after he had heard that Lincoln had been renominated, "forbid that we are to have two terms of the rottenest, most stinking ruin-working small pox ever conceived by fiends or mortals in the shape of two terms of Abe Lincoln's Administration."[123] Pomeroy put a picture of Lincoln in one issue of his paper and over it placed the caption, "The Widow-Maker of the Nineteenth Century."[124]

Pomeroy's editorials became exercises in name-calling. The campaign technique was one of desperation. He labeled Lincoln "an orphan maker," "a teller of smutty jokes," "a clown, buffoon and story-teller," "the fanatical tool of fanatics," and "the poorest apology for a Chief Magistrate the world ever saw." He said that the President was "a usurper who wears a No. 5 hat and No. 14 boots." He claimed that President Lincoln had violated his oath of office, "spit upon the Constitution," opened the door of the treasury to speculators and thieves, "strangled the Goddess of Liberty," and "woven the chain of slavery about the people." "Lincoln," Pomeroy wrote, "has been a worse tyrant and more inhuman butcher than has existed since the days of Nero. He has listened to the counsels of fools, and millions of mourners weep over the result of his incompetency."[125]

Pomeroy even suggested that assassination might yet save the country. In a moment of despair and despondency he wrote:

The man who votes for Lincoln now is a traitor. Lincoln is a traitor and murderer. He who, pretending to war for, wars against the constitution of our country is a traitor, and Lincoln is one of these men. . . . And if he is elected to misgovern for another four years, we trust some bold hand will pierce his heart with dagger point for the public good.[126]

The bloodthirsty editor of the La Crosse *Democrat* even suggested an epitaph he deemed appropriate:

> Beneath this turf, the widow-maker lies,
> Little in everything, except in size.[127]

"Brick" Pomeroy turned to verse as well as editorials to condemn Lincoln and advance the cause of McClellan in the presidential campaign of 1864. For example, he suggested new words for the popular tune "When Johnny Comes Marching Home." One of the stanzas read:

> The widow maker soon must cave!
>   Hurrah! Hurrah!
> We'll plant him in some nigger's grave!
>   Hurrah! Hurrah!
> Torn from your farm, your shop, your raft:
> Conscript! How do you like the draft?
>   And we'll stop that too,
>   When Little Mac takes the helm![128]

Pomeroy's rancorous rantings embarrassed his less vindictive Copperhead colleagues. They recognized that his extreme utterances hurt their cause and stigmatized them all. They campaigned with more reserve and more dignity—and with more effect. They also recognized that Vallandigham's participation in the presidential contest hindered rather than helped the Democratic cause.[129] The Chicago platform, with its peace plank, was a Democratic liability, even though candidate McClellan had repudiated it. The balance slowly and surely shifted back toward Lincoln in September. The note of despair which had characterized some of Lincoln's acts in August of 1864 gave way to a note of optimism. The activity of the Union Leagues and the Loyal Publication Society was reassuring. Democratic disunity and incompetency also helped, and the "treason campaign" of the Republicans was effective.

War prosperity also undermined the cause of Copperheadism while it strenghened the hands of the administration and helped re-elect Lincoln. The Midwest's commercial, agricultural, and manufacturing interests entered a "lush era"—"a prosperity so enormous as almost to challenge belief."[130] Army purchases consumed the agricultural surplus and farm prices spiraled upward. Laborers, owing to the draft and to the business prosperity, secured better wages and working conditions. The scarcity of labor as a commodity produced a situation in which workers' unions or associations grew in number and in strength. The war prosperity healed some of the wounds of the war. One newspaperman viewed that prosperity as "the lance of Achilles, healing by its touch the wounds of war and desolation."[131] The correspondent of the London *Times,* touring the upper Mississippi Valley, noted that business prosperity hardened the conscience: "Nothing is strange, nothing is unusual, nothing is unconstitutional, nothing is wicked to people who are prospering upon the war. . . ."[132]

The business prosperity affected Copperheadism adversely. A Democratic newsman, who watched Copperheadism retreat before the pressures of war prosperity, wrote of Cincinnati: "The city, like a busy, thrifty hive, is overflowing with honey. Pros-

perity smiles upon her, and, were it not for the occasional tele-
graphic bulletins, we would forget that there was such a thing
as a devastating war raging in the country."[133]

The cycle of prosperity, with its roots planted in the inflation-
ary legal-tender measures,[134] reached its climax in 1864. Lincoln's
stock rose; McClellan's declined. Republican realists recognized
that the golden rays of business prosperity would affect the election returns. ". . . keeping business steady until after the November elections," wrote an Illinois observer, would crush Copperheadism and defeat McClellan.[135] He saw the realization of his
prophecy.

While McClellan and Lincoln supporters fought a war of words
during the political campaign, Generals Sherman and Sheridan
gave the lie to the Copperhead contention that the war was a failure. Admiral David G. Farragut helped Sheridan and Sherman
to discredit the Copperhead thesis that the South could not be
conquered. Farragut captured Fort Morgan and Mobile Bay in
August. General Sheridan, during the months of September and
October, whipped Confederate armies in three separate battles in
the Shenandoah Valley. He then proceeded to put that region to
the torch. General Sherman captured Atlanta and watched it go
up in flames whose glow brightened Republican hopes on the eve
of the presidential election.[136]

The election returns of November, 1864, were as
resounding a victory for Lincoln as they were a decisive defeat for
McClellan and midwestern Copperheadism. Republicans retained
control of every governor's chair which they held before the
election in the Midwest. They strengthened their control of the
state legislatures and reversed the results of the elections of 1862
in Indiana and Illinois. They increased their majority in Congress
and several prominent Copperheads fell by the wayside. They
returned Lincoln to the White House for another four years. They
had full control of all the machinery of government plus the
know-how to keep it functioning smoothly and effectively.

Democrats drank the dregs of defeat. At their post-mortem

sessions, the defeated Democrats tried their hand at analysis and dissection. But the discredited political doctors—the Republicans would have labeled them "quacks"—could not agree upon the cause of their defeat at the polls or on the reasons why Copperheadism collapsed. The editor of the Dayton *Empire*, like an ostrich hiding its head in the sand, blamed the election on fraud.[137] Everyone admitted that the controlled soldier vote and other Republican stratagems had a bearing upon the result.[138] War prosperity and military victories on the eve of the elections bore heavily upon the way the political wind blew. Rampant nationalism was a factor. Republican propaganda and the treason tales appealed to the gullible, whether or not Democrats believed them unfair, fictitious, and false.[139] The Republican treason campaign paid enormous dividends; it contributed considerably to the quashing of Copperheadism.

Copperheads would not admit that Lincoln's qualities of leadership were linked to the demise of Copperheadism. Lincoln grew with the war; he was a party politician when he was elected president in 1860, but he was a statesman by the time the war was in its closing days. Furthermore, he possessed the common touch and the ability to gain the sympathy and the support of the many. They were magnetized by his sincerity and his integrity. His human qualities made him seem one of them. He had the knack of appealing to their good sense and their ideals. The public recognized the Copperhead-made charges of despotism and slander were out of character. ". . . he is in the hearts of *the people*," wrote one who was charmed by the wartime president; "they believe in him, in his *integrity of purpose;* they regard him as one of themselves."[140] Lincoln's quality of character, in an immeasurable way, contributed to his own re-election and to the recession of the Copperhead high tide of 1863.

Furthermore, the Copperheads refused to accept any of the blame for their post-election dilemma. No proven leader in the Midwest arose in the Democratic ranks, and the Democrats of 1864 would not admit that they had failed to keep abreast of the changing times. They refused to admit that the winds of change were blowing and that they had failed to trim their sails. Times changed, but most Copperheads did not. Some continued to delude themselves—even in early 1865—that it was still possible to return the nation to its prewar status, federal Union and all. They continued to look backward and to repeat the phrases of Jefferson. They refused to look forward, for they were blinded by their fears.

In the remaining months of the war midwestern Copperheadism died a tortuous death. Some of the prominent Democratic critics of the Lincoln administration looked "worse than if they had been struck by lightning."[141] Some still prayed for peace and pretended that it was a possibility. Henry Clay Dean, saddened by the election returns, wanted a national peace association established in hope that it might force Lincoln to sheath the sword.[142] Some retired from politics and devoted themselves to business. Others studied the election returns and held their tongues. The military collapse of the Confederacy in March and April of 1865 brought an end to the war. Events at Appomattox proved that the South could be conquered. Copperheads choked on their words and gasped for breath.

VIII

Aftermath

COPPERHEAD DREAMS of influencing the course of events on the American scene dissipated after the October and November, 1864, elections. It seemed as if Copperheadism had been repudiated by the electorate in every sector and section of the upper Mississippi Valley. The Republicans swept both the state and the national elections. Lincoln's supporters held victory celebrations and victory parades. Lincoln's midwestern critics read the election returns sadly. Copperheadism was doomed.

Although some of the defeated Democrats took their political medicine gracefully, others spoke bitter words and expressed their hate publicly. The editor of the Dubuque *Herald* was one who took the defeat in good grace. He wove a touch of humor into a news note:

Stock market—The market for McClellan stock is dull and drooping, with more buyers than sellers at fifty per cent discount. Holders are anxious to effect sales and are not particular about rates. Copperhead 64–90's have overstocked the market and another supply will not be needed in four years for national use. McClellan badges and medals are given away, holders having no further use for them. A whole torchlight parade could be bought for a song; small lots are in demand for sale at auction.[1]

Although a few of the bitter-enders claimed that the elections were won by fraud and by controlled soldiers' votes, the majority of the Copperheads recognized that the public preferred the administration to the loyal opposition. Throughout the war the Copperheads had always expressed great faith in democratic processes, in the law, and in the Constitution. As constitutionalists and conservatives, they had no course but to bow to the election returns.[2] That policy of acquiescence and acknowledgment was well stated by a longtime adviser to Vallandigham:

I recognize the fact that the great majority of the people of this country have given expression of opinions widely different than those which I have entertained and I feel like submitting to it in the same spirit as I would to the deliberate verdict of an intelligent jury. The policy of the Administration has become the policy of the American people, and I am willing that that policy should have a full, fair and impartial trial, and if it shall result in restoring peace, Union, harmony and prosperity, I shall rejoice as much as anybody and will be ready to admit my own mistake.[3]

While Democratic political leaders were counting their losses and pondering their party's future, the military phase of the Civil War came to an end. General Robert E. Lee and his demoralized forces allowed Federal troops to occupy Richmond. Several days later Lee surrendered the remnant of a once famous army to General Grant. Soon after, General Joseph E. Johnston turned his sword over to General Sherman. The Lincoln administration had carried the war to a successful conclusion. Democrats and peace men who had shouted that the South could not be conquered were silent, and the military victories of Grant and Sherman added other nails to the Copperhead coffin.

While the victory celebrations were in progress, word spread that President Lincoln had fallen victim to an assassin's bullet. Those who had once bitterly assailed the President turned mourners in April of 1865. They had watched the President feud with the Radical Republicans over Reconstruction policy, and their sympathy went to the man in the White House. Some of the Copperheads who had been harsh critics feared that Lincoln's death might allow the harsh and vengeful Reconstruction policies of the Radical Republicans to prevail. The editor of the Milwaukee *See-Bote* claimed that Copperheads could mourn with "pure conscience." He wrote:

... we have voted against Lincoln's election, written against it, spoken against it—that we have done, and as we believe with pure conscience.

But we may say with an equally pure conscience that there are no more sincere mourners today—none who deplore the death of the President more than the Democracy of the Northern States.[4]

Even "Brick" Pomeroy of the La Crosse *Democrat*, a calumniator who had slandered Lincoln during the war years, made a show of mourning. He decked his newspaper in black and turned the column rules to express regret at the death of Lincoln. The man who hoped for Lincoln's assassination in August of 1864 deprecated Booth's mad act of April 14, 1865. He who had at one time labeled Lincoln "fiend" and "fool" wrote an editorial regret:

We mourn with the people, for a great man has fallen. President Lincoln was not a Napoleon—was not a Jackson—was not a Webster—was not a Douglas. But we believe he was a man of genius—a lover of his country—an honest man—a statesman.[5]

For good measure, Pomeroy suggested that Benjamin Butler might have been responsible for Lincoln's death and that Booth might have been Butler's tool. Heaping insult upon insinuation, Pomeroy wrote that he knew no one "more wicked and less principled"[6] than Butler. Pomeroy's political rivals countered with insinuation of their own. They reprinted Pomeroy's editorial of August 29, 1864, in which he had suggested that "some bold hand" drive a dagger into Lincoln's heart "for the public good." They circulated rumors that Pomeroy was soon to be arrested and that the finger of guilt pointed in his direction.[7]

While Northerners mourned the death of Lincoln, some Republicans tried to link the assassination plot to Confederate leaders and to the Knights of the Golden Circle. While rumors circulated that the Golden Circle and the Peace Democrats were somehow involved, Judge Advocate General Joseph Holt took a hand in investigating the murder. Holt built a fantastic tale from lies and perjury—a concoction which traced the assassination plot to Jefferson Davis' doorstep and stirred anew the fires of emotionalism.[8]

Such prominent prisoners as Phineas C. Wright, creator of the Order of American Knights, and George W. L. Bickley, originator of the Knights of the Golden Circle, were also interrogated regarding Lincoln's death. One of the investigators tried to convince Wright that he "unquestionably" was a "party to the conspiracy."[9] Bickley, incarcerated in Fort Warren, also had the blame for Lincoln's death put at his feet.[10] Both Wright and Bickley, of course, denied complicity and were kept in confinement for some months more. Wright was finally released in August of 1865 and Bickley a short time later. No specific charges were ever made against either of the two, nor were any trials ever accorded them.

Republicans did more than try to link Confederate leaders to Lincoln's assassination. They extended their treason campaign into the Reconstruction period. The practice of "waving the bloody shirt" had its roots in the political campaigns of 1863 and 1864. The Republicans claimed that their party had a monopoly upon patriotism and that the Democrats, South and North, were rebels and traitors. The anti-Copperhead tirades of 1863–64 and the "bloody shirt" practices of the postwar years were cut from the same cloth, both resting on an emotional base, and were both used to win elections.

The Republican practice of "waving the bloody shirt" helped to keep that party in control of state governments and the federal government, despite the popular reaction to fraud and corruption in high places. The "bloody shirt" slogans put Democrats at a disadvantage. They spent more time denying that they had been wartime traitors than in discussing the issues of the day.

The "bloody shirt" smear, for example, was used effectively by Republicans in the tenth congressional district of Indiana in the elections of 1866. Robert Lowry, a Copperhead who had denounced Lincoln's Emancipation Proclamation, sought a congressional seat and won his party's nomination. Republicans conducted a campaign of abuse and vilification. They "exposed" his wartime record as an "obstructionist" and "traitor." A Republican-circulated flyer contained several poems dedicated to

245

Lowry, denounced as the "Dirty Dog, Dead and Damned." The shorter of the two poems read:

> To Congress poor Bobby is anxious to go,
> But his "democratic horse" always travels too slow;
> And the soldiers, whom he says have been taught to *steal*,
> Will stamp the vile Copperhead under their heel.

> When he dies, all the Cops. will draw nigh to his "bier,"
> And drop o'er his grave each a crocodile tear,
> And, as in the wave of oblivion he sinks,
> The people'l cry out, "Good God, how he—smells."[11]

The "bloody shirt" era, an extension of the "loyalty crusade" of the Civil War days, lasted into the 1880's. Grover Cleveland, supported by "ex-Copperheads" and "ex-rebels," broke the Republican strangle hold upon the presidency in 1884. There had still been considerable "waving of the bloody shirt" by some Republicans in that election contest, and the Democrats were referred to as the party of "Rum, Romanism, and Rebellion."

Cleveland's conservative course helped to dispel the myth that Democrats in general would pursue a course inimical to the general welfare of the nation. He did, however, arouse a host of Republican critics in 1887, when he sanctioned the return of captured rebel flags to former Confederate regiments. Lucius W. Fairchild, the patriotic commander of the Grand Army of the Republic, was one who put his public protest into the record books. "May God," shouted Fairchild, "palsy the hand that wrote that order!" The many protests produced a wave of hysteria, and President Cleveland judiciously withdrew his order. Nineteen years later, President Theodore Roosevelt returned the captured banners to their respective regiments. It was, evidently, less "traitorous" for a Republican president to return the Confederate flags to the South.

Although Cleveland retreated before "patriotic pressure" in 1887, the "bloody shirt" technique was slowly dying. Several incidents the next year indicated that "waving the bloody shirt" had lost much of its appeal and influence. In 1888 the Senate of the United States confirmed the appointment of Melville W. Fuller as Chief Justice of the Supreme Court. Fuller had been one of the leading Copperheads in Illinois during the war. As a member of the Illinois Copperhead legislature of 1863, he had criticized Lincoln mercilessly, led the movement to bring about a national convention, and preached the cause of peace and compromise. Fuller won the Senate indorsement even though some Republicans "exposed" his wartime record and despite a smear campaign conducted in some quarters. His nomination was a triumph for moderation and a defeat for the "bloody shirt" crowd.[12]

Public reaction to the Ingalls-Voorhees feud of 1888 also tended to prove that the era of the "bloody shirt" was coming to an end. John W. Ingalls, U.S. senator from Kansas and a politician known for his mastery of vituperation, launched a personal attack on a fellow senator, Daniel W. Voorhees of Indiana. Ingalls publicly accused Voorhees of having been a wartime Copperhead and traitor. He said that both Voorhees and General McClellan were "allies of the Confederacy" and men of black hearts and weak minds. Voorhees retaliated with bitter invective. He questioned Ingalls' honesty, integrity, and sanity. He called the Kansan "a great liar and dirty dog." The cup of animosity and bitterness overflowed.

Neither senator, of course, emerged from the guttersniping with clean hands. Sensible senators and intelligent editors deplored the feud and expressed disgust with both participants. The editor of the New York *Times* labeled the feud "fatal nonsense." Then the editor reprimanded Ingalls for using the "bloody shirt" technique, pointing out that it was an outdated and irresponsible political stratagem. That editorial, in effect, was proof that an era had come to an end. "It is well enough in political warfare to rake over the past for all the weapons that can fairly be used," wrote the *Times*'s editor, "but it is also to be remembered that it is the past and that the issues on which the next election is to be decided are not those of a quarter of a century ago."[13]

While Republicans were "waving the bloody shirt" in the postwar decades, they also set to work with pen and pencil to write their point of view into history. Some wrote memoirs, some prepared articles and books, while others wrote "history."

Such well-known Republicans as Horace Greeley and Charles A. Dana wrote recollections which justified their stand on the issues of the day. Carl Schurz, who mixed politics and soldiering, contributed his reminiscences in three bulky volumes. Benjamin Butler wrote his autobiography and recorded his hatred of "Brick" Pomeroy. James G. Blaine presented the Republican interpretation in a two-volume account entitled *Twenty Years of Congress*.[14]

Midwestern Republicans added to the stack with a variety of works. George W. Julian, Radical Republican from Indiana, justified emancipation in a volume entitled *Political Recollections, 1840–1872*.[15] Lew Wallace contributed a well-written autobiography.[16] Shelby Cullom, a Know-Nothing who nestled down comfortably in the Republican party in Illinois, added a volume of recollections.[17] Whitelaw Reid, a Republican newsman of Ohio, turned to writing history. He told the story—with a Republican twist—of Ohio's role in the conflict in a two-volume work entitled *Ohio in the War*.[18] Governor Oliver P. Morton's friends were busy getting their story into print. William R. Holloway, Morton's private secretary and brother-in-law, took a hand in putting a hero's halo upon the head of Indiana's wartime governor. Holloway wrote a volume with the title *History of Indianapolis and Marion County*.[19] That biased account helped to fasten the treason label upon the Peace Democrats and the Copperheads. It also helped to place the story of subversive societies into the written record. Henry B. Carrington, who served Morton most loyally and helped to expose subversive societies in Indiana, wrote a dozen articles. Some were published, others were not. The Carrington articles depicted the Indiana Copperheads as villains and lauded Morton's energy, ability, and patriotism. Carrington, who had bungled while commanding the military district of Indiana, had a vested interest in depicting Morton's views as the true views and in justifying some of his own questionable acts.[20] It was an official biography of Morton, written by a lawyer-devotee named

William Dudley Foulke, which put the frosting on the cake.[21] Foulke's two-volume work won widespread acceptance, even in historical circles. It painted Governor Morton's every act in bright hues and portrayed Copperhead activities in somber black. It wove traitors' cloaks for Daniel Voorhees, Dodd, and Milligan. Foulke's highly colored biography seemed to substantiate the treason tales recorded by W. H. H. Terrell, wartime confidant of Governor Morton and adjutant general of the state of Indiana. Terrell compiled an eight-volume *Report of the Adjutant General of Indiana.*[22] Terrell's reports included a generous portion of Republican propaganda. Terrell and Morton held the same political views and the same anti-Copperhead prejudices. Terrell, like Foulke and Holloway, depicted Morton as the "savior of Indiana," and they gilded the many arbitrary acts of the energetic governor. Terrell's eight-volume *Report of the Adjutant General of Indiana* was printed at the state's expense—even Democratic taxpayers helped to pay for the apotheosizing of Oliver P. Morton.

Other Republican writers contributed their bit too. The Republican critics of Pomeroy, for example, carried their anti-Copperhead campaign into the postwar years. The editor of the La Crosse *Republican* wrote a "newspaper history" of his county and praised the patriotism of his party, dwelling at length on the "treasonable views" of "Brick" Pomeroy and his Copperhead newspaper. That Republican wrapped up his anti-Pomeroy prejudices in a capsule: "He [Pomeroy] out-jeffed Jeff Davis in treasonable utterances and out-deviled the Devil in deviltry."[23]

Some of the detectives or agents who helped to expose the various "treason plots" and thereby discredit Copperheadism also set to work to get their stories into print. I. Winslow Ayer, the questionable character who gave shape to the "Camp Douglas Conspiracy," published two exposés. In each he was the central figure—the lion of the occasion. The first, entitled *The Great Northwestern Conspiracy in All Its Startling Details . . . ,*[24] was published soon after the close of the war. The second, entitled *The Great Treason Plot in the North during the War . . . ,* was put into print thirty years later.[25] The two pamphlets, in time, became the chief sources from which writers of fiction and of history drew information regarding the "Camp Douglas Conspiracy." The creator of the legend, thus, took a hand in building it bigger and better. Thomas H. Keefe, a government agent in the Chicago area, made a contribution to the "Camp Douglas Conspiracy" story by publishing his memoirs in *Everybody's Magazine*.[26] James R. Gilmore, whose veracity has since been questioned, collected an author's fee for a composition entitled "The Chicago Conspiracy," which appeared in the *Atlantic Monthly*.[27] Gilmore's article and Ayer's first pamphlet were the chief sources from which Confederate agents like Thomas H. Hines, John B. Castleman, and John W. Headly culled information for their postwar tales of adventure and wartime activity.[28]

Felix G. Stidger, detective extraordinary, wrote at length about the Indianapolis treason plots which he helped to expose. Stidger, who styled himself "the Spy Complete," wove the threads of treason into his exposé of Dodd, Milligan, and their cohorts. Stidger was the chief witness in the Indianapolis treason trials and in his book he tried to put the pieces of the puzzle together. Although the book, *Treason History of the Order of the Sons of Liberty* . . .[29] was replete with errors of contradiction and omission, it became a best seller. Stidger, thus, helped to put his deeds on the rolls of history, and his readers swallowed the tales he told and accepted the legends to which he contributed. The shorthand scribe who occupied a table at the military proceedings at which Dodd, Milligan, and others were tried also put the "treason trials" into print. The publication of *The Trials for Treason at Indianapolis*, edited by Benn Pitman,[30] convinced the credulous. It found a large audience and helped to fasten the badge of treason to the Copperhead cause.

Authors, detectives, and politicians of Republican persuasion combined their talents to shape public opinion in postwar years. They created the atmosphere in which it was acceptable to "wave the bloody shirt"; they turned legends and myths into history and they fastened the stigma of treason on wartime Copperheadism.

While men of Republican persuasion were busy with pen and ink and the Union Clubs and the GAR sounded the drums of patriotism, ex-Copperheads set to work to justify their wartime views and activities.

Some of those who had gained a reputation as critics of Lincoln restated their conservative and sectional views in books, pamphlets, and speeches. Henry Clay Dean and Pomeroy, for example, continued to condemn Wall Street, bemoan the ascendancy of industrialism, and insist that they were still disciples of Jeffersonianism. Dean, dismissed by some of his Republican cronies as an eccentric, labored over a book manuscript for months on end. That work, published in 1868, challenged the course of events and attacked the "vested interests" of the East. He claimed that he was still an apostle of liberty, a defender of the poor, a spokesman for the agricultural interests, and a champion of the West. In his lengthy book he wrote of four "curses" or "crimes" which he laid at the door of the Lincoln administration: (*a*) the funding system, (*b*) the banking system, (*c*) the tariff, and (*d*) despotism.[31] He railed against the centralization of the government and the ascendancy of industrialism as he had during the war. He claimed that war had destroyed the people's democracy and had put the money men in power. He claimed that westerners lost their liberties and their hard-earned money to a Wall Street oligarchy. He bemoaned the passing of Jeffersonian doctrine and the triumph of grab-and-hold. The dollar sign was the new American god and Christian principles were shunted aside. Small wonder then that Dean served the cause of such sectional protest movements as Grangerism, Greenbackism, and Populism. He put his prejudices against Wall Street and strong government into verse:

> War is the statesman's game, the priest's delight,
> The lawyer's jest, the hired assassin's trade.
> And to those royal murderers whose mean thrones
> Are bought by crimes of treachery and gore,
> The bread they eat, the staff on which they lean,

> Guards, garbed in blood-red livery, surround
> Their palaces, participate the crimes
> That force defends, and from a nation's rage
> Secures the crown, which all the curses reach
> That famine, frenzy, woe and penury breathe.
> These are the hired bravoes who defend
> The tyrant's throne—the bullies of his fear;
> These are the sinks and channels of worst vice,
> The refuse of society, the dregs
> Of all that is most vile; their cold hearts blend
> Deceit with sternness, ignorance with pride,
> All that is mean and villainous with rage,
> Which hopelessness of good, and self-contempt
> Alone might kindle. They are decked in wealth,
> Honor and power, then are sent abroad
> To do their work. The pestilence that stalks
> In gloomy triumph through some eastern land
> Is less destroying. They cajole with gold
> And promises of fame, the thoughtless youth
> Already crushed with servitude; he knows
> His wretchedness too late, and cherishes
> Repentance for his ruin, when his doom
> Is sealed in gold and blood.[32]

Dean hated men of wealth and influence; he mistrusted monopolists of every kind. In time, his hatred of wealth became an obsession. Quite naturally, he turned to repudiation of the national debt as proper policy, for he argued that the money monopoly had clamped its hold upon the country unconstitutionally. He summed up his views on repudiation tersely:

Repudiation offers the only hope of relief to the country. First—It takes the corrupting influence of money out of legislation. Second—It rids the country of the whole plague and curse of assessors' clerks, collectors, spies, pimps, stamps, tariff, excises and excisemen that now enslave us. Third—It equalizes the general burdens of the war. The poor men gave their lives in battle. This demands that the rich, who grew fat on blood, shall surrender the plunder of war to save the poor who fought in battle from being further ground by direct and indirect taxation.[33]

Dean objected to the course which the reconstruction of the South was taking. He objected to the program of the Radical

Republicans. As in Civil War days, he was at heart a sectionalist and a defender of western interests.

Like Dean, Pomeroy viciously denounced the tariff program and the national bank system in postwar days. Like the economic determinists of a later day, he claimed that vested interests had used the war as a means of fastening their hold on the country. He bellowed his anti–New England and anti–Wall Street sentiments in speeches and turned to the pamphlet as a medium of expression. In 1866 he wrote: ". . . western men—we made fools of ourselves; we fought our true friends, to help our worst enemies."[34] He argued that the Civil War had turned into a curse for both the West and the South; agricultural interests suffered because of the ascendancy of capital and industry. He put his hatred of Wall Street into a soliloquy which he credited to a bondholder. In that soliloquy he credited "the Bondholder" with chortling: "Work away, you poor fools. Toil your fingers to the bone, and die poor men for my sake."[35]

After a short fling as editor of a New York newspaper, Pomeroy turned to Greenbackism as an outlet for his energy. He wrote a short history of the war, dealing chiefly with its causes and results.[36] The main theme of this subjective work was equalitarianism, and the interpretations were those of a Wall Street critic and a western sectionalist. Pomeroy became a big chief in the Greenback wigwam. In fact, he became director of the membership campaign which was so effective in the late 1860's. In the twilight of his life he began to write his memoirs, finishing only the first volume of a two-volume project.[37] It was full of distortions and prejudices just as his wartime editorials had been.

Pomeroy was not the only midwestern Copperhead to write his memoirs and to justify his wartime views. S. S. Cox, ebullient Ohioan, presented his thirty years of public life in printed form.[38] It blended history and personal justification in readable form. Daniel Voorhees, the leading Copperhead of Indiana during the war, combined autobiography and speeches into a two-volume work.[39] David Turpie, elected to the U.S. Senate by Indiana's Copperhead-manned legislature of 1863, also wrote of his personal experiences and the history of the times.[40] Vallandigham, whose death came dramatically in 1871, failed to get his side of the story into print. A nephew, however, tried to vindicate his uncle and prepared a sympathetic biography which became a best seller in Ohio.[41] This partisan volume debunked the Radical Republican contention that Vallandigham was a traitor and that Copperheadism was an American heresy.

Midwestern Copperheads also contributed much material for another book which was published in the postwar era. John A. Marshall, a Marylander who was arrested arbitrarily in 1861, compiled a volume which he entitled *American Bastille: A History of the Illegal Arrests and Imprisonment of American Citizens during the Late Civil War.*[42] Such prominent midwestern Copperheads as Milligan, Mahony, Vallandigham, and Edson B. Olds contributed accounts of their arrests and incarceration to the editor. The volume was a severe indictment of the arbitrary arrests which President Lincoln's agents made and which the midwestern Copperheads had so vigorously opposed.

Midwestern Copperheads turned to the courts as well as to the printed page to vindicate their honor and to repudiate the wartime administration. In the complex story of the postwar court cases, the name of Lambdin P. Milligan leads all the rest.

Milligan had been one of the four Hoosiers convicted by a military commission in December of 1864. The others were William A. Bowles, Stephen Horsey, and Harrison H. Dodd, who was convicted and sentenced to death *in absentia* after he fled to Canada. At the time, Copperheads protested that the military trials were illegal and viewed the verdict as a miscarriage of justice and a violation of constitutional guarantees. Those who called themselves the champions of civil liberties turned to President Andrew Johnson, the Congress, and the courts to stay the executions and redress grievances.

Daniel Voorhees and other Copperhead congressmen introduced a resolution which challenged the authority of the military officials who tried Milligan and his friends. The House of Representatives adopted it by an 80 to 64 vote. In part, the resolution read: "That no person shall be tried by court martial or military commission, in any State or Territory where the courts of the United States are open. . . . "[43]

Delaying the executions of Milligan, Horsey, and Bowles and the assassination of Lincoln put the fate of the prisoners in the hands of Andrew Johnson. Bothered less by constitutional scruples than Lincoln had been, Johnson bowed to pressure of the Radical Republicans and ordered the executions to take place on May 19, 1865.[44]

Democrats and conservative Republicans voiced their opposition. Judge David Davis of the U.S. Supreme Court, while on circuit duty in Indiana, turned his atention to the case. He urged President Johnson to commute the sentence to life imprisonment. He also conferred with Governor Morton and evidently convinced the strong-minded governor that the military commission which had tried the prisoners was illegal, for the regular courts were open. Morton, formerly firm for execution, suddenly reversed himself and favored changing the sentence to life imprisonment.[45] The Indianapolis *Journal,* owned by the governor's brother-in-law, joined the campaign for commutation and suggested that the cases be retried in the federal courts. The editor of the *Journal* also questioned the legality of the Indianapolis treason trials.[46] Democrats cried "Amen" and added their petitions to the others.

President Johnson eventually bowed to pressure exerted in behalf of commutation. Three days before the date he had earlier set for the execution, he commuted the sentence of Stephen Horsey and postponed the fateful day for Milligan and Bowles to June 2.[47]

Attorneys for the convicted Copperheads, meanwhile, turned to the federal courts to overthrow the ruling of the military tribunal. They asked the federal judges of the Indiana district of the circuit court to assume jurisdiction or to order the prisoners discharged. The two judges disagreed in order that the case could be taken to the U.S. Supreme Court. President Johnson then commuted the sentences of Milligan and Bowles to life imprisonment,[48] and everyone waited to see what the decision of the U.S. Supreme Court would be.

At length the case came up for argument before the Supreme Court, both sides having added counsel.[49] In accepting jurisdiction the Court repudiated the stand it had taken earlier in *Ex parte Vallandigham*.

The defense of Milligan featured an eloquent and erudite argument by Jeremiah Black—an argument which ranks with the greatest forensic efforts in the history of the nation. The Court's decision, read by Justice David Davis on April 3, 1866, was a great victory for Milligan and the ex-Copperheads. The decision, in fact, became "one of the bulwarks of American civil liberties":

... the Constitution of the United States is a law for rulers and people, equally in war and peace, and covers with the shield of protection all classes of men, at all times and under all circumstances. No doctrine involving more pernicious consequences was ever invented by the wit of man than that any of its provisions can be suspended during any of the great exigencies of Government.[50]

With trumpet-like clarity the Court admonished Governor Morton and General Alvin P. Hovey for sponsoring military trials in areas where the civil courts were open and where the civil government was functioning. "A citizen, not connected with the military service, and resident in a State where the courts are all open, and in the proper exercise of their jurisdiction," Judge Davis stated in *Ex parte Milligan*, "cannot, even when the privilege of habeas corpus is suspended, be tried, convicted, or sentenced otherwise than by the ordinary courts of law."[51]

Ex-Copperheads like Mahony, Vallandigham, and Voorhees lauded the Court's decision. They claimed that it validated their contention that they were the defenders of civil liberties as well as critics of the wartime administration. It proved, they contended, that their criticism of wartime despotism was valid. *Ex parte Milligan* was balm to their wounds.

Radical Republicans, on the other hand, either ignored the decision or denounced it. Some like John A. Bingham of Ohio and the noted Wendell Phillips criticized both the Court and its decision. They proved themselves real radicals by suggesting that the Court be abolished.

Federal officials took steps to release the prisoners; and, at the direction of President Johnson, the Secretary of War ordered the prisoners discharged on April 10, 1866. Milligan, Horsey, and Bowles returned to their Indiana homes to await action by the civil authorities. A short time later they were indicted by the civil authorities in the federal courts. Milligan was arrested and forced to post bail. But the case never came to trial and the three ex-Copperheads felt that they had won partial vindication.

Milligan followed with interest a case begun by Andrew Humphreys, another of the principals in the Indiana treason trials of November and December, 1864. Humphreys, like Milligan, had been arrested in the October, 1864, roundup which Governor Morton had engineered on the eve of the fall elections. At the time, Milligan was sentenced to be hanged; Humphreys was ordered imprisoned at hard labor. In January of 1865, however, Humphreys' penalty was changed to detention within the limits of two townships in his home county. About a year after the war had ended, Humphreys took steps to gain revenge. On February 1, 1866, he filed a complaint in the circuit court of Sullivan County against Samuel McCormack and ten others for assault and battery and false imprisonment.

McCormack, who was captain of the army detail which arrested Humphreys, was found guilty of the charges and ex-Copperheads who dominated the jury set damages at $25,000. McCormack, through his attorneys, moved to have the case taken into a federal court and out of the realm of partisan politics. The judge of the state circuit court overruled the motion to move the case into the federal courts. The defendants then attempted to appeal their cause to the Indiana state Supreme Court. But that court avoided a decision and the case then bogged down on legal technicalities. In the end Humphreys failed to collect any damages, and his victory was only partial.[52]

Milligan also turned to the courts to seek damages. His case had a stranger ending. The suit dragged on for three years without hearings, as the attorneys for both parties played a game of cat and rat. Finally in 1871, with Thomas A. Hendricks representing Milligan, the court took up the case in which the plaintiff sought damages from the members of the military court which had found him guilty of treason. The jury brought in a verdict of "guilty," but awarded him only the sum of five dollars. The victory was a hollow one. Ex-Copperheads and Radical Republicans debated the meaning of the decision and the paltry award for damages. Milligan claimed that he had been vindicated and that the decision indicted both the Lincoln administration and the Morton regime. Republicans, on the other hand, claimed that five dollars were all that a Copperhead's time and trouble were worth.

A sequel to the Milligan case was written in the neighboring state of Illinois. Madison Y. Johnson became the central figure in the litigation, as he sought to clear his name, smear his enemies, and collect damages. The case dated back to August 28, 1862, when Mr. Johnson was arrested by a federal marshal at the direction of the Secretary of War. Although no charges were filed, the Galena Copperhead was hustled off to Fort Lafayette and placed behind bars. Johnson's pleas to President Lincoln, a onetime personal friend and political ally, went unanswered. After the elections of 1862, however, Madison Y. Johnson and many others were discharged and sent home. After his release, he commenced legal proceedings against those whom he held responsible for his arrest and incarceration.

The case of "Madison Y. Johnson *vs.* J. Russel Jones, John C. Hawkins, O. P. Hopkins, E. B. Washburne, and Bradner Smith— Trespass for false imprisonment," was tried in the state circuit court.[53] The decision in the lower state court was unfavorable to Mr. Johnson; the state circuit court released all causes of action and damages to the "injured party." The decision, in effect, contended that no one arrested by President Lincoln's order had any rights that a "loyal court" was bound to respect. Madison Johnson and his lawyers immediately appealed the case to the state

Supreme Court, where they had hopes of a more favorable decision. The Illinois state Supreme Court reversed the judgment of
the lower court and reprimanded the circuit judge. The decision,
Copperhead in tone and principle, indicted the Lincoln administration for its unconstitutional acts. The decision held: (*a*) that
the President had no such powers as those exercised in the arrest
of Mr. Johnson, (*b*) that in his military capacity, the President's
authority was restricted by the lines of the army, (*c*) that the
President could not declare martial law, or suspend the writ of
habeas corpus, except in districts where war actually existed, and,
(*d*) that such power, as claimed for the President and his subordinates, could not safely be intrusted to any government by a
people claiming to be free. Finally, after striking out all the defense, the state Supreme Court sent the case back to the circuit
court to have the plaintiff's damages assessed.[54]

The circuit court, in turn, carried out the order and entered a
judgment upon the record. In part, that judgment read:

And inasmuch as said suit was brought by said plantiff for a personal
vindication of his character and conduct as a citizen, he releases the
said damages, except as to the sum of one thousand dollars for costs
and expenses incurred by said plaintiff on account of said wrongful
seizure and imprisonment. It is thereupon considered by the Court,
that the said plaintiff have and recover of and from the said defendents
. . . the sum of one thousand dollars, and cost of suit, and that execution issue therefore.[55]

Madison Y. Johnson claimed that the decision exculpated him
and at the same time censured the Lincoln administration. Republicans, however, paid slight attention to the decision of the state
Supreme Court. They noted that the most influential jurist of the
Court was Sidney Breese—one of the state's better-known Copperheads in the days of the Civil War. Copperheads, like leop-
ards, the Republicans concluded, never changed their spots.

The suit brought by George Wallace Jones against William H.
Seward, wartime Secretary of State, also made headlines in the
postwar years. Jones was one of the first Iowans arrested—in December of 1861, soon after his return to New York from a minis-

tership at Bogotá, South America. No charges of any kind were ever filed against Mr. Jones. He was released on February 22, 1862, after sixty-four days of imprisonment. He lived under a cloud during the remaining years of the war. Not only had he been arrested arbitrarily, but two of his sons served in the Confederate army.

Although George Wallace Jones was a Copperhead at heart, he was in no position to be a vocal critic of Lincoln or the course of wartime events. After the war, however, Mr. Jones decided to bring suit for false imprisonment to clear himself of disloyalty charges. He was spurred to action by Edwin R. Meade,[56] a notable attorney who offered his services free, if Jones would bring a suit for false imprisonment against Secretary of State William H. Seward. Jones naturally agreed and Meade subsequently engaged Charles O'Connor, counsel for Jefferson Davis, and John McKeon to assist him. Through his lawyers, Jones sued for $50,000 damages. Seward's attorney offered Meade $5,000 if he would withdraw the suit. Meade refused, saying that he had sued for fifty thousand dollars. Seward's death, in 1872, ended the case at a time when both Jones and Meade were sanguine that the case would end in victory for their side.[57]

Suits against the government for false arrest and imprisonment would have numbered in the thousands had not Seward and Secretary of War Stanton taken precautionary measures when those arrested arbitrarily were released. A condition of their release was the signing of a promise not to bring suit or to hold the government responsible for their arrest. Wearied of waiting, most of them signed the promise. After their release they were in no position to vindicate themselves or gain revenge.

Most of those who challenged the Lincoln administration and who served as Copperheads during the war years fared well in the postwar era. Their friends and acquaintances did not believe the traitor and treason charges which Republican propagandists circulated for political gain. Some served long and well in the field of politics in spite of the handicaps which the times set in their way. Others gained reputations in the professions, mostly as judges or lawyers. Still others scored in the field of business. The postwar successes of the ex-Copperheads gives the lie to the legend that the critics of the Lincoln administration were men of weak heart and blank mind.

Many of the Copperheads who jousted in the political arena in the war years enjoyed political success in the postwar era. Democrats were at a disadvantage during the postwar years, for the 1865–80 era was one in which the Republican party had a virtual monopoly on the national government. Democrats were at a disadvantage when Republicans "waved the bloody shirt" and mouthed patriotic platitudes. Nevertheless, a large number of those who served as members of the opposition party during the war sat in Congress and opposed the Reconstruction policy of the Radical Republicans.

Daniel W. Voorhees, Indiana's leading Copperhead in the war years, served in Congress for more than two decades after Appomattox. He served two postwar terms in the House of Representatives, and then sat in the U.S. Senate twenty years more. He was chairman of the Senate Finance Committee during President Grover Cleveland's second term and gradually gained the stature of a statesman.[58] Thomas A. Hendricks, another of the more prominent Democrats of Indiana, was as successful in postwar politics as Voorhees. Hendricks served in the U.S. Senate from 1863 to 1869. In 1872 he was elected governor of his state. He was a contender for the presidential nomination at the Democratic national convention of 1876 and led on the first ballot. When the nomination finally went to Samuel J. Tilden, Hendricks accepted second place on the national ticket. When the election commissioners in what is sometimes termed "the Stolen Election" gave the contested electoral votes to Rutherford B. Hayes, Hendricks lost his bid for the vice-presidency. Eight years later he was again nominated, and this time he was elected Vice-President on the ticket headed by Grover Cleveland.[59]

Hendricks and Voorhees were not the only ex-Copperheads of

Indiana who enjoyed considerable political succeess. Joseph E. McDonald, Democratic gubernatorial candidate against Morton in 1864, served three postwar terms in the U.S. Senate. William H. Hamilton, critic of Lincoln and Morton during the war, served in the House of Representatives.

George H. Pendleton, one of the principal Ohio Copperheads during the war, also became a well-known public figure in the years that followed. His was a checkered career, yet he was always in the limelight. After his defeat for re-election in 1866, Pendleton became the best-known advocate of the "Ohio idea" —a plan to issue legal tender notes, or greenbacks, to pay the U.S. bonds as they matured. He was a contender for the top spot on his party's ticket in 1868, but he failed to get the nomination. He suffered another political disappointment the following year when he lost the gubernatorial contest in Ohio to Rutherford B. Hayes. Later, Pendleton served a six-year term in the U.S. Senate, where he led the fight for civil service reform. The Pendleton Act of 1883 immortalized his name in American history.

Other Ohio ex-Copperheads also served in Congress. Allen G. Thurman, who campaigned for Vallandigham in 1863, held a seat in the Senate for eighteen years. George L. Converse, advocate of peace and compromise throughout 1864, served a term in the House of Representatives. So did Hugh J. Jewett, another active Ohio Democrat. S. S. Cox, whose private papers prove him to be more of a Copperhead than his public utterances, moved from Ohio to New York City in the postwar years because he wanted a greater outlet for his legal talents. New York Democratic leaders noted his oratorical ability and qualities of leadership and soon drafted him to run for Congress. He was elected from his district, and in Congress he opposed most of the Reconstruction bills introduced by Radical Republicans.[60]

Illinois politicos who bore the Copperhead brand also scored in the political arena. William R. Morrison, maligned by Radical Republicans as a "Southern sympathizer" during the war, gained a measure of success in both law and politics. He represented his district in Congress for a long time, and he was repeatedly boomed as presidential timber. Samuel S. Marshall, linked to the KGC by Republicans, served three terms in the lower house of Congress. James W. Singleton, preacher of peace in 1863 and 1864, also served in the House of Representatives. James C. Robinson served two terms in the House during the 1870's, and Robert M. Knapp, John R. Eden, and Carter H. Harrison—all Democratic regulars in the 1860's—also were elected to Congress in the following decade. Carter H. Harrison, "Copperhead" mayor of Chicago during the last half of the war, gained a remarkable reputation in the years that followed. He served five terms as mayor and two as congressman. When Harrison was assassinated by a political fanatic in 1893, his son stepped forward and continued to wear the mayor's mantle for twelve years. Father and son served the city of Chicago for twenty-two years.[61]

Several other ex-Copperheads enjoyed considerable success in the political arena. Charles A. Eldridge, who voted with the Democrats in Congress during the war, served three postwar terms as a congressman from Wisconsin. Garrett Davis, a Kentuckian who was very critical of the course which the Lincoln administration was pursuing, continued to serve in the U.S. Senate until his death in 1872.

Vallandigham and Long, the two best-known advocates of an armistice policy in 1863 and 1864, contributed little to postwar politics. Long, like Achilles, sulked in his tent. Not until 1876 would he vote for a presidential candidate. Vallandigham wishfully hoped to be nominated as his party's choice for a U.S. Senate seat in 1867, but he failed to get much support from his Democratic friends. He attended the Democratic national convention as a delegate in 1868. That same year he was nominated for Congress in his district but failed to unseat the incumbent. It was difficult for an ex-Copperhead to compete with an ex-soldier in politics.

In the judicial field the ex-Copperheads blazed brilliant trails. Melville W. Fuller, leader of the "peace convention" crowd in the

Illinois Copperhead legislature of 1863, served as a federal judge with distinction in the postwar era. In 1888, President Cleveland named him to head the U.S. Supreme Court—a position which he filled with ability and dignity for twenty-two years.[62]

Sidney Breese and Edward G. Ryan also left their influence upon their respective courts. Breese, a member of the Illinois State Supreme Court and a backstage Copperhead, gained stature as a jurist in the postwar years. Breese wrote some of the best-known decisions of the court, including the majority decision in *Munn* v. *Illinois*. At a later date the U.S. Supreme Court affirmed the decision written by Breese. That famous decision challenged the laissez-faire doctrines of earlier years, and it established the principle that quasi-public enterprises "must submit to be controlled by the public for the common good."[63]

Ryan, as chief justice of the Wisconsin state Supreme Court, also gave his approval to the "Granger idea"—the right of the states to regulate the railroads in the interests of the general welfare. He held the spotlight on several occasions in the postwar decades. In 1873 he made a famous and eloquent protest against wealth. Robert M. La Follette heard that speech and later traced his political views back to that day.[64] Later Ryan was appointed to the Wisconsin state Supreme Court. As a jurist, he became the idol of the Grangers, writing the decision in *Pike* v. *The Chicago, Milwaukee & St. Paul Railway Company*.[65] His argument was closely followed by Chief Justice Morrison R. Waite when the U.S. Supreme Court validated the Granger laws in 1876–77. Ryan's reputation as a jurist grew with the years and later students of the law considered him the foremost jurist in Wisconsin history.[66]

Most of the Copperhead editors of the war years were surprisingly successful in the postwar decades. Wilbur F. Storey, much maligned by Radical Republicans for his forthright criticism of the Lincoln administration, made the Chicago *Times* a respected newspaper and a financial success. The Cincinnati *En-*

quirer, as critical of Lincolnian policies as any midwestern newspaper, gained an enviable reputation in the remaining years of the nineteenth century. The Detroit *Free Press* and the Cleveland *Plain Dealer,* both critical of the course of wartime events, came to be classed with the better midwestern newspapers. Peter V. Deuster, of the Milwaukee *See-Bote,* became one of the city's most influential and respected citizens in the postwar era. Samuel Medary, did not survive the war. He was in ill health in 1864, and the mobbing of his press and his arrest for "disloyal utterances" gave him no rest. He died on the eve of the November election of 1864, so he did not live to see Lincoln re-elected. Some said that his death was hastened by the results of the October, 1864, elections in Indiana and Ohio.

Two of the Midwest's most notorious Copperhead editors, allies in their newspaper war on Lincoln and "despotism," went separate ways in the postwar era. Dennis A. Mahony and "Brick" Pomeroy centered their efforts in the field of publication, but they dabbled in other activities. Mahony was re-elected sheriff of Dubuque County in 1865. Then, after a period in St. Louis where he revived the St. Louis *Times,* he returned to his old stamping grounds, purchased the Dubuque *Telegraph* in 1871, and continued to edit it until his death eight years later at the age of fifty-eight.[67]

Pomeroy, who regularly labeled Lincoln "imbecile" and "fool"—even suggesting assassination in August of 1864— added to his notoriety and fame in the postwar era. He built the La Crosse *Democrat* into the best-known weekly in the country, and its circulation, according to him, reached 100,000.[68] Editor Pomeroy boasted that the La Crosse *Democrat* had subscribers in every state, many of them in the South. He built lush newspaper offices and gloried in the attention which came his way. Pomeroy was more than a newspaperman. He gained a reputation as a humorist and as the author of best sellers. He carried on feuds with prominent people. His feud with Benjamin Butler, noted soldier-congressman, bordered on the ridiculous. It was

Pomeroy who fastened the monicker "Spoon" to Butler's name, and then enjoyed the discomfort it caused Butler. Once Butler sued Pomeroy for libel. Then, to gain revenge, Butler served as attorney for Mrs. Pomeroy in her divorce suit. Pomeroy challenged Butler to a duel. The two recalcitrants continued to exchange insulting remarks and choice epithets for years.[69]

Pomeroy found the La Crosse puddle too small for the splash he was making and sought new and bigger ponds. At the invitation of "Boss" Tweed, Pomeroy went east to edit the New York *Democrat*. Pomeroy soon quarreled with "Boss" Tweed and the scrupulous scribe laid the charges which helped to break up the infamous "Tweed Ring." He started his own newspaper, *Pomeroy's Democrat*. He soon moved that paper to Chicago, and he returned to the Midwest to become one of the top chieftains in the Greenback clan.

Such ex-Copperheads as Pomeroy, Ryan, William Allen, George H. Pendleton, and Sidney Breese provide a link between midwestern Copperheadism and the postwar movements known as Greenbackism and Grangerism. Pomeroy, Allen, Dean, and George H. Pendleton were especially active in pushing and propagandizing the "Ohio idea." Breese's decision in *Munn* v. *Illinois* and Ryan's in *Pike* v. *The Chicago, Milwaukee & St. Paul Railway Company* link the Copperhead movement to the "Granger idea." The principle, proclaimed by Ryan in 1876, that a state could regulate a business which was "public in nature though privately owned and managed" was stated repeatedly at the Copperhead-dominated Illinois Constitutional Convention of 1862.[70] At that convention Daniel Reilly, a downstate Democrat, enunciated beliefs later incorporated into Granger arguments:

We believe down in Egypt—in that part of Egypt [seven southernmost Illinois counties] I have the honor of representing—that all our railroad corporations are creatures of the State; that what rights and immunities they have were all derived from the State; that they have derived their existence from the State. And we believe also, that railroad corporations are a power in the State not to be despised, but rather to be treated with favor; but that these establishments are not worthy of favor if they do not favor the interests of the people. . . .[71]

Both Grangerism and midwestern Copperheadism flaunted the banner of states' rights. Each was a protest against revived Whiggery and the ascendancy of industrialism over agriculture. Both emphasized human rights as against property rights. Both recited common economic grievances. Eastern capital and eastern domination were repeatedly criticized by both. Each objected to the emergence of the new America, a country of mills and cities and of a stronger central government.

The plantation South of the prewar era, the midwestern Copperheads of Civil War days, and the Grangers and Greenbackers of the postwar years could not stem the progress of the Industrial Revolution in America. They saw Jeffersonian doctrines discarded and twisted. By the end of the century the new nation, forged in the crucible of the Civil War, was one of urban centers and big business. It advocated Andrew Carnegie's "gospel of wealth" as its unofficial doctrine. Stephen Vincent Benét, in his epic poem, visualized what the Copperheads had feared might happen. Addicted to the past, midwestern Copperheads were wary of the "process": *

> Out of his body grows revolving steel,
> Out of his body grows the spinning wheel
> Made up of wheels, the new, mechanic birth,
> No longer bound by toil
> To the unsparing soil
> Or the old furrow-line,
> The great metallic beast
> Expanding West and East,
> His heart a spinning coil
> His body serpentine.
> Out of John Brown's strong sinews the tall skyscrapers grow,

Out of his heart the chanting buildings rise,
Rivet and girder, motor and dynamo,
Pillar of smoke by day and fire by night,
The steel-faced cities reaching at the skies,
The whole enormous and rotating cage
Hung with hard jewels of electric light,
Smoky with sorrow, black with splendor, dyed
Whiter than damask for a crystal bride
With metal suns, the engine-handed Age,
The genie we have raised to rule the earth,
Obsequious to our will
But servant-master still,
The tireless serf already half a god.

Notes

CHAPTER I

1. Chicago *Prairie Farmer*, June 6, 1861.
2. Adam Gurowski, *Diary . . . from March 4, 1861, to November 2, 1862* (Boston, 1862), p. 23.
3. Gideon Welles, *Diary of Gideon Welles, Secretary of the Navy under Lincoln and Johnson*, ed. John T. Morse (3 vols.; Boston, 1911), I, 89–90.
4. Appleton's *American Annual Cyclopaedia and Register of Important Events, 1861*, pp. 311–13.
5. Columbus *Crisis*, Nov. 28, 1861; Cincinnati *Daily Gazette*, Dec. 27, 1861; *Congressional Globe*, 37 Cong., 2 sess., p. 169; Chicago Board of Trade, *Annual Report, 1862* (Chicago, 1863), p. 32; James A. Headley to "My dear Father," Aug. 13, 1861, Thomas Henry Hines Papers, University of Kentucky Library.
6. Carlyle (Ill.) *Constitution and Union*, Oct. 3, 1863.
7. Edward Dicey, *Six Months in the Federal States* (2 vols.; London, 1863), II, 53–54, 62; *Crisis*, May 16, 1861. Also see Charles R. Wilson, "Cincinnati, a Southern Outpost in 1861?" *Mississippi Valley Historical Review*, XXIV (March, 1938), 473–82, and "Cincinnati's Reputation during the Civil War," *Journal of Southern History*, II (Apr., 1933), 268–79.
8. David Gass to John D. Caton, June 7, 1861, John D. Caton Papers, Library of Congress.
9. Matt Martin to S. S. Cox, Dec. 3, 1861, Samuel Sullivan Cox Papers, Brown University Library (microfilm, Hayes Memorial Library, Fremont, Ohio).
10. Dubuque *Herald*, Nov. 23, 1860.
11. Detroit *Free Press*, Apr. 4, 1861.
12. Indianapolis *Daily State Sentinel*, Jan. 9, 1862. The relation of economic conditions to the anti-Lincoln movement is treated summarily

in Frank Klement, "Economic Aspects of Middle Western Copperhead-ism," *Historian*, XIV (Autumn, 1951), pp. 27–44.

13. *Cong. Globe*, 36 Cong., 1 sess., Appendix, p. 43.

14. Milwaukee *See-Bote*, Apr. 30, 1862; Marcus Mills "Brick" Pom-eroy, *Condensed History of the War: Its Causes and Results* (n.p., 1868), pp. 4–7; *Crisis*, Jan. 28, 1863.

15. *Cong. Globe*, 37 Cong., 3 sess., Appendix, p. 58; Clement L. Val-landigham, *Speeches, Arguments, Addresses, and Letters of Clement L. Vallandigham* (New York, 1864), pp. 7, 211; Samuel Sullivan Cox, *Puritanism in Politics: Speech of Hon. S. S. Cox of Ohio before the Demo-cratic Union Association, Jan. 13, 1863* (New York, 1863), *passim*. See also Richard L. Power, *Planting Corn Belt Culture: The Impress of the Upland Southerner and Yankee in the Old Northwest* (Indianapolis, 1953).

16. Cincinnati *Daily Enquirer*, Feb. 12, 1861. It should be pointed out that Michael Faren, coeditor of the *Enquirer*, had a financial interest in several boiler-plate factories and a vested interest in the river trade.

17. *Crisis*, Apr. 4, 28, 1861.

18. *See-Bote*, Apr. 20, 1862.

19. Hastings (Minn.) *Democrat*, March, 30, 1861.

20. Canton (Ohio) *Stark County Democrat*, Jan. 9, 1861.

21. *Ibid.*, July 17, 1861; Clement L. Vallandigham, *The Record of Hon. C. L. Vallandigham on Abolition, the Union, and the Civil War* (Columbus, 1863), p. 71.

22. F. W. Horn to Gov. Alexander Randall, Apr. 18, 1861, Wisconsin Civil War Governors' Letters, Wisconsin State Historical Society.

23. Quoted in John H. Holliday, *Indianapolis and the Civil War* (In-dianapolis, 1911), pp. 572–73.

24. James A. Cravens to William H. English, Apr. 9, July 28, 1861, William H. English Papers, Indiana State Historical Society.

25. Sheboygan *Journal*, Feb. 18, 1862.

26. Huntington (Ind.) *Democrat*, Dec. 18, 1862, quoted in Indianapolis *State Sentinel*, Dec. 25, 1862.

27. *Cong. Globe*, 37 Cong., 2 sess., p. 1150; Indianapolis *Daily Jour-nal*, July 16, 1862; Indianapolis *State Sentinel*, July 17, 1862; William S. Holman to Allen Hamilton, March 2, 1862, Allen Hamilton Papers, In-diana Division, Indiana State Library.

28. O. Ballentine to E. B. Washburne, March 4, 1862, Elihu B. Wash-burne Papers, Library of Congress.

29. O. B. Niles to S. S. Cox, Feb. 4, 1862, Cox Papers; *See-Bote*, May 7, 1862; Chicago *Weekly Journal*, Jan. 9, 1863; Cox, *Puritanism in Poli-tics*, pp. 3, 6, *passim*.

30. *Eighth Census of the United States: Agriculture*, Introduction, p. xli.

31. *Crisis*, Jan. 28, 1863.

32. William F. Faren to Elihu B. Washburne, Jan. 19, 1862, Washburne Papers.

33. The link between midwestern Copperheadism and postwar Grangerism is treated in Frank L. Klement, "Middle Western Copperheadism and the Genesis of the Granger Movement," *Mississippi Valley Historical Review*, XXXVIII (March, 1952), 679–94.

34. "Proceedings of the Illinois State Constitutional Convention, Jan. 21, 1862," published in the Springfield *Illinois State Register*, Jan. 22, 1862; *Journal of the Constitutional Convention of the State of Illinois convened at Springfield on January 7, 1862* (Springfield, 1862), pp. 941–44; *Illinois State Journal*, Feb. 6, 11, 12, 18, 1862; William H. Osborn to Thomas S. Walker, Feb. 7, March 12, 1862, in "President's Letter Book, W. H. Osborn, November 19, 1861–July 1, 1862," Illinois Central Rail Road Co. Papers, Newberry Library; Stanley L. Jones, "Agrarian Radicalism in the Illinois Constitutional Convention of 1862," *Journal of the Illinois State Historical Society*, XLVIII (Autumn, 1955), 271–82.

35. Chicago *Times*, June 20, 1862.

36. E. B. McCagg to Charles Butler, Jan. 20, 1863, Charles Butler Papers, Library of Congress. Earle D. Ross, "Northern Sectionalism in the Civil War Era," *Iowa Journal of History and Politics*, XXX (October, 1932), 455–512, recognizes that western sectionalism was a part of the Civil War story.

37. William H. Osborn to H. V. Poor, Feb. 18, 1863, in "President's Letter Book, W. H. Osborn, November 19, 1861—July 1, 1862," Illinois Central Rail Road Co. Papers.

38. *Official Records of the Union and Confederate Armies* (128 vols., 1880–1901), Ser. 1, XVII, Part 2, 332–33; John A. McClernand to S. S. Cox, Dec. 4, 1861, Cox Papers; Peter Zinn to Benjamin Wade, Apr. 15, 1862, Timothy C. Day to Wade, Feb. 2, 1862, Benjamin Wade Papers, Library of Congress.

39. Vallandigham, *The Record of Hon. C. L. Vallandigham on Abolition, the Union, and the Civil War*, p. 51.

40. Reynolds, onetime governor of Illinois and an elder statesman in his party, indorsed the doctrine that the Negro was inferior to the white man in *"The Balm of Gilead": An Inquiry into the Right of American Slavery* (Belleville, Ill., 1860). Rev. C. F. W. Walther of St. Louis wrote a theological defense of slavery; his arguments are summarized in Joel S. Torstenson, "The Attitude of the Lutheran Church toward Slavery" (M.A. thesis, University of Minnesota, 1940).

41. *Cong. Globe*, 36 Cong., 2 sess., Appendix, p. 168.

42. *Official Records*, Ser. 1, II, 466–67; Indianapolis *State Sentinel*, Sept. 9, Oct. 22, 1861; Louisville *Journal* (n.d.), quoted in *ibid.*, Sept. 17, 1861; Detroit *Free Press*, Sept. 19, Oct. 4, 25, 1861; Chatfield *Democrat*, Sept. 21, Oct. 19, 26, 1861; Thomas Ewing, Sr., to Thomas Ewing, Jr., Nov. 2, 1861, Thomas Ewing Papers, Library of Congress.

43. Indianapolis *State Sentinel*, Jan. 9, 28, 1862.

44. The editor of one Democratic newspaper protested thus in his editorial columns: "Congress has the negro-phobia. It is nigger in the Senate and nigger in the House. It is nigger in the forenoon and nigger in the afternoon. It is nigger in motions and nigger in speeches. It was nigger the first day and it has been nigger every day. Nigger is in every man's eye, and nigger in every man's mouth. It's nigger in the lobby and nigger in the hall. Congress smells of nigger and the proceedings are black with nigger. . . . The nigger vapor is a moral pestilence that blunts the sense of duty to the constitution and destroys the instinct of obedience to the law." Macomb *Eagle* (n.d.), quoted in Indianapolis *State Sentinel*, Dec. 23, 1861.

45. *Western Railroad Gazette* (Chicago), Apr. 25, 1863; Cincinnati *Commercial*, Jan. 15, 1862; Indianapolis *State Sentinel*, Jan. 15, 1862.

46. London *Times*, Dec. 1, 1863.

47. *See-Bote*, Apr. 9, 23, 30, Oct. 15, Nov. 3, 1862.

48. *Crisis*, Jan. 16, July 2, 1862, Feb. 7, 1863; Cincinnati *Weekly Gazette*, Sept. 2, 1862; Cincinnati *Enquirer*, Apr. 18, 1862; Chicago *Times*, Sept. 26, Oct. 5, 19, 1862; Appleton's *American Annual Cyclopaedia . . . 1862*, p. 754. Also see Williston H. Lofton, "Northern Labor and the Negro during the Civil War," *Journal of Negro History*, XXXIV (July, 1949), 251–73; Bernard Mandel, "The Northern Working Class and the Abolition of Slavery" (Ph.D. diss., Western Reserve University, 1952); Emma Lou Thornborough, "The Race Issue in Indiana Politics during the Civil War," *Indiana Magazine of History*, XLVII (June, 1951), 165–88; Roy H. Abrams, "The Copperhead Newspapers and the Negro," *Journal of Negro History*, XX (April, 1935), 131–52.

49. The socioeconomic aspects of Ohio Copperheadism are explored in a scholarly fashion in John Stipp, "Economic and Political Aspects of Western Copperheadism" (Ph.D. diss., Ohio State University, 1942). Jasper W. Cross, "Divided Loyalties in Southern Illinois during the Civil War" (Ph.D. diss., University of Illinois, 1942), views "Egypt" residents as pro-Southern in many ways. Harvey L. Carter's "The Origins of Political Patterns in the Older Middle West, 1856–1864" (manuscript in possession of the author, Colorado College) probes the religious, social, and political relationships of Republicans and Democrats.

50. La Crosse *Weekly Democrat*, Dec. 13, 1861; Robert McClelland to "Mr. Pritchette," Jan. 20, 1862, in McClelland "Letterbook, 1860–1862," Robert McClelland Papers, Burton Historical Collection, Detroit Public Library; Frederic W. Horn to George H. Paul, May 21, 1861, George H. Paul Papers, Wisconsin State Historical Society; George S. Converse to S. S. Cox, March 15, 1862, Cox Papers.

51. O. H. Betrick to Joseph A. Wright, March 13, 1862, Joseph A. Wright Papers, Indiana Division, Indiana State Library; Detroit *Free Press*, March 8, 1862; Indianapolis *State Sentinel*, March 15, 18, 1862; *Cong. Globe*, 37 Cong., 2 sess., p. 1112.

52. La Crosse *Democrat,* April 18, 1862.

53. John W. Kees to S. S. Cox, Apr. 12, 1862, and T. H. Marriott to S. S. Cox, Apr. 28, 1862, Cox Papers.

54. Circleville *Watchman* (n.d.), quoted in Indianapolis *State Sentinel,* April 28, 1862.

55. David Christy's *Pulpit Politics: Ecclesiastical Legislation on Slavery, in Its Disturbing Influences upon the American Union* (New York, 1862) was a 624-page book selling at two dollars per copy.

56. Chatfield *Democrat,* May 24, 1862.

57. E. M. Huntington to "My dear Son," Aug 30, 1862, Elisha M. Huntington Papers, Indiana University Library.

58. Chatfield *Democrat,* Sept. 27, 1862.

59. Indianapolis *State Sentinel,* Sept. 24, 1862.

60. *See-Bote,* Oct. 1, 8, 15, 1862.

61. Louisville *Journal,* Sept. 25, 1862.

62. Detroit *Free Press,* Oct. 3, 1862; *See-Bote,* Oct. 1, 5, 15, Nov. 3, 1862; Canton, O., *Stark County Democrat,* Sept. 24, 1862; Louisville *Journal,* Sept. 25, 1862; *Dubuque Herald,* Oct. 8, 1862; Hamilton (Ohio) *True Telegraph,* Oct. 30, 1862; Indianapolis *State Sentinel,* Sept. 24, Oct. 8, 1862; W. R. Hanley to J. J. Crittenden, Oct. 3, 1862, John J. Crittenden Papers, Library of Congress; George B. Smith, "Diary, 1862," Dec. 31, 1862, George B. Smith Papers, Wisconsin State Historical Society Library.

63. William Caton to John D. Caton, Nov. 16, 1862, Caton Papers.

64. C. K. Williams to Elihu B. Washburne, Dec. 22, 1862, Washburne Papers.

65. Robert Owen to "Ass't Adjt. Gen'l" (General Boyle), Dec. 4, 1862, Richard Owen Papers, Indiana University Library.

66. Indianapolis *State Sentinel,* Oct. 16, 1862.

67. *Illinois State Register,* Nov. 5, 1862.

68. John Reynolds to Lyman C. Draper, Nov. 8, 1862, Lyman C. Draper Papers, Wisconsin State Historical Society Library.

69. Isaac Welsh to Ben Wade, Jan. 31, 1863, Ben Wade Papers; William T. Coggeshall "Diary," Jan. 2, 1863, William T. Coggeshall Collection, Ohio Historical Society.

70. Dubuque *Herald,* May 18, 1861.

71. Cincinnati *Daily Enquirer,* Jan. 22, 1861.

72. *Crisis,* Dec. 12, 1861.

73. *Cong. Globe,* 37 Cong., 2 sess., p. 67.

74. *Ibid.,* pp. 67–68, 93.

75. The "Address of the Democratic Members of the House of Representatives of the United States to the Democracy of the United States" was published in most Democratic newspapers of the Midwest. It can be found in Vallandigham, *Speeches, Arguments, Addresses, and Letters,* pp. 362–69.

76. David L. Phillips to Hon. Edwin M. Stanton, Sept. 4, 1862, La-

fayette C. Baker–Levi C. Turner Papers, War Department Records, National Archives; William J. Allen to General McClellan, Sept. 6, 1862, *ibid.*; Israel Blanchard, "Statement" (n.d.), *ibid.; Illinois State Journal,* Aug. 21, 1862.

77. Madison Y. Johnson, "Diary," *passim,* Chicago Historical Society Library; *Illinois State Journal,* Feb. 13, 1863.

78. Lancaster *Eagle,* Jan. 8, Feb. 26, 1863; "Report of the Select Committee on Military Arrests," in *Journal of the House of Representatives of the State of Ohio, 1863* (Columbus, 1863).

79. Mrs. D. E. Sheward to "My Dear husband," Sept. 24, 1862, copy in Charles Mason Papers, State Department of History and Archives, Historical Library, Des Moines, Iowa.

80. *Stark County Democrat,* Oct. 22, 1862.

81. The *Address to the Democracy of Wisconsin Adopted at the State Convention on September 3, 1862* (Madison, 1862) became known as the "Ryan Address," after its author, Edward G. Ryan. This noted "address" became the "Copperhead Bible" in Wisconsin and its author, subsequently, became the best-known Copperhead in the state. Ryan's role as a critic of President Lincoln and of Republican policy is treated, in part, in Frank L. Klement's *Lincoln's Critics in Wisconsin* (Historical Bulletin No. 14, Lincoln Fellowship of Wisconsin [Madison, 1956]), and "Copperheads and Copperheadism in Wisconsin: Democratic Opposition to the Lincoln Administration," *Wisconsin Magazine of History,* XLII (Spring, 1959), 182–88, and in A. J. Beitzinger's "The Father of Copperheadism in Wisconsin," *Wis. Mag. Hist.,* XXXIX (Autumn, 1955), 17–25. An analysis of the "Morrison Address," Michigan's counterpart to the "Ryan Address," can be found in John B. Pritchett, "Michigan Democracy in the Civil War," *Michigan History Magazine,* XI (January, 1927), 92–110.

82. *Illinois State Register,* Sept. 9, 1862.

83. Charles Mason to Horatio Seymour, Oct. 6, 1862, copy in Mason Papers.

84. Chicago *Times,* (n.d.), in Hamilton *True Telegraph,* Nov. 7, 1862.

85. Indianapolis *State Sentinel,* Oct. 8, 1862.

86. *Stark County Democrat,* Oct. 22, 1862.

87. Lancaster *Ohio Eagle,* Dec. 25, 1862.

88. *Stark County Democrat,* Nov. 12, 1862.

89. Dubuque *Times,* Nov. 18, 1862.

90. *Cong. Globe,* 37 Cong., 3 sess., pp. 28, 36; W. I. Van Arsdale to S. S. Cox, Dec. 8, 1862, Cox Papers; Indianapolis *State Sentinel,* Dec. 20, 1862.

91. *Cong. Globe,* 37 Cong., 3 sess., p. 36.

92. Hamilton *True Telegraph,* Nov. 13, 1862.

93. Sheboygan *Journal,* July 3, 1861.

94. William G. Beggs to S. S. Cox, March 25, 1862, and O. Reinhard to S. S. Cox. Apr. 18, 1862, Cox Papers. That portion of Vallandigham's

old district still within the revamped one gave him an increased majority in the 1862 elections, but he went down to defeat. Wisconsin, too, was effectively redistricted by a Republican-controlled legislature. Even some Republicans were ashamed of the "outrageous injustice" which their party perpetrated.

95. The Wisconsin draft riots of 1862 need a thorough and scholarly analysis. John W. Oliver's "Draft Riots in Wisconsin during the Civil War," *Wisconsin Magazine of History*, II, 334–37, is a short and superficial article. Lynn I. Schoonover, "A History of the Civil War Draft in Wisconsin" (M.A. thesis, University of Wisconsin, 1915) is badly outdated. Peter Leo Johnson's "Port Washington Draft Riot of 1862," *Mid-America*, I (January, 1930), 212–20, contributes the thesis that the anti-Catholic policy in the naming of an army chaplain brought on the disorders in Ozaukee County. The best narrative account (with a minimum of interpretation) is in a volume devoted to local history; see *History of Washington and Ozaukee Counties* (Chicago, 1881), pp. 360–66, 493–96.

96. Sheboygan *Journal*, Nov. 21, 1862.

97. *Illinois State Register*, March 20, 1862.

98. Richard Yates to Thomas J. Henderson, Feb. 4, 1862, Richard Yates Papers, Illinois State Historical Library.

99. Lacon *Illinois Gazette*, June 25, 1862.

100. Indianapolis *State Sentinel*, Jan. 9, 1862; Detroit *Free Press*, July 2, 1862; La Crosse *Democrat*, July 16, 1862.

101. Detroit *Free Press*, July 2, 1862.

102. Davis, quoted in the Indianapolis *State Sentinel*, Jan. 9, 1862.

103. *Cong. Globe*, 37 Cong., 2 sess., p. 2268.

104. *Ibid.*, p. 1888. The resolution was passed April 30, 1862, three and a half months after Cameron's resignation.

105. Joe Caston to S. S. Cox, Feb. 18, 1862, Cox Papers.

106. *Cong. Globe*, 37 Cong., 2 sess., pp. 903–7.

107. T. Maple to Lyman Trumbull, Dec. 28, 1862, Lyman Trumbull Papers, Library of Congress.

108. Detroit *Free Press*, Nov. 14, 1862; *Illinois State Register*, May 6, 1863; Hamilton *True Telegraph*, Nov. 20, 1862; George S. Converse to S. S. Cox, March 15, 1862, Cox Papers.

109. Robert McClelland to John Kennedy, Nov. 17, 1862, McClelland Papers.

110. Robert M. Knapp to C. H. Lanphier, Dec. 22, 1862, Charles H. Lanphier Papers, Illinois State Historical Library.

111. A. Mahan to Z. Chandler, May 5, 1863, Zachariah Chandler Papers, Library of Congress.

112. Dubuque *Daily Times*, July 12, 1861; Dubuque *Herald*, July 13, Oct. 22, 1861.

113. Orestes Brownson, in *Brownson's Quarterly Review*, Ser. 3, IV (March, 1863), 404–6; Allen G. Wells to Gov. Blair, July 14, 1862, Austin Blair Papers, Burton Historical Collection, Detroit Public Li-

brary; Calvin Fletcher, "Diary," Nov. 12, 1864, Calvin Fletcher Papers, Indiana State Historical Society; Benjamin F. Child to Hon. O. M. Hatch, July 14, 1862, Orville M. Hatch Papers, Illinois State Historical Library; Frederic W. Horn to Governor Alexander Randall, Apr. 18, 1861, Wisconsin Civil War Governors' Letters; *See-Bote,* Oct. 31, 1860. Also see such works as: Carl F. Brand, "History of the Know-Nothing Party in Indiana" (Ph.D. diss., Indiana University, 1916); Dorothy E. Johnson, "Attitude of the Germans in Minnesota towards the Republican Party to 1865" (M.A. thesis, University of Minnesota, 1945); Elfrieda Lang, "German Migration to Dubois County, Indiana" (M.A. thesis, Indiana University, 1944); Charles W. Emery, "The Iowa Germans in the Election of 1860" (M.A. thesis, State University of Iowa, 1940); Colman J. Barry, *The Catholic Church and German Americans* (Milwaukee, 1953); Benjamin J. Blied, *Catholics and the Civil War* (Milwaukee, 1945); Carl E. Schneider, *The German Church on the American Frontier: A Study of the Rise of Religion among the Germans of the West, 1840–1866* (St. Louis, 1939).

114. *The Times* (London), Sept. 26, Dec. 1, 1863.

115. John R. Commons *et al., Documentary History of American Industrial Society* (10 vols.; Cleveland, 1910–11), II, 5.

116. Cincinnati *Daily Commercial,* Jan. 15, 1862; Indianapolis *State Sentinel,* Jan. 15, 1862.

117. Detroit *Advertiser and Tribune,* quoted in Detroit *Free Press,* Sept. 13, 1863.

118. The editor gave his vocabulary a workout when he wrote his critique of Chicago's Irish voters: "It was sight enough to sicken a decent man to behold the kind of voting cattle (each with a Dimmecratic ticket in hand) brought in interminable rows at the ward voting places. Such beastly faces, bloated carcases, filthy, stinking, God-forsaken wretches; jail birds turned loose; dirty offal vomited forth from the sinks, and gutters, and sloughs of Kilgubbin; men whose vile countenances, fiery with rum, suggested proficiency in every crime from perjury to murder as a fine art; men swearing, cursing, blaspheming; men who couldn't read a single letter of a single word of the ticket they voted; men who signed their name with a cross; the upturned substrata of city corruption; human swine all blotched and reeking with congenial mire; loathsome, blear-eyed sots, staggering under a load of whiskey; men ignorant, brutal, disgusting, debased in body and mind to a level with the beasts of the field; excrescences and running sores upon the unhealthy body politic—*such* votes . . . elected the Copperhead municipal ticket." *Western Railroad Gazette* (Chicago) Apr. 25, 1863.

119. Chicago *Tribune,* Dec. 31, 1863; *Illinois State Register,* Jan. 5, 1864.

120. The conflict of Southern and Yankee culture is admirably treated in Richard L. Power's *Planting Corn Belt Culture* (see n. 15, above). The author is indebted to Harvey L. Carter of Colorado College for the use of two unpublished manuscripts ("Persistent Political Patterns in

Indiana Presidential Elections" and "The Origins of Political Patterns in the Older Middle West, 1856–1864") which show the importance of religious and political ties. John Stipp's "Economic and Political Aspects of Western Copperheadism" (Ph.D. diss., Ohio State University, 1944) puts a microscope upon Ohio and concludes that Ohio Copperheads lived on poorer soils, had smaller homesteads, and were more illiterate than their Republican opponents. See also such studies as: Joseph E. Layton, "Sources of Population in Indiana, 1816–1850," *Indiana State Library Bulletin*, XI (Indianapolis, 1916); John D. Barnhart, "The Migration of Kentuckians across the Ohio River," *Filson Club Historical Quarterly*, XXV (January, 1951), 24–32; Mildred Throne, *A History of Agriculture in Southern Iowa, 1833–1890* (Ph.D. diss., State University of Iowa, 1946); W. E. Henry, *Some Elements of Indiana's Population, Indiana Historical Society Publications*, IV, No. 6 (Indianapolis, 1908), 375–96; Henry C. Hubbart, "Pro-Southern Influences in the Free West, 1840–1865," *Mississippi Valley Historical Review*, XX (June, 1933), 42–62; William C. Lynch, "The Flow of Colonists to and from Indiana before the Civil War," *Indiana Magazine of History*, XI (March, 1915), 1–8; William V. Pooley, *The Settlement of Illinois from 1830 to 1850* (University of Wisconsin Bulletin, Ser. 1 [Madison, 1908]), pp. 307–74; Adolph Rogers, "North Carolina and Indiana: A Tie That Binds," *Indiana Magazine of History*, V (June, 1909), 49–56; David C. Schilling, "The Relation of Southern Ohio to the South during the Decade Preceding the Civil War," *Quarterly of the Historical and Philosophical Society of Ohio*, VIII (January–March, 1913), 3–19; Daniel S. Curtis, *Western Portraiture* (New York, 1851), pp. 244 ff.; John D. Barnhart, "The Southern Element in the Leadership of the Old Northwest," *Journal of Southern History*, I (May, 1935), 189–97; N. M. Baker, "The Pioneers of Macon County and the Civil War," *Journal of the Illinois State Historical Society*, XVI (April, 1923), 117–28; E. L. Godkin, "Aristocratic Opinions of Democracy," *North American Review*, C (January, 1865), 194–232; Cardinal Goodwin, "The American Occupation of Iowa, 1833 to 1860," *Iowa Journal of History and Politics*, XVIII (January, 1919), 83–102.

121. Eugene H. Roseboom's "Southern Ohio and the Union in 1863," *Mississippi Valley Historical Review*, XXXIX (June, 1952), 29–42, effectively disproves the myth that the counties bordering the Ohio River were the most "disloyal" (i.e., voted Democratic). Jasper Cross's "Divided Loyalties in Southern Illinois during the Civil War" (Ph.D. diss., University of Illinois, 1942) deals with "dark Egypt," as does Ford Messamore's "Copperheadism in Southern Illinois from 1861 to 1865" (M.A. thesis, University of Kentucky, 1935). Buford Wilson's "Southern Illinois in the Civil War," *Transactions of the Illinois State Historical Society, 1911*, XII (Springfield, 1913), 93–103, is an outdated study.

122. Samuel P. Heintzelman, "Journal," Oct. 20, 1864, Samuel P. Heintzelman Papers, Library of Congress.

123. New Albany *Ledger*, quoted in Indianapolis *State Sentinel*, Aug. 9, 1862.

124. Indianapolis *State Sentinel*, Aug. 1, 1862.
125. I. F. Landes to "Dear Sister," Nov. 28, 1862, Lucius C. Embree Papers, Indiana Division, Indiana State Library.
126. J. T. Embree to "Dear Mary" (wife), Nov. 7, 1862, *ibid.*
127. Appleton's *American Annual Cyclopaedia . . . 1862*, pp. 519–20, 525–26, 697; Chicago *Tribune Almanac for 1863* (Chicago, 1863), pp. 18–19.
128. *Crisis*, Oct. 22, 1862.
129. Indianapolis *State Sentinel*, Nov. 2, 1862.
130. *Fulton County Ledger* (Canton, Ill.), Dec. 23, 1862; *Illinois State Register*, Nov. 5, 1862; Milwaukee *Banner & Volksfreund*, Nov. 12, 18, 1862; Lexington *Observer* (n.d.), quoted in Indianapolis *State Sentinel*, Dec. 17, 1862; Indianapolis *State Sentinel*, Oct. 16, Dec. 2, 1862. See also Harry E. Pratt, "The Repudiation of Lincoln's War Policy in 1862— Stuart-Swett Congressional Campaign," *Journal of the Illinois State Historical Society*, XXIV (April, 1931), 129–40; Winfred A. Harbison, "The Election of 1862 as a Vote of Want of Confidence in President Lincoln," *Michigan Academy of Science, Arts, and Letters Papers* (1930), 499–513.
131. Thomas P. Dudley to John J. Crittenden, Dec. 8, 1862, Crittenden Papers.
132. James D. Richardson (ed.), *Messages and Papers of the Presidents* (10 vols.; New York, 1896–99), VI 126–42. The paragraph which alarmed conservatives read: "The dogmas of the quiet past, are inadequate to the stormy present. The occasion is piled high with difficulty, and we must rise with the occasion. As our cause is new, so we must think anew. We must disenthrall ourselves, and then we shall save the country."
133. George B. Smith, final entry in "Diary, 1862," George B. Smith Papers.
134. *Crisis*, Dec. 31, 1862.
135. Gurowski, *Diary . . .*, II, 60.

CHAPTER II

1. *Congressional Globe*, 37 Cong., 3 sess., Appendix, pp. 52–60.
2. Dubuque *Democratic Herald*, Jan. 20, 1863.
3. Columbus *Crisis*, March 18, 1863; *Official Records of the Union and Confederate Armies* (128 vols., 1880–1901), Ser. 1, XVII, Part 2, 332–34.
4. Dayton *Empire*, Jan. 31, 1863; Hamilton *True Telegraph*, Jan. 29, 1863; Indianapolis *State Sentinel*, Feb. 3, 1863.
5. "Mitchell Y. Jackson Diary," Jan. 1, 1863, in Rodney C. Loehr (ed.), *Minnesota Farmers' Diaries* (St. Paul, 1939), p. 214; St. Cloud *Democrat*, Feb. 26, 1863; St. Paul *Daily Press*, Jan. 3, 1863; St. Paul *Pioneer and Democrat*, Jan. 9, 1863; Cleveland *Herald*, May 23, 1863;

New York *Tribune*, Jan. 23, 1863; Charles Blanchard, *Chief Justice Caton's Seymour Letter* (Ottawa, Ill., 1863), p. 9.

6. William O. Stoddard, Jr. (ed.), *Lincoln's Third Secretary: The Memoirs of William O. Stoddard* (New York, 1955), p. 170.

7. Dubuque *Democratic Herald*, Jan. 1, 3, 6, 10, 18, 1863.

8. *Ibid.*, Jan. 10, 1863.

9. *Ibid.*, Jan. 3, 1863.

10. *Ibid.*, Jan. 3, 6, 10, 18, 1863. Mahony's role as a Lincoln critic is treated in Roger J. Sullivan, "Mahony the Unterrified" (B.A. thesis, Loras College, Dubuque, 1938); Edward J. Goodman, "Copperheadism in Dubuque during the Civil War" (M.A. thesis, Loras College, 1938); Helen Wukow, "Dubuque in the Civil War Period" (M.A. thesis, Northwestern University, 1941); Hubert W. Wubben, "Dennis Mahony and the Dubuque Herald, 1860–1863," *Iowa Journal of History*, LVI (October, 1958), 289–320; and Robert Rutland, "The Copperheads of Iowa: A Re-evaluation," *Iowa Jour. Hist.*, LII (January, 1954), 1–30.

11. Ashland *Union*, Jan. 7, 1863.

12. Chatfield (Minn.) *Democrat*, Jan. 10, 1863.

13. Green Bay *Advocate*, March 3, 1863.

14. Oshkosh *Courier*, Jan. 1, Oct. 31, 1863.

15. Sheboygan *Journal*, May 7, 1863.

16. Milwaukee *See-Bote*, Jan. 3, Feb. 11, 1863.

17. Milwaukee *Banner & Volksfreund*, Jan. 6, 1863.

18. Thomas O. Lowe to "Dear Will" (brother), Jan. 23, 1863, Thomas O. Lowe Papers, Dayton Public Library.

19. *Ibid.*, March 28, 1863.

20. Detroit *Free Press*, Jan. 1, 4, 1863. Editor Henry N. Walker's conduct as a critic of the Lincoln administration is treated in Margaret J. Applegate's "The Detroit Free Press during the Civil War" (M.A. thesis, Wayne University, 1938).

21. Chicago *Times*, Jan. 3, 1863.

22. La Crosse *Weekly Democrat*, Jan. 8, 1863. The author has treated Pomeroy as a Copperhead in two different articles. See Frank L. Klement, "'Brick' Pomeroy: Copperhead and Curmudgeon," *Wisconsin Magazine of History*, XXXV (Winter, 1951), 106–13, 156–57, and "A Small-Town Editor Criticizes Lincoln: A Study in Editorial Abuse," *Lincoln Herald*, LV (Summer, 1952), 27–32, 60.

23. Springfield *Illinois State Register*, Jan. 2, 3, 27, 1863.

24. Chicago *Daily Tribune*, Jan. 9, 1863; Springfield *Illinois State Journal*, Jan. 6, 7, 1863; *Illinois State Register*, Jan. 6, 8, 1863.

25. *Crisis*, Jan. 14, 1863. Thurman's role in the meeting is discussed in John Hare, "Allen G. Thurman: A Political Study" (Ph.D. diss., Ohio State University, 1933).

26. Detroit *Free Press*, Feb. 12, 1863.

27. Chicago *Times*, Jan. 24, 1863; *Illinois State Register*, Jan. 26, 1863.

28. Indianapolis *Sentinel,* Jan. 7, 9, Feb. 14, 1863.

29. *Illinois State Register,* Jan. 10, 1863; Dubuque *Times,* Jan. 20, 1863.

30. *Ibid.,* Feb. 16, 1863; *Fulton County Ledger* (Canton, Ill.), May 5, 1863.

31. *Illinois State Register,* Jan. 17, 1863; *Illinois State Journal,* June 17, 18, 1863; Chicago *Tribune,* June 20, 1863.

32. John Reynolds to "Gentlemen," Jan. 9, 1863, published in the *Illinois State Register,* Jan. 12, 1863.

33. Amos Kendall to John D. Caton, Jan. 27, 1863, John D. Caton Papers, Library of Congress.

34. *Cong. Globe,* 37 Cong., 2 sess., p. 2537, Appendix, pp. 242–49; *Crisis,* Jan. 21, 1863.

35. Clement L. Vallandigham, *Speeches, Arguments, Addresses, and Letters of Clement L. Vallandigham* (New York, 1864), p. 438; *Cong. Globe,* 37 Cong., 3 sess., p. 130; *Crisis,* Jan. 28, 1863.

36. *Cong. Globe,* 37 Cong., 3 sess., pp. 783–86.

37. Chicago *Weekly Journal,* Jan. 3, 1863.

38. *Cong. Globe,* 37 Cong., 3 sess., p. 76.

39. Hamilton *True Telegraph,* Jan. 15, 1863.

40. Cincinnati *Gazette,* March 3, 1863.

41. "Proceedings, Twenty-third General Assembly, Jan. 29, 1863," published in *Illinois State Register,* Jan. 30, 1863; *Illinois State Register,* Jan. 9, 1863.

42. Indianapolis *Daily Journal,* Jan. 30, 1863; Indianapolis *State Sentinel,* Jan. 15, 1863.

43. State of Wisconsin, *Journal of the House, 1863* (Madison, 1863), pp. 148–49, 424–27, 482.

44. *Illinois State Journal,* Jan. 30, 1863, quoting letter in St. Louis *Missouri Democrat* (n.d.).

45. R. George Dun to S. S. Cox, Feb. 18, 1863, Samuel Sullivan Cox Papers, microfilm copy, Hayes Memorial Library.

46. Dr. George F. Chittenden to "My Dear Wife," Feb. 8, 1863, George F. Chittenden Papers, Indiana Division, Indiana State Library.

47. Indianapolis *State Sentinel,* Jan. 23, 1863; W. H. H. Terrell, *Report of the Adjutant General of Indiana* (8 vols.; Indianapolis, 1866–69), I, 79.

48. Chicago *Weekly Journal,* Feb. 9, 1863.

49. J. W. Kincheloe to Joseph Holt, Jan. 18, 1863; Joseph Holt Papers, Library of Congress.

50. Joseph Miller to Pvt. William A. Wilmoth, Jan. 25, 1863, Illinois 11th Cavalry Folder, Illinois Civil War Files and Records, Illinois State Archives.

51. Indianapolis *Daily Journal,* Nov. 10, 1862.

52. *Ibid.,* Oct. 17, 25, 26, 28, 1862, Jan. 9, 1863; Terrell, *Report . . . ,* I, 296–97.

53. Morton to Secretary of War Edwin M. Stanton, Jan. 3, 1863, Telegrams Received (Vol. IV, Part 2, 759), War Department Records, The National Archives.

54. State of Indiana, *Brevier Legislative Reports*, compiled by Ariel and William H. Drapier, VI (1863), 10, 12.

55. *Ibid.*, p. 13; Calvin Fletcher, "Diary," Jan. 8, 1863, Calvin Fletcher Papers, Indiana State Historical Society; Indianapolis *State Sentinel*, Jan. 9, 1863. One of the senators was elected for the term starting in March of 1863, the other was supposed to serve out the rest of Jesse Bright's term (Bright had been expelled early in 1862).

56. Indianapolis *State Sentinel*, Jan. 9, 12, 1863.

57. State of Indiana, *Brevier Legislative Reports*, VI (1863), 21, 22, 30–32; Indianapolis *State Sentinel*, Jan. 10, 1863; Indianapolis *Daily Journal*, Jan. 10, 1863.

58. Indianapolis *State Sentinel*, Jan. 15, 16, 1863; Indianapolis *Daily Journal*, Jan. 14–16, 21, 1863; State of Indiana, *Brevier Legislative Reports*, VI (1863), 37–38, 46–49, 64, 67–69, 85, 114.

59. P. Haagland to Allen Hamilton, Feb. 20, 1863, Allen Hamilton Papers, Indiana Division, Indiana State Library; Frederick W. Matthis to W. H. English, March 6, 1863, William H. English Papers, Indiana State Historical Society; Indianapolis *State Sentinel*, Feb. 27, 1863; State of Indiana, *Brevier Legislative Reports*, VI (1863) 99, 119–21, 155. The traditional view is presented in Logan Esary's *A History of Indiana* (2 vols.; Fort Wayne, 1924), II, 677–78. Kenneth M. Stampp's *Indiana Politics during the Civil War* (Indianapolis, 1949) is a welcome antidote to propaganda which passes for history.

60. Indianapolis *Daily Journal*, Jan. 13, 17, 30, 31, March 13, 1863. William Dudley Foulke's *Life of Oliver P. Morton* (2 vols.; Indianapolis, 1899) is a partisan defense of Morton; it depicts the Democratic-Republican struggle as a contest between truth and patriotism, on the one hand, and between perfidy and treason, on the other.

61. W. H. H. Terrell to Col. J. T. Wilder, Jan. 24, 1863, John T. Wilder Papers, Indiana Division, Indiana State Library; W. P. Wilder to "Uncle Charley," Jan. 28, 1863, Charles B. Lasselle Collection, Indiana Division, Indiana State Library; Calvin Fletcher, "Diary," Jan. 20, Feb. 3, 12, 1863, Fletcher Papers; Indianapolis *Daily Journal*, Jan. 9, 16, 17, Feb. 3, 1863; Indianapolis *State Sentinel*, Feb. 27, 1863; Terrell, *Report* . . . , I, Appendix, 355–56.

62. Schuyler Colfax to "Dear Sir," Feb. 7, 1863, Schuyler Colfax Papers, Indiana Division, Indiana State Library.

63. State of Indiana, *Journal of the House of Representatives of the State of Indiana, 1863* (Indianapolis, 1863), p. 216; Indianapolis *State Sentinel*, Jan. 27, 1863.

64. State of Indiana, *Brevier Legislative Reports*, VI (1863), 175–76; B. F. Claypool to Allen Hamilton, Feb. 6, 1863, Hamilton Papers; N. S.

LaRose to C. B. Lasselle, Feb. 2, 1863, Lasselle Collection; Frederick W. Matthis to W. H. English, March 6, 1863, English Papers.

65. "Propositions of the Bolting Members, House of Representatives, 1863," Oliver P. Morton Papers, Indiana Division, Indiana State Library.

66. Calvin Fletcher, "Diary," June 9, 1863, Fletcher Papers.

67. A. Teagarden to O. P. Morton, Sept. 11, 1863, Chicago-Morton Papers, Archives Division, Indiana State Library; Indianapolis *Daily Journal*, May 12, June 12, 13, July 2, 6, Dec. 11, 1863.

68. Indianapolis *State Sentinel*, March 12, Apr. 16, June 9, 10, 17, 18, 22, Aug. 4, 1863.

69. Frederick W. Matthis to W. H. English, March 6, 1863, English Papers.

70. William S. Pope to Governor Yates, Nov. 7, 1862, Governor Richard Yates Papers, Illinois State Historical Library.

71. D. S. Phillips to Lyman Trumbull, Dec. 24, 1862, Lyman Trumbull Papers, Library of Congress.

72. *Illinois State Journal*, Jan. 6, 1863; Chicago *Tribune*, Jan. 7, 1863.

73. Chicago *Weekly Journal*, Jan. 16, 1863; *Illinois State Register*, Jan. 9, 1863.

74. *Illinois State Journal*, Jan. 9, 1863.

75. *Ibid.*, Jan. 10, 1863; *Illinois State Register*, Jan. 10, 1863.

76. E. W. Haines to Elihu B. Washburne, Jan. 10, 1863, and J. F. Chapman to E. B. Washburne, Jan. 12, 1863, Elihu B. Washburne Papers, Library of Congress; *Illinois State Journal*, Jan. 13, 1863.

77. *Journal of the House of Representatives, Illinois, 1863* (Springfield, 1863), pp. 155, 175; Chicago *Tri-Weekly Tribune*, Jan. 13, 21, 1863; W. C. Flagg to Lyman Trumbull, Jan. 17, 1863, Trumbull Papers.

78. "Proceedings . . . , Jan. 20, 1863," *Illinois State Register*, Jan. 31, 1863; *Illinois State Register*, Jan. 28, 30, 31, 1863.

79. "Proceedings . . . , Jan. 17, 1863," *ibid.*, Jan. 19, 1863; *Illinois State Register*, Jan. 20, 30, 1863; Chicago *Weekly Journal*, Feb. 6, 1863; Chicago *Tri-Weekly Tribune*, Feb. 16, 1863.

80. "Proceedings . . . , Jan. 29, 1863," *Illinois State Register*, Jan. 30, 1863.

81. *Fulton County Ledger* (Canton, Ill.), Jan. 20, 1863.

82. Jesse K. Dubois to Lyman Trumbull, Feb. 2, 1863, Trumbull Papers.

83. "Proceedings . . . , Feb. 6, 1863," *Illinois State Register*, Feb. 7, 1863.

84. Charles H. Ray to Elihu B. Washburne, Feb. 10, 1863, Washburne Papers.

85. James M. Blades (assistant sergeant-at-arms, Illinois State Senate, 1863) to "Mr. Editor" (n.d.), published in *Illinois State Register*, Feb. 13, 1863; *Fulton County Ledger* (Canton, Ill.), Feb. 17, 1863.

86. *Journal of the Senate . . . Illinois . . . 1863* (Springfield, 1863), p. 339; *Journal of the House of Representatives . . . Illinois . . . 1863* (Springfield, 1863), p. 653.

87. D. Richards to Elihu B. Washburne, April 14, 1863, and S. W. McMaster to Washburne, Feb. 7, 1863, Washburne Papers; Chicago *Morning Post*, Feb. 8, 1863; *Fulton County Ledger* (Canton, Ill.), Feb. 17, 1863; *Illinois State Register*, Feb. 9, 1863.

88. "Proceedings . . . , Feb. 14, 1863," *Illinois State Register*, Feb. 16, 1863. William H. Green had been arrested in the fall roundup of 1862; he was later released without any charge being filed. His arrest in February, 1863, seemed to be part of a deliberate plan to give the Republicans control of the upper house.

89. Chicago *Tribune*, Feb. 16, 1863.

90. Richard Yates, William Butler, O. M. Hatch, and Jesse K. Dubois to President Lincoln, March 1, 1863, Robert Todd Lincoln Papers, Library of Congress; William Butler to Lyman Trumbull, Jan. 28, 1863, Trumbull Papers.

91. *Copperheads under the Heel of an Illinois Farmer: Speech of Mr. Funk in the Illinois State Legislature, February 28, 1863* (n.p., n.d.). The date given in the title is incorrect, for Mr. Funk's speech was made on February 13, 1863.

92. "Proceedings . . . , June 3, 1863," *Illinois State Register*, June 4, 1863.

93. Governor Yates to General A. C. Fuller, June 10, 1863, copy of telegram in Yates Papers; "Address of Protest" of the Democratic Legislative Committee, June 10, 1863, published in Chicago *Post*, June 12, 1863; Chicago *Tri-Weekly Tribune*, June 12, 1863; *Illinois State Register*, June 11, 25, 1863.

94. Chicago *Times*, June 12, 1863.

95. *Illinois State Register*, June 16, 1863.

96. New York *World* (n.d.), quoted in *ibid.*, June 13, 1863.

97. Springfield *Illinois State Journal*, June 11, 1863.

98. Chicago *Weekly Journal*, June 19, 1863; Chicago *Tri-Weekly Tribune*, June 12, 1863.

99. *Western Railroad Gazette* (Chicago), June 13, 1863. "Wabash" Fuller proved to be Melville W. Fuller, later a chief justice of the United States Supreme Court. Fuller's role as a Copperhead is included in Willard L. King, *Melville Weston Fuller, Chief Justice of the United States, 1888–1910* (New York, 1950).

100. *Illinois State Register*, Dec. 13, 1863, Jan. 10, 1864.

101. Madison *Wisconsin Patriot*, Dec. 23, 1862.

102. *In re Kemp*, 16 Wisconsin 396 (1863); Appleton's *American Annual Cyclopaedia and Register of Important Events, 1863*, pp. 469–70.

103. Edward Bates to Edwin M. Stanton, Jan. 31, 1863, Edwin M. Stanton Papers, Library of Congress.

104. *In re Griner*, 16 Wisconsin 447 (1863); Madison *Wisconsin State Journal*, Feb. 18, 1863.

105. Appleton's *American Annual Cyclopaedia . . . 1863*, p. 472. Col. Carrington's side of the story is told in Henry B. Carrington, "The Constable Case," Henry B. Carrington Papers, Archives Division, Indiana

State Library. There is conflicting evidence as to whether the four were "deserters" or "parolees," James Gamron, one of the four, served with the 130th Illinois; he was taken prisoner during a campaign in Tennessee and subsequently paroled. He had returned to his home near Marshall when he was arrested by Col. Carrington's agents.

106. H. B. Carrington to Governor Yates, March 10, 1863, telegram in Yates Papers.

107. Carrington, "The Constable Case," Carrington Papers.

108. Appleton's *American Annual Cyclopaedia . . . 1863,* pp. 606–9.

109. Indianapolis *Daily Journal,* Feb. 3, 4, March 18, 1863; Indianapolis *State Sentinel,* Feb. 1, 1863.

110. Indiana State Supreme Court, *Reports,* XX, 345–83; Indianapolis *Daily Journal,* May 12, 1863; Indianapolis *State Sentinel,* May 14, 16, June 12, 14, 1863. It is interesting to compare the highly partisan, pro-Morton account in William D. Foulke, *Life of Oliver P. Morton: Including His Important Speeches* (2 vols.; New York, 1899), I, 257–59, with the objective treatment accorded Indiana issues in Kenneth Stampp, *Indiana Politics during the Civil War* (Indianapolis, 1949), 178–85.

111. Jackson (Mich.) *Weekly Patriot,* March 4, 1863, quoting New York *Independent* (n.d.).

CHAPTER III

1. Calvin Fletcher, "Diary," Jan. 4, 1863, Calvin Fletcher Papers, Indiana State Historical Society.

2. George Hay to E. B. Washburne, Feb. 12, 1863, Elihu B. Washburne Papers, Library of Congress.

3. *Official Records of the Union and Confederate Armies* (128 vols., 1880–1901), Ser. 3, V, 757–58.

4. Dr. Humphrey H. Hood to "My Dear Wife," Jan. 11, 1863, Dr. Humphrey H. Hood Papers, Illinois State Historical Library.

5. March 26, 1863, *ibid.*

6. Edward Mosher to Richard Speake, March 1, 1863, published in the Canton (Ill.) *Weekly Register,* April 20, 1863; Springfield *Illinois State Journal,* Jan. 30, 1863; Dr. Humphrey H. Hood to "My Dear Wife," Jan. 29, Feb. 26, 1863, Hood Papers; Frank L. Klement (ed.), "Edwin B. Bigelow: A Michigan Sergeant in the Civil War," *Michigan History,* XXXVIII (September, 1954), 205; Bell Irvin Wiley, *The Life of Billy Yank* (Indianapolis, 1951), pp. 86–91, 205–7, 277.

7. Roy P. Basler (ed.), *The Collected Works of Abraham Lincoln* (9 vols.; New Brunswick, 1953), VI, 369–70.

8. S. S. Cox, quoted in *Illinois State Register,* March 3, 1863.

9. Dayton *Weekly Empire,* Feb. 21, 1863.

10. Hamilton *True Telegraph,* Feb. 26, 1863.

11. Indianapolis *State Sentinel,* July 30, 1863.

12. Herman B. Keel to "Mr. Editor" (n.d.), published in the *Fulton County Ledger* (Canton, Ill.), Aug. 4, 1863.

13. Quoted in Indianapolis *State Sentinel,* March 12, 1863.

14. Chatfield (Minn.) *Democrat,* March 7, 1863.

15. La Crosse *Weekly Democrat,* Feb. 17 1863.

16. Dayton *Weekly Empire,* March 7, 1863.

17. Milwaukee *See-Bote,* Feb. 11, March 25, April 20, 1863.

18. *Official Records,* Ser. 1, XXXIX, Part 2, 35.

19. *Ibid.,* Ser. 3, III, 371, 392.

20. *Ibid.,* pp. 370–71, 375, 391–98.

21. Dr. Alexander McPheeters to "Dear Son," June 10, 1863, Dr. John S. McPheeters Papers, Indiana State Historical Society.

22. *Official Records,* Ser. 3, III, 338–40. Also see Charles E. Canup, "Conscription and Draft in Indiana during the Civil War," *Indiana Magazine of History,* X (June, 1914), 70–83; and Marjorie Anita Perry, *Opposition to the Civil War in Indiana* (M.S. thesis, University of Washington, Seattle, 1932).

23. Chicago *Tribune,* June 26, 27, 28, 1863.

24. Springfield *Illinois State Register,* Aug. 10, 1863; Chicago *Tribune,* Aug. 16, 1863; *Illinois State Journal,* Aug. 20, 1863. The rumors were circulated by Joseph K. C. Forrest, Springfield correspondent for the Chicago *Tribune.*

25. *Official Records,* Ser. 3, III, 247–48, 395–96.

26. S. W. Shepherd to Gov. Kirkwood, May 6, 1863, Samuel J. Kirkwood Papers, State Department of History and Archives, Historical Library, Des Moines, Iowa.

27. Laz Noble to Allen Hamilton, Apr. 2, 1863, Allen Hamilton Papers, Indiana Division, Indiana State Library; *Official Records,* Ser. 3, III, 370–71, 375, 391–98.

28. *Official Records,* Ser. 3, III, 339–40; Indianapolis *State Sentinel,* June 18, 19, 26, 1863; Indianapolis *Daily Journal,* June 27, 1863; Clement L. Vallandigham, *Speeches, Arguments, Addresses, and Letters of Clement L. Vallandigham* (New York, 1864), pp. 42–43, 502–4; Charles Roll, *Colonel Dick Thompson* ("Indiana Historical Collections," Vol. XXX [Indianapolis, 1948]), p. 212.

29. John D. Caton to Messrs. John W. Merritt, Silas L. Bryan, and H. K. S. O'Melveny, March 24, 1863, John D. Caton Papers, Library of Congress.

30. *Ibid.*

31. W. B. Pritchett to Gov. Yates, June 23, 1863, Richard Yates Papers, Illinois State Historical Library; Ralph Emerson, Jr. to Elihu B. Washburne, Jan. 26, 1863, Washburne Papers; R. H. Stephenson to William Henry Smith, Aug. 25, 1863, William Henry Smith Papers, Ohio Historical Society.

32. *United States Statutes at Large,* XII, 755.

33. *Congressional Globe,* 37 Cong., 3 sess., p. 1103.

34. *Ibid.,* p. 1465.

35. *Ibid.,* pp. 1057–63. Forrest Seal's "The Political Speaking of Senator Daniel Voorhees of Indiana" (Ph.D. diss., Purdue University, 1955) treats Voorhees, as an orator, in scholarly fashion. Two M.A.

theses worthy of mention are Herbert V. Cordier, "The Oratory of Daniel W. Voorhees" (Michigan State University, 1952), and Orland S. Lefforge, "Daniel Wolsey Voorhees, Indiana Orator" (University of Wisconsin, 1940).

36. Dayton *Weekly Empire*, March 14, 1863.

37. Ira Harris to O. H. Browning, May 30, 1863, Orville H. Browning Papers, Illinois State Historical Library.

38. *Cong. Globe*, 37 Cong., 3 sess., p. 599.

39. *Ibid.*, Appendix, p. 73.

40. *Ibid.*, 39 Cong., 3 sess., p. 897; James G. Blaine, *Twenty Years in Congress: From Lincoln to Garfield* (2 vols.; New York, 1884–86), I, 480.

41. Columbus *Crisis*, March 4, 18, 1863.

42. Cincinnati *Daily Enquirer*, Feb. 24, 1863.

43. Detroit *Free Press*, Apr. 1, Sept. 3, 1863; Indianapolis *State Sentinel*, Sept. 25, 1863; Milwaukee *Daily News* (n.d.), quoted in Indianapolis *State Sentinel*, Apr. 29, 1863; Chicago *Times*, Sept. 30, 1863.

44. State of Minnesota, *House Journal, 1863* (St. Paul, 1863), p. 223; Indianapolis *State Sentinel*, Sept. 25, 1863; E. B. Warner to Elihu B. Washburne, Jan. 16, 1863, Washburne Papers; *Cong. Globe*, 39 Cong., 3 sess., p. 897; Henry Clay Dean, *Crimes of the Civil War and Curse of the Funding System* (Baltimore, 1868), pp. 7–8, 436 ff.; Dennis A. Mahony, *Four Acts of Despotism . . .* (New York, 1863), *passim*.

45. Dayton *Weekly Empire*, March 14, 1863; Hamilton *True Telegraph*, March 19, 1863.

46. La Crosse *Democrat*, Sept. 28, 1862, Jan. 8, 1863. An autobiography, M. M. Pomeroy, *Journey of Life: Reminiscences and Recollections of "Brick" Pomeroy* (New York, 1890), rationalizes the author's contribution to the Copperhead cause.

47. La Crosse *Democrat*, Dec. 9, 16, 1862.

48. *Ibid.*, April 7, 1863.

49. Pomeroy, *Journey of Life*, pp. 184 ff.

50. La Crosse *Democrat*, March 17, 1863.

51. *Ibid.*, Feb. 10, 17, March 3, 17, Apr. 7, 1863.

52. Brig. General Benjamin M. Prentiss, "General Order No. 19," District of Eastern Arkansas, Civil War Commands, War Department Records, National Archives. Pomeroy's version is dramatically given in Pomeroy, *Journey of Life*, pp. 187–89.

53. General A. E. Burnside to Henry B. Carrington, Apr. 21, 1863, Henry B. Carrington Papers, Archives Division, Indiana State Library.

54. Dayton *Weekly Empire*, March 14, 1863.

55. La Crosse *Weekly Democrat*, Feb. 19, Oct. 10, 1864.

56. Dayton *Weekly Empire*, March 14, 1863.

57. *Official Records*, Ser. 3, XXIII, Part 1, 398, 728; Governor Oliver P. Morton to General Burnside, July 11, 1863, Oliver P. Morton Papers, Archives Division, Indiana State Library.

58. Dayton *Weekly Empire*, March 21, 1863.
59. Edwin B. Morgan to Elihu B. Washburne, Jan. 21, 1863, Washburne Papers.
60. *Official Records*, Ser. 1, XXIII, Part 2, 237.
61. W. P. Penn to John D. Caton, Apr. 15, 1863, Caton Papers.
62. Vallandigham to Hon. Franklin Pierce, Apr. 11, 1862, photostatic copy in Franklin Pierce Papers, Library of Congress. Vallandigham needs an objective biographer. His side of the controversy appears in J. L. Vallandigham, *A Life of Clement L. Vallandigham* (Baltimore, 1872), and in E. N. Vallandigham, "Clement L. Vallandigham, 'Copperhead,' " *Putnam's Monthly Magazine*, II (August, 1907), 590–99. The traditional anti-Vallandigham interpretation is presented in George Fort Milton, *Abraham Lincoln and the Fifth Column* (New York, 1942).
63. "Report on Vallandigham's Military Trial," Citizens' File, 1861–65, War Department Collection of Confederate Records, National Archives.
64. *Ibid.; Official Records*, Ser. 2, V, 634; Appleton's *American Annual Cyclopaedia and Register of Important Events, 1863*, pp. 234–35.
65. Thomas O. Lowe to "My dear brother" (William), May 11, 1863, Thomas O. Lowe Papers, Dayton Public Library.
66. Dayton *Empire*, May 5, 1863.
67. *Ibid.*
68. Thomas O. Lowe to "Brother Will," May 11, 1863, Lowe Papers. The Lowe letters offer the best description of the riot, for Thomas O. Lowe was a close observer. Two M.A. theses deal with the Dayton Democrat: Florence E. Boyd, "Dayton, Ohio, during the Civil War" (Ohio State University, 1939), and Irving L. Schwartz, "Dayton, Ohio, during the Civil War" (Miami University, Oxford, Ohio, 1949).
69. Thomas O. Lowe, "Open Letter" (n.d.), Lowe Papers. The letter was published in the Dayton *Journal*, May 7, 1863. After the riot the *Journal* was published for a time on the presses of the *Religious Telescope*, a weekly issue of the United Brethren Church.
70. "Report on Vallandigham's Military Trial," Citizens' File 1861–65, War Department Collection of Confederate Records.
71. Thomas O. Lowe to "Brother Will," May 11, 14, 1863, Lowe Papers.
72. "Proceedings of a Military Commission Convened at Cincinnati, May 6, 1863," Citizens' File, 1861–65, War Department Collection of Confederate Records; *Official Records*, Ser. 2, V, 633 ff.; Samuel Sullivan Cox, *Union, Disunion, Reunion: Three Decades of Federal Legislation* (Providence, 1885), p. 83; Appleton's *American Annual Cyclopaedia . . . 1863*, pp. 473–84.
73. John T. Morse (ed.), *Diary of Gideon Welles, Secretary of the Navy under Lincoln and Johnson* (3 vols.; New York, 1911), I, 306.
74. Merritt Miller to "Bro. Clement," May 30, 1863, Merritt Miller Papers, in possession of Mr. V. L. Rockwell, Union Grove, Wis.
75. Report of Maj. William M. Wiles to Brig. Gen. James A. Garfield,

May 25, 1863, Citizens' File, 1861–65, War Department Collection of Confederate Papers. The "dumped down" interpretation is given in A. J. L. Freemantle, *Three Months in the Southern States: April, June, 1863* (London, 1863).

76. James Ford Rhodes, *History of the United States from the Compromise of 1850* . . . (7 vols.; New York, 1893–1906), IV, 353. Storey's contribution to midwestern Copperheadism is treated in Cecil C. Blair, "The Chicago Democratic Press in the Civil War" (Ph.D. diss., University of Chicago, 1949); Mrs. L. E. Ellis, "The Chicago *Times* during the Civil War," *Transactions of the Illinois State Historical Society, 1932,* pp. 135–82; and Donald B. Sanger, "The Chicago *Times* and the Civil War," *Mississippi Valley Historical Review,* XVII (March, 1931), 557–80.

77. *Official Records,* Ser. 2, XXIII, Part 2, 381.

78. "Argument of Hon. James F. Joy on the Preliminary Application of the Chicago *Times* for an Injunction in the United States Court," Detroit *Free Press,* June 9, 1863.

79. *Official Records,* Ser. 2, XXIII, Part 2, 725, 752; Appleton's *American Annual Cyclopaedia* . . . *1863,* pp. 484 ff. It should be mentioned that Gen. Milo S. Hascall, who succeeded Brig. Gen. Henry B. Carrington as commander of the District of Indiana, had earlier suppressed the South Bend *Forum* and the Columbia City *News.*

80. Dubuque *Herald,* May 14, 1863.

81. Iowa City *State Press,* May 9, 1863.

82. Hamilton *True Telegraph,* June 11, 1863.

83. Chatfield *Democrat,* May 23, 1863; Milwaukee *See-Bote,* May 13, 1863; St. Paul *Pioneer and Democrat,* June 26, July 3, 1863; Iowa City *State Press,* May 9, 1863; Hamilton *True Telegraph,* June 18, 1863; Detroit *Free Press,* May 8, 26, June 7, 1863.

84. *Official Records,* Ser. 2, V, 485.

85. Indianapolis *State Sentinel,* May 21, 1863.

86. *Ibid.*

87. Indianapolis *Daily Journal,* May 21, 1863; Milo S. Hascall, "Autobiography," Milo S. Hascall Papers, Archives Division, Indiana State Library. Typically biased accounts are included in William D. Foulke, *Life of Oliver P. Morton, Including His Important Speeches* (2 vols.; Indianapolis, 1899), I, 274–77, and Logan Esarey, *A History of Indiana* (2 vols.; Fort Wayne, 1924), II, 781–83.

88. *Illinois State Register,* June 18, 1863. The editor of the Chicago *Tribune* (in the issue of June 20, 1863) estimated that only 40,000 attended the Copperhead convention.

89. *Illinois State Journal,* June 19, 20, 1863; *Illinois State Register,* June 18, 19, 1863. Governor Yates's fears that the Springfield rally might introduce civil war into Illinois were unfounded. The five telegrams which General Ammen's agent (in Springfield) sent to his superior are interesting. The five read: (1) "A great crowd here. No appearance of trouble. Speeches last night until twelve very conserva-

tive." (2) "No soldiers on the street. All quiet. No rows yet." (3) "The crowd is going home fast. No fighting yet. Drunk men plenty. No sign of trouble." (4) "The speaking is over. No appearance of an outbreak and few fights. Very quiet." (5) "All quiet. Crowd gone." W. L. Ammen to Brig. Gen. Jacob Ammen, June 18, 1863, "Telegram Book," William P. Palmer Collection, Western Reserve Historical Society Library.

90. Milwaukee *Daily News*, July 2, 1863.

91. *Ibid.*

92. A. L. Perrill to S. S. Cox, Feb. 8, 1863, Samuel Sullivan Cox Papers, microfilm, Hayes Memorial Library, Fremont, Ohio.

93. Hamilton *True Telegraph*, May 21, 1863.

94. *Crisis*, June 4, 1863.

95. John Law to S. S. Cox, June 18, 1863, Cox Papers; Thomas O. Lowe to "My dear Brother" (Will), May 11, 1863, Lowe Papers; *Crisis*, June 13, 1863.

96. *Crisis*, June 13, 1863; *See-Bote*, June 17, 1863; La Crosse *Democrat*, June 24, 1863; Detroit *Free Press*, June 14, 1863. Benjamin Wood, prominent Peace Democrat of New York wrote: "The convention was all that I could have wished and I trust the election will be equally emphatic." Benjamin Wood to S. S. Cox, June 12, 1863, Cox Papers.

97. Paper-covered copies of the 250-page book, published by J. Walter & Co., sold for sixty cents (those bound in muslin were priced at one dollar).

98. Dayton *Daily Empire*, Apr. 25, 1863; Hamilton *True Telegraph*, Apr. 30, 1863.

99. Dubuque *Herald*, Apr. 8, 1863.

100. Dennis A. Mahony, *The Prisoner of State* (New York, 1863), pp. iii–iv.

101. Dubuque *Herald*, Apr. 11, 1863.

102. Mahony, *Four Acts of Despotism, passim.*

103. *Illinois State Register*, Jan. 15, 1863; A. D. Duff, *Letter of A. D. Duff . . .* (Springfield, 1863).

104. Edson B. Olds, *Arbitrary Arrests: Speech of Hon. Edson B. Olds for Which He Was Arrested and His Reception Speeches on His Return from the Bastile* (Lancaster, 1863). Also see Lancaster *Ohio Eagle*, Jan. 8, Feb. 26, 1863.

105. Samuel Sullivan Cox, *Puritanism in Politics: Speech before Democratic Union Association, January 13, 1863* (New York, 1863).

106. R. George Dun to S. S. Cox, Feb. 18, 1863, John Dowling to S. S. Cox, Feb. 10, 1863, Cox Papers.

107. The "Morrison Address" is capably treated in John P. Pritchett, "Michigan Democracy in the Civil War," *Michigan History Magazine*, XL (January, 1927), 92–110.

108. *Address of the Democratic State Central Committee to the People of Iowa* (Iowa City, 1863), pp. 2–3, 5, 8.

109. Edward Johnstone to Charles Mason, May 23, 1863, and Dennis

A. Mahony to Charles Mason, June 24, 1863, Charles Mason Papers, State Department of History and Archives, Historical Library, Des Moines, Iowa.

110. S. F. B. Morse to Sidney Breese, Feb. 4, 1863, Sidney Breese Papers, Illinois State Historical Library.

111. Dubuque *Daily Democratic Herald*, Apr. 11, 1863.

112. Dayton *Journal*, Apr. 9, 1863.

113. Hamilton *True Telegraph*, Apr. 16, 1863.

114. Muscatine *Courier* (n.d.), quoted in Iowa City *Republican*, June 17, 1863.

115. La Crosse *Weekly Democrat*, June 9, 1863.

CHAPTER IV

1. Democratic interest in compromise is treated in such works as: Mary Scrugham, *The Peaceable Americans of 1860–1861* (New York, 1921); Jesse L. Keane, "The Peace Convention of 1861" (Ph.D. diss., University of Florida, 1958); Carl M. Frasure, "Union Saving Forces, 1859–1861" (Ph.D. diss., Ohio State University, 1928); George Fort Milton, "Stephen A. Douglas' Efforts for Peace," *Journal of Southern History*, I (August, 1935), 261–75. The explanation of why the North adopted a policy of coercion rather than compromise is available in: Kenneth Stampp, *And the War Came: The North and the Secession Crisis* (Baton Rouge, 1950); David Potter, *Lincoln and His Party in the Secession Crisis* (New Haven, 1942); William E. Baringer, *A House Dividing: Lincoln as President Elect* (Springfield, 1945); Clinton E. Knox, "The Possibilities of Compromise in the Senate Committee of Thirteen and the Responsibility for Failure," *Journal of Negro History*, XVII (October, 1932), 437–65; Frank C. Heck, "John C. Breckinridge in the Crisis of 1860–1861," *Journal of Southern History*, XXI (August, 1955), 316–46; Allan B. Magruder, "A Piece of Secret History: President Lincoln and the Virginia Convention of 1861," *Atlantic Monthly*, XXXV (1875), 438–45; and Robert Schwab, "Wisconsin and Compromise on the Eve of the Civil War" (M.A. thesis, Marquette University, 1957). The following bear upon the question of compromise: Charles R. Wilson, "Cincinnati, a Southern Outpost in 1860–1861?" *Mississippi Valley Historical Review*, XXIV (March, 1938), 473–82; Kenneth Stampp, "Kentucky's Influence upon Indiana in the Crisis of 1861," *Indiana Magazine of History*, XXXIX (September, 1943), 263–76; Roman J. Zorn, "Minnesota Public Opinion and the Secession Controversy, December, 1860–April, 1861," *Mississippi Valley Historical Review*, XXXVI (March, 1949), 435–56; J. M. Hofer, "Development of the Peace Movement in Illinois during the Civil War," *Journal of the Illinois State Historical Society*, XXIV (April, 1931), 110–28; and E. Merton Coulter, "The Effects of Secession upon the Commerce of the Mississippi Valley," *Mississippi Valley Historical Review*, III (December, 1916), 275–300.

2. Cincinnati *Daily Enquirer*, Jan. 2, 15, Feb. 14, March 7, 12, 22, 1861. The *Enquirer*'s interpretation of events is treated in scholarly fashion in Charles R. Wilson, "Cincinnati Daily Enquirer and Civil War Politics: A Study in Copperhead Opinion" (Ph.D. diss., University of Chicago, 1934).

3. William S. McCormick (brother of Cyrus) to Alexander Steele, May 6, 1861, Cyrus H. McCormick Papers, Wisconsin State Historical Society.

4. W. Talcott to Elihu B. Washburne, Jan. 7, 1863, Elihu B. Washburne Papers, Library of Congress.

5. William H. Brisbane to Hon. George W. Julian, Jan. 31, 1861, Joshua R. Giddings–George W. Julian Papers, Library of Congress.

6. "One of Em" to "Editor," Aug. 14, 1864, Indianapolis *State Sentinel*, Aug. 16, 1864.

7. Springfield *Illinois State Register*, Apr. 26, 1861. It should be pointed out that Douglas said that the war must be fought to save and restore the Union, and that Douglas emphasized that the institutions of the South must remain untouched.

8. Madison *Wisconsin Patriot*, May 4, 1861.

9. Charles Mason, "Diary," June 18, 1861, Charles Mason Papers, State Department of History and Archives, Historical Library, Des Moines, Iowa.

10. Dubuque *Daily Herald*, Apr. 19, 28, 1861; Dennis A. Mahony, *The Prisoner of State* (New York, 1863), pp. 29–55.

11. James C. Robinson to John A. Logan, Apr. 18, 1861, John A. Logan Papers, Library of Congress.

12. C. L. Vallandigham to Messrs. Henrickson *et al.*, May 13, 1861, published in *Stark County Democrat* (Canton, Ohio), June 19, 1861.

13. Vallandigham to the "Editor of the Cincinnati *Enquirer*," Apr. 17, 1861, open letter in Cincinnati *Daily Enquirer*, Apr. 20, 1861; Indianapolis *State Sentinel*, Apr. 22, 1861.

14. Columbus *Crisis*, May 21, 28, June 4, 1861.

15. Indianapolis *State Sentinel*, May 4, July 13, 17, 1861.

16. John A. Logan to "Dear Wife," July 16, 20, 1861, Logan Papers.

17. Cincinnati *Daily Commercial*, Sept. 9, 1861.

18. *Congressional Globe*, 37 Cong., 1 sess., p. 331.

19. Cox suggested that the seven could be: Edward Everett (Mass.), Millard Fillmore (N.Y.), Reverdy Johnson (Md.), Martin Van Buren (N.Y.), Thomas Ewing (Ohio), Franklin Pierce (N.H.), and James Guthrie (Ky.).

20. *Cong. Globe*, 37 Cong., 1 sess., pp. 331–32.

21. Indianapolis *State Sentinel*, Aug. 26, 1861.

22. Thomas O. Lowe to "Dear Johnnie" (brother), Aug. 24, 1861, Thomas O. Lowe Papers, Dayton Public Library.

23. Louisville *Democrat* (n.d.), quoted in the Indianapolis *State Sentinel*, Aug. 27, 1861.

24. Crawfordsville *Review* (n.d.), quoted in Indianapolis *State Sentinel*, Dec. 18, 1861.

25. Detroit *Free Press*, Dec. 27, 1861.

26. Indianapolis *State Sentinel*, Aug. 17, 1861.

27. Columbus *Ohio Statesman*, Aug. 11, 1861; Indianapolis *State Sentinel*, Aug. 16, 25, 1861; Detroit *Free Press*, Nov. 15, 22, 1861.

28. *Cong. Globe*, 37 Cong., 2 sess., Part 4, pp. 891–92; Indianapolis *State Sentinel*, March 10, 1862.

29. Dubuque *Herald*, Feb. 5, 1862.

30. P. H. Walker to John D. Caton, Feb. 19, 1862, Caton Papers, Library of Congress.

31. Robert McClelland to George C. Whiting, March 26, 1862, "Letterbook, 1860–62," Robert McClelland Papers, Burton Historical Collection, Detroit Public Library.

32. Detroit *Free Press*, May 21, 1862.

33. John Reynolds to John Crittenden, May 8, 1862, John J. Crittenden Papers, Library of Congress.

34. Hugh Campbell to Joseph Holt, Sept. 26, 1862, Joseph Holt Papers, Library of Congress.

35. As early as 1861 the editor of a Cincinnati Democratic daily had written: "We hold that a proclamation freeing the negro slaves would not assist us in conquering the South and restoring the Union, but that it would render the task far more difficult if not totally impossible. It would unite the South as one man against us, make the lukewarm and conservative in Border States vehement and active against us, and divide and distract the North to an alarming extent." Cincinnati *Daily Enquirer*, July 24, Nov. 12, 1861.

36. Each of the two was the subject of a special study. See Josephine Harper, "John Reynolds, the 'Old Ranger' of Illinois, 1788–1865" (Ph.D. diss., University of Illinois, 1942); and Reginald C. McGrane, *William Allen, 1803–1879: A Study in Western Democracy* (Columbus, 1925).

37. A. Ferguson Trousdate to Secretary of War Stanton, Oct. 5, 1862, Lafayette C. Baker–Levi C. Turner Papers, 1862–65, War Department Records, National Archives.

38. George B. Smith, "Diary, 1862," Dec. 31, 1862, George B. Smith Papers, Wisconsin State Historical Society.

39. J. W. Bryant to Charles Mason, July 16, 1862, Mason Papers.

40. Cincinnati *Daily Enquirer*, Oct. 17, 1862.

41. Mahony, *Prisoner of State*, p. 204.

42. LeGrand Byington, "Address of the Democratic State Central Committee to the People of Iowa," Mason Papers.

43. Detroit *Free Press*, Nov. 22, 1862; Circleville *Watchman*, March 21, 1861; Chatfield (Minn.) *Democrat*, Dec. 20, 1862; John D. Caton, *The Position and Policy of the Democratic Party* (Ottawa, Ill., 1862), pp. 4–5.

44. John D. Martin to Philip Ewing, July 9, 1862, Thomas Ewing Papers, Ohio Historical Society.

45. Huntington (Ind.) *Democrat,* Dec. 18, 1862, quoted in the Indianapolis *State Sentinel,* Dec. 25, 1862.

46. Hamilton *True Telegraph,* Oct. 30, 1862. (That editorial followed the October elections in Ohio.)

47. Detroit *Free Press,* Nov. 25, 1862.

48. *Cong. Globe,* 37 Cong., 3 sess., XXX, Part 2, pp. 39–41.

49. Dubuque *Herald,* Jan. 10, 1863; Hamilton *True Telegraph,* Jan. 8, 1863; Dayton *Empire,* Jan. 8, 10, 1863.

50. Ashland *Union,* Jan. 28, 1863; Indianapolis *State Sentinel,* Jan. 9, 1863; Huntington *Democrat,* Dec. 18, 1862, quoted in *ibid.,* Dec. 25, 1862.

51. *Cong. Globe,* 37 Cong., 3 sess., Appendix, pp. 52–58.

52. *Ibid.,* p. 59.

53. Dayton *Empire,* Jan. 31, 1863; Indianapolis *State Sentinel,* Feb. 5, 1863.

54. Dubuque *Herald,* Jan. 20, 1863.

55. Hamilton *True Telegraph,* Jan. 31, 1863.

56. John W. Finnell to John J. Crittenden, Feb. 9, 1863, Crittenden Papers.

57. Jonesboro (Ill.) *Gazette,* Jan. 14, 1863, quoted in William F. Hart, "Aspects of the Copperhead Movement: From 1860 to 1865" (M.A. thesis, State University of Iowa, 1941), p. 34.

58. Charleston *Coles County Ledger* (n.d.), quoted in *Illinois State Register,* Feb. 7, 1863.

59. Jonesboro *Gazette,* Feb. 7, 1863, quoted in Hart, *Aspects of the Copperhead Movement,* p. 34.

60. "Proceedings, Twenty-third General Assembly, January 29, 1863," printed in the *Illinois State Register,* Jan. 30, 1863. 61. *Ibid.*

62. The speech of the Hon. C. A. Keyes (Sangamon County) of Feb. 9, 1863, was published in full in the *Illinois State Register,* Feb. 13, 1863.

63. Cos Lansing to Elihu B. Washburne, Feb. 21, 1861, Washburne Papers; (Canton, Ohio), *Fulton County Ledger,* Feb. 24, 1863.

64. *Journal of the Senate . . . of the State of Illinois . . . 1863* (Springfield, 1863), p. 399; *Illinois State Register,* Feb. 16, 1863; *Fulton County Ledger,* Feb. 24, 1863.

65. State of Indiana, *Senate Journal, 1863* (Indianapolis, 1863), pp. 695–700.

66. Oliver P. Morton to Edwin M. Stanton, Jan. 3, 1863, in *Official Records of the Union and Confederate Armies* (128 vols.; 1880–1901), Ser. 1, XX, Part 2, 297.

67. La Crosse *Weekly Democrat,* Apr. 20, 1863.

68. Henry Clay Dean, *Crimes of the Civil War and Curse of the Funding System* (Baltimore, 1868), p. 142; Dubuque *Herald,* Feb. 13, 1863; Iowa City *Iowa State Register,* Apr. 8, 1863.

69. Dayton *Weekly Empire,* Jan. 3, 1863.

70. Sheboygan *Journal,* Apr. 9, 1863.

71. Iowa City *State Press,* Feb. 28, 1863.

72. *Ibid.*

73. P. G. T. Beauregard to General Braxton Bragg, Sept. 2, 1862, William P. Palmer Collection, Western Reserve Historical Society Library.

74. *Official Records,* Ser. 1, XIV, 667, LIII, 270.

75. P. G. T. Beauregard to Charles J. Villere, May 26, 1863, *ibid.,* XIV, 955.

76. Basil W. Duke and Thomas H. Hines both testified to the hostility of the Indiana and Ohio countryside. See Basil W. Duke, *History of Morgan's Cavalry* (Miami, Ohio, 1867), p. 439, and Thomas H. Hines, "The Northwestern Conspiracy," *Southern Bivouac,* II (December, 1886), 442. Morgan's dramatic and ineffective raid (made in violation of orders of his superior) has drawn the attention of nearly a score of writers. The best brief account of the raid is William E. Wilson, "Thunderbolt of the Confederacy, or 'King of Horse Thieves' (General John H. Morgan)," *Indiana Magazine of History,* LIV (June, 1958), 119–30. See also: Margarette Boyer, "Morgan's Raid in Indiana," *Indiana Magazine of History,* VIII (December, 1912), 149–65; Basil W. Duke, *Reminiscences of General Basil W. Duke, CSA* (New York, 1910) ; R. W. McFarland, "The John Morgan Raid in Ohio," *Ohio Archaeological and Historical Publications,* XVII (1908), 243–46; Cecil Holland, *Morgan and His Raiders* (New York, 1943) ; Louis B. Ewbank, "Morgan's Raid in Indiana," *Publications of the Indiana State Historical Society,* VII, 131–83; Don D. John, *The Great Indiana-Ohio Raid* (Louisville, n.d.) ; and Duke, *History of Morgan's Cavalry.*

77. *Illinois State Register,* July 11, 1863.

78. *Ibid.*

79. Detroit *Free Press,* July 22, 1863.

80. Louisville *Daily Democrat,* July 24, 1863; Betsy Stevens to John D. Caton, July 20, 1863; Caton Papers; J. S. King to Thomas Ewing, Sr., July 24, 1863, Thomas Ewing Papers, Library of Congress.

81. Alexander H. Stephens, *Recollections of Alexander H. Stephens: His Diary Kept When a Prisoner at Fort Warren, Boston Harbour, 1865; Giving Incidents and Reflections of His Prison Life and Some Letters and Reminiscences* (New York, 1910), pp. 78–79, 446. "From the beginning," Stephens wrote (p. 374), "I had been of the opinion that if reason should once be permitted to get control of the questions, peace and harmony would soon be restored."

82. A. H. Stephens to Jefferson Davis, June 12, 1863, in Dunbar Rowland (ed.), *Jefferson Davis, Constitutionalist: His Letters, Papers, and Speeches* (10 vols.; Jackson, Miss,. 1923), V, 513–15.

83. Gideon Welles, *The Diary of Gideon Welles,* ed. John T. Morse (3 vols.; New York, 1911), I, 358–63.

84. *Official Records,* Ser. 2, VI, 79–80, 84–85, 94.

85. I. Zacharie to Gen. N. P. Banks, Dec. 23, 1863, in Fred Harrington, "A Peace Mission of 1863," *American Historical Review,* XLVI (October, 1940), 76–86.

86. I. Zacharie to Gen. N. P. Banks, Dec. 28, 1863, *ibid.*, p. 86.

87. Lincoln to his wife, Aug. 8, 1863, Robert Todd Lincoln Papers, Library of Congress.

88. *Crisis,* June 17, 1863.

89. *Ibid.,* July 22, 1863; C. L. Vallandigham, *Speeches, Arguments, Addresses, and Letters of Clement L. Vallandigham* (New York, 1864), pp. 507–20; Detroit *Free Press,* Oct. 9, 1863.

90. Cleveland *Plain Dealer,* Aug. 24, 1863; *Crisis,* July 22, Aug. 19, Sept. 16, 23, 30, Oct. 7, 1863.

91. Detroit *Free Press,* Oct. 8, 1863.

92. *Crisis,* Sept. 16, 1863.

93. Dayton *Empire,* Oct. 8, 1863.

94. *Vallandigham Song Book: Songs for the Times* (Columbus, 1863).

95. Detroit *Free Press,* Oct. 29, 1863.

96. Cincinnati *Weekly Gazette,* Sept. 30, 1863.

97. Dayton *Journal,* Oct. 2, 1863.

98. *The Peace Democracy, Alias Copperheads: Their Record, Speeches, and Votes of Vallandigham and Others* (Columbus, 1863), p. 5 and *passim.*

99. Cincinnati *Gazette* (n.d.), quoted in the Indianapolis *State Sentinel,* Oct. 13, 1863.

100. Madison *Patriot,* May 4, 1863.

101. Cincinnati *Gazette* (n.d.), quoted in the Indianapolis *State Sentinel,* Oct. 13, 1863.

102. Othneil Beeson to Allen Hamilton, Oct. 22, 1863, Allen Hamilton Papers, Indiana Division, Indiana State Library; Calvin Fletcher, "Diary, 1863," Oct. 14, 15, 1863, Calvin Fletcher Papers, Indiana State Historical Society; John P. Sanderson, "Journal," Oct. 17, 1863, John P. Sanderson Collection, Ohio Historical Society; T. S. Bell to Joseph Holt, Oct. 16, 1863, Holt Papers; Appleton's *American Annual Cyclopaedia and Register of Important Events, 1863,* p. 647.

103. Quoted in the Indianapolis *State Sentinel,* Oct. 16, 1863.

104. Indianapolis *Journal,* Oct. 21, 1863.

105. Thomas O. Lowe to "Brother Will," Nov. 8, 1863, Lowe Papers.

106. *Cong. Globe,* 38 Cong., 1 sess., p. 38.

107. Sidney Breese to Messrs. S. S. Brown, J. W. Merritt, and H. K. S. O'Melvany, Sept. 15, 1863, and Wilbur F. Storey to Breese, Dec. 2, 1863, Sidney Breese Papers, Illinois State Historical Library.

108. Detroit *Free Press,* Dec. 23, 1863.

109. Indianapolis *State Sentinel,* Dec. 25, 1863.

CHAPTER V

1. The traditional interpretation of the wartime secret societies is best summarized in Bethania Meradith Smith, "Civil War Subversives," *Journal of the Illinois State Historical Society,* XLV (Autumn, 1952), 220–40. Mayo Fesler's "Secret Political Societies in the North during the

Civil War," *Indiana Magazine of History*, XIV (September, 1918), 183–286, served as the standard work for years. The secret-society legends were also fully accepted in such works as: Elbert J. Benton, *The Movement for Peace without Victory during the Civil War* ("Western Reserve Historical Society Collections," Publication No. 99 [Cleveland, 1909]); George Fort Milton, *Lincoln and the Fifth Column* (New York, 1942); Wood Gray, *The Hidden Civil War* (New York, 1942; Edward C. Smith, *The Borderland in the Civil War* (New York, 1927); William D. Foulke, *Life of Oliver P. Morton: Including His Important Speeches* (2 vols.; New York, 1899); Jasper Cross, "Divided Loyalties in Southern Illinois during the Civil War" (Ph.D. diss., University of Illinois, 1942); William F. Hart, "Aspects of the Copperhead Movement: From 1860 to 1865" (M.A. thesis, State University of Iowa, 1941); and Curtis H. Morrow, "Politico-Military Secret Societies of the Northwest," *Social Science*, IV (November, 1928–August, 1929), 9–31, 222–42, 348–61, 463–76), V (November, 1929), 73–84. The traditional story is challenged, in part, in Frank L. Klement, "Copperhead Secret Societies in Illinois during the Civil War," *Journal of the Illinois State Historical Society*, XLVIII (Summer, 1955), 152–80.

2. Reconstructing the Bickley story is difficult, for his conflicting contentions and his mendacity make his "explanations" of questionable worth. Some Bickley writings, some newspaper clippings, and other interesting items constitute the George W. L. Bickley Papers (War Department Records, National Archives). Several Bickley letters are in the John Nicolay–John Hay Papers (Illinois State Historical Society). While a prisoner, Bickley prepared an "explanation" and it appeared in the Columbus *Crisis*, Dec. 30, 1863. Ollinger Crenshaw, "The Knights of the Golden Circle: The Career of George Bickley," *American Historical Review*, XLVII (October, 1941), 23–50, should be supplemented by the Dr. A. A. Urban exposé in the Louisville *Journal* and the exposé which appeared in the Cincinnati *Daily Gazette*, Aug. 6, 1863.

3. *Rules, Regulations and Principles of the K.G.C., Issued by Order of the Congress of the K.G.C. and the General President* (New York, 1859), pp. 4 ff. There is no evidence that any KGC congress ever met.

4. KGC degree booklet (untitled, n.p., n.d.), p. 2, Bickley Papers.

5. George W. L. Bickley, "Statement of Facts," Aug. 8, 1863, Bickley Papers.

6. General Bickley, *Address* (a printed pamphlet, n.p., n.d.), p. 29, Bickley Papers.

7. General Bickley, open letter to "Fellow Soldiers," July 17, 1860, clipping from Richmond *Whig* (n.d.), Bickley Papers.

8. Letter (unsigned) to "Mr. Holt," Jan. 5, 1861, Joseph Holt Papers, Library of Congress.

9. House of Representatives, *House Reports of Committees*, 36 Cong., 2 sess., "Report No. 79," pp. 5, 145. The select committee was headed by a Republican congressman, William A. Howard. It is interesting to

note that Mr. Howard, who discredited KGC rumors in early 1861, later took the lead in making KGC charges and manufacturing KGC rumors in his home state.

10. George Bickley, who at one time or other contradicted most of what he wrote or said, gave two different versions of his activities about this time. "I have built up practical secession," he stated at one time, "and inaugurated the greatest war of modern times." Later, in a letter to Lincoln, Bickley said that he suppressed his secret order after the start of hostilities. Bickley to Lincoln, July 10, 1864, Nicolay–Hay Papers; George W. L. Bickley, "Statement," Dec. 14, 1862, and H. A. Hosmer to Stanton, July 17, 1865, Bickley Papers.

11. Louisville *Journal*, May 22, 1861.

12. State of Kentucky, *Journal of the Called Session of the House of Representatives of the Commonwealth of Kentucky* (Frankfort, 1861), p. 138; *Senate Journal* (Frankfort, 1861), p. 146.

13. Mary K. Stevens to Joseph Holt, May 28, 1861, Holt Papers.

14. William H. Osborn to Pell and Grinnel, May 30, 1861, "William H. Osborn Letter-Book," Illinois Central Rail Road Co. Papers, Newberry Library; Parker Earle and Charles Colby to Governor Richard Yates, Apr. 21, 1861, and James Gage to Yates, Apr. 23, 1861, Richard Yates Papers, Illinois State Historical Library.

15. J. W. Pomfrey, *A True Disclosure and Exposition of the Knights of the Golden Circle, including the Secret Signs, Grips, and Charges, of the Three Degrees, as Practiced by the Order* (Cincinnati, 1861). The finger of suspicion points to William Henry Smith (writing under a pseudonym) as the author.

16. [Dr. J. M. Hiatt], *An Authentic Exposition of the "K.G.C.," Knights of the Golden Circle: A History of Secession from 1834 to 1861 by a Member of the Order* (Indianapolis, 1861). General Bickley, at a later date, ridiculed the exposé of the "catchpenny concern" in Indianapolis, denying the authorship of the speeches and bulletins which Dr. Hiatt attributed to him. George W. L. Bickley to Lincoln, July 10, 1864, Nicolay–Hay Papers.

17. Indianapolis *State Sentinel*, July 8, 1861.

18. At the time of its publication, Dr. Hiatt's exposé was praised by the editor of the Indianapolis *State Sentinel*, who encouraged its sale and circulation. The editor of the Indianapolis *Journal* (the unofficial Republican party newspaper in Indiana), on the other hand, debunked and criticized Dr. Hiatt's handiwork. Later in the war the *Journal* helped to fashion the KGC straw man in Indiana and the *State Sentinel* denied the existence of the KGC in Indiana.

19. Clipping from Louisville *Journal* (n.d.) (letter to editors dated June 6, 1861), Bickley Papers.

20. The John C. Brain Papers (Civil War Political Prisoners' Records, State Department Records, National Archives) discredit the self-styled KGC agent.

21. "Arrests for Disloyalty," State Department Records, National Archives; W. H. H. Terrell, *Report of the Adjutant General of Indiana* (8 vols.; Indianapolis, 1866–69), 1, 294.

22. John B. Thomas to "Sheriff of LaPorte Co., Indiana," Sept. 7, 1861, Brain Papers.

23. Calvin Fletcher, "Diary," Aug. 21, 29, 30, Sept. 26, 1861, Calvin Fletcher Papers, Indiana State Historical Society.

24. Cleveland *Leader*, Oct. 18, 1861.

25. Columbus *Ohio State Journal*, Oct. 8, 1861; Columbus *Ohio Statesman*, Oct. 8, 12, 15, 16, 19, 1861; Cleveland *Leader*, Oct. 10, 16, 18, 1861; Mansfield *Shield and Banner*, Nov. 14, 1861, paraphrased in the Detroit *Free Press*, Nov. 20, 1861; Columbia City (Ind.) *Times*, quoted in *Crisis*, Nov. 7, 1861; *History of Marion County, Ohio* (Chicago, 1883), pp. 448–49. The so-called second oath of the inner council read: "And I further promise and swear in the presence of Almighty God, and the members of the Golden Circle that I will not rest or sleep until Abraham Lincoln, now president, shall be removed out of the President's chair, and I will wade in blood up to my knees as soon as Jefferson Davis sees proper to march with his army to take the city of Washington and the White House, to do the same." The absurdity of the bogus oath seemed to enhance rather than restrict its circulation.

26. *Crisis*, Nov. 7, 1861.

27. Columbus *Ohio Statesman*, Oct. 15, 1861.

28. Cleveland *Leader*, Oct. 16, 1861; *Ohio Statesman*, Oct. 18, 1861; *Crisis*, Nov. 28, 1861.

29. "Grand Jury Report," *Ohio Statesman*, Dec. 22, 1861. "Men who knew all about it [KGC activity] before the election," wrote Manypenny about Republican editors who had appeared before the Grand Jury, "never heard of such a thing when they were sworn before the Grand Jury."

30. Mansfield *Shield and Banner*, Nov. 14, 1861, in Detroit *Free Press*, Nov. 20, 1861.

31. *Crisis*, Nov. 28, 1861.

32. Indianapolis *State Sentinel*, Jan. 3, 1862; Detroit *Free Press*, Oct. 11, 1861.

33. Detroit *Tribune* (n.d.), quoted in the Detroit *Free Press*, Sept. 25, 1861.

34. Guy S. Hopkins to William H. Seward, Nov. 29, 1861, Guy S. Hopkins Papers, State Department Records, National Archives.

35. Hoax letter, signed in "code" and addressed to "R.M.C., Esq." [Robert McClelland], Oct. 5, 1861, Hopkins Papers.

36. Detroit *Tribune*, March 18, 1862; Detroit *Advertiser*, March 18, 1862. The *Tribune* and the *Advertiser* merged in July of 1862, and the paper henceforth was called the Detroit *Advertiser and Tribune*.

37. Robert McClelland to K. Pritchette, Apr. 1, 1862, "Robert McClelland Letterbook, 1860–62," in Robert McClelland Papers, Burton Historical Collection, Detroit Public Library.

38. Detroit *Free Press*, March 8, 1862.

39. *Congressional Globe*, 37 Cong., 2 sess., p. 1371.

40. Chicago *Tribune*, Feb. 11, 1862.

41. *Ibid.*

42. "Proceedings of the Constitutional Convention, Feb. 12, 1862," Springfield *Illinois State Register*, Feb. 13, 1862.

43. *Ibid.*

44. *Ibid.*

45. *Journal of the Constitutional Convention of the State of Illinois, Convened at Springfield on January 7, 1862* (Springfield, 1862), pp. 942–43.

46. Detroit *Free Press*, Apr. 6, 1862.

47. Chicago *Tribune*, May 15, June 5, 7, 14, 16, 1862.

48. *Ibid.*, June 21, July 11, 1862.

49. Lacon *Illinois Gazette*, June 25, 1862.

50. James F. Robinson to John J. Crittenden, Feb. 6, 1862, John J. Crittenden Papers, Library of Congress. E. Merton Coulter, *The Civil War and Readjustment in Kentucky* (Chapel Hill, N.C., 1926), treats Kentucky's role in the war in scholarly fashion. Thomas Speed, *The Union Cause in Kentucky, 1860–1865* (New York, 1907), and Smith, *The Borderland in the Civil War*, also deal with conditions in wartime Kentucky.

51. Pamphlet, quoted extensively in a three-column letter published in the Dubuque *Weekly Times*, Apr. 17, 1862.

52. Indianapolis *State Sentinel*, Aug. 7, Dec. 31, 1861, Jan. 3, March 29, 1862; Indianapolis *Journal*, Dec. 31, 1861.

53. Indianapolis *Journal*, May 16, 1862; Calvin Fletcher, "Diary," May 16–22, 1862, Calvin Fletcher Papers; Indianapolis *State Sentinel*, May 22, 1862.

54. Judge James Hughes to Gov. Oliver P. Morton, June 16, 1862, in Indianapolis *Journal*, June 19, 1862; Indianapolis *State Sentinel*, June 19, 1862.

55. Indianapolis *State Sentinel*, June 24, 1862.

56. *Ibid.*, Aug. 5, 1862; Indianapolis *Journal*, Aug. 4, 1862.

57. O. P. Morton to E. B. Allen, July 14, 1862, Edward B. Allen Papers, Indiana State Historical Society.

58. "Report of United States Grand Jury, in District Court of the United States, for the District of Indiana, May term, 1862," in "United States District Court Order Book, May 21, 1860 to November 24, 1863" (Federal Building, Indianapolis), pp. 224–48.

59. Indianapolis *State Sentinel*, Aug. 5, 1862.

60. *Ibid.*, Aug. 5–8, 14, 21, 1862; *Illinois State Register*, Aug. 21, 1862; Springfield *Illinois State Journal*, Aug. 21, 1862.

61. It could be pointed out here that the KGC revelation was published on August 26, 1862, the day before a Union League reorganization meeting was scheduled to take place in Bloomington, Illinois.

62. The *Missouri Democrat* represented the views of the Radical Republicans of St. Louis despite its misleading name.

63. Joseph K. C. Forrest to Governor Yates, July 30, 1862, Yates Papers.

64. Letter (anonymous) addressed to "Dear Sir," Aug. 18, 1862, *ibid.*

65. T. C. Estes to Yates, Sept. 7, 1862, *ibid.*

66. J. F. Cochran to Yates, Apr. 24, 1862, *ibid.*

67. Thomas Yardley and T. R. Bates to Yates, March 20, 1862, *ibid.*

68. John H. Brown and S. M. Thrift to Lyman Trumbull, May 26, 1862, Lyman Trumbull Papers, Library of Congress; Grant Goodrich to E. B. Washburne, May 29, 1862, Elihu B. Washburne Papers, Library of Congress; Mrs. Kate Anderson to Yates, May 3, 1862, A. B. Bassett to Yates, Aug. 22, 1862, T. P. Robb to Yates, Aug. 12, 1862, anonymous letter (signed "Union Forever") to Yates, Aug. 25, 1862, and D. D. C. Porter to Yates, July 12, 1862, Yates Papers. One of the letter-writers misspelled "roughest" as "rouggest."

69. The *Tribune* exposé of August 26, 1862 has, unfortunately, been accepted as prima facie evidence.

70. Affidavits, signed "X" (of James Hamilton and George Meyers) and dated Aug. 11, 1862, Lafayette C. Baker—Levi C. Turner Papers, 1862–65, Adjutant General's Records, War Department Files, National Archives.

71. Affidavit, signed "X" (Joseph T. Williams), Aug. 11, 1862, *ibid.*

72. Affidavit, signed "X" (Drenascus Hall), Aug. 11, 1862, *ibid.*

73. David L. Phillips to Edwin M. Stanton, Sept. 4, 1862, Baker-Turner Papers; D. L. Phillips to Governor Yates, Sept. 8, 1862, copy in Logan Letterbook, John A. Logan Papers, Library of Congress; D. L. Phillips to F. W. Seward, Feb. 23, 1862, Dr. John P. Clemenson File, Civil War Political Prisoners' Records, State Department Files, National Archives.

74. Chicago *Tribune*, Aug. 26, 1862. The August exposé is debunked in Frank L. Klement, "Copperhead Secret Societies in Illinois during the Civil War," *Journal of the Illinois State Historical Society*, XLVIII (Summer, 1955), 152–80.

75. Carbondale *Times* (n.d.), quoted in the *Illinois State Journal*, Sept. 10, 1862.

76. New York *Evening Post* (n.d.), quoted in *Illinois State Register*, Aug. 30, 1862.

77. *Illinois State Register*, Aug. 28, 29, 30, Sept. 3, 1862.

78. Jonesboro *Gazette*, Aug. 23, 1862; Chicago *Times*, Aug. 27, 28, 1862; *Illinois State Register*, Aug. 29, 1862.

79. William J. Allen to Maj. Gen. George B. McClellan, Sept. 6, 1862, Baker-Turner Papers.

80. "Statement of Hon. Andrew D. Duff," in Dennis A. Mahony, *The Prisoner of State* (New York, 1863), pp. 357–62.

81. William R. Morrison to "Dear Sir," Aug. 15, 1862, copy in William R. Morrison Papers, Illinois State Historical Library; statement of Israel

Blanchard to David L. Phillips (n.d.), attached to Phillips' report of Sept. 4, 1862, to Edwin M. Stanton, Madison Y. Johnson to Edwin M. Stanton, Oct. 20, 1862, Amos Green to Levi C. Turner, Sept. 16, 1862, "Statement of Frank A. O'Dell, Old Capitol Prison," (n.d.), and affidavit, signed by Amos Green *et al.*, Nov. 11, 1862, Baker-Turner Papers; *Illinois State Register*, Sept. 16, 1862.

82. Provost Marshal Records, 13th District of Illinois, Provost Marshal General's Records, War Department Files, National Archives; Indianapolis *Journal*, Oct. 30, 1862; Indianapolis *State Sentinel*, Oct. 31, 1862; Calvin Fletcher, "Diary," Dec. 30, 1862, Fletcher Papers; telegram, Gov. Richard Yates to Edwin M. Stanton, Aug. 7, 1862, copy in Baker-Turner Papers. Gov. Yates sought Stanton's permission to institute martial law in Illinois before the elections and later wanted to prorogue the legislature with force.

83. *Official Records*, Ser. 2, V, 108; Calvin Fletcher, "Diary," Dec. 30, 1862, Fletcher Papers.

84. William T. Coggeshall, "Diary," June 1, 1861, William T. Coggeshall Collection, Ohio Historical Society; *Official Records*, Ser. 1, XXIII, Part 2, 193. Carrington's role in the Constable case counts against him. Later, during Morgan's raid, Carrington was guilty of drunkenness. Nevertheless, a legend concerning Carrington's competence and ability still exists in Indiana.

85. O. P. Morton to Secretary of War Edwin M. Stanton, Jan. 2, 1863, typewritten copy in Henry B. Carrington Papers, Archives Division, Indiana State Library.

86. Indianapolis *Journal*, Oct. 30, 1862; Indianapolis *State Sentinel*, Oct. 31, 1862.

87. *Official Records*, Ser. 2, V, 108.

88. Indianapolis *Journal*, Jan. 15, 25, Feb. 13, 1863; Indianapolis *State Sentinel*, Jan. 15, 25, 26, Feb. 13, 1863.

89. Indianapolis *Journal*, Jan. 19, 1863.

90. *Ibid.*, Feb. 1, 1863; Indianapolis *State Sentinel*, Feb. 2, 1863.

91. Indianapolis *Journal*, Feb. 19, 1863; Indianapolis *State Sentinel*, Feb. 20, 1863.

92. Indianapolis *Journal*, Feb. 21, 1863.

93. Henry B. Carrington To Lincoln, Jan. 14, 1863, Robert Todd Lincoln Papers, Library of Congress.

94. This item, intended to be circulated by and for the Union Leagues, seems to be little more than a reprint of a previously published pamphlet entitled *An Authentic Exposition of the K.G.C.* . . . (Indianapolis, 1861).

95. "Private instructions to Presidents of Subordinate Clubs" (n.p., n.d.), a pamphlet concerning Union League activity in the Henry K. English Papers, Indiana Division, Indiana State Library.

96. Indianapolis *Journal*, Feb. 26, 1863.

97. Report by Carrington to Brig. Gen. Lorenzo Thomas, Feb. 2, 1863, Carrington Papers; Indianapolis *Journal*, Feb. 26, March 27, Apr. 6, 1863; Indianapolis *State Sentinel*, Feb. 3, 1863.

98. Indianapolis *Journal*, March 25, 1863.

99. *Ibid.*, March 23, 1863.

100. Winchester *Randolph County Journal* (n.d.), in New Castle *Courier*, May 19, 1863 (clipping in "Newspaper Readings" in the *History of New Castle, Indiana*, compiled for the Indiana State Historical Society Library); Terrell, *Report of the Adjutant General of Indiana*, I, 262; Indianapolis *State Sentinel*, Apr. 20, 1863.

101. The author is indebted to Messrs. Francis M. Potts and Willard Jordon for use of the Thomas Hough manuscript in the possession of the Greenforks Township Historical Society, Lynn, Indiana.

102. Carrington, "Memorandum on Condition of Public Affairs in Indiana, To Be Submitted to the President and the Honorable Secretary of War," March 19, 1863, Robert Todd Lincoln Papers.

103. Calvin Fletcher, "Diary," March 21, 1863, Fletcher Papers.

104. Carrington to Lincoln, March 2, 1863, Robert Todd Lincoln Papers.

105. Henry B. Carrington, "The Morgan Raid through Indiana, 1863," *passim*, Carrington Papers; Indianapolis *Journal*, July 15, 22, 23, 25, 1863. The myth that Morgan's raid was linked to KGC activity in Indiana received a tremendous assist in Mayo Fesler's "Secret Political Societies in the North during the Civil War," *Indiana Magazine of History*, XIV (September, 1918), 213–14. James D. Horan's *Confederate Agent: A Discovery in History* (New York, 1954) is an example of a recent work that helps (pp. 7–14) to popularize the myth.

106. Willis William, "Report," dated July 20, 1863, Bickley Papers.

107. Statement of Eli Kenney (Bickley's brother-in-law) and Daniel K. Cady, Feb. 7, 1864, Bickley Papers.

108. Report of Maj. Gen. W. S. Rosecrans, Feb. 12, 1864, *ibid.*

109. *Ibid.*; Statement of George L. Gibbs, July 23, 1863, and Statement (unsigned), dated May 25, 1865, Bickley Papers.

110. "List of Items Confiscated," dated July 17, 1863, Bickley Papers.

111. Major I. M. Wright to Brig. Gen. N. C. McLean, Aug. 8, 1863, Bickley Papers.

112. Cincinnati *Gazette*, Aug. 6, 1863; Indianapolis *Journal*, July 20, 21, 1863; Indianapolis *State Sentinel*, July 21, 1863.

113. Report of Brig. Gen. N. C. McLean, March 5, 1864, and Lars Anderson to "Dear General" (McLean), Feb. 6, 1864, Bickley Papers.

114. Bickley was a prisoner in the State Penitentiary at Columbus from Aug. 18, 1863, to March 17, 1864. Then he was transferred to Fort Lafayette and kept there until March 14, 1865. He was then kept at Fort Warren from March 15 to October 14, 1865.

115. Bickley to Lincoln, Dec. 18, 1863, Bickley Papers.

116. Bickley to Hon. William H. Seward, Aug. 14, 1863, Baker-Turner Papers; Bickley to John Hay, July 11, 1864, and Bickley to Lincoln, July 10, 1864, Nicolay-Hay Papers; Bickley's explanation was prepared exclusively for *Crisis*, Dec. 30, 1863.

117. Chicago *Tribune*, Jan. 13, 1863.

118. St. Louis *Missouri Democrat*, Jan. 7, 1863; *Illinois State Journal*, Jan. 7, 8, 1863; *Illinois State Register*, Jan. 7, 8, 1863.

119. Chicago *Journal*, May 15, 1863; *Illinois State Register*, May 14, 16, 21, 1863.

120. *Illinois State Journal*, March 31, 1863.

121. *Illinois State Register*, Jan. 10, 1863. According to Lanphier, Forrest "acknowledged himself the poorest of inventors."

122. *Ibid.*, May 16, 22, 1863.

123. *Ibid.*, May 14, 1863.

124. *Ibid.*, Sept. 9, 1863. Editor Lanphier then called Forrest "a deliberate, studied, and infamous LIAR," one who "lies without even the liar's excuse for lying."

125. W. F. Wells to Yates, Aug. 2, 1863, Yates Papers; St. Louis *Missouri Democrat*, Aug. 8, 1863; Chicago *Tribune*, Aug. 4, 1863.

126. *Illinois State Register*, Aug. 5, 1863.

127. Springfield *Illinois State Journal*, Aug. 20, 1863; Chicago *Tribune*, Aug. 15, 1863.

128. *Illinois State Register*, Aug. 5, 1863.

129. LeGrand Byington to R. H. Sylvester, March 23, 1863, in Iowa City *State Press*, Apr. 4, 1863; Dayton *Weekly Empire*, Feb. 24, March 17, Apr. 11, 1863; Ashland (Ohio) *Union*, May 20, 1863; Fletcher, "Diary," Apr. 6, 1863, Fletcher Papers; Indianapolis *State Sentinel*, Feb. 25, March 17, Apr. 7, 27, 1863; *Alton Democrat* (n.d.), quoted in *Illinois State Register*, Feb. 12, 1863; Dubuque *Daily Times*, Apr. 5, 1863; *Illinois State Register*, March 6, 1863.

130. Thomas O. Lowe to "Dear Brother" (Will), March 23, 1863, Thomas O. Lowe Papers, Dayton Public Library.

131. Detroit *Free Press*, June 5, 1863; LeGrand Byington to R. H. Sylvester, March 23, 1863, in Iowa City *State Press*, Apr. 4, 1863.

132. Dayton *Empire*, Feb. 28, 1863.

133. Charles Negus to Charles Mason, Feb. 14, 1863, Charles Mason Papers, State Department of History and Archives, Historical Library, Des Moines, Iowa; testimony of S. Corning Judd, March 31, 1863, before the Cincinnati Military Commission, published in the Cincinnati *Daily Enquirer*, Apr. 2, 1865.

134. *Illinois State Register*, Feb. 24, 1863.

135. Chicago *Times*, March 6, 1863.

136. Indianapolis *State Sentinel*, June 24, 1862.

137. The Jackson County resolves were published in the Indianapolis *State Sentinel*, June 12, 1862.

138. Indianapolis *State Sentinel*, Oct. 15, 1862.

139. *Ibid.*, March 30, 1863.

140. Indianapolis *Journal*, May 2, 6, 1863; Indianapolis *State Sentinel*, May 2, 3, 1863.

141. John Harding to "My Dear Cousin," Feb. 15, 1863, John Harding Papers, Filson Club Library, Louisville; Milwaukee *See-Bote*, Apr. 30,

June 10, 1863; La Crosse *Democrat*, March 17, 1863; Indianapolis *State Sentinel*, May 2, 3, 1863.

142. S. Corning Judd to Lincoln, March 3, 1865, Nicolay-Hay Papers.

143. *Ibid.*

144. The evidence given later in the Indiana treason trials was somewhat contradictory. Republican evidence was often mere conjecture, e.g., Affidavit, Nov. 25, 1863, notarized by Thomas Hough, J.P., in possession of the Greenforks Township Historical Society, Lynn, Ind.

145. *Fulton County Ledger* (Lewiston) Oct. 6, 1863; S. Corning Judd to Lincoln, March 3, 1865, Nicolay-Hay Papers.

146. Statement of P. C. Wright, Apr. 27, 1863, Holt Papers.

147. Phineas C. Wright to John D. Caton, Nov. 1, 1862, John D. Caton Papers, Library of Congress.

148. Francis P. Blair, *The Jacobins of Missouri and Maryland: Speech of the Hon. F. P. Blair of Missouri, Delivered in the House of Representatives, February 27, 1864* (n.p., n.d), pp. 1, 11.

149. Statement of P. C. Wright, Apr. 27, 1865, Holt Papers; P. Caius Urbanus, "Occasional Address of Supreme Commander," Dec. 8, 1863, in John P. Sanderson Papers, Ohio Historical Society.

150. "Interrogation of Charles L. Hunt," June 17, 1864, Citizens' File, 1861–65, War Department Collection of Confederate Records, National Archives.

151. Testimony of S. Corning Judd, March 31, 1865, before the Cincinnati Military Commission, published in Cincinnati *Enquirer*, Apr. 2, 1865.

CHAPTER VI

1. Circular (printed letter), Feb. 8, 1864, and Charles Mason, "Diary," Feb. 4, 1864, Charles Mason Papers, State Department of History and Archives, Historical Library, Des Moines, Iowa.

2. Fernando Wood was a New York congressman and a spokesman for the Peace Democrats in New York. James A. McMaster edited the New York *Freeman's Journal.* The two invited midwestern anti-McClellan Democrats to meet in New York. Edward C. Kirkland's *The Peacemakers of 1864* (New York, 1927) makes no mention of this New York meeting.

3. Indianapolis *State Sentinel*, Sept. 14, 1863.

4. *Ibid.*, Jan. 9, 1864; Indianapolis *Journal*, Jan. 9, 10, 1864.

5. James A. Barret, letter of resignation, dated May 2, 1862, Adjutant General's Records, National Archives.

6. Testimony of Clement L. Vallandigham, March 29, 1865, before the Cincinnati Military Commission, published in Cincinnati *Enquirer*, March 30, 1865.

7. *Ibid.*

8. Virginia (Ill.) *Cass County Union* (n.d.), quoted in the Springfield *Illinois State Register*, Jan. 17, 1864. The editor of the *Illinois State*

Register indorsed Judd's candidacy, characterizing him as "one of the soundest and most reliable democrats in the State."

9. Testimony of S. Corning Judd, March 31, 1865, before the Cincinnati Military Commission, published in Cincinnati *Enquirer*, Apr. 2, 1865.

10. *Congressional Globe*, 38 Cong., 1 sess., p. 1501; Columbus *Crisis*, Apr. 20, 1864.

11. Testimony of S. Corning Judd, March 31, 1865, before the Cincinnati Military Commission, published in Cincinnati *Enquirer*, Apr. 2, 1865.

12. Testimony of Clement L. Vallandigham, March 29, 1865, before the Cincinnati Military Commission, published in Cincinnati *Enquirer*, March 30, 1865.

13. John P. Sanderson, "Journal," Feb. 13, 16, 23, March 2, 5, 18, 1864, John P. Sanderson Papers, Ohio Historical Society.

14. *Ibid.*, March 10, 1864.

15. *Ibid.*; Francis P. Blair, *The Jacobins of Missouri and Maryland: Speech of the Hon. F. P. Blair of Missouri, Delivered in the House of Representatives, February 27, 1864* (n.p., n.d.), pp. 7, 11–15. See also: Sceva Bright Laughlin, *Missouri Politics during the Civil War* (Ph.D. diss., State University of Iowa, 1921); *Letters of President Lincoln to the Missouri Radicals and Speech of S. T. Glover at the Court House in Jefferson City, Missouri, Saturday, October 17, 1863* (n.p., 1863); David D. March, "The Missouri Radicals and the Re-election of Lincoln," *Mid-America*, XXXVII (July, 1952), 172–87; Lucy L. Tasher, "The *Missouri Democrat* and the Civil War," *Missouri Historical Review*, XXXI (July, 1937), 402–19; Galusha Anderson, *Story of a Border City* [St. Louis] *during the Civil War* (Boston, 1908); Virgil C. Blum, "The Political and Military Activities of the German Element in St. Louis, 1859–1861," *Missouri Historical Review*, XLIII (January, 1948), 103–29.

16. Sanderson, "Journal," March 7, 9, 1863, Sanderson Papers.

17. This "address" (see p. 168 above) was dated Dec. 8, 1863. A copy is included in the Sanderson Papers.

18. Christian Kribben to Robert M. Renick, Aug. 16, 1863, Sanderson Papers.

19. Sanderson, "Journal," March 9, 1864, Sanderson Papers.

20. *Official Records*, Ser. 2, VII, 239–40. Earlier Jones had used the name James C. Johnston.

21. Sanderson, Report of June 12, 1864, to Maj. Gen. William S. Rosecrans, and Sanderson "Journal," March 9, 10, 1864, Sanderson Papers.

22. Sanderson, Report of June 12, 1864, to Maj. Gen. William S. Rosecrans, Sanderson Papers.

23. Blair, *The Jacobins of Missouri and Maryland*, p. 9.

24. *Official Records*, Ser. 3, III, 68–69. H. M. Hoxie, who served as U.S. marshal for the Iowa district, also functioned as titular head of the Republican party in his state.

25. Paris, Illinois, *Times,* Feb. 4, 1864, quoted in the Indianapolis *State Sentinel,* Feb. 9, 1864. Furloughed soldiers brought on the incident when they tried to intimidate some Copperheads. Gun-play and violence were the result.

26. Quincy *Whig,* May 6, 1864, in the *Illinois State Register,* May 8, 1864.

27. Samuel P. Heintzelman, "Journal," March 2, 4, 5, 1864, Samuel P. Heintzelman Papers, Library of Congress; Indianapolis *Daily Journal,* Apr. 1, 1864. The Republican reports on the "insurrection" were grossly exaggerated.

28. Brig. Gen. H. T. Reid to Maj. Gen. W. S. Rosecrans, March 8, 1864, and reports by Provost Marshal Isaac M. Tallmadge, Feb. 18, March 8, 1864, Sanderson Papers.

29. Brig. Gen. H. T. Reid to Maj. Gen. W. S. Rosecrans, March 8, 1864, Sanderson Papers.

30. Samuel Pollock to Richard Yates, March 30, 1864, Richard Yates Papers, Illinois State Historical Library.

31. Indianapolis *Journal,* Feb. 3, 4, March 18, 1864; Indianapolis *State Sentinel,* Feb. 1, 1864. Judge Perkins challenged the propriety of military proclamations and arbitrary arrests in the decision in *Griffin* v. *Willcox.*

32. Indianapolis *State Sentinel,* Jan. 9, 12, 13, 16, 19, 1864.

33. Calvin Fletcher, "Diary," March 31, 1864, Calvin Fletcher Papers, Indiana State Historical Library; Indianapolis *Journal,* Apr. 30, 1864.

34. Indianapolis *Journal,* Apr. 8, 1864; Indianapolis *State Sentinel,* Apr. 8, 1864.

35. Samuel P. Heintzelman, "Journal," Jan. 14, 24, Apr. 21, 1864, Heintzelman Papers.

36. *Ibid.,* Feb. 19, 20, 21, 1864.

37. Indianapolis *State Sentinel,* Apr. 23, 25, 1864; Indianapolis *Journal,* Apr. 30, 1864.

38. Orders for Arrest of Byron H. Robb, Aug. 10, Oct. 24, 1863, Citizens' File, 1861–65, War Department Collection of Confederate Records, National Archives.

39. Byron H. Robb to James A. Garfield, Jan. 9, 1864, Joseph Holt Papers, Library of Congress.

40. Report from Col. Paul von Radowitz to Capt. C. H. Potter, A.A.G., May 6, 1864, Lafayette C. Baker–Levi C. Turner Papers, 1862–65, Adjutant General's Records, National Archives; Samuel P. Heintzelman, "Journal," Apr. 23, 1864, Heintzelman Papers; Detroit *Free Press,* Apr. 1, 1864. Phineas C. Wright's story is included in John A. Marshall, *American Bastile: A History of the Illegal Arrests and Imprisonment of American Citizens during the Late Civil War* (Philadelphia, 1878), pp. 218–35.

41. In January, 1864, Gen. Heintzelman was placed in charge of the newly created Northern Department (comprising the states of Ohio, Indiana, Illinois, and Michigan). Gov. Oliver P. Morton was responsible

for the transfer of Gen. Orlando B. Willcox (commanding the District of
Michigan and Indiana) because the forthright general had ordered both
Republicans and Democrats to abandon their secret societies. Morton
had no intention of disbanding the Union or Lincoln Leagues. Further-
more, Gen. Willcox had gained Morton's displeasure for arresting Col.
Carrington for drunkenness and failure to do his duty.

42. Samuel P. Heintzelman, "Diary," Apr. 15, 1864, and "Journal,"
March 4, 5, 6, Apr. 16, 1864, Heintzelman Papers; Indianapolis *State
Sentinel*, Apr. 16, 1864.

43. Report from Col. John P. Sanderson to Maj. Gen. W. S. Rosecrans,
June 12, 1864, Records of the Office of the Judge Advocate General, War
Department Records, National Archives. This report and the added evi-
dence is included in the *Official Records*, Ser. 2, VII, 228–314.

44. The three were Charles L. Hunt (linked to both the Corps de
Belgique and the OAK), Charles E. Dunn, and Dr. James A. Barret,
formerly of Illinois and an acquaintance of Gen. U. S. Grant. See Sanderson, Special Orders, No. 139, May 27, 1864, Charles E. Dunn Papers,
Citizens' File, 1861–65, War Department Collection of Confederate Records; see also the Charles L. Hunt Papers in the same collection.

45. Rosecrans to Heintzelman, May 25, 1864, Heintzelman Papers;
Rosecrans to Garfield, June 4, 1864, James A. Garfield Papers, Library
of Congress; telegrams, Rosecrans to Lincoln, June 2, 8, 1864, Robert
Todd Lincoln Papers, Library of Congress.

46. Rosecrans to James A. Garfield, March 22, 1864, Garfield Papers.

47. Tyler Dennett (ed.), *Lincoln and the Civil War in the Diaries and
Letters of John Hay* (New York, 1939), pp. 187–94.

48. Lincoln, "Order to John Hay," June 10, 1864, in Roy P. Basler
(ed.), *The Collected Works of Abraham Lincoln* (9 vols.; New Brunswick, N.J., 1953), VII, 386.

49. Maj. Gen. W. S. Rosecrans to President Lincoln, June 14, 1864,
Robert Todd Lincoln Papers.

50. Dennett (ed.), *Lincoln and the Civil War in the Diaries and Letters of John Hay*, p. 188.

51. Rosecrans to Lincoln, June 14, 1864, Robert Todd Lincoln Papers.

52. *Official Records*, Ser. 1, XXXIV, Part 4, 337.

53. *Ibid.*, Ser. 2, VII, 411, 417, 447.

54. Report from Col. John P. Sanderson to Maj. Gen. W. S. Rosecrans,
June 22, 1864, Records of the Office of the Judge Advocate General,
National Archives. This report and the sheaf of evidence is available in
Official Records, Ser. 2, VII, 314–66.

55. Rosecrans to Lincoln, June 14, 1864, and telegrams, Rosecrans to
Lincoln, June 21, 22, July 9, 1864, Robert Todd Lincoln Papers.

56. James O. Broadhead to Hon. Edward Bates, July 24, 1864, copy in
Robert Todd Lincoln Papers.

57. Sanderson's copy of this long document forms a portion of the
Sanderson Papers, in the archives of the Ohio Historical Society. This
"final report," strangely enough, does not appear in the *Official Records*.

58. St. Louis *Missouri Democrat,* July 28, 1864.

59. Sanderson, "O.A.K. Scrapbook," Sanderson Papers.

60. Cincinnati *Gazette,* July 30, 1864, Chicago *Tribune,* July 31, 1864; Springfield *Illinois State Journal,* Aug. 2, 1864.

61. New York *Tribune,* July 20, 1864.

62. Clipping (undated), in Sanderson, "O.A.K. Scrapbook," Sanderson Papers.

63. Richmond *Daily Dispatch,* Aug. 26, 1864, and an undated penciled note, in Nicolay-Hay Papers, Illinois State Historical Library.

64. Samuel P. Heintzelman, "Journal," June 24, 1864, Heintzelman Papers.

65. Sanderson, indorsement to Governor Yates on letter from L. Newland to "Editor *Dem*" [*Missouri Democrat*], July 28, 1864, Yates Papers.

66. St. Louis *Missouri Republican,* July 29, 1864.

67. Clipping (undated), in the "Col. John P. Sanderson Scrapbook, 1864," Sanderson Papers.

68. Chicago *Times,* July 30, 1864.

69. Detroit *Free Press,* Aug. 2, 1864.

70. *Illinois State Register,* Aug. 2, 1864.

71. Samuel P. Heintzelman, "Journal," June 14, 15, 1864, Heintzelman Papers. Heintzelman wisely refused to let Govs. Morton and Brough stampede him into rearresting Vallandigham.

72. Indianapolis *Journal,* June 17, 21, 1864.

73. *Ibid.,* June 24, 1864; Indianapolis *State Sentinel,* June 24, 1864.

74. Felix G. Stidger to Capt. Stephen E. Jones, June 2, 1864, Felix G. Stidger Papers, Records of the Office of the Judge Advocate General, National Archives. It should be pointed out that Capt. Jones, Gen. Burbridge's provost marshal, was a political disciple of Gov. Oliver P. Morton. Stidger was later transferred from Burbridge's to Morton's (or Carrington's) employ.

75. "Carrington Report," in Indianapolis *Journal,* June 29, 1864.

76. *Ibid.*

77. S. Corning Judd to Lincoln, March 3, 1865, Nicolay-Hay Papers.

78. Testimony, S. Corning Judd, March 31, 1865, before the Cincinnati Military Commission, published in Cincinnati *Enquirer,* Apr. 21, 1865.

79. Samuel P. Heintzelman, "Journal," July 29, 1864, Heintzelman Papers; S. Corning Judd to Lincoln, March 3, 1865, Nicolay-Hay Papers; clipping, Indianapolis *People,* March 10, 1883, in the (Indiana State Historical Society) Indiana Scrap-Book Collection (compiled by George S. Cottman), III, 33–34; Benn Pitman (ed.), *The Trials for Treason at Indianapolis Disclosing the Plans for Establishing a North-Western Confederacy* (Cincinnati, 1865) pp. 92, 106–19.

80. William S. Hall to Charles B. Lasselle, Aug. 4, 1864, Charles B. Lasselle Papers, Indiana Division, Indiana State Library; Indianapolis *State Sentinel,* June 27, 1864; *Illinois State Register,* Oct. 13, 1864.

81. William S. Hall to Charles B. Lasselle, Aug. 4, 1864, Lasselle Papers.

82. Report of Edward F. Hoffman (one of Sanderson's agents), May 28, 1864, *Official Records*, Ser. 2, VII, 270–71.

83. Henry B. Carrington, "Indiana War Documents Cleared of Error," (undated), p. 8, Henry B. Carrington Papers, Archives Division, Indiana State Library; *Official Records*, Ser. 1, XXXIX, Part 2, 228; Felix G. Stidger to Lt. Col. Thomas B. Farleigh, Aug. 3, 1864, Stidger Papers.

84. Samuel P. Heintzelman, "Journal," July 29, 1864, Heintzelman Papers; Carrington, "Indiana War Documents Cleared of Error," p. 8, Carrington Papers.

85. Felix G. Stidger to Lt. Col. Thomas B. Farleigh, June 29, 1864, Stidger Papers.

86. Stidger to Farleigh, July 10, 1864, *ibid.*

87. Stidger to Farleigh, Aug. 3, Sept. 4, 1864, *ibid.*

88. "Anonymous" to Col. J. R. Smith (n.d.), Heintzelman Papers.

89. Indianapolis *State Sentinel*, Aug. 8, 1864.

90. Samuel P. Heintzelman, "Journal," July 29, 1864, Heintzelman Papers.

91. D. T. Yeakel, "To the People of Indiana" (a printed statement), Oct. 28, 1864, Lasselle Papers.

92. *Ibid.*

93. Indianapolis *State Sentinel*, July 13, 1864. Before accepting the chairmanship on July 12, 1864, Bingham had served as executive secretary of the Democratic State Central Committee.

94. *Ibid.*, Aug. 15, 1864.

95. Yeakel, "To the People of Indiana."

96. The reports of Felix G. Stidger indicate that he was not in Indianapolis at the time of Dodd's proposal that open rebellion be attempted. In fact, Stidger was not even aware that the Order of the American Cincinnatus had replaced the defunct Sons of Liberty.

97. Heintzelman, "Journal," Aug. 8, 1864, Heintzelman Papers; William Henry Smith, "Private Memoranda: Wartime," Aug. 8, 1864, William Henry Smith Papers (Indiana State Historical Society).

98. Indiana *State Sentinel*, Aug. 22, 1864.

99. Heintzelman, "Journal," Aug. 20, 1864, Heintzelman Papers; Indianapolis *State Sentinel*, Aug. 23, 1864.

100. W. H. H. Terrell to Col. A. J. Werner, Aug. 22, 1864, A. J. Werner Papers, William P. Palmer Collection, Western Reserve Historical Society; New York *Times*, Aug. 25, 1864; Indianapolis *Journal*, Aug. 22, 1864.

101. Indianapolis *Journal*, Aug. 22, 1864.

102. Henry B. Carrington, "Seizures at the Treason Headquarters Noticed" (undated), p. 2, Carrington Papers; *Official Records*, Ser. 1, XXXIX, Part 2, 295.

103. Indianapolis *Journal*, Aug. 23, 1864.

104. Indianapolis *State Sentinel*, Sept. 5, 1864. The co-worker was William H. Harrison, Grand Secretary of Dodd's organization in Indiana.

105. *Ibid.*

106. *Ibid.*, Aug. 22, Sept. 8, 1864.

107. Louisville *Democrat* (n.d.), quoted in Indianapolis *State Sentinel*, Aug. 30, 1864.

108. James C. Walker to Gov. Morton, Aug. 25, 1864, in Indianapolis *State Sentinel*, Aug. 30, 1864.

109. William H. H. Terrell to John T. Wilder, Sept. 6, 1864, John T. Wilder Papers, Indiana Division, Indiana State Library.

110. Indianapolis *State Sentinel*, Sept. 9, 1864.

111. Yeakel, "To the People of Indiana," Oct. 28, 1864, Lasselle Papers.

112. Clipping, Indianapolis *People*, March 10, 1883, in Indiana Scrap-Book Collection, III, 34.

113. Yeakel, "To the People of Indiana."

114. *Ibid.* Morton's use of the treason charges in the 1864 elections is treated in Kenneth M. Stampp, "The Milligan Case and the Election of 1864 in Indiana," *Mississippi Valley Historical Review*, XXXI (June, 1944), 41–58; also see William F. Zornow, "Treason as a Campaign Issue in the Re-election of Lincoln," *Abraham Lincoln Quarterly*, V (June, 1949), 348–63.

115. *Official Records*, Ser. 2, VII, 1215.

116. Silas F. Miller to Oliver P. Morton, May 15, 1865, Miscellaneous Letter File, Indiana State Historical Society.

117. In testimony before the Cincinnati Military Commisson, Ayer admitted that his diplomas were forged. Dr. Ayer also admitted that he kept a mistress in his office in the McCormack Building.

118. I. Winslow Ayer to Yates, Dec. 2, 1864, Yates Papers.

119. *Ibid.*; testimony before the Cincinnati Military Commission, published in the Cincinnati *Enquirer*, March 15, 1865.

120. Testimony published in Cincinnati *Enquirer*, Feb. 1, to Apr. 1, 1865. The traditional interpretation of the "Camp Douglas Conspiracy" is to be found in: Andrew W. Renfrew, "Copperheads, Confederates, and Conspiracies on the Detroit-Canadian Border (M.A. thesis, Wayne University, Detroit, 1952); James D. Horan, *Confederate Agent: A Discovery in History* (New York, 1954); and Wilfred Bovey, "Confederate Agents in Canada during the American Civil War," *Canadian Historical Review*, II (March, 1921), 46–67. I. Winslow Ayer, *The Great Northwest Conspiracy . . .* (Chicago, 1865), should be recognized as sheer propaganda.

121. Clipping, Richmond *Daily Dispatch*, Aug. 26, 1864, in Nicolay-Hay Papers; *Official Records*, Ser. 1, XIV, 955; Thomas Henry Hines, "Memorandum" [1864], in Thomas Henry Hines Papers, University of Kentucky Library, Lexington; John W. Headley, *Confederate Operations in Canada and New York* (New York, 1906), p. 264; Jacob Thompson

to Judah P. Benjamin, Dec. 3, 1864, Jacob Thompson Papers, Library of Congress; Thomas H. Hines [John B. Castleman], "The Northwestern Conspiracy," *Southern Bivouac: A Monthly Literary and Historical Magazine*, N.S., II (December, 1886–March, 1887), 437–55, 500–510, 567–74, 699–704; John B. Castleman, *Active Service* (Louisville, 1917).

122. Buckner S. Morris Papers, Citizens' File, 1861–65, War Department Collection of Confederate Records.

123. Testimony of Dr. I. Winslow Ayer before the Cincinnati Military Commission, published in Cincinnati *Enquirer*, March 11, Apr. 1, 1865.

124. Charles Walsh Papers, Citizens' File, 1861–65, War Department Collection of Confederate Records.

125. Vincent Marmaduke to Maj. Gen. Joseph Hooker, Dec. 22, 1864, Citizens' File, *ibid.*

126. Detroit *Free Press*, Nov. 11, 1864.

127. Louisville *Daily Democrat*, Nov. 9, 1864.

128. Chicago *Post*, Nov. 7, 1864.

129. Gustave Koerner, later a Republican governor of Illinois, viewed the "conspiracy" as "incredible." Thomas J. McCormack (ed.), *Memoirs of Gustave Koerner, 1809–1896* (2 vols.; Cedar Rapids, 1909), II, 437. Lincoln's disbelief is recorded, in part, in Dennett (ed.), *Lincoln and the Civil War in the Diaries and Letters of John Hay*, pp. 187–94. The Yates Papers fail to substantiate any of the exposés which originated in the mind of Joseph K. C. Forrest or in the editorial offices of the Chicago *Tribune*.

130. Judd to Lincoln, March 3, 1865, Nicolay-Hay Papers; testimony, S. Corning Judd before the Cincinnati Military Commission on March 31, 1865, published in Cincinnati *Enquirer*, Apr. 2, 1865.

131. Judd to Lincoln, March 3, 1865, Nicolay-Hay Papers.

132. *Ibid.*

133. Testimony of Clement L. Vallandigham, March 29, 1865, before the Cincinnati Military Commission, published in Cincinnati *Enquirer*, March 30, 1865.

134. In addition to the booklet *The Great Northwestern Conspiracy* (published in 1865) Ayer contributed a second propaganda pamphlet thirty years later—*The Great Treason Plot in the North during the Civil War* (Chicago, 1895).

135. Lafayette C. Baker to Charles A. Dana, Sept. 3, 1864, Holt Papers.

136. Edwin M. Stanton to Carrington, Sept. 19, 1864, in Carrington, "War Telegrams of 1864" (typed volume), Carrington Papers; Felix G. Stidger to Thomas C. Farleigh, Sept. 7, 1864, Stidger Papers; Carrington, "Complications during the Draft," Carrington Papers.

137. Colonel Sanderson died in St. Louis less than a week after Holt completed his report. The St. Louis *Missouri Democrat*, Oct. 15, 1864, carries a notation on Sanderson's death.

138. Report by Joseph Holt to Hon. E. M. Stanton, Oct. 8, 1864, in *Official Records*, Ser. 2, VII, 930–53.

139. *Ibid.*, pp. 931–33, 935, 942–51, 953.

140. This pamphlet-report carried the imprint of the Washington *Chronicle.*

141. D. N. Cooley to Elihu B. Washburne, Oct. 20, 1864, Elihu B. Washburne Papers, Library of Congress.

142. John McGaffey to W. H. Smith, Nov. 17, 1864, W. H. Smith Papers; William B. Lord to Joseph Holt, Nov. 13, 1864, Holt Papers.

143. Detroit *Free Press*, Oct. 23, 1864; Cincinnati *Enquirer*, Oct. 16, 19, 1864; newspaper clippings, (n.d.), Holt Papers.

144. *Illinois State Register*, Oct. 18, 21, 1864.

145. Detroit *Free Press*, Oct. 23, 1864.

146. George I. King to Yates, Sept. 9, 1864, Yates Papers.

147. Vallandigham to "Editor of the New York *News*," Oct. 22, 1864, Sanderson, "Scrapbook, 1864," Sanderson Papers.

148. P. C. Wright to Joseph Holt, Oct. 17, 1864, Holt Papers.

149. P. C. Wright to "Friend Romeyn" (Theodore Romeyn of Detroit), Nov. 27, 1864, Holt Papers.

150. William Blair Lord to Joseph Holt, Nov. 13, 1864, Holt Papers.

CHAPTER VII

1. Timothy O. Howe to Horace Rublee, July 3, 1861, in Milwaukee *Sentinel*, Dec. 15, 1889.

2. William T. Coggeshall, "Diary," July 19, 1861, William T. Coggeshall Collection, Ohio Historical Society; Chatfield (Minn.) *Democrat*, Aug. 31, 1861; Winona *Republican*, Sept. 11, 1861.

3. William H. Green to John A. Logan, Apr. 25, 1861, John A. Logan Papers, Library of Congress.

4. Indianapolis *Journal*, Aug. 20, 1861.

5. Indianapolis *State Sentinel*, Aug. 19, 1861.

6. George B. Smith, "Diary," Sept. 17, 1861, George B. Smith Papers, Wisconsin State Historical Society; La Crosse *Democrat*, Sept. 20, Oct. 4, 11, 1861; Fond du Lac *Saturday Reporter*, Nov. 8, 1861; Sheboygan *Journal*, Oct. 7, 1862; Madison *Patriot*, May 10, 1862.

7. Sty. W. Lowel to Zachariah Chandler, Feb. 6, 1863, Zachariah Chandler Papers, Library of Congress; J. E. Beebe to "My dear Son," Nov. 18, 1862, J. E. Beebe Papers, Michigan Historical Collections, University of Michigan Library; N. Bailey to C. S. May, Oct. 26, 1862, Charles Sedgewick Papers, Burton Historical Collection, Detroit Public Library; L. S. Church to Shelby Cullom, March 29, 1862, Richard Yates Papers, Illinois State Historical Library; James A. Cravens to William H. English, June 25, 1862, William H. English Papers, Indiana State Historical Society; Terre Haute *Journal* (n.d.), quoted in the Indianapolis *State Sentinel*, June 25, 1862.

8. Timothy O. Howe to Horace Rublee, Aug. 31, 1861, Timothy O. Howe Papers, Wisconsin State Historical Society.

9. Detroit *Free Press,* Sept. 6, 1864.

10. Clement M. Silvestro's "None But Patriots: Union Leagues in Civil War and Reconstruction" (Ph.D. diss., University of Wisconsin, 1959) counteracts the patriotic interpretation evinced in Guy Gibson's "Lincoln's League: The Union League Movement during the Civil War" (Ph.D. diss. University of Illinois, 1957) and E. Bently Hamilton's "The Union League: Its Origins and Achievements in the Civil War," *Transactions of the Illinois State Historical Society, 1921* (Springfield), pp. 110–15. Since the S.B. organization (Spartan Band or Strong Band) never gained respectability and influence, it is bypassed as an instrument used to quash Copperheadism. The S.B. story remains to be written —it awaits someone interested in historical detective work.

11. The charter for the Indianapolis Club of the Union or Loyal League is in the Henry K. English Papers, Indiana Division, Indiana State Library. An item entitled "Cryptographic Alphabet and Signs" is in the same set of manuscripts.

12. The eastern branch of the Union League arose out of the "Patriots' League" of Connecticut, the Union League of Maryland, and the Union Clubs of Philadelphia and New York. The latter two eventually "took over" the eastern branch—actually it was less a branch than a separate entity.

13. William O. Stoddard, Jr. (ed.), *Lincoln's Third Secretary: The Memoirs of William O. Stoddard* (New York, 1955), pp. 100–101.

14. *Ibid.,* pp. 101–2.

15. Calvin Fletcher, "Diary," Jan. 2, 1863, Calvin Fletcher Papers, Indiana State Historical Society; George H. Harlow, "Secretary's Report," *Proceedings of the State Grand Council of the N.L.A., Illinois, 1863,* pp. 12–13.

16. Grant Goodrich to Elihu B. Washburne, May 29, 1862, and S. W. McMaster to Elihu B. Washburne, Dec. 28, 1862, Elihu B. Washburne Papers, Library of Congress; Calvin Fletcher, "Diary," Jan. 2, 1863, Fletcher Papers.

17. Harlow, "Secretary's Report," *Proceedings of the State Grand Council of N.L.A., Illinois, 1863,* p. 12; testimony of Dr. J. A. Kennicott before the Cincinnati Military Commission, published in Cincinnati *Enquirer,* March 11, 1865.

18. George W. O'Brien to Governor Samuel Kirkwood, Apr. 7, 1863, Samuel J. Kirkwood Papers, Iowa State Department of History and Archives, Historical Library, Des Moines; Iowa City *Iowa State Register,* June 24, 1863.

19. O. W. Smith to S. F. B. Morse, May 28, 1863, Samuel Finley Breese Morse Papers, Library of Congress.

20. Indianapolis *State Sentinel,* Apr. 6, 1863; *ibid.* (n.d.), quoted in the Springfield *Illinois State Register,* Apr. 28, 1863.

21. Hamilton *True Telegraph,* May 7, 1863.

22. *Illinois State Register,* March 16, 1863.

23. E. A. Small to Elihu B. Washburne, Feb. 5, 1864, and J. B. Brown to Washburne, Jan. 8, 1864, Washburne Papers; *Illinois State Register,* Jan. 26, 1864; Charles Negus to Charles Mason, Feb. 14, 1863, Charles Mason Papers, State Department of History and Archives, Historical Library, Des Moines. Also see Mrs. Ann Smith Hardie, "The Influence of the Union League of America on the Second Election of Lincoln" (Ph.D. diss., Louisiana State University, 1937), and George Winston Smith, "Generative Forces of Union Propaganda: A Study in Civil War Pressure Groups" (Ph.D. diss., University of Wisconsin, 1950).

24. Francis Lieber directed the work of the Loyal Publication Society of New York. Its first item, a fifteen-page pamphlet entitled *The Future of the Northwest,* came from the pen of Robert Dale Owen. An item entitled *Copperhead Conspiracy in the North-West* (New York, 1864) was circulated as an election propaganda pamphlet in 1864. The work of the "publication societies" is capably treated in G. W. Smith, "Generative Forces," and in Frank Freidel, "The Loyal Publication Society: A Pro-Union Propaganda Agency," *Mississippi Valley Historical Review,* XXVI (December, 1939), 359–76.

25. Madison *Patriot,* Nov. 17, 1862.

26. S. B. Gaskill to Gov. Austin Blair, July 15, 1862, Austin Blair Papers, Burton Historical Collection, Detroit Public Library; W. H. Green to John A. Logan, Apr. 15, 1861, Logan Papers; Charles Mason, "Diary, 1861," July 5, 1861, Mason Papers. Letters written to such prominent Republicans as Benjamin Wade, Zachariah Chandler, and Salmon P. Chase are filled with the contention that Republicans should monopolize the army appointments.

27. George Arnold *et al.* to Governor Oliver P. Morton (n.d.), Chicago-Morton Collection, Archives Division, Indiana State Library.

28. Donn Piatt to Joseph Holt, Nov. 30, 1862, Joseph Holt Papers, Library of Congress.

29. Fred Brown to Elihu B. Washburne, Feb. 28, 1862, Washburne Papers.

30. Brig. Gen. R. H. Milroy to Schuyler Colfax, added to printed copy of "General Orders, No. 28," Oct. 27, 1862, Schuyler Colfax Papers, Indiana Division, Indiana State Library.

31. Col. W. H. Blake to Schuyler Colfax, Nov. 7, 1862, *ibid.*

32. S. P. Heintzelman to James A. Garfield, Feb. 13, 1864, James A. Garfield Papers, Library of Congress.

33. Sgt. Eli R. Pickett to "My Dear Wife," March 27, 1863, Eli Pickett Papers, Minnesota State Historical Society.

34. W. H. H. Terrell to "My dear Wilder," Jan. 24, 1863, John T. Wilder Papers, Indiana Division, Indiana State Library.

35. William B. Lasselle to Charles B. Lasselle Jan. 28, 1863, Charles B. Lasselle Papers, Indiana Division, Indiana State Library; Indianapolis *Journal,* Feb. 12, 1863; W. H. H. Terrell, *Report of the Adjutant General of Indiana* (8 vols.; Indianapolis, 1866–69), I, Appendix, 355–56.

36. Calvin Fletcher, "Diary," Feb. 3, 1863, Fletcher Papers.

37. James S. Whitmore to Governor Richard Yates, March 18, 1863, Yates Papers; Dr. Humphrey H. Hood to his wife, Feb. 13, 17, 19, 1863, Humphrey H. Hood Papers, Illinois State Historical Library; "Resolutions on the Conduct of the War Adopted by the Officers and Enlisted Men from Illinois" (stationed at Bolivar, Tenn.), Feb. 13, 1863, Yates Papers.

38. Joseph Miller to William A. Wilmoth, Jan. 23, 1863, Eleventh Illinois Cavalry Regiment Folder, Illinois State Archives; J. W. Dok to R. G. Campbell, July 19, 1864, R. H. Campbell Papers, Illinois State Historical Library; "Nick" to "My dear General" (W. W. Orme), March 25, 1864, William Ward Orme Papers, Illinois State Historical Library.

39. Pontiac *Weekly Gazette*, March 11, 1864.

40. Jackson *Weekly Citizen*, Feb. 21, 1864.

41. Dayton *Empire*, Nov. 14, 1864; Detroit *Free Press*, Apr. 19, 1864.

42. Timothy O. Howe to Horace Rublee, Aug. 31, 1862, Howe Papers; Chatfield *Democrat*, Sept. 27, 1862; Ignatius Donnelly to wife, Aug. 28, 1862, Ignatius Donnelly Papers, Minnesota State Historical Society; E. P. Ferry to Elihu B. Washburne, May 22, 1862, Washburne Papers; John Tilleson to John Moses, July 7, 1862, Yates Papers.

43. State of Wisconsin, *Senate Journal, 1862, Extra Session* (Madison, 1862), pp. 22–30, and *Assembly Journal, 1862, Extra Session* (Madison, 1862), pp. 42, 60–61, 93–94; *Laws of Iowa, 1862, Extra Session* (Des Moines, 1862), pp. 28–37, quoted in Olynthus Clark, *The Politics of Iowa during the Civil War and Reconstruction* (Iowa City, 1911), p. 161; St. Paul *Press*, Aug. 20, 1862; St. Paul *Pioneer & Press*, Oct. 7, 1862.

44. In Minnesota, William J. Cullen (Dem.) out-polled Ignatius Donnelly (Rep.) in the home vote, but the one-sided returns from the soldier vote gave Donnelly the edge in total votes cast. In Iowa's fourth congressional district, Henry M. Martin (Dem.) out-polled James B. Grinnell (Rep.) by a vote of 10,393 to 9,534 at home. After the soldier vote was tabulated, the grand totals were 12,900 to 11,529 in Grinnell's favor.

45. Madison *Patriot*, Nov. 8, 1862.

46. Milwaukee *News* (n.d.), quoted in the Madison *Patriot*, Nov. 25, 1862; St. Cloud *Democrat*, Oct. 30, 1862.

47. Dubuque *Times* (n.d.), quoted in Dubuque *Herald*, Oct. 18, 1862.

48. A. E. O. to "Editor," Nov. 21, 1862, Madison *Patriot*, Nov. 24, 1862.

49. Madison *Patriot*, Sept. 19, 1862; Dubuque *Herald*, Oct. 31, 1862; St. Cloud *Democrat*, Oct. 30, 1862; Green Bay *Advocate*, Nov. 6, 1862, *Illinois State Register*, Oct. 25, 1862.

The definitive story of voting-in-the-field during the Civil War still remains to be written. Josiah H. Benton, *Voting in the Field: The Forgotten Chapter of the Civil War* (Boston, 1915), contains some valuable information but contains little about the execution of the vote. Frank L.

Klement, "The Soldier Vote in Wisconsin during the Civil War," *Wisconsin Magazine of History*, XXVII (September, 1944), 37–47, reveals the workings of the stratagem in one state. Lynwood G. Downs, "The Soldier Vote and Minnesota Politics, 1862–65," *Minnesota History*, XXVI (September, 1945), 187–210, puts the historical microscope upon a second midwestern state. The soldier vote is also treated in: T. Harry Williams, "Voters in Blue: The Citizen Soldiers of the Civil War," *Mississippi Valley Historical Review*, XXXI (September, 1944), 187–204; William L. Young, "Soldier Voting in Ohio during the Civil War" (M.A. thesis, Ohio State University, 1948) ; and William F. Zornow, "Lincoln Voters among the Boys in Blue," *Lincoln Herald*, LIV (Fall, 1952), 22–25.

50. Col. Cyrus Bussey to "Dear Governor," Oct. 19, 1862, Kirkwood Papers.

51. I. F. Christiancy to Gov. Blair, Jan. 24, 1862, Blair Papers; Detroit *Free Press*, June 26, 1864.

52. *Ex. Rel. Chandler* v. *Main*, 16 Wisconsin 422; Madison *Patriot*, Nov. 10, 11, 1862, Apr. 21, 1863. The home vote for the two candidates was as follows: M. M. Cothern (Dem.), 56,840 votes, and Luther S. Dixon (Rep.), 51,948. The soldier vote (9,440 for Dixon and 1,747 for Cothern) gave the election to Dixon, the incumbent. The decision was timely!

53. Morton to Lincoln, Oct. 13, 1864, telegram in Robert Todd Lincoln Papers, Library of Congress.

54. James C. Wetmon to W. H. Smith, Oct. 22, 1864, William Henry Smith Papers, Indiana State Historical Society. To justify their action, the Republicans had circulated a pamphlet, William E. Chandler, *The Soldiers' Right to Vote* (Washington, 1864).

55. William R. Holloway to "Friend Smith," July 29, 1864, William Henry Smith Papers, Ohio Historical Society; H. Noble to Richard Yates, July 18, 1864, Yates Papers; John McKay to Richard Yates, Aug. 29, 1864, *ibid.*

56. T. S. Bell to Joseph Holt, Aug. 28, 1864, Holt Papers.

57. Hon. Z. C. Cook to Richard Yates, Sept. 19, 1864, Yates Papers.

58. William H. Ladd to Elihu B. Washburne, Sept. 24, 1864, Washburne Papers.

59. John Lellyett to Charles Mason, Oct. 25, 1864, Mason Papers; Calvin Fletcher, "Diary," Oct. 14, 1862, Fletcher Papers; Thomas O. Lowe to "My dear Brother," March 19, 1864, Thomas O. Lowe Papers, Dayton Public Library; Indianapolis *State Sentinel*, Oct. 15, 1862; Dayton *Daily Empire*, March 8, 12, 1864; *Illinois State Register*, June 12, Aug. 4, 1864.

60. Dubuque *Democratic Herald*, March 15, 1863.

61. *Ibid.*, (n.d.), quoted in Franklin T. Oldt (ed.), *History of Dubuque County, Iowa* (Chicago, n.d.), p. 293.

62. Dubuque *Democratic Herald*, Nov. 14, 1862.

63. Martha Cumming to "Dear Uncle," Aug. 27, 1861, John D. Caton Papers, Library of Congress.

64. Indianapolis *State Sentinel,* May 6, 1861.

65. Marcus Mills Pomeroy, *Journey of Life: Reminiscences and Recollections of "Brick" Pomeroy* (New York, 1890), p. 169.

66. Iowa City *State Press,* May 16, 1863; Clarence R. Aurner, *Leading Events in Johnson County, Iowa, History* (Cedar Rapids, 1912), p. 524.

67. William M. Pratt, "Diary," June 12, 1862, Rev. William M. Pratt Papers, University of Kentucky Library.

68. C. M. Gould to S. S. Cox, Oct. 15, 1863, S. S. Cox Papers (microfilm copy, Hayes Memorial Library, Fremont, Ohio).

69. The incident was incorporated into Florence Edna Boyd, "Dayton, Ohio, during the Civil War" (M.A. thesis, Ohio State University, 1939), pp. 25–26. Also see Charlotte Reeve Conover, *The Story of Dayton* (Dayton, 1919), p. 85.

70. Rev. Wesson G. Miller, *Thirty Years in the Itinerary* (Milwaukee, 1875), p. 244.

71. Chicago *Tribune,* Apr. 22, 1861.

72. Quoted in William W. Sweet, *The Methodist Episcopal Church and the Civil War* (Cincinnati, 1912), p. 144.

73. Columbus *Crisis,* Jan. 13, 1864. Also see Edward McPherson, *The Political History of the United States of America during the Great Rebellion* (Washington, 1882), pp. 498–99; and Chester F. Dunham, *The Attitude of Northern Clergy toward the South, 1860–1865* (Toledo, 1942), pp. 121–22.

74. *Illinois State Register,* Oct. 13, 1863. The two clergymen were Rev. W. R. Howard and Rev. W. P. Paxson. Both laid aside their clerical garb rather than surrender their political convictions.

75. Rev. P. S. Bennett, *History of Methodism in Wisconsin* (Cincinnati, 1890), p. 207.

76. Circleville *Democrat,* June 26, 1863, cited in Mildred O. Wertman, "The Democracy of Pickaway County during the Civil War" (M.A. thesis, Ohio State University, 1942), p. 73.

77. *Illinois State Register,* Nov. 14, 1863.

78. Cincinnati *Daily Gazette,* Nov. 12, 1863.

79. Cited by James Woodburn, *Scotch-Irish Presbyterians in Monroe County, Indiana* ("Indiana Historical Society Publications," Vol. IX [Indianapolis, 1911]), p. 593.

80. William S. McCormick to Cyrus H. McCormick, Feb. 15, Nov. 22, 1863, Cyrus H. McCormick Papers, Wisconsin State Historical Society.

81. John C. Haines to Richard Yates, Aug. 11, 1862, Yates Papers. The role of the Catholic hierarchy in the Civil War is treated summarily in Benjamin J. Blied, *Catholics and the Civil War* (Milwaukee, 1945). Bishop Rosecrans was the brother of Maj. Gen. William S. Rosecrans.

82. Dubuque *Democratic Herald* (n.d.), quoted in Edward J. Goodman, "Copperheadism in Dubuque during the Civil War" (M.A. thesis Loras College, Dubuque, 1938), p. 35.

83. *Ibid.*

84. *Stark County Democrat* (Canton, Ohio), July 17, 1861; Dayton *Journal,* May 23, June 11, 1861.

85. Indianapolis *State Sentinel,* Aug. 10, 1861.

86. William J. Ferrick to S. S. Cox, Apr. 21, 1862, Cox Papers.

87. Chicago *Tribune,* June 6, 7, 1862; *Illinois State Register,* June 12, 1862; Dubuque *Times,* April 8, 9, 1862.

88. O. T. Fishback to Thomas O. Lowe, Apr. 22, 1862, Lowe Papers.

89. Dubuque *Times,* Dec. 7, 1862.

90. Thomas O. Lowe to "Brother Will," Nov. 8, 1863, Lowe Papers.

91. Edward H. Beck to Elihu B. Washburne, Jan. 28, 1864, Washburne Papers.

92. Charles Negus to Charles Mason, Nov. 2, 1863, Mason Papers; Thomas O. Lowe to "Brother Will," Nov. 8, 1863, Lowe Papers.

93. *Crisis,* Jan. 20, 1864.

94. *Congressional Globe,* 38 Cong., 1 sess., pp. 95–96, 177.

95. *Ibid.,* p. 32.

96. Letter, written in Lincoln's hand and with the names "Gen'l Singleton" and "P. C. Wright" penciled on the back of the first page, dated January, 1864, R. T. Lincoln Papers.

97. *Ibid.*

98. A. R. Jenkins to Elihu B. Washburne, Feb. 14, 1864, Washburne Papers.

99. *Cong. Globe,* 38 Cong., 1 sess., pp. 1499–1503; *Crisis,* Apr. 20, 1864; James G. Blaine, *Twenty Years of Congress: From Lincoln to Garfield* (2 vols.; Norwich, Conn., 1884–86), I, 526. Long's speech was given on Apr. 8, 1864.

100. *Cong. Globe,* 38 Cong., 1 sess., pp. 1499–1503.

101. Noah Brooks, *Washington in Lincoln's Time* (New York, 1895), pp. 98 ff.

102. *Cong. Globe,* 38 Cong., 1 sess., pp. 1505–1635; *Crisis,* Apr. 20, 1864.

103. Hamilton *True Telegraph,* June 16, 1864.

104. Quoted in the Indianapolis *State Sentinel,* June 28, 1864.

105. The clique included: Benjamin Wood, three-time mayor and owner of the New York *News;* Fernando Wood, a brother who served in Congress; James A. McMaster, editor of the New York *Freeman's Journal;* and Manton Marble, editor of the pro-peace New York *World.*

106. St. Louis *Missouri Democrat,* July 14, 1864.

107. Stephen D. Cone, *Biographical and Historical Sketches: A Narrative of Hamilton and Its Residents from 1792 to 1896* (Hamilton, 1896), p. 198; Dayton *Empire,* June 17, 1864; Hamilton *True Telegraph,* June 16, 1864.

108. "Report" of William Thorpe, June 18, 1864, John P. Sanderson Papers, Ohio Historical Society.

109. John Reynolds to Sidney Breese (n.d.), Sidney Breese Papers,

Illinois State Historical Library; Breese to Thomas Hayne, Aug. 12, 1863, *ibid.;* Indianapolis *State Sentinel,* July 23, 27, Aug. 16, 1864.

110. La Crosse *Democrat,* July 19, 1864.

111. Charles Medary to "Dear Father," July 20, 1864, Samuel Medary Papers, Ohio Historical Society; "Report" of William Thorpe, June 18, 1864, Sanderson Papers.

112. Charles Medary to "Dear Father," July 20, 1864, Medary Papers. Charles Medary took over the editorship of *Crisis* due to the serious sickness of his father.

113. Greeley to Lincoln, July 7, 1864, Robert Todd Lincoln Papers.

114. Roy Basler (ed.), *The Collected Works of Abraham Lincoln* (9 vols.; New Brunswick, N.J., 1953), VII, 441–42, 446.

115. The Confederate "commissioners" were Clement C. Clay (Alabama), Jacob Thompson (Mississippi), James P. Holcomb (Virginia), and George W. Sanders (Kentucky). The papers of Sanders and Thompson, in the Library of Congress, throw no light upon the Niagara Falls convention. Harlan Hoyt Horner, *Lincoln and Greeley* (Urbana, 1953), incorporates most of the pertinent documents relative to the Niagara Falls "peace puff" into a chapter entitled "Peace Overtures" (pp. 289–330). Edward C. Kirkland, *The Peacemakers of 1864* (New York, 1927), devotes considerable space to Greeley's trip to Canada. See also: Ralph R. Fahrney, *Horace Greeley and the Tribune in the Civil War* (Cedar Rapids, Iowa, 1936); Elbert J. Benton, *Movement for Peace without Victory during the Civil War* ("Western Reserve Historical Society Collections," No. 99 [Cleveland, 1919]); J. N. Hofer, "Development of the Peace Movement in Illinois during the Civil War," *Journal of the Illinois State Historical Society,* XXIV (April, 1931), 119–28; Tyler Dennett (ed), *Lincoln and the Civil War in the Diaries and Letters of John Hay* (New York, 1939); and Andrew W. Renfrew, "Copperheads, Confederates, and Conspiracies on the Detroit-Canadian Border (M.A. thesis, Wayne University, Detroit, 1952).

116. Elihu B. Pond, "Diary, 1864," July 22, 1864, Elihu B. Pond Papers, Michigan Historical Collections, University of Michigan Library; Basler (ed.), *Collected Works of Lincoln,* VII, 451; Detroit *Free Press,* July 22, Aug. 3, 1864; Milwaukee *See-Bote,* July 27, 1864; Charles Mason "Diary, 1864," July 24, 1864, Mason Papers.

117. "Report" of William Thorpe, June 18, 1864, Sanderson Papers.

118. St. Louis *Missouri Republican,* Aug. 28 to Sept. 2, 1864. Lincoln recognized that the Democrats must compromise. "They must nominate a Peace Democrat on a war platform, or a War Democrat on a peace platform." Brooks, *Washington in Lincoln's Time,* p. 180. See also: Chicago *Times,* Aug. 28 to Sept. 1, 1864; Noah Brooks, "Two War-Time Conventions," *Century Magazine,* XLIX (March, 1895), 723–36; and William F. Zornow, "McClellan and Seymour in the Chicago Convention of 1864," *Journal of the Illinois State Historical Society,* XLIII (Winter, 1950), 282–85.

119. W. H. West to William Henry Smith, Aug. 31, 1864, W. H. Smith Papers; Charles R. Wilson, "McClellan's Changing Views on the Peace Plank of 1864," *American Historical Review*, XXXVIII (April, 1933), 498–510.

120. Lambdin P. Milligan to Charles B. Lasselle, Sept. 8, 1864, Lasselle Papers; *Crisis*, Sept. 9, Oct. 26, 1864; *Cincinnati Convention, October 18, 1864, for the Organization of a Peace Party upon States-Rights, Jeffersonian, Democratic Principles and for the Promotion of Peace and Independent Nominations for President and Vice-President of the United States* (n.p., n.d.).

121. *Crisis*, Sept. 9, Nov. 23, 1864; Columbus *Ohio State Journal*, Nov. 8, 1864.

122. The first was a publication (New York, 1864) of the Society for the Diffusion of Political Knowledge; the second was published (New York, 1864) by the Democratic National Committee.

123. La Crosse *Weekly Democrat*, July 5, 1864.

124. *Ibid.*, Aug. 23, 1864.

125. *Ibid.*, Aug. 2, 9, 16, 23, 24, Oct. 17, 24, 1864.

126. *Ibid.*, Aug. 29, 1864.

127. *Ibid.*, reprinted from the Appleton *Crescent* (n.d.)

128. *Ibid.*, Oct. 3, 1864.

129. Mrs. Plattenburg to Philip (son), Oct. 31, 1864, Philip Plattenburg Letter (copy in the Illinois State Historical Library; original in the hands of Mr. Wilbur Duncan, Decatur, Ill.); Evans Blake to Elihu B. Washburne, Sept. 20, 1864, Washburne Papers.

130. *The Times* (London), Sept. 25, 1863; *Chicago in 1864* (a bulletin prepared by the Chicago *Tribune*; Chicago, 1865), p. 1.

131. Cincinnati *Daily Gazette*, Nov. 9, 1863.

132. *The Times* (London), March 17, 1863.

133. Cincinnati *Enquirer*, Nov. 11, 1863.

134. Courtland Palmer to Thomas Ewing, Apr. 17, 1862, Thomas Ewing Papers, Library of Congress; A. Campbell to Elihu B. Washburne, Feb. 18, 1863, Washburne Papers; *Chicago in 1864*, pp. 4 ff.; Madison *Wisconsin State Journal*, Apr. 20, 1864.

135. Samuel J. Riddle to Elihu B. Washburne, May 16, 1864, Washburne Papers.

136. Charles Mason, "Journal, 1865," Feb. 26, 1865, Mason Papers. "If Sherman had not met with success," Mason wrote, "those who expect[ed] peace through subjugation would have lost hope."

137. Dayton *Empire*, Nov. 14, 1864.

138. *Ibid.*

139. Robert McClelland to "Dear Bess" (daughter), Dec. 28, 1864, Robert McClelland Papers, Burton Historical Collection, Detroit Public Library.

140. Mary Giddings to "My dear friend" (George W. Julian), Sept. 4, 1863, Joshua R. Giddings–George W. Julian Papers, Library of Congress.

141. C. B. Smith to H. P. B. Bromwell, Nov. 10, 1864, Henry Pelham Bromwell Papers, Library of Congress.

142. Henry Clay Dean to Charles Mason, Nov. 20, 1864, Mason Papers.

CHAPTER VIII

1. Dubuque *Herald*, Nov. 12, 1864.

2. "The cheerful acquiescence of the democracy in the recent expression of a majority of the people testifies their loyalty and love of law. . . . Smarting under defeat, branded as a disloyal organization, denounced as the left wing of the rebel army, it gracefully yields and bows to the popular verdict, expressed in a consitutional way." Detroit *Free Press*, Nov. 17, 1864.

3. John McGuffey to W. H. Smith, Nov. 17, 1864, William Henry Smith Papers, Ohio Historical Society.

4. Milwaukee *See-Bote*, Apr. 26, 1865.

5. La Crosse *Weekly Democrat*, Apr. 17, 1865. Pomeroy's show of sorrow was of brief duration. An editorial, written in June, boldly and baldly claimed that the assassination was an act of God; and he wrote: "God generously permitted an agent to make a martyr of the late president. . . ." Six months later Pomeroy's editorials again bordered on blasphemy. "We deprecate assassination," wrote the stiff-necked critic as he dipped his pen in venom, "yet we feel to thank God for calling Lincoln home, wherever that may be." Pomeroy then contended that assassination had "halted the advance of usurpation most effectively"—it had also given the country "a statesman for a President." La Crosse *Weekly Democrat*, June 19, Oct. 2, 1865.

6. *Ibid.*, Apr. 14, 1865.

7. Milwaukee *Sentinel*, May 8, 1865.

8. Efforts of the Radical Republicans to link Confederate leaders to the assassination is effectively exposed in Seymour Frank, "The Conspiracy To Implicate the Confederate Leaders in Lincoln's Assassination," *Mississippi Valley Historical Review*, XL (March, 1954), 629–56.

9. John A. Marshall, *American Bastile: A History of the Illegal Arrests and Imprisonment of American Citizens during the Late Civil War* (Philadelphia, 1878), p. 230.

10. James R. Gilmore to Joseph Holt, Apr. 22, 1865, Joseph Holt Papers, Library of Congress; La Crosse *Weekly Democrat*, May 8, 1865; Milwaukee *Sentinel*, May 8, 1865; Ollinger Crenshaw, "The Knights of the Golden Circle: The Career of George Bickley," *American Historical Review*, XLVII (October, 1941), 47 n.

11. Flyer, entitled *Elkhart Review* (Elkhart, 1866), in the files of the Indiana State Historical Society.

12. Willard L. King's *Melville Weston Fuller, Chief Justice of the United States, 1888–1910* (New York, 1950) is a recent biography that treats Fuller's Civil War years as well as the controversy over his appointment to head the nation's highest court.

13. New York *Times,* May 2, 1888. The Ingalls-Voorhees feud and Voorhees' postwar career are well treated in Forrest L. Seal, "The Political Speaking of Sen. Daniel W. Voorhees" (Ph.D. diss., Purdue University, 1955).

14. Horace Greeley, *Recollections of a Busy Life* . . . (New York, 1868); Charles A. Dana, *Recollections of the Civil War* (New York, 1892); Carl Schurz, *The Reminiscences of Carl Schurz* (3 vols.; New York, 1907–8); Benjamin F. Butler, *Autobiography . . . of . . . Benjamin F. Butler . . . [Butler's Book]* (New York, 1892); James G. Blaine, *Twenty Years of Congress: From Lincoln to Garfield* (2 vols.; Norwich, Conn., 1884–86).

15. See George W. Julian, *Political Recollections, 1840–1872* (Chicago, 1872), and *Speeches on Political Questions* . . . (New York, 1872).

16. Lew Wallace, *Lew Wallace: An Autobiography* (2 vols.; New York, 1907).

17. Shelby Cullom, *Fifty Years of Public Service: Personal Recollections* (Chicago, 1911).

18. Whitelaw Reid, *Ohio in the War* (2 vols.; Cincinnati, 1868).

19. William R. Holloway, *History of Indianapolis and Marion County* (Philadelphia, 1884).

20. The Henry B. Carrington Papers (Archives Division, Indiana State Library) include an even dozen typewritten manuscripts. Typical titles include: "Indiana War Documents Cleared of Error," "The Constable Case," "Complications during the Draft, 1864," and "Seizures at the Treason Headquarters."

21. William Dudley Foulke, *Life of Oliver P. Morton, Including His Important Speeches* (2 vols.; Indianapolis, 1899). Foulke's work has been one of the chief sources for information about the Sons of Liberty in the Hoosier State. The biography is a highly partisan one.

22. W. H. H. Terrell, *Report of the Adjutant General of Indiana* (8 vols.; Indianapolis, 1866–68).

23. Charles Seymour, "The Press," in *History of La Crosse County, Wisconsin* (Chicago, 1881), p. 545.

24. I[saiah] Winslow Ayer, *The Great Northwestern Conspiracy in All Its Startling Details* . . . (Chicago, 1865).

25. I. Winslow Ayer, *The Great Treason Plot in the North during the War* . . . (Chicago, 1895).

26. Thomas H. Keefe, "Personal Memoirs of Colonel Thomas H. Keefe," *Everybody's Magazine,* II (June, 1900), 82–91.

27. Edmund Kirke (pseud. of James R. Gilmore), "The Chicago Conspiracy," *Atlantic Monthly,* XVI (July, 1865), 108–20.

28. See such publications as Thomas H. Hines [John B. Castleman], "The Northwestern Conspiracy," *Southern Bivouac,* II (December, 1886–March, 1887), 437–55, 500–570, 567–74, 699–704; John B. Castleman, *Active Service* (Louisville, 1917); and John W. Headley, *Confederate Operations in Canada and New York* (New York, 1906).

29. Felix G. Stidger, *Treason History of the Order of the Sons of Liberty, Formerly Circle of Honor, Succeeded by Knights of the Golden Circle, Afterward Order of American Knights: The Most Gigantic Treasonable Conspiracy the World Has Ever Known* (Chicago, 1903). Stidger and his book need a critical and complete treatment.

30. Benn Pitman (ed.), *The Trials for Treason at Indianapolis, Disclosing the Plans for Establishing a North-Western Confederacy . . .* (Cincinnati, 1865).

31. Henry Clay Dean, *Crimes of the Civil War and Curse of the Funding System* (Baltimore, 1868).

32. *Ibid.*, p. 511.

33. *Ibid.*, pp. 9–10.

34. Marcus Mills "Brick" Pomeroy, *Soliloquies of the Bondholder, the Poor Farmer, the Soldier's Widow, the Political Preacher, the Poor Mechanic, the Freed Negro, the "Radical" Congressman, the Returned Soldier, the Southerner, and Other Political Articles* (New York, 1866), p. 22.

35. *Ibid.*, p. 5.

36. Marcus Mills "Brick" Pomeroy, *Condensed History of the War: Its Causes and Results: Plain Home-Told Facts for the Young Men and Working Men of the United States* (n.p., 1868).

37. Marcus Mills Pomeroy, *Journey of Life: Reminiscences and Recollections of "Brick" Pomeroy* (New York, 1890). The second volume, scheduled to deal with the postwar years, never was written.

38. Samuel S. Cox, *Union—Disunion—Reunion: Three Decades of Federal Legislation, 1855–1885* (Providence, 1885).

39. Daniel Voorhees, *Forty Years of Oratory . . . Lectures, Addresses and Speeches* (2 vols.; Indianapolis, 1898).

40. David Turpie, *Sketches of My Own Times* (Indianapolis, 1903).

41. James L. Vallandigham, *A Life of Clement L. Vallandigham* (Baltimore, 1872).

42. Marshall's volume was published by Thomas W. Hartley of Philadelphia in 1878.

43. *Congressional Globe*, 38 Cong., 2 sess., II, 1323; Detroit *Free Press*, March 4, 1865. The resolution was passed on March 2, more than a month before Lincoln's death.

44. *Official Records*, Ser. 2, VIII, 548–49.

45. Gov. Oliver P. Morton to President Andrew Johnson, May 13, 22, 1865, Telegram Dispatch Books, Oliver P. Morton, 1861–65, Archives Division, Indiana State Library.

46. Indianapolis *Daily Journal*, May 15, 17, 1863.

47. *Official Records*, Ser. 2, VIII, 587.

48. *Ibid.*, p. 637; Indianapolis *State Sentinel*, June 1, 1865; Indianapolis *Daily Journal*, June 2, 1865.

49. Messrs. Joseph E. McDonald, Jeremiah S. Black, James A. Garfield, and David Dudley Field served as counsel for Milligan. U.S. At-

torney General James Speed, Henry Stanbery, and Benjamin Butler represented the government.

50. *Ex parte Milligan,* 4 Wallace 2 (1866).

51. *Ibid.* The case is treated in Samuel Klaus (ed.), *American Trials* (New York, 1929), and in Charles Warren, *The Supreme Court in United States History* (2 vols.; New York, 1937).

52. Newspaper clipping, Indianapolis *Daily Journal,* Feb. 19, 1867, in the Colonel A. J. Warner Papers, Western Reserve Historical Society Library.

53. State of Illinois, Jo Daviess County, May Term, 1869.

54. *Madison Y. Johnson v. J. Russel Jones, John C. Hawkins, Oliver P. Hopkins, Elihu B. Washburne, and Bradner Smith: Appeal from Jo Daviess County: Abstract, Brief: Argument of the Plaintiff with Opinion and Judgment of Court* (Dubuque, 1869). This item came off the press of the Dubuque *Herald,* and the decision, without doubt, must have pleased ex-Copperhead Dennis A. Mahony. At the time of the decision J. Russel Jones (a federal marshal responsible for the arrest) was the U.S. minister to Belgium and Elihu B. Washburne (congressman from Johnson's district in 1862) was the U.S. ambassador to France.

55. *Ibid.* The text of the judgment of the circuit court is also given in full in Marshall, *American Bastile,* pp. 534–35.

56. Meade, a New York lawyer, later represented his district in the Forty-fourth Congress.

57. George Wallace Jones, "Autobiography," in John D. Parish (ed.), *George Wallace Jones* (2 vols.; Iowa City, 1912), Part II, p. 247.

58. Voorhees' career has interested students of American politics and of public speaking. His postwar years are treated in such studies as: Frank S. Bogardus, "Daniel W. Voorhees," *Indiana Magazine of History,* XXVII (June, 1931), 91–103; Hubert V. Cordier, "The Oratory of Daniel W. Voorhees" (M.A. thesis, Michigan State College, 1942); Ruth M. Harsh, "The Congressional Career of D. W. Voorhees" (M.A. thesis, University of Chicago, 1935); Henry D. Jordan, "Daniel Wolsey Voorhees," *Mississippi Valley Historical Review,* VI (March, 1920), 532–55; Leonard S. Kenworthy, *The Tall Sycamore of the Wabash: Daniel Wolsey Voorhees* (Boston, 1936); Orland S. Lefforge, "Daniel Wolsey Voorhees, Indiana Orator" (M.A. thesis, University of Wisconsin, 1940); and Forrest L. Seal, "The Political Speaking of Sen. Daniel W. Voorhees of Indiana" (Ph.D. diss., Purdue University, 1955). The works of Seal and Kenworthy stand out above the rest.

59. Hendrick's postwar career can be reconstructed from such sources as: John W. Holcomb and Robert M. Skinner, *The Life and Public Services of Thomas A. Hendricks, with Selected Speeches and Writings* (Indianapolis, 1886); Francis Trissal, *Public Men of Indiana: A Political History from 1860 to 1890* (2 vols.; Hammond, 1922); and Turpie, *Sketches of My Own Times.*

60. John S. Hare's "Allen G. Thurman: A Study in Politics" (Ph.D. diss., Ohio State University, 1933) is a solid piece of scholarship; so is David Lindsay's Samuel Sullivan Cox, 1824–1889 (Ph.D. diss., University

of Chicago, 1950) ; Lindsay devotes considerable space to Cox's postwar career. Lindsay's work should be supplemented by Cox's *Union—Disunion—Reunion*. William Van Zandt Cox and M. A. Northrup, *The Life of Samuel Sullivan Cox* (Syracuse, 1899), is badly outdated.

61. The postwar years of some of the Illinois Copperheads are treated in such works as: Franklin D. Scott, "The Political Career of William R. Morrison," *Illinois State Historical Transactions, 1926* (Springfield), pp. 134–71; Joseph Gillespie, *Recollections of Early Illinois and Her Noted Men* (Chicago, 1880); Robert Holt, "The Political Career of William A. Richardson," *Journal of the Illinois State Historical Society,* XXVI (October, 1933), 222–69. One should balance the scales with such accounts as Gustave Koerner's *Memoirs, 1809–1896* (2 vols.; Cedar Rapids, 1909) and Shelby Cullom's *Fifty Years of Public Service.*

62. The controversy over Fuller's nomination is treated earlier in the chapter. Willard L. King's biography of Fuller is highly recommended.

63. 94 U.S. 113 (1876).

64. Robert M. La Follette, *La Follette's Autobiography: A Personal Narrative of Political Experience* (Madison, 1911), pp. 22–24.

65. 40 Wis. 538 (1876).

66. Ryan's contribution to legal history receives scholarly treatment in A. J. Beitzinger, "Chief Justice Ryan of the Wisconsin Supreme Court" (Ph.D. diss., University of Wisconsin, 1955).

Ryan, Breese and Fuller were not the only ex-Copperheads who became noted jurists after the war. William Joshua Allen, for example, was appointed to a federal (U.S. District Court for the Southern District of Illinois) judgeship and filled the post with honor and dignity. This was the same Allen who was arrested in 1862 and accused of "disloyal sentiments."

67. The best account of Mahony's postwar activities is found in Roger J. Sullivan, "Mahony the Unterrified" (B.A. thesis, Loras College, 1948) and in Franklin T. Oldt (ed.), *History of Dubuque County, Iowa* (Chicago, n.d.).

68. Pomeroy, *Journey of Life,* p. 203. L. H. Pammel, *Some Reminiscences of La Crosse and Vicinity* (La Crosse, 1928), p. 68, states that the circulation of Pomeroy's paper was "some 90,000 copies per issue."

69. Butler, *Autobiography* . . . [Butler's Book], p. 43; Milwaukee *Sentinel,* Jan. 10, 1867, May 3, 5, 8, 1871, Feb. 1, March 28, May 14, 1872.

70. The link between midwestern Copperheadism and postwar Grangerism is explored in Frank L. Klement, "Middle Western Copperheadism and the Genesis of the Granger Movement," *Mississippi Valley Historical Review,* XXXIII (March, 1952), 679–94. Also see Stanley L. Jones "Agrarian Radicalism in the Illinois Constitutional Convention of 1862," *Journal of the Illinois State Historical Society,* XLVIII (Autumn, 1955), 271–82.

71. "Proceedings of the Illinois State Constitutional Convention . . . Jan. 21, 1862," published in the Springfield *Illinois State Register,* Jan. 22, 1862.

Bibliographical Essay

ABOUT A DOZEN of the more than 150 manuscript collections used in this study of midwestern Copperheadism merit more than mention in the footnotes. The Thomas O. Lowe Papers (Dayton Public Library) best reveal the views of the Copperheads. Young lawyer Lowe, a disciple of Clement L. Vallandigham, wrote many letters to his soldier-brother and commented freely upon political events and Copperhead prejudices. Since the soldier-brother tended to accept the Republican interpretation of affairs, Thomas O. Lowe's letters became masterpieces of explanation and justification.

The Charles Mason Papers (State Department of History and Archives, Historical Library, Des Moines, Iowa) also throw light on the Copperhead mind. The collection includes diaries and journals as well as letters. Mason, successful Iowa lawyer and active Democratic politician, was a graduate of West Point—he is the one who finished ahead of Robert E. Lee in the class of 1829.

The Sidney Breese Papers (Illinois State Historical Library) include letters and miscellaneous items. Since Breese was a member of his state's highest court, his observations were confined to letters and seldom made the newspapers. The jurist frequently exchanged opinions on public affairs wth his cousin, Samuel Finley Breese Morse—both were dyed-in-the-wool Copperheads. The Samuel F. B. Morse Papers (Library of Congress) have a bearing upon midwestern Copperheadism, for Morse founded the Society for the Diffusion of Political Knowledge.

The Samuel Sullivan Cox Papers (originals in Brown University Library; microfilm copies at the Hayes Memorial Library, Fremont, Ohio) indicate the intensity of Cox's Copperheadism. The letters prove that S. S. Cox subsidized the Circleville *Watchman,* which was especially critical of the Lincoln administration. The LeGrand Byington Papers (microfilm copies, State Historical Society of Iowa) indicate that Byington was an adamant Copperhead and an ardent Democrat. The Robert McClelland Papers (Burton Historical Collection, Detroit Public Library) are invaluable for the 1861–62 period; the letter books especially show a growing hostility to the political party in power. The George B. Smith Papers (Wisconsin State Historical Society) include diaries for each of the war years; the entries are written in an almost illegible hand. It was Smith who wanted President Lincoln impeached "for his many unconstitutional acts."

In the William H. English Papers (Indiana State Historical Society) two folders dealing with the years 1858–65 offer insights into Indiana politics. The Charles H. Lanphier Papers (Illinois State Historical Library) reveal the bitter partisanship which characterized Illinois politics, especially in 1863. A diary kept by Madison Y. Johnson during the time he was a "political prisoner" contains many interesting entries. The diary is in the archives of the Chicago Historical Society. The Cyrus H. McCormick Papers (Wisconsin State Historical Society) reveal the economic views and political interests of a former Virginian and Chicagoan. Mrs. Elizabeth Black, wife of an Iowa doctor who suffered persecution for his Copperhead proclivities, wrote her memoirs late in life and never lost her convictions regarding his righteousness; the three manuscript volumes are in the Newberry Library. The William R. Morrison Papers (Illinois State Historical Library) reveal the reactions of a soldier-politician who resented being called a Copperhead and labeled a subversive.

Other manuscript sources which reveal the Copperhead line of thought and which merit mention include: the George H. Paul Papers (Wisconsin State Historical Society); the Allen Hamilton Papers and the Charles B. Lasselle Papers (both in the Indiana Division, Indiana State Library); and the Samuel Medary Papers (Ohio Historical Society). There are no collected papers of Clement L. Vallandigham— they were supposedly lost in the Dayton flood of 1913—but letters written by Vallandigham can be found in such collections as the S. S. Cox Papers or the Franklin Pierce Papers (Library of Congress).

Manuscript collections which reveal the Republican point of view are numerous, outnumbering Copperhead collections two to one. The Calvin Fletcher Papers (Indiana State Historical Society) include an invaluable diary, for Fletcher was a prominent Indianapolis banker and a back-scenes adviser to Governor Oliver P. Morton. Such prominent Republican politicos as Lyman Trumbull, Elihu B. Washburne, Zachariah Chandler, and Benjamin Wade kept most of the letters they received from their constituents, and those letters are needed to balance the story of Civil War policy and politics; the collected papers of each of the four are in the Library of Congress.

The Richard Yates Papers (Illinois State Historical Library) are a mine of information (it took two months to work through the hundreds of letters) and contain more than twice the number of letters found in any other collection of Civil War governors' papers. The Samuel J. Kirkwood Papers (State Department of History and Archives, Historical Library, Des Moines, Iowa) and the Austin Blair Papers (Burton Historical Collection, Detroit Public Library) reveal facets of the political controversy in Iowa and Michigan, respectively. Both Kirkwood and Blair were energetic Republicans anxious to put Democrats at a disadvantage. The Oliver P. Morton Papers are in four separate collections in the Indiana State Library. They include, among other things, eighteen dispatch books (telegrams sent and received) and nine letter-press books. The Henry B. Carrington Papers (Archives Division, Indiana State Library) complement the Morton papers. The Carrington collection includes five letter books and a dozen typewritten compositions which attempt to justify and glorify the military aide's Civil War career.

The John Nicolay–John Hay Papers (Illinois State Historical Library) and the Robert Todd Lincoln Papers (Library of Congress) throw considerable light upon some facets of the Copperhead story. The Joseph Holt Papers (Library of Congress) should not be bypassed, because Holt was named Judge Advocate General in 1862. The Samuel P. Heintzelman Papers (Library of Congress) have a bearing upon midwestern Copperheadism, for Heintzelman commanded the Department of the Ohio for a time. A journal, kept by the punctilious commander has a bearing upon events of 1864.

Footnotes which accompany the text refer to other manuscripts utilized in gathering material for the Copperhead story.

The Copperhead mind is also revealed in the editorial columns of many Civil War newspapers. Samuel Medary launched the *Crisis* (Columbus) in January of 1861 as an outlet for his partisan and sectional views and gained national notoriety with it. Dennis Mahony of the Dubuque *Herald* also waged a war of words against the Lincoln administration. The co-editors of the Cincinnati *Enquirer* were as partisan as Medary and Mahony but more temperate in criticizing government policy. The Chicago *Times*, the Chatfield *Democrat*, and the Detroit *Free Press* were edited by Democrats who were mild critics early in the war and rabid Copperheads in the later years. Editors William T. Logan of the Dayton *Empire* and John McElwee of the Hamilton *True Telegraph* asked no quarter and gave none. Marcus Mills "Brick" Pomeroy turned the La Crosse *Democrat* into a paper that spewed hate and partisanship—no Copperhead called Lincoln as many vile names as this petulant editor-publisher.

The Indianapolis *State Sentinel* and the *Illinois State Register* (Springfield) served as the official organs of the Democrats of Indiana and Illinois, respectively. In each state the titular head of the party edited the newspaper. The *Fulton County Ledger* (Canton, Ill.) and the *Stark County Democrat* (Canton, Ohio) are well worth the time of anyone interested in midwestern Copperheadism. The Milwaukee *See-Bote,* edited by the capable Peter V. Deuster, shaped the political views of the many German Catholics who lived in southeastern Wisconsin. Scattered footnotes indicate what other Democratic newspapers were occasionally consulted.

The Republican side of the story is revealed in such well-known newspapers as the Indianapolis *Journal,* the Chicago *Tribune,* the Cincinnati *Commercial,* and the (Springfield) *Illinois State Journal.*

The anti-administration line of thought is presented in a variety of other primary sources besides Copperhead newspaper and manuscript collections. Scores of pamphlets were circulated as campaign propaganda preceding each election. Copperheads turned to the printing presses to justify their actions and to defend their views. Dennis Mahony, for example, wrote two books which indicted the Lincoln administration. Both *The Prisoner of State* and *The Four Acts of Despotism* were published in New York in 1863. Stephen D. Carpenter's *Logic of History* (Madison, 1864) is an interesting collection of miscellany intended to influence voters during the presidential campaign of 1864. "Brick" Pomeroy's *Condensed History of the War* . . . (n.p., 1868) and Henry Clay Dean's *The Crimes of the Civil War and the Curse of the Funding System* (Baltimore, 1869) carried the anti-Republican campaign into the postwar era.

Addresses, prepared by individuals or by state Democratic committees, survive as proof that opposition to the Lincoln administration was intensive, extensive, and rational. Many Midwesterners signed the *Address of the Democratic Members of Congress to the Democracy of the United States* (dated April 9, 1862, and published in Washington, D.C.). Edward G. Ryan prepared a scholarly political treatise, critical of administration policy and steeped in Jeffersonian doctrine; it was published in 1862 as the platform of the Badger State Democratic party under the title *Address to the People by the Democracy of Wis-*

consin Adopted in State Convention in Milwaukee, September 3, 1862 (Milwaukee, 1862).

Government records, both published and unpublished, contribute material for any Copperhead study. The *Congressional Globe* and the *War of the Rebellion: Official Records of the Union and Confederate Armies* (128 vols.; Washington, 1880–1901), of course, head the list of published governmental sources. State executive and legislative records also make a contribution to the story of the times.

The Lafayette C. Baker–Levi C. Turner Papers, 1862–65 (Adjutant General's Records, War Department Division, National Archives) were finally opened to research students in 1953—the author was one of the first to use these materials. The stack of records, in eighty steel boxes (32 cubic feet) contains information concerning "investigations of fraud, examinations of civilians and military prisoners, and other matter pertaining generally to subversive activities in connection with the Civil War." The Records of the Office of Judge Advocate General (National Archives) include the George W. L. Bickley Papers and the Reports on the Order of American Knights. The Provost Marshal Generals' Records (also in the National Archives) contain information upon diverse subjects and individual Copperheads. The Civil War Political Prisoners' Records (State Department files, National Archives) are in twenty steel files. These records contain information on individuals arrested upon the orders of William H. Seward, Secretary of State, in 1861–62. Grand jury reports and court records contribute to aspects of the Copperhead movement.

Since the footnotes contain many bibliographical analyses and indicate secondary sources having a bearing upon certain subjects or problems, it seems unnecessary to list here the hundreds of secondary sources consulted; the original bibliography included thirty-five typewritten pages (double space) of printed secondary sources. Readers who check the footnotes will notice that this study is based, practically in entirety, upon primary sources.

Index

PRINTED IN U.S.A.

Date Due

NOV 13 '68			
	PRINTED IN U. S. A.		